THE MICROVERSE

THE MICROVERSE

BYRON PREISS
EDITOR

WILLIAM R. ALSCHULER
SCIENTIFIC EDITOR

A BYRON PREISS BOOK

BANTAM BOOKS
NEW YORK • TORONTO • LONDON • SYDNEY • AUCKLAND

To Sandi, with much love.

—B. P.

To my children, Elise and Rachel,
who are the future.

—W. R. A.

THE MICROVERSE

A Bantam Book / November 1989

*Thanks especially to George Brecher, M.D., for critical assistance; Emily and
Richard Alschuler along with Kenneth Brecher for inspiration; Karen B.
Alschuler for faith, encouragement, and critical reading; and Rebecca Ruopp
for critical reading; to Alan Friedman for suggesting me to BPVP.*
—William R. Alschuler

Associate Editor for Science: *Ruth Ashby*
Associate Editor for Science Fiction:
David M. Harris
Photo Editor: *Patty Delahanty*
Book design by Alex Jay/Studio J
*Mechanicals by Mary Griffin
and Elizabeth Driesbach*

Library of Congress Cataloging-in-Publication Data
The Microverse / Byron Preiss, editor.
      p.   cm.
   ISBN 0-553-05705-7
   1. Microscope and microscopy.   I. Preiss, Byron.
   II. Alschuler, William R.
   QH211.M55   1989
   502'.8'2—dc20   89-17561
                                                CIP

Published simultaneously in the United States and Canada

Bantam Books are published by Bantam Books, a division of Bantam
Doubleday Dell Publishing Group, Inc. Its trademark, consisting of the
words "Bantam Books" and the portrayal of a rooster, is Registered in U.S.
Patent and Trademark Office and in other countries. Marca Registrada.
Bantam Books, 666 Fifth Avenue, New York, New York 10103.

PRINTED IN THE UNITED STATES OF AMERICA

DW 0 9 8 7 6 5 4 3 2 1

CONTENTS

WE ARE NOT ALONE
BYRON PREISS

AS WE HEAD TOWARD THE MILLENNIUM, IT SEEMS IMPOSSIBLE that in a world where instantaneous communication is a reality, there is so much loneliness. As a million faxes are fired from one coast to another, as satellites silently rebound a billion bits of information back to Earth, millions of people cry out for some contact with another soul. The plights of the hungry, the homeless, and the aged are pervasive realties of late twentieth-century civilization. Superconductivity at room temperature, cold fusion, and the fifth force are not.

It is ironic that as we try to map out every gene in the twenty-three pairs of human chromosomes, as we wonder whether the quark and the lepton will always be viewed as the "smallest" particles in the universe, the highest court in the most technologically advanced country on the planet still debates the legal rights of human beings based on race. If we can't agree on the meaninglessness of pigmentation of the skin, how important is it to our society to identify the structure of matter? If we cannot agree to provide food to every person on the planet while we have the means to do so, what right do we have to try biological engineering of human genes? If we cannot agree to love each other, what reason is there to explore an invisible world?

The answers that this book provides will intrigue you.

In our lifetime, we have postulated a definition of physical reality that binds our concept of the cosmos (outer space) with our concept of matter (inner space). Through the use of high-energy accelerators (high technology descendants of what the press used to call "atom smashers"), we have isolated two basic and so far indivisible types of particles, the quark and the lepton, that may constitute all known matter in the universe. Scientists have defined four forces that govern all interactivity between these building blocks: *gravity* (the attraction that one body exerts on another); the *strong force* (that holds the nucleus together); the *weak force* (that accounts for radioactive decay); and the *electromagnetic force* (responsible for electricity, magnetism, light, radio waves, and microwaves). Moreover, scientists theorize that these four forces were once a unified force present at the evolutionary start of the universe. Through the use of supercolliders, such as the superconducting supercollider proposed for Texas, scientists hope to learn how—and if—the four forces unify. They will attempt to do this by literally "smashing" protons together in a supercollider, to simulate, for a highly split second, the unified state in which these particles may have originally existed. In doing so, they will simultaneously be working toward the simulation of the conditions at the outset of the history of the universe. Thus the momentary actions of the very smallest mass and confirm the grand unified theory of matter, which posits that our bodies, our genes, and our atoms are an infinitesimal part of the same process that resulted in the formation of the planets.

Planets, people, protons . . . all threads in the fabric of reality we call the universe.

The Microverse was developed to help us understand the invisible world of particle physics and microbiology and the interconnectivity of the small scale of inner space and the large scale of the cosmos. The word "microverse" suggests the microscopic and the universal. We hope this book will enlighten you, the reader, about humanity's role in these two worlds and suggest, through science and speculation, how our understanding of the microverse can have real benefits for civilization.

Just as the much-derided Apollo space program defied its detractors by providing far more benefits to society than its cost, explorations into the invisible world may yield a new horizon of scientific merit. For example, by carefully delving into the genetic code of all living things, we have an opportunity to produce, under strict controls, transgenic organisms (lifeforms containing genes transplanted from one living thing into another) which may potentially supply the world with needed food and pharmaceuticals. By launching the genome project to identify the estimated 100,000 human genes, we may be able to detect and treat early abnormalities such as diabetes and multiple sclerosis that have their origins in genetic defects. By exploring the world of fusion (the same process by which the sun sustains its energy), we are on the road to self-sustaining fusion reactions in which as much energy is put in as is taken out. The next step, a process that produces more energy than it requires, holds out the hope of cheap and plentiful electricity for developing nations.

All of these possibilities stem from our entry into the microverse but cannot be taken for granted in an age of budget cuts and conservatism. Fundamental scientific research is one of humanity's highest callings. Thank G-d for a democratic process that allows us to lobby for the exploration of the world inside all of us for the common good.

If science, art, religion, commerce, and government are the "five forces" of late twentieth-century civilization, then it is our responsibility to interact with these forces to ensure a safe, progressive, and nurturing policy of research to benefit all people.

We are not alone. We are bound together in history with the planets above us, with the microscopic worlds within us, and with the subatomic worlds within them. When we look up at the stars at night, we see elements in them that also burn within us. We must choose whether to understand those elements and use that knowledge to make a better planet, or to be consumed by the fires of ignorance and injustice.

It is my hope that *The Microverse* will contribute to the process of enlightenment for all people.

I would like to thank William Alschuler for his heroic efforts in getting the scientists for this book and Ruth Ashby and David Harris, Associate Editors, for their work on the science and science fiction contributions respectively. Alex Jay, an award-winning designer, was responsible for the outstanding interior design of this book. Patty Delahanty, Photo Editor, diligently tracked down some of the best sources for photographs. To all of them, and to Lou Aronica, publisher of Bantam Spectra books, our sincere appreciation and friendship.

Following pages. This graphic symbolizes the current view of the evolution of the universe. It starts with a tiny singularity, which forms spontaneously out of nothing. Then the big bang fills the microverse with radiation. A tiny fraction of a second after the origin, the universe expands with incredible rapidity. This brief "inflation" from a state of complete uniformity accounts for the smoothness of the leftover universal background radiation today.

Originally only one force and two kinds of particles are created. As the expansion continues, this "superforce" separates into the four forces we see today, and the fundamental particles combine to make the nucleons and other particles. The light elements form, but the universe is still expanding too fast for the heavy elements to form. As the universe "fans out," protogalaxies condense out of clumpy matter and the first generation of stars is born. When they explode, they expel the heavy elements they have made, which are then incorporated into the next generation of stars and eventually into the sun, the planets, and all life on Earth. (Illustration by Ron Miller)

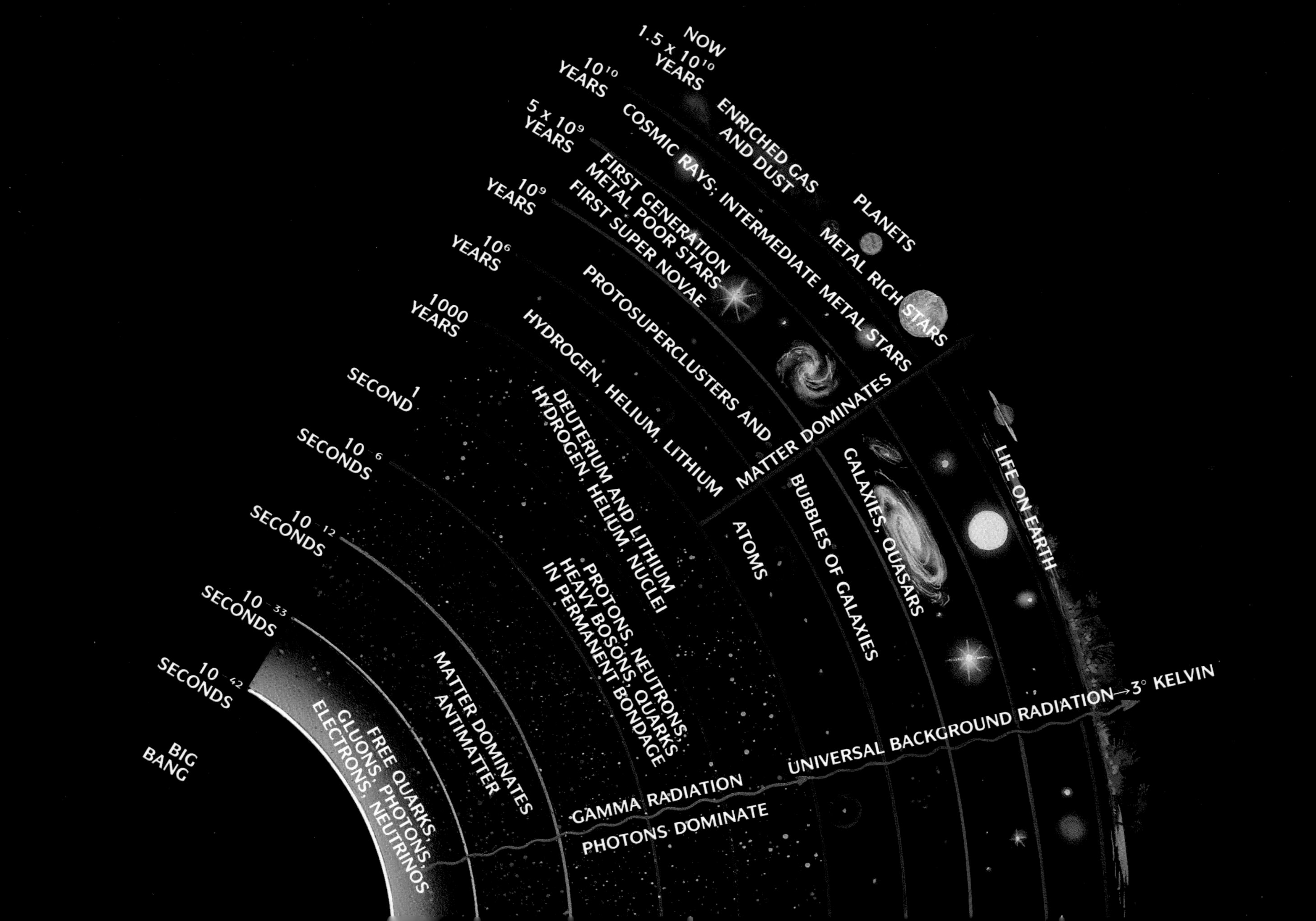

BIG BANG
10^{-42} SECONDS
10^{-33} SECONDS
10^{-12} SECONDS
10^{-6} SECONDS
1 SECOND
1000 YEARS
10^{6} YEARS
10^{9} YEARS
5×10^{9} YEARS
10^{10} YEARS
NOW 1.5×10^{10} YEARS
FREE QUARKS, GLUONS, PHOTONS, ELECTRONS, NEUTRINOS
MATTER DOMINATES ANTIMATTER
PROTONS, NEUTRONS, HEAVY BOSONS, QUARKS IN PERMANENT BONDAGE
DEUTERIUM AND LITHIUM HYDROGEN, HELIUM, NUCLEI
HYDROGEN, HELIUM, LITHIUM
PROTOSUPERCLUSTERS AND
FIRST GENERATION METAL POOR STARS FIRST SUPER NOVAE
COSMIC RAYS; INTERMEDIATE METAL STARS
ENRICHED GAS AND DUST
PLANETS
METAL RICH STARS
MATTER DOMINATES
ATOMS
BUBBLES OF GALAXIES
GALAXIES, QUASARS
LIFE ON EARTH
GAMMA RADIATION
PHOTONS DOMINATE
UNIVERSAL BACKGROUND RADIATION→3° KELVIN

NOW
1.5×10^{10} YEARS

10^{10} YEARS

5×10^9 YEARS

10^9 YEARS

10^6 YEARS

1000 YEARS

1 SECOND

10^{-6} SECONDS

10^{-12} SECONDS

10^{-33} SECONDS

10^{-42} SECONDS

BIG BANG

SOLAR SYSTEM FORMS

SECOND GENERATION STARS

PROTOGALAXIES: HEAVY ELEMENT SYNTHESIS IN FIRST GENERATION STARS AND SUPERNOVAE

SUPERGALACTIC LUMPINESS OF MATTER

HYDROGEN NUCELI COMBINE WITH ELECTRONS UNIVERSE OPAQUE TO RADIATION

BIG BANG NUCLEOSYNTHESIS OF LIGHT ELEMENTS

QUARKS COMBINE INTO NUCLEONS AND HEAVY BOSONS

END OF ELECTROWEAK UNIFICATION.

END OF GRAND UNIFICATION OF FORCES (ELECTROWEAK AND STRONG)

QUANTUM GRAVITY (EXTRA DIMENSIONS)

INTRODUCTION
WILLIAM R. ALSCHULER

THIS BOOK IS ABOUT THE VERY LARGE AND THE VERY SMALL, the relations between them, and the great efforts of human imagination and experimentation that have led to our present understanding of them. It attempts to give the clearest answer possible to the question: Does the structure of the universe at the very largest scale reflect the structure and interactions of its very smallest constituents?

Large-scale things must be built on smaller, ultimately tiny, fundamental parts. This concept seems self-evident to most of us today, though it was only about 180 years ago that scientists first performed chemistry experiments able to support it. However, that there are fundamental constituents is an old idea; it was first recorded, about 430 BC, as the idea of *atomos*, which means "indivisible," by the Greek philosophers Leucippus and his student, Democritus. Most contemporary scientists think the idea is quite true, as far as it goes, though what particles of matter are truly fundamental is still a matter of some doubt. In the 1920s, electrons and protons were thought to be fundamental; now, electrons, quarks, and neutrinos occupy that niche. Scientists are reasonably sure of this because the current theory, which encompasses these particles, seems reasonably tidy and calls for just a few types of fundamental particles. This relative simplicity is in itself an important reason why scientists believe in the theory and in these particles as being fundamental. However, the next experiment on subatomic particles may reveal a new and even smaller particle, and thus the historic regression in scale may continue.

There is a second answer to the question of whether there are fundamental particles in everything, an answer sometimes encountered in science fiction. It is that we and our universe are nothing more than atoms in a gemstone on the finger of a being living in a much larger universe. In turn, we ourselves wear rings containing universe upon smaller universe. This metaphor suggests an infinite regression of universes, which as mentioned above, may be something like the real state of affairs. Echoes of this notion can be heard in some of the theories of multiple simultaneous universes lately proposed to resolve certain paradoxes of quantum mechanics. Quantum mechanics is the twentieth-century theory that explains the behavior of matter, energy, and forces on atomic and subatomic scales. It underlies all of nuclear physics, atomic physics, solid-state physics (used in modern electronics), and the behavior of matter in extremely compressed states, as are postulated to exist inside black holes and to have existed at the time of the big bang, when the universe exploded from nothingness.

However, both the idea that all matter is made of just a few types of indivisible particles, and the idea that the universe repeats its structure endlessly at every scale, miss the main discoveries and insights of modern science about the fundamental nature of the universe. The discovery in the early 1900s of the finite speed of light affected our picture of the age, structure, and scale of the universe. The discovery in 1965 of the cold remnants of the hot event (the big bang) that created the universe, and the determination of the atomic composition of the sun, stars, and galaxies, showed the connection of our era to the physical conditions of a distant past. The dissection of nuclei by bombarding them with subatomic particles, along with work on the nature of the fundamental forces (gravity, electromagnetism, the "glue" or strong force, and the weak force) and the work on particle physics in the last 30 years, led to the insights that the universe has evolved and that the character of its evolution rests on the properties of the fundamental particles and a single underlying force. This force is no longer present in our part of the universe in its original form; it has evolved into the four forces we now observe. It is this evolutionary connection that scientists see as the true tie between the very large and the very small.

To cover all the territory from the smallest to the largest of the universe's constituents in one compact book is a major task. This book follows a semihistorical approach in its ordering of topics, roughly parallel to the history of experimental discovery of the different scales of existence, and each essay attempts to provide a brief history of its field. The book starts with an essay on the descent from the visible world of everyday existence to the just invisible, the quite invisible, the submicroscopic, and finally the unthinkably small. Then follow essays that tour cells in groups, examine how the giant molecules of the genetic code control the machinery of life on the cellular level, and view how molecules in general are constructed in nature and in the lab. We next track the electron and trace the natural history and properties of atomic nuclei. After rest stops at the fundamental particles and their interactions, in one giant leap we come back up past ordinary human existence to the most gigantic structures of the visible universe and how they originated.

A history of this sort is, in part, a history of the images we have made of the world, of the progression of imaging techniques that carry us beyond our normal senses. My personal history of images has flowed from a lifetime of experiences: an early look through a microscope at a drop of pond water; the first night I took my homemade telescope outside to look at the moon, planets, and nebulae; the evanescent tracks of cosmic rays I viewed in my coffee-can cloud chamber. It also has meant using some of the largest telescopes in the world, in winter cold and summer heat, rock music keeping me awake. I re-corded sky images on film and on TV-like detectors. I collected an indelible image standing in the spark chamber room at an accelerator outside of Paris, watching as test shots of subatomic particles were fired and their spark trails leapt across the chamber with the crack of doom. The essays and illustrations collected in this book hint at some of the thrills that come in discovering new ways of looking at the world and in the chase after the unknown, as well as in the actual glimpse of the unexpected. The images offered here can become yours.

Each science essay in this book is accompanied by a science fiction story. Unlike the science essays, the stories frequently explore technologies that are not yet here. For example, you will notice that many of the stories have as a backdrop or theme the use of micromachines (called "nanotechnology" in the engineering journals). The idea that you can travel in a world at a much smaller scale than our ordinary one is not quite a new idea; remember the movies *The Incredible Shrinking Man* and *Fantastic Voyage* (or for that matter, certain as-pects of *Gulliver's Travels*). Nanotechnology is now popular as a science fiction theme because it has recently appeared as the subject of serious engineering papers and because we feel besieged by microscopic enemies, such as the mole-cules and viruses of pollution, cholesterol, cancer, and AIDS, which attack on an invisible scale. Several versions of nanomachines are envisioned by scientists, but in general they will probably be built up from a few atoms or molecules, rather than miniaturized by shrinking machines, as proposed in the stories. Recent attempts at "microtechnology" have resulted in equipment small by ordinary standards, but not nearly so small as the envisioned molecular ma-chines. AT&T Bell Laboratories, for example, has built a complete 24,000 rpm turbine of under three-quarters of a millimeter in diameter, made out of silicon using computer chipmaking techniques.

The discovery of cells in living things was one of the first fundamental observations made when microscopes were invented. The history of this dis-covery and of other discoveries in both biology and materials science is covered in the first essay, "The Invisible World," by Linn W. Hobbs and Jean Paul Revel, which surveys the development of microscopy.

The next essay, "Cell Ecology," by Marcel Bessis, concentrates on advances in our knowledge about cell differentiation, growth, interaction, and death. The relatively new field of cell ecology is especially relevant in studies of aging, abnormalities of development, and cancer. The range of cell "behaviors" in groups is extraordinarily large, and the behavioral repertoire to a great extent parallels that of the whole organism. Some of these behaviors, including cell "feeding frenzies," are caught in the photos that accompany this essay.

Next, "The Genetic Code," by William A. Haseltine, surveys a field exploding on many fronts. The cell's machinery for creating the proteins of life is a major focus of the essay, which is full of recent results. Not the least of these is the picture of DNA's mutability, its internal redundancy, its apparently useless molecular fillers, and the presence in it of fragments of ancient viral interlopers, all of which contribute to the present character of human beings and all other living things.

We will likely see in the next decade an enterprise on the scale of the Manhattan Project* to completely map the human genetic code. Even if this costs only a few dollars per "bit" of genetic information, the human genome (the set of 46 chromosomes, made of long strands of DNA molecules, found in every human cell), is so large that this will be a multibillion-dollar project.

It is worth noting that several of society's biggest ethical challenges are tied up with advances in our understanding of the genetic code. A number have to do with AIDS. The AIDS virus probably has the most complex behavior of any virus ever encountered. It destroys the body's disease-fighting machinery at several levels, by interfering with precisely the RNA- and protein-producing machinery described in "The Genetic Code." Society must deal with the issues of education and health care, as well as the issue of how to test new medical treatments, and AIDS throws these issues into sharp relief.

Another major ethical challenge lies in the rapid advance of genetic engineering, in our increasing control of our macroscopic world based on our newly developed control of the microscopic. Consider these examples: We have seen the successful implantation of the gene for human insulin production into the genome of the common intestinal bacterium E. coli, and the bacteria can be grown to mass produce insulin. As this book went to press, a team of Italian researchers announced a simple technique for gene transplantation to any egg: bathing sperm cells in a bath of tailored gene fragments. The sperm take up the fragments and pass them into the eggs they fertilize. Kits are now available for under one hundred dollars that will allow high school and college students to do bacterial clones. Yesterday, this was a technique that required massive lab resources and many years of experience in microbiology! How can society regulate this process?

Even more incredible are cross-species genetic experiments. In 1987, one

Figure 1 (*left*).   A contented *geep* (goat/sheep chimera) basking in the California sun. (Photo credit: University of California, Davis) *Figure 2* (*right*).   A griffin, a mythical beast, part bird and part lion. Detail from an Iranian gold plaque, about 650 B.C. (Photo credit: Metropolitan Museum of Art)

of these produced the "geep," a combination species, or chimera. (See Figure 1.) This animal, part goat and part sheep, falls into the realm of mythical beasts, such as the griffin, the centaur, and the sphinx. (See Figure 2.) And yet there it is, chewing its cud on page 21 of *The New York Times*! The geep was created by combining fragments of sheep and goat cells at the embryo stage, a crude but apparently successful way to grow unheard-of combinations. The United States Patent Office has already declared an engineered mouse species as patentable, and the geep is also therefore likely to be patentable. Other techniques that use viruses to transplant genetic material may have equally radical results. The creation, by human intervention, of living things that could not naturally evolve themselves, is a signal event, on a par with exploding the atomic bomb and landing on the moon. The full implications of this part of our "brave new world" have not been explored. At the very least, our notion of biological evolution will be changed, as we have become creators of new forms of life.

In the next essay, "The Molecular World," William M. Gelbart details our basic understanding of the principles that structure all molecules and discusses the role of new, single-molecule experiments and computer-aided molecular simulations. These are at the heart of creating new materials by design.

From molecules, our tour drops down to their constituents: atoms and their cores, the nuclei, in the essay "The Nuclear World," coauthored by Philip Morrison and myself. Scientists already have considerable experience in creating new atomic species (new nuclei). Most are quite unstable and have been created in accelerators. The alchemist's dream of transmuting dross into gold has been achieved, but the gold so generated is worth more than its own weight! The essay discusses the properties of the new and the natural nuclei, their origin, and their important uses. It also speculates on whether the whole universe is really mostly made up of the known forms of matter, and it looks at major recent research in the tearing apart of nuclei into tinier and more fundamental constituents. This takes us into the realm of particle physics.

The first fundamental particle discussed was the first discovered and is the most prominent in everyday life: the electron. In "The Electron," Gerald Feinberg covers the electron's nature and discovery, along with exciting new work. High-temperature superconductors are a sensational development that was not widely expected. Only a bit more than two years after their discovery, superconductors will likely appear in their first commercial application, as SQUIDS, extremely sensitive detectors of electric and magnetic fields, which can be used to study the extremely weak signals in human nerves and measure subtle variations in the earth's magnetic field. The experimental work on superconductors is proceeding rapidly in many laboratories, and new superconductors are being found by trying materials with properties similar to those of the first successes, and by inspired guesses, since there is no good theory to explain their behavior or predict the configuration of new materials. At present, the predominant opinion is that there is no upper limit to the critical temperature of superconductivity in this new group of materials. The prospects for lossless power transmission, high-speed levitating monorail trains, and more powerful particle accelerators are very exciting, though their realization is at least 10 years away.

The research enterprise described in Leon M. Lederman's essay on particle physics is typical of the high-energy particle physics work going on worldwide, which has brought into captivity the "particle zoo." The essay concentrates on the investigation of just one particle, the neutrino. It is a fundamental particle, so far as we know, and massless; it is important in the energy-producing reactions in the sun and stars and in some types of radioactivity, and yet it interacts with other matter only via the weak force, a very slight interaction that we do not directly experience. Neutrinos may also be the most numerous particles and, in total, the greatest part of the mass in the universe, if they have just a little mass.

The "particle zoo" was teeming with seemingly independent species of subatomic particles, until the work described in Alvaro De Rújula's essay on quarks showed that the various species of mesons and heavy particles like protons are really made up of just a few types of quarks. Our understanding of quarks goes hand in hand with our understanding of the fundamental forces, discussed in Sheldon Lee Glashow's essay, "The Four Forces." Both of these essays provide insights into how scientists think about the questions they face and how they have attempted to give the simplest possible theoretical explanations for what they observe.

As higher and higher energies are achieved, the conditions in accelerator experiments approach closer to those of the earliest moments of the universe. At present, the energies achieved are equivalent to those in a gas of 10^{16} degrees Kelvin, which is believed to have occurred about 10^{-12} seconds after the big bang, when the universe was still smaller than an atomic nucleus. The exploration of this connection is the subject of the last essay, "Inner Space/Outer Space," by Edward W. Kolb. It presents what in some quarters is known as the "standard model" of the universe, along with the evidence for that model. A word of caution: 25 years ago this theory, then known as the "evolutionary model," competed with another theory, called the "steady-state model," which explained many of the same observations but postulated no moment of origin for the universe. Instead, it supposed that at the very largest scale the universe always looks the same and that matter is being continuously created everywhere, out of nothing, at a rate too small to detect but sufficient to keep the average density of the universe constant in the face of its expansion. The steady-state theory is out of favor now, but improved observations of the microwave background or of quasars could revive it.

As you can see, the aim of this enterprise is to unriddle the large by looking at the small, and vice versa. The observations of the very large can place incredible constraints on the very small. For example, the faint afterglow of the big bang, which fills the sky and is the ultimate background in every direction, is found to be very uniform. It varies in color and intensity by less than one part in 10,000 from one direction to another. Its constancy suggests that the matter by which it was last absorbed and radiated must itself have been very smoothly distributed. Yet that same matter, shortly thereafter, somehow was lumpy enough to start to form galaxies and clusters of galaxies. To avoid this dilemma, consideration of quantum physics phenomena (which were important for the universe as a whole when it was tiny, just after the big bang) and the possibility that the electromagnetic, weak, and strong forces were all unified as one force yielded the idea of an early period of rapid expansion when there was no mass (10^{-32} to 10^{-12} seconds after the bang), called the "inflationary period." During this period the universal background radiation could have achieved its great uniformity. This is the very small at the heart of the very large!

If you wish to get a more personal sense of this grand connection without going to graduate school or performing an experiment yourself, consider this: take a cubic centimeter from your body (a gram of flesh!) and unravel it. Place all the atoms in it side by side. The resulting monoatomic filament would stretch way beyond the edge of the solar system, into interstellar space! Five billion years ago, your atoms were spread out in a cloud of gas and dust of that diameter. Contemplate what has happened since to bring you to your present occupation: reading this book!

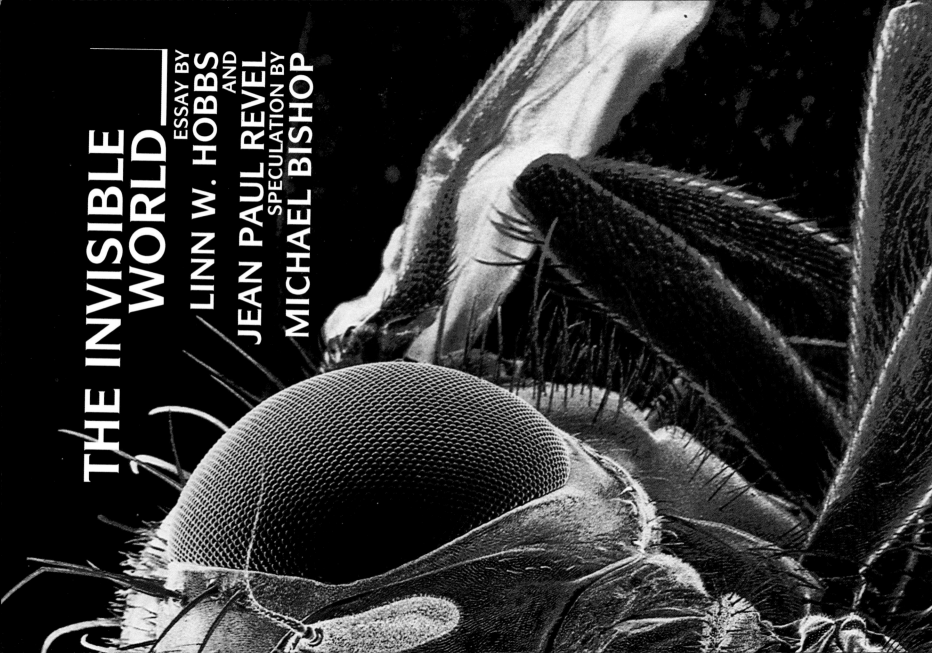

THE INVISIBLE WORLD

ESSAY BY
LINN W. HOBBS AND
JEAN PAUL REVEL
SPECULATION BY
MICHAEL BISHOP

THE INVISIBLE WORLD

LINN W. HOBBS
MASSACHUSETTS INSTITUTE OF TECHNOLOGY
JEAN PAUL REVEL
CALIFORNIA INSTITUTE OF TECHNOLOGY

"'Yes, I have a pair of eyes,' replied Sam, 'and that's
just it. If't they wos a pair o' patent double million
magnifyin' gas microscopes of hextra power, p'raps I
might be able to see you through a flight o' stairs and
a deal door; but bein' only eyes, you see, my wision's
limited.'"

—Charles Dickens, *Pickwick Papers*

THE DESIRE TO DISCOVER THE NATURE OF THINGS BY VISUAL-
izing ever finer detail has been a human dream of long standing.
Our progressive realization of this dream is the story of the instruments we have developed to help us see with, beginning with the
initial successes of the first light microscopes using glass lenses,
followed by the development of the electron microscope using magnetic lenses,
and continuing with the recent invention of microscopes with no lenses at all.

How small an object we can resolve *without* the help of instruments is
limited by our eyes. With the object as close as possible to the eye and still in
focus, the cornea and lens working together produce an image reduced about
10 times on the retina. There, the incoming light is registered by photoreceptors (rods and cones), each about 2.5 micrometers (μm), or about 1/10,000 inch
wide. In the simplest analysis, we can intuitively assume that to resolve two
luminous points the photoreceptors receiving their images must be separated
by at least one other that remains in the dark. The luminous objects must
therefore be more than 50 μm (0.05 mm or 1/500 inch) apart, so their images
on the retina will be at least 5 μm apart. To distinguish clearly objects that are
more closely spaced than this requires that a magnified image be presented to
our eye. Magnifying glasses were already used in Roman times, and possibly
even as early as the Minoan civilization 2,500 years ago, and the use of magnifying eyeglasses for correction of nearsightedness can be traced to the thirteenth
century. Progress in producing magnified images has been sporadic. Geometrical optics was studied by the Greeks, but the first real treatment of the properties
of lenses was by the eleventh-century Arabian scholar Ibn-al-Haytham. Significant additional advances, both theoretical and practical, were made in the seven-

22

teenth century with the invention of the microscope, then in the nineteenth century, and again in the last 50 years.

Besides the limit set by the structure of the receptors in our eyes, there is also a limit set by the wavelength of the radiation used in imaging. This limitation is fundamental and can be seen as an inevitable consequence of Heisenberg's uncertainty principle (1927), an axiom more usually associated with the field of quantum physics. Werner Heisenberg's principle posits a fundamental uncertainty in the position of a particle whose momentum (essentially speed and direction) is known. This means that we cannot know the exact position and the precise momentum of a particle at the same time. Light (or any radiation) is scattered ("diffracted") by objects and so changes the direction of its propagation and thus its momentum. If the extent of the momentum change is established, say by interposing an aperture or lens that accepts radiation scattered through some maximum angle, there is a corresponding uncertainty in the position of the object from which the radiation emanated, which sets the resolution limit. Even if we collect scattered radiation over all angles in front of the object, the positional uncertainty is about half the wavelength of the radiation used. With visible light, this theoretical resolving power is about 0.2 μm (about 1/125,000 inch).

To resolve objects down to this limit means that magnifications of at least 250X (50 μm/0.2 μm = 250), or better, 500 to 1,000X are needed. Of course, these requirements are relaxed if one does not need the highest resolution. The magnifications needed for top resolution are difficult to produce with a single lens such as a magnifying glass. Lenses made of just one kind of material also suffer from aberrations, which limit the quality of images. Aberrations are most readily corrected by using several lenses (often made of different types of glass) acting together as a single optical element. Visualization of small details first became possible with the development of "compound" microscopes, in which the magnified image produced by the first lens (the objective) is further enlarged by a second lens (the eyepiece).

THE LIGHT MICROSCOPE

The first microscopes we know of seem to have been built in the Netherlands by the Janssens, Hans and his son Zacharias, between 1590 and 1609. By 1610, Galileo had made a microscope "that made a fly look as big as a hen." The seventeenth-century English scientist Robert Hooke, whose job it was to prepare demonstrations for fellow members of the Royal Society in London, made free-hand sections through pieces of cork and examined them in a microscope he had made himself. He saw "cells," the small chambers in which the living structures we now call cells used to reside. "Methought . . . ," he exclaimed, "I had with the discovery of them [cells] presently hinted to me the true and intelligible nature of all the phenomena of cork." He calculated that there were "in a cubick Inch above 12 hundred Millions, a thing most incredible." These and many other of Hooke' microscopical explorations are chronicled in his remarkable book *Micrographia*, published in 1665. But it was the seventeenth-century Dutch merchant-draper Anthony van Leeuwenhoek who made some of the most telling and significant early biological discoveries. Surprisingly, he was not using a compound microscope. Leeuwenhoek's microscopes (there was one for each sample he examined!) were only single-lens magnifying glasses of high power (short focus and small diameter). (See Figure 1.) It is a measure of his craft that he was able to manufacture lenses of sufficient quality to allow him to resolve protozoans that live in pond water, as well as bacteria and spermatozoa. In fact, it is likely that the aberrations inherent in such lenses helped him, because they produced contrast even though they hindered resolution.

Leeuwenhoek saw details in his specimens whose significance he did not always appreciate. A drawing of his of a red blood cell from a frog shows a central dot that we would now recognize as its nucleus, the repository of the genetic code that shapes us all. (The discovery of the nucleus is generally attributed to Robert Brown in 1831 because he correctly appreciated it as an important organ in the cell.)

There were many ingenious advances in microscope construction from the time of Leeuwenhoek to that of Brown, most of them arrived at empirically. The foremost *optical* problem was correction of two serious lens aberrations: chromatic aberration and spherical aberration. The first occurs because the refractive index of glass lenses, which is a measure of the speed of light in the glass and determines how much each light wave is bent, is a function of the wavelength of light (a property known as dispersion, first investigated by Isaac Newton with his glass prism, which dispersed white light into its constituent colors). Thus images formed by the different wavelengths occurred at different magnifications and were confusingly superimposed. The second arises when rays passing through different regions of a large aperture lens do not come to the same focus. Early microscopes were restricted to small apertures as the only way of minimizing both aberrations, an inconvenient compromise well known to Hooke.

Newton had incorrectly adduced from his experiments with prisms that chromatic aberration could be corrected by a series of similar lenses. In experimenting with such multiple lenses, an English barrister, Chester More Hall, accidentally discovered in 1733 that a *compound* lens, consisting of a convex lens made of low-dispersion (crown) glass and a concave lens of lead-containing high-dispersion glass (flint glass) cemented together, had the property of reducing the chromatic aberration; multiple elements can correct it more completely. The principle was not, however, applied to microscopes until 1791 by François Beeldsnyder, a colonel in the Amsterdam cavalry and an amateur

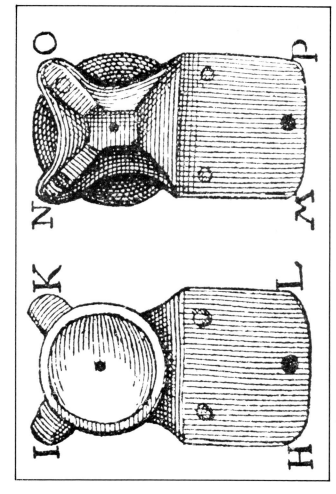

Figure 1. A drawing of Leeuwenhoek's microscope. With one tiny lens held almost touching his eye, he achieved 400x's magnification and good resolution. (Source: *Growth of Biology,* W. A. Locy, 1925.)

physicist. And it was not until 1830 that Joseph Lister, writing in the *Philosophical Transactions* of the Royal Society, set forth the principles underlying correction of spherical aberration, so that design of aberration-corrected objective lenses became at last feasible. In keeping with the amateur tradition of the times, Lister was, like Hall, a London barrister and a founding member of the Royal Microscopical Society in 1839.

The development of light microscopes of ultimate optical quality was due to the work of the nineteenth-century, German physicist Ernst Abbe who teamed up with the microscope maker Carl Zeiss in a systematic program to construct better lenses. Abbe realized that it was essential for lenses to have high *numerical apertures,* that is, high acceptance angles for the rays diffracted by the sample. The more closely spaced the objects to be resolved, the greater the angle of acceptance has to be (recall Heisenberg's principle). As well as increasing the acceptance angle, it is also possible to increase the numerical aperture by immersing the specimen and lens in a fluid of higher refractive index than air, for example water or oil; this is routinely practiced for light microscopy at the highest resolution. In addition, Abbe formulated an optical theory of image formation that replaced geometrical optics and today bears his name. It must be remarked parenthetically that Abbe was a social activist who paid close attention to conditions at the Zeiss factory. He was instrumental in creating a medical insurance fund and a retirement fund and instituting an eight-hour working day. The result of his work, and that of others at the time, was that microscopes made in the last part of the nineteenth century were limited in resolution only by the wavelength of the light used to illuminate the specimen.

There were significant consequences to pushing back this technological frontier. Bacteriology progressed very much in tandem with the evolution of microscope resolving power. The anthrax bacillus (measuring 1×5 μm) was first seen in 1850. Viruses are much smaller, and the first observation of a virus, that responsible for cowpox (measuring 0.25 μm), had to wait until 1887, when microscope resolution caught up. Among the most important practical developments at around this time was the application of photographic methods for the recording of microscope images. The adoption of photomicrography obviated the tedious drawing and subsequent engraving of images for reproduction and facilitated dissemination. Previously, many microscopists had, of necessity, been skilled illustrators—Hooke's drawings in his *Micrographia* are a good example of the art—though Leeuwenhoek, who was bad at drawing, employed a surrogate draftsman. Thomas Wedgwood and Humphry Davy experimented with taking photographs of microscopic objects as early as about 1800, but apparently without notable success. The first real photomicrography setup was an elaborate projection arrangement utilizing a camera obscura, and the first photomicrograph taken with this apparatus was presented to the Academy of Sciences in Paris by A. Donne in 1840. By the 1880s, August Köhler in Germany had installed a bellows camera onto the microscope itself, and by the end of the century photomicrographs had become the standard vehicle for communicating the results of microscopical investigations.

THE LIGHT MICROSCOPE IN BIOLOGY

Until the 1930s, few further fundamental advances in microscope design were forthcoming. One of the major problems encountered by the early microscopists interested in biology is caused by the fact that our eyes are sensitive to intensity and color, but most biological objects at microscopic scale are completely transparent and many also nearly colorless. Specimen preparation techniques that provided contrast had to be invented in order to reap the benefits of high resolution. One way is to impart color to different parts of the object. Natural dyes such as carmine had long been used to differentially tint different parts of organisms. The invention of synthetic dyes in 1856 by William Henry Perkins, then 18 years old, opened the way for a much greater variety of dyes with different properties. One important contributor to the development of techniques for specific staining of different structures was Paul Ehrlich, whose later major contribution was the development of Salvarsan as an antisyphillis drug. Tissue preparation also often involved a "fixation" step to prevent decay, yet retain as nearly lifelike an appearance as possible. Fixation made cells permeable to the dyes and hardened them to allow the preparation of transparent thin sections from bulk tissue, the only way to see internal structures. To help in preparing thin slices, material for study was embedded in molten waxes that solidify as they cool or in a material such as celloidin in organic solvents. Microtomes, essentially automated razor blades set up like tiny sausage slicers, were developed to prepare sections as thin as a few micrometers. These techniques worked well, but because of the many steps involved, they raised doubts about the reality of the structures that were seen.

In retrospect, using today's much broader range of approaches and thus armed with a great deal more confidence in our observations, we cannot help being impressed by the results that the microscopists of the eighteenth and nineteenth centuries were able to obtain. Use of improved microscopes and techniques resulted in an explosion of knowledge about the cells that make up all living organisms and about the constituent parts of cells, their organelles. The cell nucleus, which had already been represented by Leeuwenhoek, was discovered to be a feature of nearly all animal cells (except mammalian red blood cells) by Brown in Scotland, and this fact was confirmed in plants by Eduard Strasburger. Brown, like Leeuwenhoek, used only simple microscopes. Among other influential workers were the cytologists Matthias Schleiden and Theodor Schwann, who, despite some misguided notions, are usually credited with the development of the modern concept of "cell"; the pathologist Ernst Rudolf Virchow, who pointed out in 1859 that new cells arise only from other cells; Walther Flemming, famous for his description of mitosis (1878), the complex mechanism by which (we now realize) genetic material is evenly distributed to the daughters of dividing cells; Robert Koch, the discoverer of the tubercle bacillus; and Louis Pasteur, whose many contributions need not be enumerated here. A famous portrait of Pasteur shows him leaning pensively next to his trusty microscope.

Even today, medical students hear the names of many pioneers, remembered by a staining technique they originated or by a structure named after them. Perhaps the pinnacle of nineteenth-century microscopy was reached by Santiago Ramon y Cajal, a Spanish microscopist who adapted the silver staining technique of his contemporary, the Italian scientist Camillo Golgi. Ramon y Cajal made such astute and profound observations about the organization of cells in the nervous system that his work is still a starting point for modern neurobiologists. His illustrations and observations still provide indispensable guidance today. Camillo Golgi used his technique to describe the cellular compartment involved in packaging and export of secretion products, the Golgi apparatus, the one cellular organelle still commonly called after its discoverer. Golgi shared the Nobel Prize with Ramon y Cajal in 1906.

Interpretation of the material and of the images obtained required that one be a very knowledgeable interpreter. Not everyone could appreciate what the masters could see in their preparations. Methods for the specific staining of particular classes of cells were essentially nonexistent. Even so, specific stains could be very useful, as shown by the example of Johann Friedrich Miescher, who made use of the staining of nucleic acids to purify DNA from cells for the first time in 1869.

Since the resolution of the light microscope is limited by the wavelength of light used, one way to obtain higher resolution is to work at shorter wavelengths. Ultraviolet (UV) light can be used if special glass or quartz is used for the optics (normal optical glass absorbs UV light), and one can bypass the necessity of direct examination (our eyes are not sensitive to UV light) by using photography instead. Such a microscope was originally proposed by Köhler. Torbjorn Caspersson and Jean Brachet showed in 1941 that different parts of cells absorbed short wavelengths to different degrees, thus providing improved contrast as well as higher resolution. Some regions were quite opaque, particularly the nucleus and portions of the cytoplasm, the very same portions that could also be stained using basic dyes. We now understand that the reason is that these regions contain large concentrations of nucleic acids (see "The Genetic Code," by William A. Haseltine). There is ribonucleic acid (RNA) in the cytoplasm in those regions where proteins are being made.

While the use of the ultraviolet microscope led to the recognition that there was a link between the presence of nucleic acids and the synthesis of proteins, the instrument has become much more important today because UV light can be used to excite fluorescence in many regions of the cells. Thanks to techniques pioneered by Albert Coons in 1941, fluorescent tags have become some of the most widely used subcell labels in research. They are often used to tag antibodies, which are exquisitely sensitive and specific in recognizing the molecules and agents against which they have been raised. An optical arrangement (epifluorescence) that has proved extremely convenient and efficient uses a single objective to illuminate the sample with "exciting" UV radiation and to collect the "emitted" visible light fluorescence signal.

NONBIOLOGICAL OBJECTS

Hooke's demonstrations to his Royal Society colleagues in 1663–65 included, in addition to experiments on biological objects, images of many nonbiological subjects, such as needle points and razor blade edges. A contemporary London microscopist, Henry Power, also mentions his observations of polished metal surfaces in 1664 and of the globular nature of spark chips struck from steel by a flint (which showed that the metal had locally melted). But the first really scientific application of the microscope to the physical sciences took place some 80 years later. Henry Baker was a London poet and polymath who, among other pastimes, rhymed couplets about crocodiles, studied freshwater polyps, and played around with electricity. A year after his election to the Royal Society in 1741, he published his first scientific book, *The Microscope Made Easy*. While his principal contribution to science was as a popularizer, his original observations on the crystallization of salts under the microscope represented the first documented study of dynamic processes in the microscopical world.

Baker's study was incidentally responsible for the present-day form of the microscope, owing to the inconvenience he encountered in using the popular eighteenth-century tripod design of Edmund Culpeper for his crystallization studies. In his book *Employment of the Microscope* (1753), Baker complains that "when examining daily the Configurations of Saline Substances, the Legs were continual Impediments to my turning about the Slips of Glass; and indeed I had found them frequently so on other Occasions. Pulling the Body of the Instrument up and down was likewise subject to Jerks which caused a Difficulty in fixing it exactly at the Focus: there was no good Contrivance for viewing opake Objects. Complaining of these Inconveniences, Mr. Cuff, the Optician, applyed his Thoughts to fashion a Microscope in another Manner, leaving the stage intirely free and open by taking away the Legs, applying a fine threaded Screw to regulate and adjust its Motions, and adding a concave Speculum for Objects that are opake." The result was a design in brass by John Cuff which closely resembles the modern instrument for both transmitted and reflected light. (See Figure 2.)

Further interest in applying the microscope to the nonbiological arena was surprisingly absent until about 1860, even though significant empirical advances in mineralogy and metallurgy had taken place over the previous 200 years and many of the important phenomena in these fields can be easily observed with magnifications of less than 100X, available even in Hooke's time. The man responsible for the resurgence was Henry Sorby, an English geologist who pioneered modern microscopical petrology and physical metallurgy. In 1848, at the age of 22, Sorby was introduced to the technique of making thin sections of hard substances and recognized immediately the possibilities for examination of geological specimens by transmitted-light microscopy. Within a few years, he was challenging the fundamental tenets of geological origins with his microscopical observations, first of sedimentary accumulations and later of igneous rocks. His recipe for preparation and impregnation of petrographic thin sections (typically 25–30 μm, or 1/1,000 inch, thick) is largely followed unaltered even today.

Viewing petrographic thin sections benefits particularly from examination in transmission with polarized light. (See Figure 3.) Light, in common with radiant heat, radio waves, and X rays, is a traveling electromagnetic disturbance in which separate electric and magnetic field vibrations occur at right angles (transverse) to the direction of propagation and to each other. Normal light exhibits such vibrations in all transverse directions at random, but light reflected from surfaces has a unique vibration direction, or *polarization*, a fact discovered in 1808 by E. L. Malus. Many minerals, with noncubic crystalline atomic arrangements, most notably calcite (crystalline calcium carbonate), exhibit very different refractive indices in different transmission directions. This was noticed as early as 1669 by Erasmus Bartolinus and later studied by Christian Huygens, a clever Dutch contemporary of Newton who proposed a wave theory for the propagation of light. The Frenchman Augustin Fresnel showed in 1816 that the two rays in calcite were polarized at right angles to each other, an observation that formed the basis for a method of producing polarized light, described in 1829 by the Englishman William Nicol, using calcite prisms that ever since have been called "nicols." (Today we more conveniently use correctly aligned sheets of a material containing a highly oriented polymer developed by Edwin Land's Polaroid Corporation to effect strong polarization. These act like a Venetian blind for polarized light, which is why polaroid sunglasses are effective in suppressing the glare reflected from smooth surfaces like water.) When examined in a *petrographic microscope* with polarizers situated both above and below the sample, thin sections of birefringent minerals (i.e., minerals having different refractive indices in different directions) exhibit colors that are signatures of particular minerals and were first catalogued by Albert Michel-Lévy in 1906.

In 1863, Sorby turned his attention to the microstructure of meteorites, metallic iron-nickel alloys of extraterrestrial origin, which had been studied earlier without the aid of a microscope by Aloys von Widmanstätten. That same year, Sorby observed similar Widmanstätten structures in man-made steel, initiating the field of metallography. These studies were conducted in reflected light on highly-polished specimens that had been etched in acid to erode differentially the different constituents of the microscopical assemblage, the standard metallographic preparation procedure even today. Early metallurgical investigations were all concentrated on understanding the microstructure of cast iron and steel, the most economically important metals of the day. There was special interest in the roles played by carbon, heat treatment, and the addition of other alloying elements. (See Figure 4.)

One of the significant discoveries at this time was that metals are crystalline (like most minerals) and not glassy (like obsidian, window glass, or slags). Even well into this century, it was popularly thought that metals were amorphous and only "crystallized" when fractured. It would have to await the discovery of

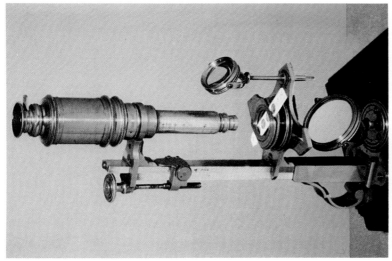

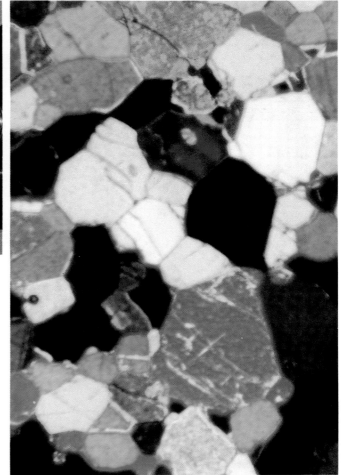

Figure 2 (right). Classical brass compound microscope with fine screw focusing and movable stage for specimens. By John Cuff, London, made in 1744. (Source: *Microscopy to the End of the Nineteenth Century* by F. W. Palmer and A. B. Sahiar, HMSO, London, 1971) *Figure 3 (below).* Thin section of the mineral hornblend, seen in transmitted polarized light. The colors of the crystalline grains show that they have varied compositions, formation history, molecular structure and orientation. (Photo credit: Dr. Linn W. Hobbs)

X-ray diffraction in 1912 to deduce, and the advent of atomic-resolution electron microscopy in the 1970s to actually demonstrate, that crystallinity, in metals and in other solids, arises from the regularly-repeated arrangements of atoms.

REFINEMENTS IN LIGHT MICROSCOPY

New techniques that overcame some of the limitations of the light microscope began to appear in the 1930s. Frits Zernike developed a *phase contrast microscope*, which allowed researchers to visualize transparent colorless objects, so long as there were differences in the refractive index, meaning that the light passing through the object traveled at different speeds through different parts. This causes differences in the phase of the light waves coming out of the object, which can be used to produce contrast by an ingenious optical sleight of hand involving the use of transparent *phase grating plates*. Luckily, there are large differences in refractive index in cells. Cell membranes and membrane-bounded organelles, for example, could now be distinguished, even though the membranes themselves were transparent and 20 times thinner (about 0.01 μm) than can be resolved with visible light.

Another method that allows the detection of objects smaller than the theoretical resolution limit of the microscope is interference microscopy. The incoming beam is split into two polarized, spatially separated components by a doubly refracting prism and then recombined by a second double prism after passing through the specimen. This technique provides superbly crisp images, whereas in phase contrast there is always a diffuse halo around the objects visualized. Interference microscopy has now been replaced by differential interference, a variant technique developed by G. Nomarski, which is simpler to implement from the point of view of the user and effectively displays phase differences across interfaces, producing striking images that look three dimensional, where the apparent height of the object is a function of its refractive index rather than of its shape. Nomarski contrast is much used in reflection as well in metallurgical applications where sharp contrast at edges or at interfaces is sought. Here, too, the level of recognizable detail far outstrips the theoretical resolution limit. Abbe would have been happy to see such developments. During a visit to London in 1876 he said, "There is a limit to our vision which we cannot exceed. This limit is set by the nature of light itself. Perhaps the human genius will contrive a way, quite different from the one we use now, to bypass these limitations which we now feel unsurmountable." The several approaches just outlined do not change the resolution, only the ability to utilize the available information, using optical tricks that were simpler to discover than expected.

Still further improvements in imaging have been made thanks to modern

Figure 4.   Tip of a samurai sword, showing gross difference in grain structure between blade edge and center. The center was covered with clay before rapid cooling to yield a less brittle microstructure. (Photo credit: Dr. Linn W. Hobbs)

electronics. Just a few years ago the cytologists Robert Allen and Shinya Inoué began investigating the usefulness of video enhancement techniques. Most biological objects are almost invisible, because the background is almost as dark (or bright) as the object, which is another way of saying there is little contrast. It is simple, however, to stretch the image signal electronically. By altering the zero level, one can readily provide conditions where a small percentage difference in even a weak signal can be stretched and detected over a strong background. Using differential interference contrast combined with video enhancement, Allen showed that one could observe and portray microtubules in live cells. Microtubules are only about 0.02 μm wide, 10 times smaller than the resolution of the light microscope, and had previously been seen only in the electron microscope. Polarized light microscopy has also profited much from the application of video enhancement. Digitization of image information, whether by using video cameras on the microscope or by later conversion of photographs, opens up the whole world of computer-aided image enhancement that has been much developed for the fields of astronomy, forensic science, and pattern recognition in military applications.

A most exciting recent advance in light microscopy was the invention of laser confocal scanning microscopes. Typically, a specimen 5–10 μm thick is used for most light microscopy. At the highest magnifications, only an optical slice through the object corresponding to the depth of field of the lens used (typically 0.5 μm for a high-power lens) is in sharp focus. Everything above or below contributes an out-of-focus blur superimposed on the plane of interest. This is like a photographer having to cope with a shallow depth of field: there is too much out-of-focus detail in front of and behind the object of interest. The confocal approach eliminates from the image all information above and below the focal plane and thus all the blurry out-of-focus parts of the image. The result is an extremely crisp and contrasty image. Further improvement can then be made by processing the resultant image by computer. Some types of confocal microscopes allow imaging of different focal slices in real time and thus permit the reconstruction of high-resolution three-dimensional information of very thick or even partially opaque objects, such as bone.

THE ELECTRON MICROSCOPE

In 1924, Louis de Broglie's theoretical work showed that moving electrons had wavelike properties, a finding that although coming from a totally unexpected direction led to the events that helped to cross the resolution barrier imposed by the wavelength of light. The idea of an electron microscope seems to have come to several investigators at about the same time. The advantage is that the wavelength of electrons (which depends inversely on their velocity) can be made much shorter than that associated with light photons, so that one could expect a great gain in resolution. (Light can also be thought of as particles, or "photons," as well as waves.) Electrons, which have a negative electrical charge, can be made to move by attracting them to a more electrically positive object, as anyone who has shuffled across a carpet and touched a metal doorknob on a dry day will readily attest. An electron accelerated from rest through as moderate an electrical potential as 100 volts, easily obtained with a simple battery, travels at 2% of the speed of light and exhibits a wavelength of atomic dimensions, about 0.1 nanometers (nm), or 5,000 times smaller than the wavelength of visible light.

In 1928, the physicist Leo Szilard suggested to Denis Gabor (inventor of holography) that an electron microscope should be built. Gabor is supposed to have answered, "What is the use? Everything under an electron beam would turn to cinder." Nevertheless, at just this time in Berlin, Max Knoll and his student Ernst Ruska had begun work on electron lenses, and on June 4, 1931, Knoll gave a talk where he discussed experiments they had done on a two-lens electron microscope. A few days earlier, Reinhold Rudenberg, the director of research for the electrical firm Siemens, had already filed a patent describing how several magnetic lenses could be combined into an electron microscope. Rudenberg left Germany because of the rise of fascism, and Siemens went on to become a manufacturer of electron microscopes used worldwide for many years. Ruska succeeded in bettering the resolution of the light microscope with his second electron instrument in 1933 and, rather belatedly, was awarded the Nobel Prize in physics in 1986 for his part in developing the electron microscope.

Electron microscopes differ from light microscopes in several important respects, though the design philosophies and most of the optical elements are identical. For one, lenses for electrons cannot be made of glass, or indeed any material, since their refractive index for electrons is not sufficient to bend electron paths, and even energetic electrons cannot penetrate more than a fraction of a millimeter of matter. Instead, the magnetic fields of strong electromagnets are used to deflect the electron trajectories, a principle employed in television tubes. Another difference is that electrons are strongly scattered by air molecules, so that the electron trajectories, along with the sample, have to remain in a vacuum, an obvious difficulty for biological specimens which rapidly desiccate in vacuo. Heated tungsten filaments are used as sources of electrons (as in incandescent light bulbs), and photographic emulsions, which are sensitive to both light and electron impingement, can be used to record electron images. In order to view the electron image by eye, a phosphor screen is used, which glows when struck by electrons, just like a TV screen. Electron lenses also suffer from both chromatic and spherical aberrations, as do lenses for light, only much more seriously; the present (1989) resolution limit of about 0.14 nm (about the diameter of a carbon atom) for the best electron microscopes is due to as yet uncorrectable spherical aberration. Chromatic aberration restricts the thickness of specimens to less than 1 μm (1/25,000 inch) for even modest resolutions of 10 nm or so, and to less than 10 nm (about 50 atoms thick) for the highest resolution, because electrons lose velocity and thus change their wavelength in traversing matter. Because the resolution is so much higher than in the light microscope, much higher magnifications can be tolerated and are easily achieved by adding more lenses; magnifications exceeding 1 million times are not uncommon today.

In 1934, Ladislaus Marton took the first micrograph of biological material in an electron microscope of his making in Brussels. This first image was of a section of plant tissue impregnated with osmium. Metal impregnation was deemed important to make the sample heat-conductive in an attempt to protect it from incineration by electron heating, a problem other pioneers bypassed by looking at objects not expected to burn, namely nonbiological samples. Marton's success led to a more pragmatic attitude toward electron microscopy in biology: "Let it burn, but let's look at the cinder!" Damage in the electron microscope is still a grave concern, even in nonbiological material and especially in high-resolution work. Because electrons interact so strongly with matter and because the electron beam is so highly focused at typical magnifications, a simple calculation reveals that the rate of deposition of damaging energy in a specimen under observation approaches that of a modest nuclear explosion!

Shortly after Marton's success, the first steps were taken to commercialize the new instrument in a number of countries: in Germany, where the first commercial unit was released by Siemens in 1938, but also in Japan, England, and the Netherlands. In this country, Vladimir Zworykin (the father of television) at RCA hired Marton to build a microscope. At about the same time (1940), James Hillier began working with Arthur Vance, a high-voltage engineer at RCA. Together, the three designed the RCA model EMU B electron microscope, 60 of which were made for the war effort. These instruments were largely assigned to materials research. Only Francis Schmitt at MIT had one assigned to him for biology. With a number of his colleagues, he made many remarkable observations that contributed enormously to the early understanding of biological organization at the subcellular level. Schmitt and his co-workers worked mainly with isolated parts of cells because of the restrictions imposed on the penetration of the samples by the relatively low voltages employed. Most cells are too thick to be imaged *in toto* except by today's million-volt microscopes. One ingenious way around this problem was to produce replicas of the surface of the sample, which were then directionally shadowed with evaporated films of heavy metals to emphasize the three-dimensional shapes of the objects under study. Various types of replicas and shadowing eventually played an important role in studying the structure of DNA molecules and of cell membranes.

Keith Porter, a young investigator at the Rockefeller Institute, was a pioneer in the culture of cells in vitro and sought another solution. He quickly realized that the edges of cells in culture might be thin enough to allow penetration of the beam and visualization of internal structures. So the study of the ultrastructure of cells was begun by Porter and his colleague Albert Claude. They managed to get after-hours access to an electron microscope installed at the Interchemical Company on New York's West Side. After many tries, they achieved their goal of studying the thin parts of whole cells grown on the specimen holder itself. They used osmium as a fixative because it had been shown to stabilize cellular structure very well. A heavy metal, osmium also provided contrast in the electron microscope because it scatters electrons more effectively than the lighter atoms in biological material. Of special interest to Porter and Claude were viruses that had been used to infect cells. Most viruses are too small to be detected, except in an electron microscope, and had been detected previously only by their biological activity.

Porter's contributions were very important, both for the discoveries he made and for the students he inspired. He was instrumental in designing, among other inventions, a practical microtome that permitted the cutting of slices less than 0.1 μm thick, so thin that they display interference colors like those produced by oil slicks on water. The first such microtomes advanced by thermal expansion, but there were soon mechanical advances made to produce slices of proper thinness more reliably. The blade used for cutting the sections was a piece of plate glass, still used today, although many also use diamond edges, developed in Venezuela by microscopist Humberto Fernández-Morán.

Porter, in his first series of observations using whole cultured cells, described a "reticulum," a cytoplasmic network of tubules and dilatations, which had not been previously recognized. Part of this system is associated with ribosomes, the RNA factories in which proteins are made (see "The Genetic Code," by William A. Haseltine). Many of the parameters of this process were worked out by an early collaborator of Porter's, George Palade. Along with biochemist Philip Siekevitz and others, Palade contributed much of our present understanding of the transfer of proteins from ribosomes into various cellular compartments before export via the Golgi apparatus to other cells.

Osmium tetroxide, so popular with early electron microscopists as a fixative, emphasized membrane structures at the expense of other cellular components. As a result, cells stopped being considered as bags of enzymes, and membranous intracellular organelles became the focus of attention, being correctly interpreted as subcellular compartments with specific roles in the overall cellular economy. It was also discovered that proteins were associated with membranes in a highly organized fashion. It was only with the later introduction of aldehyde fixatives that nonmembrane components were easily explored.

Because thin slices had to be used, an appreciation of the three-dimensional nature of cellular structures could be obtained only by painstaking serial sectioning. Few attempted this endeavor on a large scale. Other approaches that allow three-dimensional study became the subject of much interest. They include high-voltage microscopy (one million volts and up), pioneered by the Frenchman Gaston Dupouy at his institute in Toulouse, which allows imaging of thick objects and, especially when combined with stereoscopic viewing, provides a means of studying the three-dimensional architecture of objects. High-voltage electron microscopy has also had an impact on studies in the physical sciences, particularly for study of thick sections, which preserve more bulklike physical properties, and for *in situ* experimentation.

ELECTRON MICROSCOPY OF NONBIOLOGICAL OBJECTS

The serious application of electron microscopy to the physical sciences had a much later start, partly because there appeared little need at first to reveal details of microstructure beyond those already resolvable by light microscopy, partly because the details of atomic structure in inorganic crystals had already been worked out indirectly by X-ray diffraction in the 1920s and 1930s, and mostly because suitable methods for reducing inorganic specimens readily to electron-transparent thicknesses had not been developed. Photographic emulsions, which consist of finely divided crystalline grains of silver halides, were among the first inorganic materials to be examined, not surprisingly in the instrument built at Eastman Kodak Research Laboratories in Rochester, New York, shortly before 1940, by Cecil Hall. In common with many biological materials, halides decompose in the electron beam, a property that renders them useful for recording electron microscope images but impedes their study in the microscope. Nevertheless, observations of the conversion of light-exposed halide grains into metallic silver were made. Oxide smokes, formed by burning reactive metals such as magnesium in air, became a popular object of study because of the electron transparency of the tiny crystallites produced. Detailed information about surface morphology and surface relief became readily accessible with the development of surface replication techniques in the 1940s, paralleling those developed for biology. These were immediately applied to metallurgical problems, with a great increase in resolution over images obtained by reflection light microscopy.

The idea of looking in transmission through specimens of inorganic substances deliberately thinned to electron transparency (about 0.1 μm or less) did not occur until about 1948, when Robert Heidenreich, working at the RCA Laboratory in New Jersey, developed an electrochemical method for thinning aluminum metal sheet down to electron-transparent foils. Heidenreich's observations and their interpretation represent a classic contribution, because they provided experimental confirmation of crystalline image contrast effects, which had been predicted in theories of electron diffraction, by direct observation of thin sections. They were nevertheless ignored by metallurgists, who continued making replicas, and it was not until the later efforts of Peter Hirsch and his student Michael Whelan at the Cavendish Laboratory in Cambridge that the power of electron microscopy for revealing the internal microstructure of inorganic materials became more fully appreciated. The Cavendish professor at the time, W. L. Bragg (of X-ray diffraction fame), had an interest in the deformation of metals, and Hirsch had begun study of this phenomenon using X-ray methods.

Metals, and indeed all crystalline materials, deform permanently (plastically) by the slippage of planes in the regular array of atoms past each other, much as what happens when one pushes askew a stacked deck of cards. However, the planes do not slip monolithically over each other, but instead an atomic-scale wrinkle, like the rumple in a carpet, is propagated from one side to the other until the shift has occurred. This rumple is called a *dislocation*, and its existence had been theorized for some time. (See Figure 5.) Bragg's successor in the Cavendish chair in 1954, Neville Mott, was particularly keen

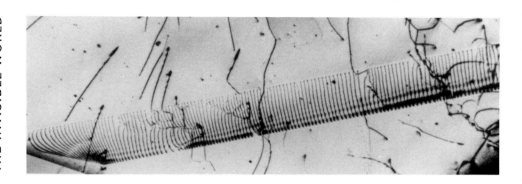

Figure 5. Dislocations in a sample of deformed stainless steel, visible due to small displacements of atoms from their original positions. Imaged at 2 million volts in the microscope at Toulouse. (Source: *The Beginnings of Electron Microscopy* by P. W. Hawkes, ed. Academic Press, Orlando, Florida, 1985).

on pursuing the atomic mechanisms of deformation in metals and encouraged Hirsch to look for dislocations in the electron microscope. Whelan began in 1954 to find ways of thinning beaten aluminum foil, and by 1955 had succeeded not only in imaging dislocations but observing their motion. Walter Bollman made similar independent observations in stainless steel at the Battelle Memorial Institute in Geneva the following year. In retrospect, Heidenreich's 1949–51 images also show dislocation features, but their significance was not appreciated at the time. Similar unappreciated images are apparent in micrographs of mica, taken by Tadatosi Hibi in 1952, and in molybdenum trioxide crystals, taken by another Japanese pioneer, Hatsujiro Hashimoto, in 1954. Hashimoto was a graduate student in electron microscopy in Hiroshima in 1945; miraculously, both he and his microscope survived the nuclear bomb dropped there by the United States on August 6, 1945.

The internal microstructure of metals below 1 μm resolution, revealed for the first time by the electron microscope, is in fact so important to their properties that it has become the main field of operations for modern metallurgy. Developments in alloy design that have made possible modern turbojet aircraft, aerospace missiles, and nuclear reactors all have their origins in microstructural features rendered visible by electron microscopy. The first observations of alloy microstructures were made by electron microscopy. Imaging of many specimens thinned by bombardment with energetic gas ions by Rudolf Castaing in Paris in 1954 in other microstructural features—rapidly followed, pursued at first in precipitates of all kinds, radiation damage—twins, stacking faults, grain boundaries, pre-Cambridge and then in other laboratories throughout the world. About 1970, Castaing's ion-thinning technique was perfected and commercialized and applied to ceramic, semiconductor, and geological materials, opening up these materials to electron microscope investigations previously pursued mostly in metals. The microstructural phenomena observed in all these materials turn out to be so widespread that a new, unified field, materials science and engineering, has arisen that addresses the properties and design of *all* materials—metals, ceramics, electronic materials, even polymers (plastics)—from the point of view of their microstructural origins. Nowhere is this more in evidence than in the development of new electronic materials and devices, in which atomic arrangements are engineered on a microstructural scale visible only with electron microscopy. (See Figure 6.)

Interpretation of the images of the internal structure of materials has formed a large part of electron microscopy in the physical sciences since about 1945, because such images cannot necessarily be naively understood. Hirsch's group at the Cavendish, and later at Oxford, as well as S. Amelinckx's group in Antwerp, have been especially active in formulating a sophisticated theory of image contrast for defects and inhomogeneities. Quite in parallel has been an Australian effort initiated in 1957 by John Cowley (later of Arizona State University) and Alex Moodie, which has been more concerned with images of perfect crystalline structures at the highest resolution. Cowley recognized the potential of high-resolution electron microscopy to reveal atomic arrangements by direct observation, rather than by inference as with X-ray methods. Under favorable conditions and with full appreciation of how the lenses and lens aberrations have manipulated the electron trajectories, it is possible to obtain high-resolution images that are perfect representations of projected positions of the actual atoms regularly repeated in a crystalline structure. (See Figure 7.) While these images are impressive, the real challenge is using such images to deduce atom arrangements at defect sites, such as the cores of dislocations, at interfaces, and on the surface of crystalline solids. An ultimate challenge is to image the arbitrary atomic arrangements in a glass, which has not been and perhaps cannot be done. High-resolution imaging of biological material has been most successful also with objects with repetitive structure, because the redundancy of repeated structural units can be used to average out the damage caused by the investigating electron beam, which ends up statistically different in each unit. Images with resolution below 0.5 nm, essentially molecular dimensions, have been obtained with the aid of computerized image processing techniques and provide important information about the role of molecular configurations in biological activity.

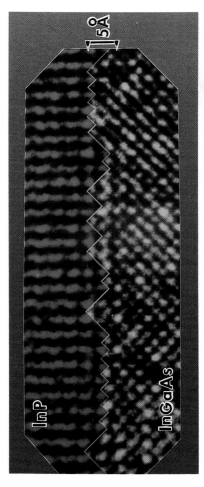

Figure 6. Electron microscope image of an engineered interface between layers of semiconductors indium phosphide (InP) and indium gallium arsenide (InGaAs). The atoms shown were deposited one at a time by a controlled atomic beam. (Photo credit: Dr. Abbas Ourmazd, AT&T Bell Laboratories, Holmdel)

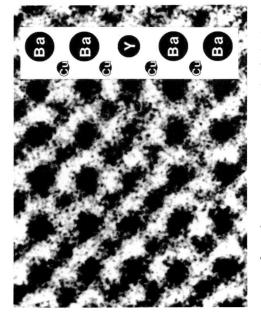

Figure 7. TEM image of metal atom positions in a sample of a high temperature superconductor of yttrium barium copper oxide, taken at 1 million volts. (Photo credit: Dr. Ronald Gronsky, Lawrence Berkeley Laboratory)

SCANNING ELECTRON MICROSCOPY

The conventional electron microscope, like the conventional light microscope, is a *flooding* instrument, in that the specimen is uniformly illuminated at all points, and images of each point are formed in parallel. An alternative way to obtain an image is to build it up point by point, as in a television picture or the scanning confocal light microscope. The idea of obtaining electron microscope images in this way was realized as early as 1937 by Manfred Baron von Ardenne, working in Berlin, whose early instrument was unfortunately destroyed in an air raid in 1944. In this type of microscope, the primary electron beam is focused to a small probe that is scanned systematically across the specimen surface. If the specimen is thin, electrons transmitted through the sample can be detected electronically, and the differences in their transmission from point to point can be used to modulate the brightness of a scanned spot in a cathode ray tube that is scanned synchronously with the electron beam on the specimen. The magnification of the image so formed is the simple geometrical ratio of the dimension scanned on the cathode ray tube to the dimension scanned by the electron beam on the specimen. This configuration is known as a scanning transmission electron microscope (STEM), to distinguish it from the conventional transmission instrument (CTEM).

Alternatively, one can collect secondary electrons that are dislodged by the primary scanned beam and escape from the sample if they originate near its surface. The ease with which secondary electrons are emitted depends on the shape of the surface, peaks being best while crevices effectively trap emission. The primary beam is scanned across the sample and secondaries collected from each point, gradually building up an image of the surface topography of solid specimens. It is this latter approach, known simply as scanning electron microscopy (SEM), that has captured the imagination of every microscopist and made microscopists of virtually everyone else: the instrument can be made as easy to use as a light microscope, requires little or no specimen preparation, and since no lenses are involved after the specimen, has an almost infinite depth of field, giving spectacular three-dimensional images. (See pages 20–21.) The initial development of the SEM was carried out in the engineering department of Cambridge University, starting in 1948, by Charles Oatley and his students Denis McMullan (who completed the first working instrument in 1953 as his Ph.D. thesis) and, later, Kenneth Smith. Invention of an improved secondary electron detector by Thomas Everhart (then a Marshall Scholar at Cambridge and now president of CalTech), together with other improvements by Oatley's group, led to commercialization of the instrument in 1965.

Scanning electron microscopy grew like Alice and brought us all into Wonderland. To the chagrin of the theoretical pessimists who suggested that there would be a limit of 5 nm, perhaps even 10 nm, in the scanning mode, the "theoretical" limits have been successively shattered, and there are now instruments capable of resolving 1 nm (within a factor of five of atomic dimensions) on a routine basis. In the physical sciences, the instrument has become the workhorse of materials scientists, with SEMs as common as light microscopes once were. In biology, it has produced fantastic micrographs of internal cellular structures. These have given us satisfying confirmation that cells are really as we had imagined them to be. Gone are the uncertainties, the difficult and time-consuming reconstructions that were beyond the patience and resources of most investigators. Now all of us are suddenly endowed with the ability to make ourselves, like little Maxwell demons, as small as needed to crawl into things and see for ourselves how organs or cells or microcircuits have been put together.

The scanning transmission electron microscope, pioneered by von Ardenne, was pursued in a quite different direction. Albert Crewe, director of the Argonne National Laboratory in the early 1960s, was convinced that individual atoms could be seen using electron beams, but being a physicist and not a microscopist he had a rather different conception of how to go about it—with a probe and a detector, rather than with conventional microscope optics. Because atoms are small, the probe had to be of atomic dimensions (less than 0.5 nm) and very bright. Crewe bootlegged time, personnel, and laboratory space at Argonne and later at the University of Chicago to develop the requisite bright electron sources and probe-forming lenses. In 1970, Crewe's team succeeded in imaging individual uranium atoms, which had been sparsely deposited on a thin carbon film, and later filmed their motion as they moved about the ledges and terraces of the carbon substrate. (See Figure 8.) Teaming up with biologist-microscopist Elmar Zeitler, their subsequent efforts were aimed at high-resolution studies of biologically significant molecules and at the correction of spherical aberration in electron lenses, the holy grail of electron optics.

NEEDLE POINTS AND TUNNELING CURRENTS

Electron microscopes are not the only way of seeing atoms. Two other methods rely on large variations in imposed electric fields in the vicinity of atoms at the surface of solid specimens. The first of these, field ion microscopy (FIM), was developed by Erwin Müller at Pennsylvania State University in 1956. By appropriate chemical machining, the specimen material is made into a sharp needle at whose tip the radius of curvature is extremely small. If a high voltage is imposed between the tip and a distant observation screen, the resulting very strong electric fields in the vicinity of the needle's tip are sufficient to pull electrons off nearby gas atoms, converting them to positively charged ions that are then accelerated along electric field lines to the observation screen, where they form an image. The electric field at the tip varies locally from atom to atom, and the gas atoms can be arranged to ionize only near the atom sites, effectively sampling atomic positions. The effective magnification, 10 million times or so, is due to the diverging electric field lines, in much the same way as a pinhole camera operates. (See Figure 9.) The local electric field is strongest for atoms at the edges of terraces formed by the stacking up of spherical atoms to form the hemispherical cap of the needle's tip—these configurations are best appreciated by stacking up arrays of marbles, a modeling activity playfully engaged in by field ion microscopists, much to the amusement of their more inhibited colleagues. Robert Hooke, who showed a magnified image of a needle's point to his Royal Society colleagues in 1663, would have been amazed at the detail in his specimen had he been able to blow it up another million times. He would doubtless have been dumbfounded by a recent variant of the technique in which individual atoms, imaged in the FIM, can be pulled off the specimen *one by one* and sent into a device to be chemically analyzed!

A second approach to imaging surface atoms began only in 1980 with an idea of Heinrich Röhrer's, a physicist at IBM's research center in Zürich. He reasoned that if a sharp needle point, of the sort used for field ion microscope tips, were brought close enough to a specimen surface, the electron clouds of a protruding atom on the tip and of a surface atom in the specimen would at some point overlap, and an electric current could be passed through them, even though the tip and the specimen were not actually touching. Such a current is called a *tunneling current* (a quantum-mechanical effect) and increases exponentially with decreasing separation between tip and specimen atom. Here, then, was an atomically sensitive probe of surface topography, which could be made to form images of a surface if the tip were mechanically scanned across the specimen an atom or two's distance above its surface. (See Figure 10.) Röhrer and his colleague Gerd Binnig spent the next year developing mechanical manipulators of the requisite precision and emerged with the scanning tunneling microscope (STM), for which they were awarded the Nobel Prize in 1986, sharing the honor with Ernst Ruska, father of a quite different sort of electron microscope 50 years before. Unlike TEM, SEM, and FIM, scanning tunneling microscopy can be carried out in air or even under water, opening up a whole field of surface chemical reactions to microscopical exploration on an atomic scale—a happy circumstance that, had it occurred 200 years earlier, would certainly have sent Henry Baker marching off to his London publisher with an idea for yet another book on the microscope!

WHERE TO, MICROSCOPY?

And what of future conquests in the invisible world? We already have reached the atomic limit, at least in inorganic materials, with the biologists not very far behind at the molecular level. There are near-atomic-scale techniques

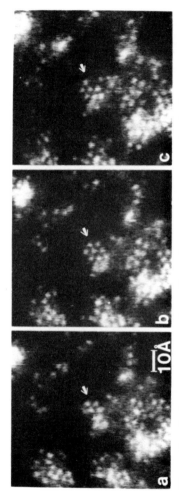

Figure 8. An image sequence from Crewe's STEM, showing individual uranium atoms on a carbon substrate. The exposures were taken at 17 second intervals, and show that the atoms moved between exposures. (Photo credit: Albert V. Crewe, University of Chicago)

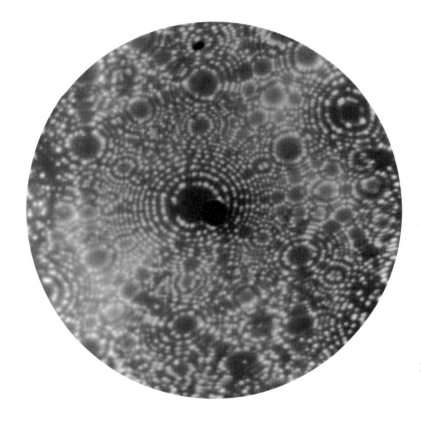

Figure 9. Field ion microscope image of iron atoms at the tip of a needle. The effective magnification is about 2 million times. The central black area is a hole through which atoms may be extracted for chemical analysis. (Photo credit: Sidney Brenner, University of Pittsburgh)

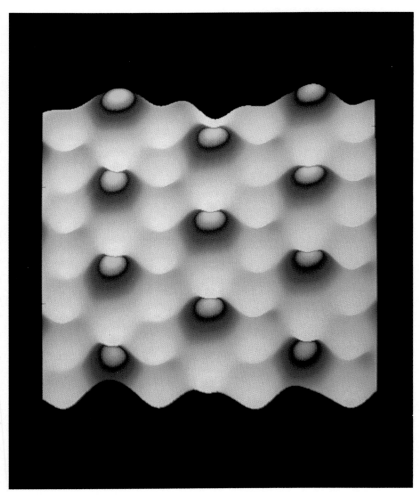

Figure 10. STM image of iodine atoms (blue) adsorbed on a platinum surface (green). This structure is important for understanding catalytic processes. Color added. (Photo credit: Bruce C. Schardt, Purdue University)

presently available for assessing not only structure, but also microscopic chemical composition, which are only now being applied to biological specimens after 30 years of use in the physical sciences. These permit one to localize biologically important ions with greater certainty and to directly measure their concentrations in different parts of the cell. All electron microscopy methods at present suffer from having to use dead samples because they have to be exposed to the high vacuum of the microscope and suffer intense radiation in the electron beam. While this is of little consequence to the materials scientist who studies inanimate objects, it is of great concern to the biologist who would like to freeze his sample's structural details in place. In fact, literal freezing of hydrated samples reduces the damage induced by both vacuum and the electron beam. Recent advances in the development of rapid freezing techniques for tissue preservation have helped to reduce the formation of ice crystals, which have heretofore distorted both morphology and distribution of ions in frozen thin sections.

There are other microscopies that hold out the promise of less damage to the specimen. X-ray microscopy has been made possible through the realization that X-rays could be focused by zone plates of the type introduced by Zernicke for phase contrast microscopy and by the availability of high-brightness X-ray sources at synchrotron accelerator installations, such as those at Hamburg, Daresbury, Stanford, and Brookhaven. Unlike electrons, X rays have high penetrating power, and they promise better resolution than the light microscope. The use of photoelectron emission microscopy, revived by Hayes Griffith in Oregon, has a bright future as another approach to looking at cellular structures that might also give chemical information. There are dark horses, too, represented by acoustic microscopy and nuclear magnetic resonance (NMR) imaging, though it is not too likely these will ever reach the resolution of any of the forms of electron microscopy. We are seemingly limited only by our ability to generate suitable probes and invent apposite acronyms! Of course we have to be ever so careful: for each futurist there are so many whose vision has proved defective, like Sam in Dickens's novel. We are more likely to mispredict than to be correct. Yet those of us who are too cautious will be rapidly passed by events. How could one have guessed that today's light microscope could detect structures much smaller than the early electron microscopes, or that electron microscopes would permit one to see molecules and even atoms? All of these achievements seemed unthinkable only a few years ago. Who could have predicted that positron emission tomography (PET) combined with NMR imaging would give information about what part of the brain is active under different conditions, and that we could see it happen in the head of a living human being, the experimenter himself?! Abbe was right not to underestimate the genius of that organism.

THE OMMATIDIUM MINIATURES

MICHAEL BISHOP

ILLUSTRATION BY
ALAN GUTIERREZ

"A IS FOR APHID." EMMONS COULD NEVER RECALL HIS MOTHER without thinking of the ABC books of microscopic phenomena that she had compiled to amuse him during long summer afternoons on Tybee Island. A microscopist of acknowledged creativity, Kathleen Emmons had published one of these books under the off-putting title *An Abecedary of the Near Invisible.* To almost everyone's surprise, it became a best-seller. For the next few years you couldn't find a home with elementary-school-age children anywhere in the country without a copy of her book lying on a coffee table or sticking out of a bookcase.

"A Is for Aphid," it asserted. And on the facing page, looking to young Emmons more like bug-eyed outer-space monsters than like microscopic insects, a herd of potato-shaped aphids elephant-walked the magnified branch of a muscadine vine. Deeper into the picture book, you learned that "D Is for Diatom," "M Is for Microchip," "R Is for Rotifer," and you saw the stunning micrographs illustrating these statements. But the siphon-nosed aphids at the outset of his mother's book were the creatures that had fascinated Emmons as a boy. Thus, he'd leapt at the invitation of International MicroDyne and begun preparing for his drop-down. He had done so not only to test the minute engines of the company's new technologies but also to solder a spiritual link with his past—when, once upon a time, *he'd* been small: an embryonic personality struggling to creep out from the shadows thrown by his mother's success and his father's international reputation.

The Incredible Shrinking Man. On the seventh floor of the IMD Sensor and Actuator Center in a northern suburb of Atlanta, Emmons sat in a conference room watching a video of a 1957 sci-fi flick he had previously avoided having to see. Watching this movie was one of the weirder requirements of the field-test training that McKay had masterminded for the pilot of the company's first microremote; and as Scott Carey, the movie's common-man protagonist, shrank to the size of a three-year-old boy, a mouse, and, finally, a bipedal cockroach, Emmons's attention wobbled.

"I can't believe you've never seen this," said McKay, leaning into him in the carpeted dark and flinching when Carey stabbed his straight pin up into the belly of an attacking spider. "It's a certifiable classic."

But Emmons thought it smart to refrain from confessing that he hated the movies, that he had always hated the movies, and that he was grateful to his parents for encouraging him to develop other interests; he kept his eyes—not his mind—on the oversized screen and said nothing. McKay, a personnel rather than a research-and-development specialist, sincerely believed that even Micro-Dyne's brightest technicians could benefit from the psychological training provided by a sci-fi "classic" like *The Incredible Shrinking Man*, and when an executive of his rank took that sort of tack, what else could you do but comply?

"To God There Is No Zero." For now, high on the screen, Scott Carey, who had squeezed into his garden from a window ledge in the basement, was gazing at the impossibly distant stars and all the muddled galaxies. "That existence begins and ends," said the actor Grant Williams in the film's final voice-over narration, "is man's conception, not nature's. And I felt my body dwindling, melting, becoming nothing. My fears melted away, and in their place came acceptance. All this vast majesty of creation, it had to mean something. And then I meant something, too. Yes, smaller than the smallest, I meant something, too. To God there is no zero. I still exist!"

And B is for bullshit, thought Emmons, for it appeared to him that all he had seen in the film—denial, alienation, degradation, struggle—refuted Carey's concluding cry of existential yea-saying; indeed, the hero's fears about his own insignificance, and life's ultimate meaninglessness, were *underscored* by the fact that Carey was going to go on shrinking forever.

Being There. McKay had the lights brought up. He still got a boost from the film's upbeat gloss on the existential ramifications of littleness.

"Going down isn't easy," he told Emmons. "It's different from light microscopy, different from electron microscopy, and different from doing hands-on manipulations with a stereo-microscope assist. *Being there*—down among the dust mites, so to speak—is an *intenser* sort of microscopy, Emmons. Even if, on the literal level, you're operating a tiny waldo, doing watchmaker tasks with silicon pincers the size of an amoeba's paws.

"You have to overcome the possibility of 'dimensional shock' and take your bearings from the point of view of a nematode, say, or a spider colt. You have a learn to see again, at what I like to call 'ground zero.' Theoretically, it seems smart to work your way to the needed redimensionalization slowly. Which is why I've asked you to watch *The Incredible Shrinking Man* and then to discuss it with me."

Emmons discussed the film with McKay, certain that his boss was enjoying their talk—as he had the movie—immeasurably more than he was.

Frogs and Philistines. During their talk, McKay noted that Science—Emmons could hear the capital—had long ago declared that certain species of frog could not see anything in their environment inapplicable to their day-to-day existence. They were selectively blind to whatever failed to advance their survival or immediate well-being. The nonessential was invisible to them. A dragonfly at mealtime would loom like a helicopter, but an animal neither edible nor threatening—a wading heifer, for example—would splash by unregarded.

Scowling, McKay noted that some human philistines had a similar trait; namely, an inability to see anything that so much as hinted at parentheticality or irrelevance, i.e., the microscopic.

Emmons's mind cast back to his mother's abecedaries: McKay was preaching to the converted. If A wasn't for "aphid," then it was for "amoeba;" if F wasn't for "follicle," then it was for "flea." The naked human eye could not distinguish two dots less than a tenth of a millimeter apart, but from an early age he had trained himself to see all that the human eye *could* see.

How, then, was he either a frog or a philistine?

His mother had helped make him sensitive to the invisible—the infusoria in a vial of creek water—and his father, whose namesake Emmons was, had made these lessons stick by seeing to it that he often felt like a mere protozoan. In fact, of late Emmons secretly saw himself as someone whom others did not fully register: a spear carrier in a play or some anonymous urban scarecrow sleeping in the gutter.

F Is for "Father," F Is for "Flea." The Emmonses' beach house on Tybee Island had always been full of dogs: Newfoundlands, poodles, Russian wolfhounds. It had also been full of fleas.

As McKay lectured, Emmons recalled his father striding shoeless in his tennis whites over the rattan mats on their concrete porch. Fleas jumped from the mats onto the damp cotton of his father's sweat socks, where their hard little bodies took on the instant visibility of commas or periods. His father picked off each flea with his thumb and forefinger and dropped it into the hot tapwater in an otherwise empty fish tank.

Lying on their pinched sides, the fleas kicked pathetically on the surface. Finger-jabbed, they spiraled, still kicking, to the bottom, where, eventually, the kicking ceased.

The elder Emmons, who seldom played very long with his namesake because his son usually netted more shots than he returned, would spend the rest of the morning decoying, seizing, and dunking fleas, moving from spot to spot on the mats to entice fresh generations of vermin to spring onto his socks. This intellectual celebrity, the computer scientist and backdoor cosmologist who had extended and redeemed his once-discredited mentor Edward Fredkin's science of "digital physics," would scold young Emmons for failing to capture fleas, too.

To the world at large, he held up the dictum that the universe is a computer—that atoms, electrons, and other subatomic particles are built from infinitesimal bits of information; that reality is grainy; and that there exists a single underlying programming rule to account for the movement and purpose of each of its constituent grains—but to his twelve-year-old son on Tybee, in the microcosmos of his family's summer retreat, he preached filial devotion, a more disciplined forehand smash, and the philosophical-cum-recreational benefits of flea-tweezering.

Microscopic Rain and a Midget's Parasol. "In a sense," Mckay was saying, "Carey was lucky. He shrank by degrees, with plenty of chances to make adjustments."

Emmons, returning from his flashback, became aware of the dense particulate rain in his boss's strangely appointed office. Decay products from the radioactive gases thrown off by the ceiling tiles and the Sheetrock walls rained down as an invisible but inescapable fallout. The air was afire. It fell in charged veils, sleeting, draping, folding back on itself to repeatedly stipple his boss with iotas of disintegrating matter. Also, the molecules on the surface of McKay's aircraft carrier of a desk were migrating aside to allow the falling particles to penetrate and rape it.

A guilty horror seized Emmons as he watched the rain, a shower clearly imperceptible to McKay, who was jawing about "acclimating declensions" and giving odd examples:

"The smallest adult human being recorded, Emmons, was a Mexican midget called Lucia Zarate. At seventeen, Señorita Zarate stood two feet and two inches tall and weighed not quite five and a half pounds. This nineteenth-century freak could have stepped from one of the Montgolfiers' balloons, popped a parasol, and floated safely to earth. On her trip down, she could have leisurely scrutinized a torrent of high-altitude plankton: pollen grains, lichen fragments, the spores of fungi, bacteria, algae, and so forth. If MicroDyne could bring off that easy a drop-down, Emmons, you'd have no sweat accepting your littleness."

But Emmons kept thinking how handy the señorita's parasol would have been: a shield against the invisible deluge.

"*Let's Get Small.*" McKay's office was a museum of the minute. It contained an elegant miniature of the living room of the Tybee Island beach house—down to a baby baby grand piano, an itsy-bitsy computer station, a dinky fireplace with even dinkier andirons and grates, a collection of foraminifer shells, and a gallery of framed Kirkuchi patterns (diffraction images of various alloy particles as created and photographed inside a transmission electron microscope) no bigger than postage stamps.

A newt-sized plastic doll of Emmons's canonized father sat in a wicker rocker in this mock-down of their old beach house, gazing at the Kirkuchi patterns and thinking godly thoughts. McKay paid no attention to these items, he'd seen them so many times before, but Emmons knew that this miniature architectural tribute to his father had triggered his flashback as surely as had McKay's jabber about frogs and philistines. The urge seized him to grab the father doll and pop it between his fingernails as if clicking the carapace of a flea—but, even as a tiny doll, his father remained a Micromegas in Emmons's view, and he couldn't do it.

Elsewhere in McKay's office there were Lilliputian cathedrals, miniature divans, Tinker Toy forts, and a display case containing gnat robots, beetle jeeps, electrostatic motors, and microdozers. The spiders that had draped some of these furnishings with gauze were living creatures, just like Emmons, but everything inanimate in the room mocked him by seeming more cunningly made.

"Ever see a tape of Steve Martin doing his classic 'Let's Get Small' routine?" McKay had just asked. "God, I love that routine. Think 'high' for 'small.' You'll get a grip on microminiaturization as a kind of occupational addiction. Look around. You can see why a shtick like that would appeal to me. . . ."

Inadequacy, Impotence, Insignificance: A Tract. That evening, in his apartment, Emmons worried that even his competence as a microremote engineer hadn't given him the sense of self possessed by a pompous company shill like McKay. Would going down—getting smaller—do the trick?

If H isn't for "humility" (an abstract noun), then it's for "hydra" (a tube-shaped freshwater polyp with a mouth at one end ringed by tentacles). And another definition of hydra is "a multifarious evil not overcome by a single effort." How to cope with the fact that the hydra he'd been struggling to defeat wasn't any sort of evil, but rather the achievements of a mother who'd led the world's scientific community toward the one computational Rule governing every nanometer of space and perhaps explaining everything?

Forget that Fredkin's Rule—as his father had dubbed it—was still incompletely teased out. Forget that many scientists still blasted both the elder Emmons and the late Fredkin as, at best, "inspired crackpots." *Emmons* was now an Olympian name. Although the son bearing it was proud of his name, he was also cowed by it, mindful of the meagerness of his own efforts in comparison to his parents'. He seemed doomed by the scale of their reputations to fall on his face in any attempt to match them. He was too small to rival their successes, a bacterium in a life-extinguishing drop of acid: Scott Carey with a Ph.D. in microengineering.

"It's a Didinium-Eat-Paramecium World." Germaine Bihaly, who lived across the complex's parking lot, showed up at his door with a tray of Cantonese carryout boxes, each one a small soggy chalet packed with steamed chestnuts, sweet-and-sour meats, plump shrimp, or vivid strings of slime defying identification.

"Share?" she said.

Emmons let her in. Bihaly was a travel agent, whom he had met over the telephone while booking a flight to a sensor-and-actuator conference in Berkeley. Later, he had coincidentally found her to be one of his neighbors.

They ate Chinese sitting on the ad sections from the *Atlanta Constitution.* Emmons explained why he felt like the incredible shrinking man and told her how, as part of his training, he'd had to watch an old sci-fi flick and then listen to McKay gab about its applicability to the piloting of microremotes.

Unsympathetic, Bihaly said, "Hey, Emmons, it's a *Didinium-eat-Paramecium* world," a joke between them ever since he had shown her his mother's sequential micrographs of a predatory ciliate seizing and absorbing another ciliate species nearly twice the *Didinium*'s size. Wasn't he a big boy? Couldn't he take care of himself in the sharkish corporate world?

Later, Emmons, frightened and tentative, hovered over Bihaly's body like a gar above the remains of a hammerhead's kill.

The Night Testimony of Leeuwenhoek. Bihaly stayed anyway, and Emmons dreamed that he was an animalcule in a moist cavern among a population explosion of such creatures, all fidgeting, feeding, and reproducing in a balmy darkness not unlike that of MicroDyne's company pool.

What most upset Emmons about his presence among these nameless microorganisms was the heightening of his own namelessness by their large numbers. The indeterminacy of the Where in which he and all the other tiny beasties multiplied also bothered him. But, at last, a voice spoke over, around, and through him—like God making a proclamation—and he knew that he and the bacteria around him were cliff-dwelling on the speaker's gums.

"I dug some stuff out of the roots of one of my teeth," boomed the dead Dutch lens grinder and scope maker, Anton van Leeuwenhoek, Emmons's host. *"And in it I found an unbelievably great company of living animalcules, amoving more nimbly than I had seen up to now. The biggest sort bent their bodies into curves in going forwards, and the number of animalcules was so extraordinarily great that 'twould take a thousand million of some of them to make up the bulk of a coarse sand grain."*

In his sleep, Emmons shriveled.

"Indeed, all the people living in our United Netherlands are not as many as the living animals I carry in my mouth." Emmons had once read that Leeuwenhoek attributed his lifelong ruddy health to a hot Ethiop beverage—coffee—that "scalded the animalcules" in his mouth. Emmons's arms reached out for Germaine Bihaly, but they could not find her.

Artificial Fauna in a Day-Care Zoo. For the past seven months, Emmons had stopped nearly every morning on the edge of the day-care courtyard. He watched the kids swarm over the fiberglass backs of pink dinosaurs and the extruded-foam statues of giraffes.

Today, he saw a mechanical crane lowering into the courtyard an armored monster so much like a menacing alien crab that most of the kids dashed into the arms of day-care workers to escape it. Emmons knew it for the jungle-gym simulacrum of a dust mite, magnified thousands of times. Its body plates and serrated front claws were gigantic. Detracting from its realism, size aside, was the absence of magnified counterparts for the carpet fibers, hair strands, and skin flakes that cling to living dust mites.

"Educational, don't you think?" said McKay, appearing behind Emmons as if from nowhere.

Emmons stayed mute. He imagined the kids climbing on the dust mite like parasites on parasites, *ad infinitum.* A team of workmen positioned the yawing statue on its base, and Emmons wondered if possibly there weren't a few situations in which it might not be so bad to be parasitized.

The Relativity of Time Consciousness. "When you're down there, Emmons, you'll feel like the Methuselah of the microverse. That's because your eyes and hands will be electronically plugged into the ommatidia and manipulators of your remote. Generations will come and go, but you'll endure.

"Your consciousness—unlike poor Scott Carey's—will be up here in the Sensor and Actuator Center with me, President Sawyer, and the kids out there in the courtyard, but you'll be interacting with critters for whom a second may be an hour and a day a lifetime. That could rattle you."

McKay pointed to the hummingbird feeder on the far edge of the fiberglass zoo and to the ruby-throats hovering about it.

"Those guys have a metabolic rate higher than that of any other bird or mammal, Emmons. About twelve times that of a pigeon, about a hundred times that of an elephant. A second for a hummingbird is equivalent to two or three minutes for a whale. Just imagine what an hour down in the microdimensions could be, and remember that as you observe and actuate, okay?

"You've got to have this conception of yourself as being in two places at once, but you've got to subordinate your real-world self to the one on microsafari. Otherwise, you'll screw up. We don't sweat the screw-ups for MicroDyne's sake, Emmons. One day, we'll mass-produce microbots in the same kind of volume that the folks in Silicon Valley do microchips. It's *your* well-being we're worried about. We don't want to take a raving loon or a mindless artichoke out of actuator harness."

McKay consulted his watch. Less than two hours to drop-down. It would roll around in either an eyeblink or an ice age, depending on which of his anxieties Emmons set his inner clock by.

Telemetry vs. Manned Redimensionalization. Bihaly could not understand why International MicroDyne, or any other multinational mass-producing flea-sized actuators and invisible sensors, thought it necessary to plug the eyes and mind of a human being into the tiny contraptions that were already evaluating the safety of space-shuttle parts, encoding new functions on gallium-arsenide chips, and overseeing the manufacture of other microbots.

"Hell, Bihaly, to boldly go where no one's ever gone before," Emmons told her. "Why weren't we satisfied to fling only a lander at Mars? Why do our astronauts perform EVAs when a machine could do the job a helluva lot more safely?"

Bihaly continued to object. Emmons wasn't going to shrink, not like that guy in the sf film; in fact, he wasn't going to go bodily to the microdimensions at all. But, according to McKay, there was a psychological hazard as forbidding as the prospect of stranding an astronaut on Titan.

"So please tell me," Bihaly said, "why you've chosen to be the first Micro-Dyne employee to accept the risk?"

"It's pretty simple, really. I want to send back this message to McKay: 'That's one baby step for amoeba-kind, one gigantic step for Yours Truly.' Ain't it a shame the lousy drop-down's not going to be televised?"

The Map Is Not the Territory, the Name Is Not the Thing Named. McKay took him into the hermetic, dust-free room in which he was to execute the drop-down and perform his mission. "Dust-free," McKay hurried to qualify, in the sense that only the target area—a bell of clear glass eighteen inches in diameter and six high—contained any dust, organic debris, or moisture. As for Emmons himself, he would not really be in this room, but in a nearby operator's booth, jacked into the microremote prototype beneath the glass bell in the center of the otherwise vacant floor of this otherwise featureless chamber. In sterile yellow boots and coveralls, the two men stared down on the bell.

"My Mildendo," Emmons said.

McKay lifted his eyebrows.

"The capital city of Lilliput," Emmons said. He saw that the dome's inner circle had been quartered into pie wedges of jungle, desert, ocean, and a landscape of Mondrianesque microcircuitry. It was a map, a relief map. As a very small boy, he had once taken a Texaco road map from the glove box of his dad's Audi and studied it as if it were a two-dimensional kingdom, convinced that the names of towns were the town themselves and that dot-sized people really lived there.

A fantasy that his mother's microscopy had given a credibility that even beginning grade school hadn't undermined.

Today the fantasy had come true. The map was the territory (even if the name was still not the thing named.) As he and McKay knelt to examine the bell more closely, Emmons had the unpleasant sensation that he was both a demiurge to this little world and one of its puny inhabitants.

O Is For "Ommatidia." What must it be like to be a gnat gazing up through the bell at McKay and him? Would the ommatidia of one of those tiny insects even register them, or would their images be fragmented into so many repeating split screens that the creature's brain rebelled against the overload?

An ommatidium—as Emmons and half the population of the United States had learned thirty years ago from *An Abecedary of the Near-Invisible*—is one of the light-sensitive facets of the compound eye of a fly, a honeybee, or a dragonfly. The dragonfly, his mother's book had said, has more of these honeycomblike optical drupes than does any other insect, nearly thirty thousand.

Emmons loved the word: *Ommatidium.*

Dragonflies saw the world fractured, divvied up, split-screened to infinity, which, of course, was also the way that Emmons lived his life and saw reality. It was the same discontinuous, grainy, particulate world amplified in his father's brilliant reworking of Fredkin's private science, digital physics. And just as thousands of ommatidia working together brought useful information out of the fundamental graininess of the world, so, too, might Fredkin's Rule precipitate from the countless information bits of the universe one crystalline truth that made perfect sense of the whole.

Emmons said it to himself as a mantra: Ommm-atiddy-ummm. Ommm-atiddy-ummm. Ommm-atiddy-ummm.

"You'll see more when you're down there," McKay said, puffing as he climbed off the floor. "From a human vantage, the bell's pretty damn empty-looking and ordinary-seeming. But there's stuff in there, all right, and you'd best get to it."

Emmons, standing, had a dizzying image of thousands of immense, cockamamie avatars of himself backing away from the dome and fading off into a vast blue muzziness.

Inside the Microtaur. Emmons entered the operator's booth and, with McKay's and two businesslike technicians' help, placed himself in harness.

His invisible vehicle—the one at the very center of the sealed dome—was smaller than a weevil nymph, much too tiny for unassisted detection. Its dimensions qualified it as a micro-, rather than a nano-, technological wonder, but it had not been manufactured by the whittle-away process employed for most of MicroDyne's current wares; instead, it had been drexlered—built up atom by atom—from virtual nothingness, so that it had not only a clear exterior shape under the scanning electron microscope, but also an intricately made interior, or cockpit, with fine one-to-one correspondences to all the controls in the human-scale operator's cab.

Outwardly, the remote resembled a cross between an armor-plated combat vehicle, moving on treads, and an eight-armed crab. Emmons regarded it as the spider-mite equivalent of a modern tank and the mythological centaur, a kind of high-tech microtaur.

Strapped into his seat and plugged into the vehicle's sensors and actuators, Emmons finally received the signal for drop-down. Obediently, he hit the switches in their proper sequences. *Wham!* Brobdingnagian landscapes bloomed, and he was there, an intruder in the pettiness and majesty of the microdimensions.

Down Among the Dust Mites. "That's one baby step for amoeba-kind," Emmons said, but the realization that he was moving forward on tiny caterpillar treads made him cut short the guff. He could float, he could tractor, he could shinny, and, by the unfurling of veil-like wings, he could even fly a little, escaping by a hair the fate of insects so nearly weightless that the Brownian movement of random molecular action could buffet them to doom.

What he couldn't do was walk—not as a person walked, anyway—and his first true dimensional shock, all training aside, was the weirdness of this lack. Simulator trials had been helpful, but not wholly to the point. After all, the incredible shrinking man had not had to give up his body as he dropped toward the infinitesimal, only the dumb assumptions that size bestowed dignity, that whatever was small was willy-nilly of no import. The great whales of the seas and the bacterial populations in the human gut, Emmons knew, were . . . well, *equally meaningless lifeforms.*

But not being able to ambulate as human beings usually do—that was a bitch. Down among the dust mites, you had to motor like dust mites. If you didn't do in Rome as the Romans did, you could count on going nowhere but crazy. Frustrated, Emmons slapped at switches like a kid trying to undercut an upright Babel of ABC blocks.

Reverberations from the Voice of God. "Emmons, you idiot, stop that!" McKay thundered from afar. "I can't believe you're behaving this way! You haven't done a blasted thing yet!"

But Emmons could believe it. He was a child again, overwhelmed by his father's disdain, lost in an utterly mystifying world.

"Easy," God advised. "Caterpillar into Quadrant Dust Jungle. We'll try the microchip wirings after you've had a chance to take your bearings there."

Emmons settled down; he headed the microtaur into Quadrant Dust Jungle, treading through a gray tangle of pet hairs, grease-coated cotton fibers, cat-flea eggs, pollen grains, skin scales, severed strands of spider webbing, and lopsided arches of unidentifiable gunk and fuzz.

Initially, this alien landscape fascinated Emmons, more by its grotesquerie than by its "beauty," but the longer he piloted the microtaur the more grim and monotonous it seemed. He was reminded of boyhood car trips across the panhandle of Oklahoma.

Boredom was settling on him when he saw a scale-freckled dust mite micrometering over the detritus-cobbled terrain, and he neared the retiring critter, a sort of cow-cum-crayfish, just to see what it would do.

It sensed the microtaur and switched directions. Thus baited, Emmons caterpillared after the mite, careful not to overtake it in his zeal to enliven things.

Relatively soon, he came among dozens—hundreds—of other such mites grazing through the spun-dust jungle of the quadrant. They were microdimensional cattle, heifers of the waste declensions of the very small.

"Reorient your vehicle and head for the EPROM chips in Quadrant Microprocessor!" demanded God.

Grudgingly, Emmons obeyed.

Taking the Tour. Over a period of days, Emmons's microtaur did a grand promenade of the bell, creeping into the separately sealed Quadrant Microprocessor to perform Herculean cutting, pasting, and wire-connecting labors on the wafers arrayed there, and incidentally clabbering them with debris from Dust Mite Territory.

Never mind, said McKay; it was the execution of the preassigned tasks that mattered, not their ultimate results, for under optimum conditions their results were entirely predictable. It was the doing of them by hands-on intervention at "ground zero" that was being tested.

"A is for A-OK," the godly McKay intoned. "Good job, Emmons."

In the control booth, Emmons took nutrients through IV stylets and fatigue-offsetting electrostimulus through the wires externally mapping his nervous system.

His microtaur entered Quadrant Living Desert, where its treads terraced a landscape of sand grains, humus particles, and buried seeds. Beneath this promise squirmed springtails and earthworms, creatures out of the *Dune* books, while beneath them unraveled miles of fungal mycelium and loop snares. The microtaur's drexlered claws seized nematodes, tardigrades, and Panta-

gruelian lice. It brought minute soil samples into its collection baskets, then tractored out of Quadrant Living Desert into its final microenvironment, Quadrant Waterworld.

Here, it unshipped flagellate oars to power it through a realm of rotifers, ciliates, and diatoms.

Despite his various energizing hookups, Emmons was exhausted. He hadn't slept for days. If he failed to get some sleep soon, he would begin—even in this hallucinatory realm—to trip out. McKay and MicroDyne were hard taskmasters. He hated them for protracting his mission and for holding him so long in actuator harness. A pox on the bastards.

A Rendezvous with Mytilina. Emmons's microtaur sculled through Quadrant Waterworld and all its light-shot, alga-forested grottoes, bucking, releasing ballast, sounding, rising again.

Eventually, it neared a branching filamentous tree, jewel-green in the submarine stillness, on which a single crystal rotifer had gingerly perched. By its thornlike toes (resembling paired tails), its red eye-spot (like a speck of blood in a minute package of egg white), and its transparent shell (or lorica), Emmons knew it for a representative of the genus *Mytilina.*

It bobbed in the currents stirred by the MicroDyne vehicle, but otherwise appeared unalarmed, even though Emmons understood that the rotifer was aware of his approach. In fact, it actually wished for him to close with it so that they could converse.

"McKay," he said, activating his throat mike, "this is weird. A goddamn rotifer wants to talk with me."

When no one in the Sensor and Actuator Center replied, Emmons knew that the *Mytilina* had willed his isolation from his co-workers and that a meeting with the creature was inevitable.

"Son," it said. "Son, what do you think you're doing?"

How Can the Perceiver Know That Which Composes Its Apparatuses of Perception? Each separate hairlike process ringing the mouth of the rotifer wiggled at its own ever-altering rate. The sound waves generated by these "smart" vibrations belled out through the water, colliding with, building upon, or subtly damping one another as the *Mytilina* itself required, so that by the time the shaped wave-front struck the sensors of his vehicle, it was—Emmons could think of no other appropriate term—"recognizable human speech." On the other hand, Emmons realized that the speaker was actually either God (not McKay & Friends, but the Living God) or his own celebrity father in the guise of a microorganism.

"Maybe this is just my way of trying to help deduce the Rule," Emmons replied. "Didn't you always claim that the basic units of reality are very small, that the universe only seems continuous because we can't see the parts from which it's made? It's like a pointillistic painting by Seurat seen from a long way away. Walk closer and you see the dots. The same with Sunday's funnies. Take a magnifying glass and you'll see the specks of colored ink making up Linus's security blanket."

The crimson eye-spot of the bobbing rotifer pulsed, growing and shrinking at the whim of some inner cadence.

"Derek," it said, "can eyes composed of the smallest units in existence perceive those units? Do you really believe such a situation possible or likely?"

(Either the Deity or my dad is scolding me, Emmons thought. Give heed.)

"Remember," the *Mytilina* said, wobbling on its algal perch. "If the universe is a computer, everything happening as a result of its existence is innately incapable of understanding that it runs at the *direction* of that computer. The software, Derek, can't know the hardware—just as ommatidia the size of the smallest grains comprising reality can never see those grains. Put another way, they can never know—perceive—themselves."

Know Thyself. The rotifer talked to Emmons for mind-made ages; the purpose of the mystic computer of the universe—to answer the question posed by its hidden creator—was obvious. But both the answer and the question itself remained obscure to the universe's sentient representatives because the algorithmic program running to provide the answer was still in process. Not even God—as the *Mytilina* itself could attest—had the answer yet, and no one could guess how much longer the program had to run before it burped out its solution.

Emmons's head began to ache. Other "wheel animalcules" drifted into view, curlecuing toward his father's emerald tree like pixels filling a computer screen.

"Join us, Derek," the rotifer said. "Escape that shell you're hiding in and join us here in Quadrant Waterworld."

It confessed that although he might never learn the question God had posed the universe, being too small to perceive anything that vast, and too integral a part of the program in process to have an objective vantage on it, he might yet learn a few things that would repay him for slipping out of harness into the amniotic warmth of the very small.

Emmons, in the submerged microtaur, saw this as the best offer he'd had in years. Doggedly, he started to prise up electrodes, unplug jacks, strip away wiring, and pull out IV stylets. Free at last, he would crawl into the ejection tube and shoot himself into the tiny water world now harboring both his father and God.

Z Is for Zero, Which to God Does Not Exist. McKay ordered two burly technicians into the barricaded control booth. But before they could restrain him,

Emmons—sweaty, pop-eyed, thick-tongued—fell back into his padded chair as if siphoned of all memory and will. The operator's cab was a shambles. (His microremote yawed in an emerald orchard of algae and glassy rotifers.) Feverishly, McKay and his cohorts worked to revive Emmons.

Bihaly's appearance wasn't providential—she had been worrying about the drop-down—but McKay's decision to let her in before the company doctor arrived may have been. "Rick," she said, using her private diminutive. "Rick, look at me."

Emmons's eyes opened. Above him, the faces of Bihaly, McKay, and the doctor orbited one another like the kaleidoscope jewels. He felt nothing—not relief, gratitude, or panic—only a fine, pervasive nothingness drifting through him like pollen through the foliage of evergreens. So what? Nothingness was okay. It might even be survivable. To God, after all, there was no zero. Nothingness was nothingness. To a man, nothingness was the thing.

Emmons had been down for slightly more than four hours, a fact McKay's blurred watch face withheld from him. Again, no matter. Eventually, his eyes would adjust. Maybe, when they did, Bihaly, who had called him back from that which cannot see itself, would still be there and, with her, he would try to understand all that had ever happened to him.

THE LIVING CELL

ESSAY BY
MARCEL BESSIS

SPECULATION BY
ISAAC ASIMOV

CELL ECOLOGY

MARCEL BESSIS
*CENTRE D'ECOLOGIE CELLULAIRE HÔPITAL
DE LA SALPÊTRIÈRE*

TRANSLATED BY GEORGE BRECHER
UNIVERSITY OF CALIFORNIA, BERKELEY

THE HISTORY OF THE STUDY OF INDIVIDUAL CELLS DATES BACK a mere 300 years—to the times of Malpighi, Swammerdam, and Leeuwenhoek. They were the first to observe and report on the wonders of the microscopic world. The enthusiastic tales written by the chroniclers of the time, after a visit to any one of the men, enable us to understand the wonder that seized those who had just realized the existence of "Living Creatures 100,000 times smaller than the Human Body." Robert Boyle says in his *Discourse on the Usefulness of Experimental Philosophy:*

Upon comparing the Structure of a Mite with that of an Elephant, the largeness and Strength of the One may strike us with Wonder and Terror, but we shall find ourselves quite lost in Amazement, if we attentively examine the several minute Parts of the Other. For the Mite has more Limbs than the Elephant, each of which is furnished with Veins and Arteries, Nerves, Muscles, Tendons, and Bones: it has Eyes, a Mouth and a Probiscis too (as well as the Elephant) to take in its Food; it has a Stomach to digest it, and Intestines to carry off what is not retained for Nourishment: it has a Heart to propel the Circulation of its Blood, a Brain to supply Nerves everywhere, and Parts of Generation as perfect as the largest Animal. Let us now stop, look back, and consider, as far as our Abilities can reach, the excessive Minuteness of all these Parts; and if we find them so surprising and beyond our Ideas, what shall we say of those many species of Animalcules, to whom a Mite itself, in Size, is as if it were an Elephant.

INSTRUMENTS AND TECHNIQUES

Boyle's amazement would have been even greater, had he been transplanted into the second half of the twentieth century. There he would have witnessed the extraordinary profusion of new chemical and physical techniques, the discovery of the electron microscope (Figures 1 and 2), the miniaturization of instruments, and new standards of measurements scaled down to the size of individual cells. (See "The Invisible World," by Linn W. Hobbs and Jean Paul Revel.) These advances have made it possible to study the anatomy, physiology, and pathology of single cells the same way one would study the whole organism, except on a scale 50,000 times smaller. With these tools, we have discovered that the organelles of cells correspond, in the functions of complex organisms, to organs.

As a result, an important new way of thinking about the cells of living beings has taken shape during the past 10 years. Now cells are considered as individuals, grouped into various "populations" (cell types) with different populations grouped in different organs. As with the whole organism, one may consider them demographically: the populations of cells are born, renew themselves, grow old, and eventually die.

The different cell types that live together in, for example, the bone marrow

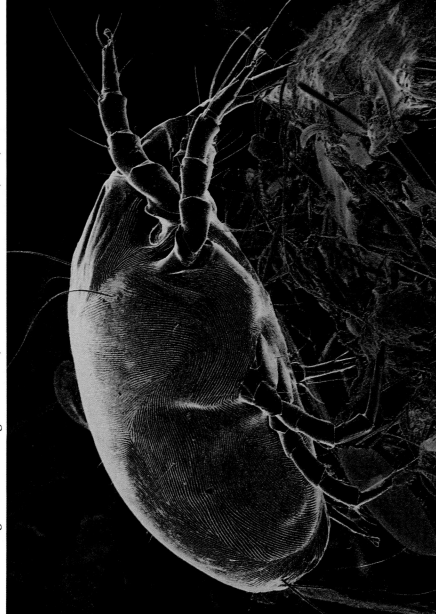

Figure 1. SEM image of a mite. (Photo credit: © David Scharf, 1986)

of an adult constitute a population of individuals that is 100 times larger than the world's human population. These large numbers suggest that it may be possible to observe events of great rarity in individual cells with sufficient frequency to see evolutionary developments within the lifetime of an individual person.

Mutations are just such rare events, and because they are heritable, and the cell population is so huge, mutations of individual cells capable of division should produce observable subpopulations of abnormal (i.e. mutated) cells. Since such subpopulations of abnormal cells are not usually observed (in healthy individuals), the organism must have means to dispose of most such cells. But we lack information on two main points:

1. The mechanisms of homeostatic equilibrium which maintain an equilibrium between cells being born and cells dying.

2. The mechanisms of selection in the elimination of abnormal cells. (According to one theory, the body may no longer recognize some altered cells as its own, and then may form antibodies against them, as it does against foreign cells, and destroy them. This process, still hypothetical, is often referred to as "immunosurveillance."

Thus, each of our organs is populated by groups of individual cells, and the whole may be likened to a large city and its subdivisions, with its own laws and with the births and deaths of its citizens. This point of view makes possible the study of the social behavior of cells, which we may call "cyto-ecology," or "cell ecology."

"Ecology" is a very recent word, proposed by Ernst Haeckel at the end of the nineteenth century. The definition is simple: Ecology is the science that studies the environments of living beings and the relationships among the living beings and the environment. Experimental ecology studies these relationships while changing the environment.

Studying the cell in its natural or artificial environment, the cellular ecologist utilizes the kinds of techniques, knowledge, and hypotheses of zoologists and human and animal sociologists. The biologist who studies the migration of whales can be enlightened by someone who studies the behavior of ants and the cytologist whose subjects are microscopic. It is tempting to think that increased size goes hand in hand with increasing complexity, and miniaturization with simplification. In fact, an individual cell is as complex as the whole organism.

Cell behavior and the interactions of a cell with its environment can be most impressively observed through an optical microscope with phase contrast optics. This type of microscope, first used in the late 1940s, converts variations of the refractive index (the ability to bend light rays) into variations of intensity, which the eye then sees as shades of gray. Since the internal structures of cells, the organelles, differ in their refraction, details of living cells can now be seen. With the conventional light microscope cells had to be killed, fixed, and stained to allow internal structures to be seen. Moreover, the phase contrast microscope reveals the organelles more distinctly in living cells then does the conventional microscope in the cadavers of killed cells (Figure 3). With a movie camera (1950s), or videocamera (1970s), observations can be made of phenomena that are inaccessible to the traditional microscopist. It is fair to say that the movie camera, the principle tool of the animal ecologist, is also the primary tool of the cell ecologist.

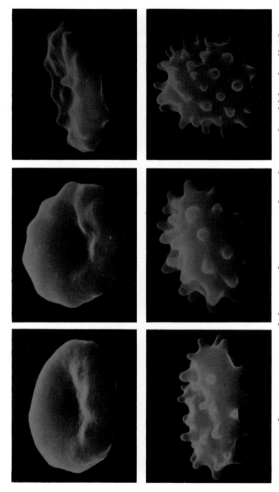

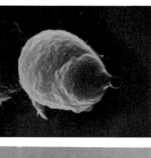

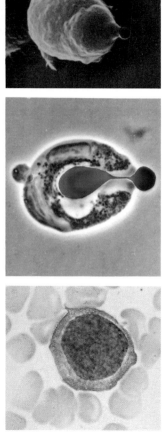

Figures 2a-f. SEM images of the transformation of an abnormal red blood cell (discocyte) into a spiny shape (echinocyte), due to changes in the cell environment. (Photo credit: © Marcel Bessis)

Figure 3a (*left*). Standard optical image of a dye-stained, dead stem cell (blood cell precursor). This kind of cell is found in bone marrow. *3b* (*center*) A phase-contrast image of a white blood cell ingesting a red cell (color added). The cells appear to be nearly transparent. *3c* (*right*) An SEM image of a white cell ingesting a red cell. Color added. (Photo credit: © Marcel Bessis)

Time-lapse cinematography transforms days into minutes, hours into seconds. Cells move so slowly that they appear to stand still if observed directly. Cells that in real-time seem to be lifeless become intensely animated on the cinematographic screen. Just as it is necessary to enlarge the cells a thousandfold or more to "see" their forms, so it is necessary to accelerate their movements greatly to "see" their behavior (Figure 4).

The combination of cinematography and other techniques permits experimentation on cell behavior. Microirradiation by lasers or by ultraviolet light can kill an individual cell or even inactivate a single intracellular organelle, permitting study of dead cell scavenging by neighboring cells, and the behavioral changes of the injured cell. With microspectrophotometers, we can identify and measure the amount of substances secreted by cells. Miniaturized culture systems make it possible to vary the physical, chemical, and cellular environments.

In the living organism, cells are always in a microenvironment, a microclimate, that has a major influence on the way cells grow and mature. Because we cannot study individual cells in the living organism, we remove living cells to artificial media for study. It was first thought that a simple salt solution was a sufficiently physiologic environment (thence the term "physiologic saline"). Biologists soon learned, however, that artificial media must more closely approximate the microenvironment of the living animal if the cells are to maintain their functions. Today such media contain growth factors, inducers of specific functions, and other molecules of the microenvironment of living animals. We can now manipulate the artificial environment so that the molecules that come in contact with the cell surface can alter it and influence the interior of the cell as well. For example, by addition of erythropoietin (blood cell growth factor) to certain growth media, we can induce the development of undifferentiated blood precursor cells (normally in the bone marrow) to ma-

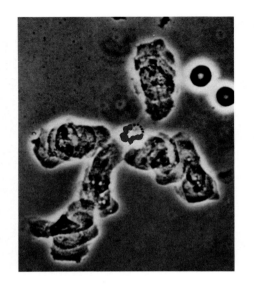

Figure 4. Necrotaxis. Phagocytes tearing apart a laser-killed red cell in a "feeding frenzy." Phase contrast, multiple exposure. Color added. (Photo credit: © Marcel Bessis)

ture red blood cells. Genetically engineered erythropoietin is just coming on the market, as a substitute for long-term blood transfusions. It promises to revolutionize dialysis and treatment of bone cancer.

ECOLOGICAL NICHES

The cyto-ecologist is particularly interested in the "protected territories" in the various organs (for example, in certain parts of the bone marrow, the intestine, and the thymus). These territories are the equivalent of ecological niches, parts of the Earth's environment where animals in the wild can survive and reproduce.

The erythroblastic island in the bone marrow is a good example of one of these niches. It consists of one or two centrally located macrophages (specialized white blood cells) surrounded by erythroblasts (nucleated precursors of red cells) at all stages of maturation. The erythroblasts remain in contact with the body of the macrophage or its long cytoplasmic extensions throughout development. The macrophages also digest red blood cells that have reached the end of their lives and then impart the remnants of the digested cells to developing young red cells, thus nourishing them (Figures 5 and 6). They are analogous to digesters such as sow bugs and bacteria in macroscopic ecological systems, recycling dead and waste products into usable materials for new growth.

Microcinematography reveals that the microphage cytoplasm is very active: its extensions move rapidly (within a minute or two) among the surrounding wreath of erythroblasts, producing intimate but fleeting intercellular contact.

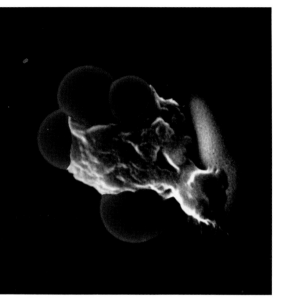

Figure 5. Polyphagocytosis. A phagocyte and three red cells, transformed from discocytes into spherocytes in the process. Color added. SEM image. (Photo credit: © Marcel Bessis)

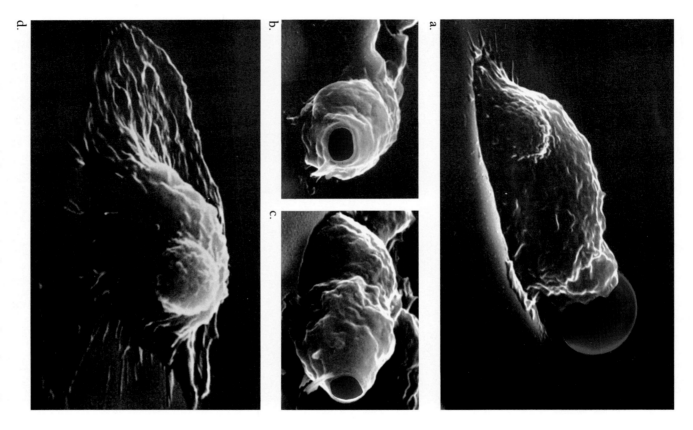

Figures 6a-d. Stages of phagocytosis of spherocytes. The white cell captures the red cell, and engulfs and digests it. Color added. SEM images. (Photo credit: © Marcel Bessis)

Viewed three-dimensionally with a scanning electron microscope, the erythroblastic island is a spongelike structure in which erythroblasts lie in pockets formed by infoldings of the surface of the macrophage. The erythroblasts are thus relatively protected and not digested by roaming macrophages, which might see the immature cells as "foreign."

As each erythroblast matures, it moves away from the main body of the macrophage, along the cytoplasmic extension, leaving in its wake a developing series of red cell precursors. When sufficiently mature, the erythroblast detaches from the cytoplasmic extension of the macrophage and eventually enters the blood circulation.

HOMING

It has been known for some time, though it has been insufficiently emphasized, that cells of a given organ can recognize other cells derived from the same organ and stick to them. If dispersed cells from liver, heart, kidney, and lung of the same embryo are placed in a tissue culture flask, selective reaggregation will occur. Liver cells adhere to liver cells, lung cells to lung cells, and kidney cells to kidney cells. Highly selective migration also occurs when bone marrow cells injected into the blood stream of irradiated mice (to cure potentially lethal marrow failure) seed and proliferate exclusively in the bone marrow.

Paul Weiss coined the term "homing" for this capacity of cells to recognize their normal environment and return to it. The mechanism of homing is only beginning to be understood: receptors have been identified on stationary cells and complementary molecules on homing cells; as the homing cells pass by they attach to the receptor cells because their complementary molecules fit like a key in a lock.

Homing must play an important role in both normal and pathologic states. For instance, cancerous cells seem to lose their ability to recognize their normal home and create metastases (secondary distant growth) throughout the body. Yet certain cancers metastasize preferentially in certain locations, which could mean that the altered (cancerous) cells are still homing but to different environments.

NECROTAXIS

The reaction of living cells to dying or dead cells varies greatly, depending on the tissue, the quantity of cells being rapidly or slowly transformed into cadavers, and the causes of death. Microirradiation with a laser beam makes it possible to kill a single cell in a group of cells. The normal lifetime of blood cells is from seven hours (granular cell), to 120 days (red cells), to many years (lymphocytes). As soon as the dying cell shows signs of distress the healthy cells

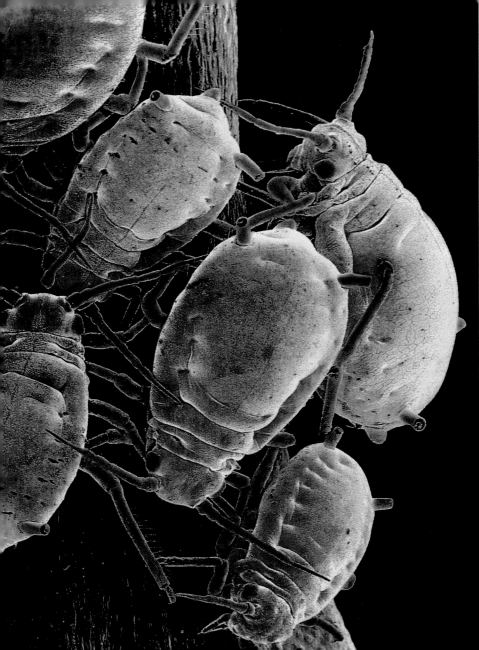

in the vicinity gather around. Within 5–10 minutes, the dead cell is surrounded by phagocytes, specialized white blood cells that can ingest and digest a variety of particulate matter. They tear the cellular corpse apart. Recently arrived phagocytes push aside the ones that have already formed a rosette around the corpse in order to obtain their share of the prey (Figure 4). This behavior, which calls to mind the "feeding frenzy" of sharks attacking other injured sharks, is called "necrotaxis." The phenomenon of necrotaxis poses a number of questions: What is the nature of the message, most likely chemical, sent by the dying cell? What receptors allow the phagocytes to recognize the message? By what mechanism can they follow the message to the target?

So far, we have only partial answers to these questions. We have known for a long time that foreign cells, whether living or dead, are attacked by phagocytes. This is an immunologic process, in which the body attacks cells that are "nonself." But in the phagocytosis of dying or dead cells, the body's own cells are attacked, as if the dying or dead cells were also "nonself." The mechanism of this apparently nonimmunologic recognition of dying or dead cells remains to be determined.

Figure 7. Aphids grazing on a lemon leaf. Part of the microscopic community that amazed Hooke and Leeuwenhoek. SEM image. (Photo credit: © David Scharf 1980)

THE ECOLOGY OF CANCER CELLS

Cancer cells are not always readily distinguishable from normal cells, hence a precise definition that fits all circumstances is impossible. As a good approximation it may be stated, however, that cancer cells are cells of the body that have become altered so as to be able to form tumors. Yet depending on the microenvironment, cancer cells do not always form tumors. Experiments concerning a particular mouse tumor, teratocarcinoma, illustrate the different behaviors of cancer cells in different environments. These experiments, and those concerning human leukemic cells, both demonstrate that cancer cells can behave like normal cells following changes in the microenvironment.

EXPERIMENTAL TERATOCARCINOMA

The interplay between cancer cells and the environment is especially striking in mouse teratocarcinomas. Injecting embryonal teratocarcinoma cells into the skin of mice causes cancer, killing the animals within a few weeks. Injection of the same cells into a mouse embryo fails to give rise to cancers. Moreover, the mice are born and develop normally. Yet the injected "cancerous" cells, which can be traced by their pigmentation (they are black) in their new hosts, are found in several of the normal tissues of the maturing mouse. This experiment shows that the environment can force cancerous cells to behave like normal cells. We have to say "behave like" normal cells, because when retransplanted into the skin of normal mice, the cancer cells again produce tumors in the new host.

HUMAN LEUKEMIAS

Remission or cure of leukemias generally requires the killing of leukemic cells. However, remission or cures have occasionally been observed during pregnancy, after certain viral infections, and after exchange transfusion without chemotherapy. Such spontaneous normalization of malignant cells after manipulation of the microenvironment is rare, but it unquestionably occurs.

Has the normal organism the potential of changing leukemic cells back to normal? Can leukemic cells be induced to behave normally by a normal microenvironment? Recent experiments in vitro (in the test tube) on the maturation of leukemic cells are beginning to answer these questions.

The cells of acute myelogenous leukemia fail to mature; their development appears irreversibly arrested at an early stage of maturation. However, if certain substances are added to cultures of these cells, the leukemic cells mature despite their malignant transformation. The substances capable of inducing such maturation are relatively ordinary and nontoxic, such as the solvent DMSO (dimethylsulfoxide), retinoic acid, certain hormones, and some growth factors.

These observations give us hope that the antileukemic therapy of the future may be based on ecological factors and their regulatory effects on cell maturation, rather than on elimination of the leukemic cells by radiation and chemotherapy. Ideally, ecological therapies will replace the present treatments, which affect not only malignant cells, but also normal cells.

CONCLUSION

In his seminal work on what he called the *milieu interieur* (internal environment) of cells, nineteenth-century French physiologist Claude Bernard posited that the relative constancy of the *milieu interieur* makes organisms independent of their environment, at least to a degree. Today that notion remains of fundamental importance, but as the preceding discussion has made clear, it needs to be modified in light of what we now know about cells and their environments.

First, close examination of the *milieu interieur* reveals that it is not truly constant. Rather, it is in a continual state of fluctuation and disequilibrium, always searching for an internal equilibrium that is distinct from that of the environment.

Second, the *milieu interieur* in turn is made up of numerous microenvironments, each different, each in search of its own equilibrium, and each a building block of the overall *milieu interieur.*

So no microenvironment is an island unto itself: each molecule, each organelle, each cell, and each organ in a living organism depends on the larger environment which surrounds it. There is a stratified ecology of life encompassing many environmental levels, from the geographical region where the organism lives (that region itself influenced by climate and other factors), to the microclimates and microenvironments of the various organs, to the subsystems of cells, and even down to the genes. Some years ago, scientists believed that genes had a rigid structural order—that they were not influenced by the environment around them, and by the organism's own environment (see "The Genetic Code," by William A. Haseltine.)

Progress in understanding life and improving health will come with increasing knowledge of the body's varied *milieux interieur* and their interaction with its various cell populations. The level of complexity in these interrelations is the equal to any among the earth's natural environments. However, since the scale of cell ecology is smaller and controlled experiments are possible, progress should be relatively rapid.

TOO BAD!

ISAAC ASIMOV

ILLUSTRATION BY
BRIAN SULLIVAN

THE THREE LAWS OF ROBOTICS

1. A robot may not injure a human being or, through inaction, allow a human being to come to harm.

2. A robot must obey the orders given it by human beings except where that would conflict with the First Law.

3. A robot must protect its own existence as long as such protection does not conflict with the First or Second Law.

GREGORY ARNFELD WAS NOT ACTUALLY DYING, BUT CERtainly there was a sharp limit to how long he might live. He had inoperable cancer and he had refused, strenuously, all suggestions of chemical treatment or of radiation therapy.

He smiled at his wife as he lay propped up against the pillows and said, "I'm the perfect case, Tertia, and Mike will handle it."

Tertia did not smile. She looked dreadfully concerned. "There are so many things that can be done, Gregory. Surely Mike is a last resort. You may not need it."

"No, no. By the time they're done drenching me with chemicals and dowsing me with radiation, I would be so far gone that it wouldn't be a reasonable test. . . . And please don't call Mike 'it.'"

"This is the twenty-second century, Greg. There are so many ways of handling cancer."

"Yes, but Mike is one of them, and I think the best. This is the twenty-second century, and we know what robots can do. Certainly, I know. I had more to do with Mike than anyone else. You know that."

"But you can't want to use him just out of pride of design. Besides, how certain are you of miniaturization? That's an even newer technique than robotics."

Arnfeld nodded. "Granted, Tertia. But the miniaturization boys seem confident. They can reduce or restore Planck's constant in what they say is a reasonably foolproof manner, and the controls that make that possible are built into Mike. He can make himself smaller or larger at will without affecting his surroundings."

"*Reasonably* foolproof," said Tertia with soft bitterness.

"That's all anyone can ask for, surely. Think of it, Tertia. I am privileged to be part of the experiment. I'll go down in history as the principal designer of Mike, but that will be secondary. My greatest feat will be that of having been successfully treated by a minirobot—by my own choice, by my own initiative."

"You know it's dangerous."

"There's danger to everything. Chemicals and radiation have their side effects. They can slow without stopping. They can allow me to live a wearying sort of half-life. And doing nothing will certainly kill me. If Mike does his job properly, I shall be completely healthy, and if it recurs"—Arnfeld smiled joyously—"Mike can recur as well."

He put out his hand to grasp hers. "Tertia, we've known this was coming, you and I. Let's make something out of this—a glorious experiment. Even if it fails—and it won't fail—it will be a glorious experiment."

Louis Secundo, of the miniaturization group, said, "No, Mrs. Arnfeld. We can't guarantee success. Miniaturization is intimately involved with quantum mechanics, and there is a strong element of the unpredictable there. As MIK-27 reduces his size, there is always the chance that a sudden unplanned reexpansion will take place, naturally killing the—the patient. The greater the reduction in size, the tinier the robot becomes, the greater the chance of reexpansion. And once he starts expanding again, the chance of a sudden accelerated burst is even higher. The reexpansion is the really dangerous part."

Tertia shook her head. "Do you think it will happen?"

"The chances are it won't, Mrs. Arnfeld. But the chance is never zero. You must understand that."

"Does Dr. Arnfeld understand that?"

"Certainly. We have discussed this in detail. He feels that the circumstances warrant the risk." He hesitated. "So do we. I know that you'll see we're not all running the risk, but a few of us will be, and we nevertheless feel the experiment to be worthwhile. More important, Dr. Arnfeld does."

"What if Mike makes a mistake or reduces himself too far because of a glitch in the mechanism. Then reexpansion would be certain, wouldn't it?"

"It never becomes quite *certain*. It remains statistical. The chances improve if he gets too small. But then the smaller he gets, the less massive he is, and at some critical point, mass will become so insignificant that the least effort on his part will send him flying off at nearly the speed of light."

"Well, won't *that* kill the doctor?"

"No. By that time, Mike would be so small he would slip between the atoms of the doctor's body without affecting them."

"But how likely would it be that he would reexpand when he's that small?"

"When MIK-27 approaches neutrino size, so to speak, his half-life would be in the neighborhood of seconds. That is, the chances are fifty-fifty that he would reexpand within seconds, but by the time he reexpanded, he would be a hundred thousand miles away in outer space and the explosion that resulted would merely produce a small burst of gamma rays for the astronomers to puzzle over. Still, none of that will happen. MIK-27 will have his instructions and he will reduce himself to no smaller than he will need to be to carry out his mission."

Mrs. Arnfeld knew she would have to face the press one way or another. She had adamantly refused to appear on holovision, and the right-to-privacy provision of the World Charter protected her. On the other hand, she could not refuse to answer questions on a voice-over basis. The right-to-know provision would not allow a blanket blackout.

She sat stiffly, while the young woman facing her said, "Aside from all that, Mrs. Arnfeld, isn't it a rather weird coincidence that your husband, chief designer of Mike the Microbot, should also be its first patient?"

"Not at all, Miss Roth," said Mrs. Arnfeld wearily. "The doctor's condition is the result of a predisposition. There have been others in his family who have had it. He told me of it when we married, so I was in no way deceived in the matter, and it was for that reason that we have had no children. It is also for that reason that my husband chose his lifework and labored so assiduously to produce a robot capable of miniaturization. He always felt he would be its patient eventually, you see."

Mrs. Arnfeld insisted on interviewing Mike and, under the circumstances, that could not be denied. Ben Johannes, who had worked with her husband for five years and whom she knew well enough to be on first-name terms with, brought her into the robot's quarters.

Mrs. Arnfeld had seen Mike soon after his construction, when he was being put through his primary tests, and he remembered her. He said, in his curiously neutral voice, too smoothly average to be quite human, "I am pleased to see you, Mrs. Arnfeld."

He was not a well-shaped robot. He looked pinheaded and very bottom heavy. He was almost conical, point upward. Mrs. Arnfeld knew that was because his miniaturization mechanism was bulky and abdominal and because his brain had to be abdominal as well in order to increase the speed of response. It was an unnecessary anthropomorphism to insist on a brain behind a tall cranium, her husband had explained. Yet it made Mike seem ridiculous, almost moronic. There were psychological advantages to anthropomorphism, Mrs. Arnfeld thought, uneasily.

"Are you sure you understand your task, Mike?" said Mrs. Arnfeld.

"Completely, Mrs. Arnfeld," said Mike. "I will see to it that every vestige of cancer is removed."

Johannes said, "I'm not sure if Gregory explained it, but Mike can easily recognize a cancer cell when he is at the proper size. The difference is unmistakable, and he can quickly destroy the nucleus of any cell that is not normal."

"I am laser equipped, Mrs. Arnfeld," said Mike, with an odd air of unexpressed pride.

"Yes, but there are millions of cancer cells all over. It would take how long to get them, one by one?"

"Not quite necessarily one by one, Tertia," said Johannes. "Even though the cancer is widespread, it exists in clumps. Mike is equipped to burn off and close capillaries leading to the clump, and a million cells could die at a stroke in that fashion. He will only occasionally have to deal with cells on an individual basis."

"And every moment of those hours will increase the chance of reexpansion."

"Still, how long would it take?"

Johannes's youngish face went into a grimace as though it were difficult to decide what to say. "It could take hours, Tertia, if we're to do a thorough job. I admit that."

Mike said, "Mrs. Arnfeld, I will labor to prevent reexpansion."

Mrs. Arnfeld turned to the robot and said earnestly, "Can you, Mike? I mean, is it possible for you to prevent it?"

"Not entirely, Mrs. Arnfeld. By monitoring my size and making an effort to keep it constant, I can minimize the random changes that might lead to a reexpansion. Naturally, it is almost impossible to do this when I am actually reexpanding under controlled conditions."

"Yes, I know. My husband has told me that reexpansion is the most dangerous time. But you will try, Mike? Please?"

"The laws of robotics ensure that I will, Mrs. Arnfeld," said Mike solemnly. As they left, Johannes said in what Mrs. Arnfeld understood to be an attempt at reassurance, "Really, Tertia, we have a holo-sonogram and a detailed cat scan of the area. Mike knows the precise location of every significant cancerous lesion. Most of his time will be spent searching for small lesions undetectable by instruments, but that can't be helped. We must get them all, if we can, you see, and that takes time. Mike is strictly instructed, however, as to how small to get, and he will get no smaller, you can be sure. A robot must obey orders."

"And the reexpansion, Ben?"

"There, Tertia, we're in the lap of the quanta. There is no way of predicting, but there is a more than reasonable chance that he will get out without trouble. Naturally, we will have him reexpand within Gregory's body as little as possible—just enough to make us reasonably certain we can find and extract him. He will then be rushed to the safe room where the rest of the reexpansion will take place. Please, Tertia, even ordinary medical procedures have their risk."

Mrs. Arnfeld was in the observation room as the miniaturization of Mike took place. So were the holovision cameras and selected media representatives. The importance of the medical experiment made it impossible to prevent that, but Mrs. Arnfeld was in a niche with only Johannes for company, and it was understood that she was not to be approached for comment, particularly if anything untoward occurred.

Untoward! A full and sudden reexpansion would blow up the entire operating room and kill every person in it. It was not for nothing it was underground and half a mile away from the viewing room.

It gave Mrs. Arnfeld a somewhat grisly sense of assurance that the three miniaturists who were working on the procedure (so calmly, it would seem, so calmly) were condemned to death as firmly as her husband was in case of—anything untoward. Surely, she could rely on them protecting their own lives to the extreme; they would not, therefore, be cavalier in the protection of her husband.

Eventually, of course, if the procedure were successful, ways would be worked out to perform it in automated fashion, and only the patient would be at risk. Then, perhaps, the patient might be more easily sacrificed through carelessness—but not now, not now. Mrs. Arnfeld keenly watched the three, working under imminent sentence of death, for any sign of discomposure.

She watched the miniaturization procedure (she had seen it before) and saw Mike grow smaller and disappear. She watched the elaborate procedure that injected him into the proper place in her husband's body. (It had been explained to her that it would have been prohibitively expensive to inject human beings in a submarine device instead. Mike, at least, needed no life-support system.)

Then matters shifted to the screen, in which the appropriate section of the body was shown in holo-sonogram. It was a three-dimensional representation, cloudy and unfocused, made imprecise through a combination of the finite size of the sound waves and the effects of Brownian motion. It showed Mike dimly and noiselessly making his way through Gregory Arnfeld's tissues by way of his bloodstream. It was almost impossible to tell what he was doing, but Johannes described the events to her in a low, satisfied manner, until she could listen to him no more and asked to be led away.

She had been mildly sedated, and she had slept until evening, when Johannes came to see her. She had not been long awake and it took her a moment to gather her faculties. Then she said, in sudden and overwhelming fear, "What has happened?"

Johannes said, hastily, "Success, Tertia. Complete success. Your husband is cured. We can't stop the cancer from recurring, but for now he is cured."

She fell back in relief. "Oh, wonderful."

"Just the same, something unexpected has happened and this will have to be explained to Gregory. We felt that it would be best if *you* did the explaining?"

"I?" Then, in a renewed access of fear, "What has happened?"

Johannes told her.

It was two days before she could see her husband for more than a moment or two. He was sitting up in bed, looking a little pale, but smiling at her.

"A new lease on life, Tertia," he said buoyantly.

"Indeed, Greg. I was quite wrong. The experiment succeeded and they tell me they can't find a trace of cancer in you."

"Well, we can't be too confident about *that*. There may be a cancerous cell here and there, but perhaps my immune system will handle it, especially with the proper medication, and if it ever builds up again, which might well take years, we'll call on Mike again."

At this point, he frowned and said, "You know, I haven't seen Mike."

Mrs. Arnfeld maintained a discreet silence.

Arnfeld said, "They've been putting me off."

"You've been weak, dear, and sedated. Mike was poking through your tissues and doing a little necessary destructive work here and there. Even with a successful operation you need time for recovery."

"If I've recovered enough to see you, surely I've recovered enough to see Mike, at least long enough to thank him."

"A robot doesn't need to receive thanks."

"Of course not, but I need to give it. Do me a favor, Tertia. Go out there and tell them I want Mike right away."

Mrs. Arnfeld hesitated, then came to a decision. Waiting would make the task harder for everyone. She said carefully, "Actually, dear, Mike is not available."

"Not available! Why not?"

"He had to make a choice, you see. He had cleaned up your tissues marvelously well; he had done a magnificent job, everyone agrees; and then he had to undergo reexpansion. That was the risky part."

"Yes, but here I am. Why are you making a long story out of it?"

"Mike decided to minimize the risk."

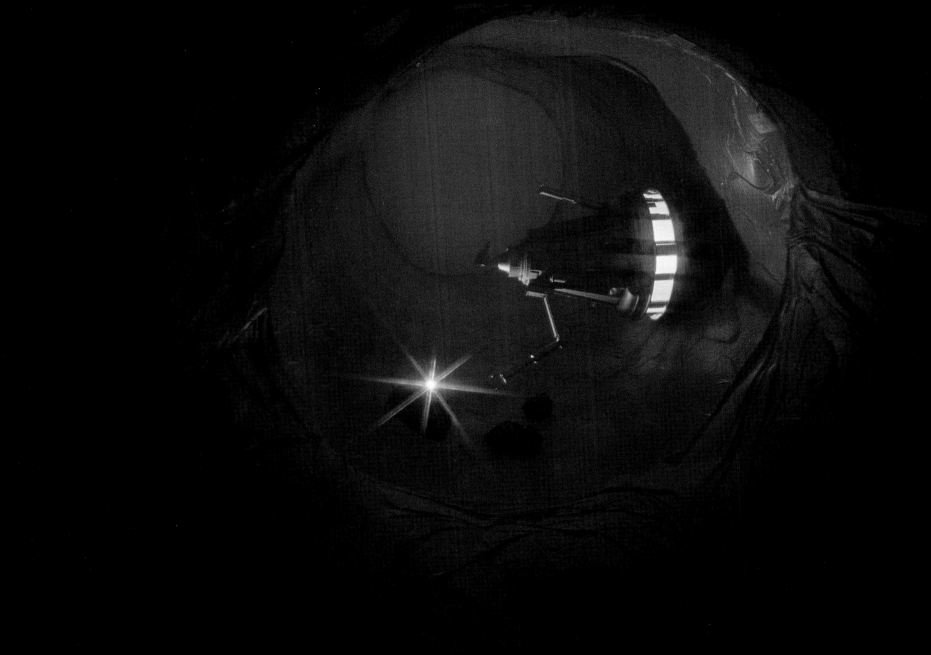

"Naturally. What did he do?"

"Well, dear, he decided to make himself smaller."

"What! He couldn't. He was ordered not to."

"That was Second Law, Greg. First Law took precedence. He wanted to make certain your life would be saved. He was equipped to control his own size, so he made himself smaller as rapidly as he could, and when he was far less massive than an electron he used his laser beam, which was by then too tiny to hurt anything in your body, and the recoil sent him flying away at nearly the speed of light. He exploded in outer space. The gamma rays were detected."

Arnfeld stared at her. "You can't mean it. Are you serious? Mike is dead?"

"That's what happened. Mike could not refuse to take an action that might keep you from harm."

"But I didn't want that. I wanted him safe for further work. He wouldn't have reexpanded uncontrollably. He would have gotten out safely."

"He couldn't be sure. He couldn't risk your life, so he sacrificed his own."

"But my life was less important than his."

"Not to me, dear. Not to those who work with you. Not to anyone. Not even to Mike." She put out her hand to him. "Come, Greg, you're alive. You're well. That's all that counts."

But he pushed her hand aside impatiently. "That's not all that counts. You don't understand. Oh, too bad. Too bad!"

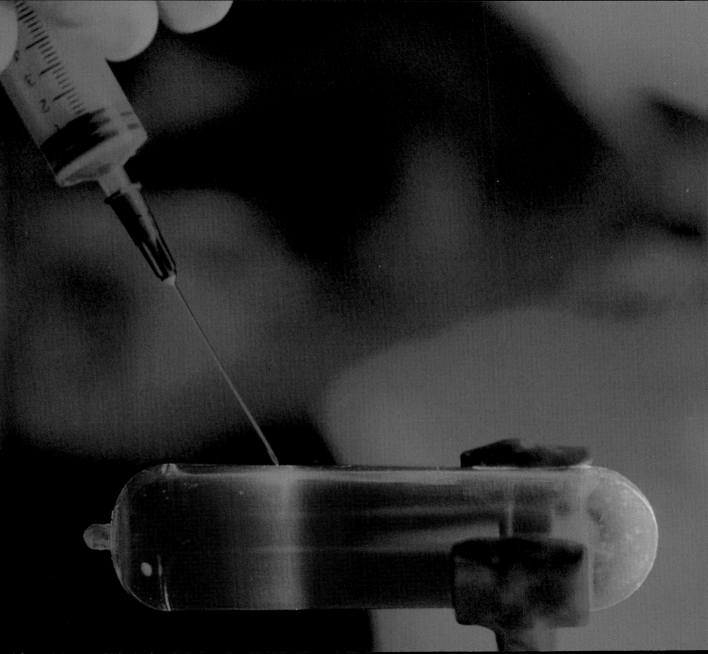

THE GENETIC CODE

ESSAY BY
WILLIAM A. HASELTINE

SPECULATION BY
HARRY HARRISON

THE GENETIC CODE
WILLIAM A. HASELTINE
DANA-FARBER CANCER INSTITUTE

A CLASSICAL VIEW

THE STORAGE AND TRANSFER OF INFORMATION LIES AT THE heart of life processes. The successful transfer of information from one generation to another, along with the ability to recover information at the right time and place, is the essence of all living systems. Include the possibility of the introduction of errors into the primary information storage and a general definition of living systems emerges, one that defines not only life on earth but, all living systems, wherever they may be.

The discovery of the process by which living systems on earth store and transfer information from one generation to the next constitutes one of humanity's greatest achievements in self-understanding. These discoveries began in the 1940s and culminated by the mid-1960s with an outline of information transfer in living systems. These 25 years of discovery changed the way we think about our origins, as well as our relationship with all other living systems. They also paved the way for a revolution in technology, by providing the tools that permit us to manipulate the biological information storehouse to our purposes.

To the surprise of many who predicted, toward the end of the 1960s, that the great age of biological discovery was drawing to a close, the past 25 years have provided as rich a harvest of knowledge as the previous 25 years. The fruits of contemporary biological research are all the more exotic as they were not anticipated. Much of the work over the past 25 years has been directed toward understanding how biological information is recovered for the construction and maintenance of complex living systems. These recent discoveries have changed our concepts of the fundamental life processes of information storage and retrieval. The view that the information transfer process follows a rigid set of instructions that is always faithfully executed has evolved to a recognition of the fluidity of the entire process—one in which there is flexibility in how the information is stored and how it is retrieved. What has seemed to be an inviolable rule regarding the unidirectional flow of genetic information and the unique role of proteins as catalysts has been overturned. Indeed, the previously proposed primacy of DNA or proteins as the original life form has been challenged. A prebiotic world populated first by self-replicating RNA molecules is now postulated. These discoveries have also provided a deeper understanding of the origin of cancer and have helped to explain the causes of many other diseases.

INFORMATION STORAGE—DNA

The golden age of molecular biology dawned in the late 1930s and early 1940s with the realization that the primary means of information storage in living systems is a chemical—deoxyribonucleic acid, or DNA—found in the cell nuclei of all living things. DNA is a polymer, a very long chain of similar chemical units linked end to end. These units, called bases or nucleotides, are of four different types, but each can link up with any other to form a long "backbone."

The links that hold the DNA together are made of a simple sugar, deoxyribose. Each link of the polymer is named according to the structure of the attached base: deoxyadenosine (dA), deoxycytosine (dC), deoxyguanosine (dG), and deoxythymidine (dT). The whole DNA molecule is a double helix formed by two backbones connected by bases, like a spiral stair in which the bases are the treads and the backbones are the banisters.

Information in DNA is stored in much the same manner as information is stored in a book. In a book, the order and spacing of the 26 letters of the alphabet stores the information. For DNA, it is the sequence of the four different nucleotides in the chemical side chains on the DNA polymer that stores the information. The DNA polymer of a human cell is approximately four billion bases long, which means there are about two billion letters in the information library of the cell, as each cell contains a duplicate set of instructions. This compares with approximately 100 million letters in the complete *Encyclopedia Britannica!* However, potential for storage of information in the *Encyclopedia Britannica* and in the human cell is approximately equal, as more information per unit can be stored in a sequence that contains 26 different units, the alphabet, than in a sequence with only four units, the DNA bases.

The observation that each cell, so small as not to be visible to the naked eye, contains as much information as the entire *Encyclopedia Britannica* emphasizes the compact nature of information storage in living systems.

COMPLEMENTARITY AND INFORMATION DUPLICATION

Complementary, the principle of mirror imaging, underlies the transfer of information from one generation to the next in living systems. Complementarity is also one of the major principles governing the selective retrieval of information.

In the DNA molecule, only certain pairs of bases join with each other between the two side chains: dA pairs with dT, and dG pairs with dC. (See Figure 1.) Other pairs, such as dA with dG, are not found. This complementary structure provided an immediate understanding of how the information stored in DNA is transferred intact from one generation to the next. Each of the two strands of the polymer provides the complete information necessary for the formation of the opposite strand. Duplication of a DNA molecule involves separating the two strands and creating the complement for each, yielding two molecules identical to the original one in the parental structure.

The mutual affinity of the dA and dT bases and of the dG and dC bases makes the process of duplication possible. This mutual affinity, which lies at the root of all living forms on earth, is achieved through a series of chemical interactions that depend on the shape and arrangement of the bases.

The chemical bond involved in forming the dA–dT and dG–dC base pairs has been known since the 1920s. It is a relatively weak type of interaction called the hydrogen bond. In this bond the atoms need not be very close to one another in order to link up. The attachment between the bases of DNA is strengthened somewhat by the formation of multiple hydrogen bonds between the base pairs: three hydrogen bonds form between dG and dC, and two form between dA and dT.

Because the bases are joined relatively weakly, the two strands can be separated with relatively little expenditure of energy. In other words, the information in double-stranded DNA is not tightly locked in. The energies required for separating the two strands are well within the range possible in liquid water, the medium of life on earth. The chemistry of DNA is adapted to the aqueous, temperate climate of our planet. (See "The World of Molecules," by William M. Gelbart.)

This process of duplicating the stored information of each organism by doubling the DNA is called DNA replication. But the picture given above lacks a definition of the cellular machinery that makes replication possible. DNA replication is carried out by a cluster of proteins, each of which performs a specialized function. Some proteins unwind the DNA, others hold the strands apart, and still others link nucleotides together to form the new, complementary DNA polymer. There are also proteins that replace nucleotides that are incorrectly inserted into the growing chain—for example, proteins that remove a dG opposite a dA and a dC opposite a dT. These error-correcting proteins assure that the stored information is faithfully passed on to daughter cells.

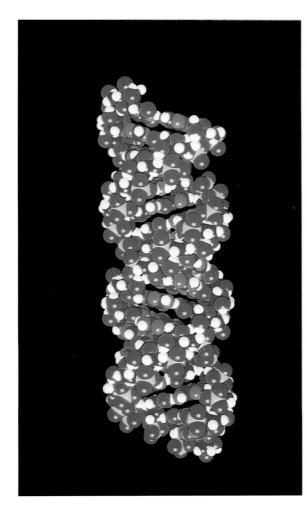

Figure 1. Computer-generated image of a crystallized form of DNA 20 base-pairs long. The base-pair units are blue-and-white, in the "treads" running in the core of the double helix. (Credit: Dr. Nelson Max, University of California, Lawrence Livermore Laboratory and the Department of Energy)

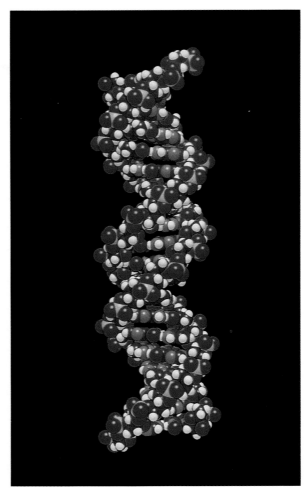

Figure 2. Computer-generated image of RNA, 20 base-pairs long. Similar to the structure of DNA, but less tightly wound, and with simpler base pairs. (Credit: Dr. Nelson Max, University of California, Lawrence Livermore Laboratory and the Department of Energy)

One reason for the great interest currently in the process that initiates DNA duplication is that it is believed that the signals that start DNA duplication are damaged in cancer cells and that DNA replication in such cells is switched on permanently. Understanding the details of replication may lead to new approaches to cancer therapy.

COMPLEMENTARITY AND INFORMATION RETRIEVAL:
THE RNA MACHINES

Living organisms depend upon the ability to select subsets of genetic information for expression at specific times and places. The information stored in DNA must be sufficient to specify *all* the properties of the living organism, including development from a single cell to adulthood, as well as the moment-to-moment functioning of each cell. Only a small part of the total stored information is needed by any one cell at any particular time. There must be a process by which information is selected for retrieval.

Complementarity is not only the principle of information retrieval. The process of information retrieval is mediated by a second type of polymer called ribonucleic acid, or RNA. RNA molecules, which contain small subsets of the information stored in the total DNA, come in two varieties. The larger are called messenger RNA (mRNA); they bring a portion of the information that is contained in DNA, usually in the nucleus of a cell, to the cytoplasm where the information can be used. A typical mRNA of a human cell contains one one-millionth of the cell's total stored information; thus it is about 4,000 bases long. (The smaller variety of RNA molecule, called transfer RNA, will be discussed later in this chapter.)

RNA is a polymer in which the backbone is composed of a sugar, ribose, that is closely related to, but simpler than, the sugar in the DNA backbone. Consequently, the structure and properties of RNA are very similar to those of DNA, except that the links that form the RNA chain are more easily broken than those of the DNA chain.

The fragile nature of the RNA molecule allows living systems to adapt to external conditions by destroying one set of RNA molecules that contain one subset of information and replacing them with a different set of RNA molecules that store a different subset of information. The chemistry of RNA helps organisms adapt to changes in their environment. For example, when one food source is present, mRNA is made that contains information necessary to make the enzymes that convert that food source to a useful form. If the food source changes, this type of mRNA is no longer made; it disappears rapidly and is replaced by mRNA that specifies enzymes appropriate for conversion of the new food source. There is an elaborate mechanism whereby cells respond to specific nutrients to achieve such regulation. The nutrients bind to specific proteins on the surface of the cell, which triggers the cell to make the type of

RNA that specifies proteins that metabolize the specific nutrients. The chemical nature of RNA is such that it degrades rapidly, so if it is not continually made, it disappears. Indeed, in some cells there are proteins that serve to destroy some RNA molecules so that they disappear even more quickly when the signal that triggers their synthesis ceases. Another RNA-mediated major change that regularly occurs in cells is the manufacture of special proteins required for each stage of the cell cycle. When the cell is at rest, one set of proteins is needed, but when the cell begins to divide, a different set of proteins is needed. A rapid change in the mRNAs that specify the proteins needed for each stage in the cell cycle occurs just prior to each stage.

The individual bases that make up the RNA polymer side chains also closely resemble those of DNA. They are called adenosine (A), cytosine (C), guanosine (G), and uracil (U). Uracil has a shape that is very similar to that of thymidine in DNA. A sophisticated complementarity applies here too: the A base of RNA will pair with U of RNA or dT of DNA, and the C of RNA will pair with G of RNA or dG of DNA. Similarly, the G of RNA will pair with C of RNA or dC of DNA, and U will pair with A of RNA or dA of DNA. (See Figure 2.)

RNA also performs other functions in cells. It serves as a structural element for subcellular components, including the machinery that is required to make new cellular components. And as we shall see, a separate form of RNA serves as a second key element in the information transfer process for making the proteins that carry on the cell's work.

PROTEINS

Most cellular structures are made of proteins. These proteins define not only the shape of the cell but also its functions. Proteins serve as the catalysts for almost all of the reactions necessary for the functioning of living organisms. For example, a specific set of proteins binds nutrient molecules and transports them within cells. Proteins also catalyze reactions that break apart these molecules and restructure them into new cellular components. Sets of proteins working in concert perform the transformations needed to supply energy in the cells, which powers living systems. The differences in the proteins present in different types of cells determine the cells' specialized functions.

The chemical makeup of proteins was elucidated before the chemical nature of DNA and RNA was unraveled. Proteins are also polymers, and like DNA and RNA, there is a common polymer linkage in each protein type. However, the chemical nature of the linkage is different and more stable than that of RNA and DNA.

There are 20 different kinds of units that can form the links of a protein polymer. These units are called amino acids. The individual units have a common protein backbone but differ in the structures that are attached to the backbone, the side chains. Some of the side chains are very small, while others are large. Some of the side chains have a high affinity for a waterlike environment; others do not mix well with water but have an affinity for oillike surroundings. Some of the side chains maintain a slight positive electric charge, whereas others maintain a negative charge. Some side chains permit the polymer a full range of flexibility. Others restrict the rotation and bending of the polymer.

Most of the important characteristics of proteins, including their functions, are determined by form. As a protein polymer is constructed it folds into a complex three-dimensional structure. The three-dimensional shape of many proteins has been determined using the tool of X-ray diffraction. (X rays are detected after they are scattered off thin layers of atoms formed in crystallized proteins. The structure of the proteins in crystalline form is thought to be closely related to that in living cells in most cases.) The position in space of each of the atoms that make up the proteins can be known with precision. (See Figure 3.) The shape of the protein is uniquely determined by the order of the amino acids that make up the polymer. The primary force that determines the protein chain shape is the affinity of the individual side chains for an aqueous or an oil environment. Clusters of adjacent amino acids will pull the aqueous-

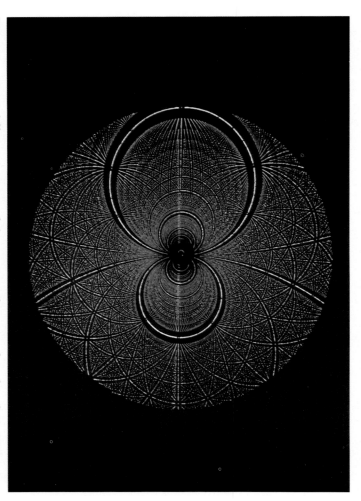

Figure 3. X-ray diffraction image of the enzyme glycogen phosphorylase. Using special mathematical techniques the internal positions of the enzyme's atoms can be derived from this image. (Credit: J. Hajdu and L. N. Johnson, University of Oxford, Oxford, England)

attracted part of the polymer to the outside of the protein and into the aqueous surroundings of the interior of the cell. Clusters of oil-soluble side chains will force their portion of the polymer away from the aqueous environment on the outside of the protein into the protein's center, or to the outside if the environment is lipid rich (for example, at a cell wall or in a fat deposit). Certain other combinations of amino acids will permit the protein to assume either a stiff coiled form or a pleated planar form.

FROM DNA TO PROTEIN

How is the information contained in DNA transferred to proteins? The first step in the process has already been described. Messenger RNA copies small segments of the much longer DNA polymer. The mRNA is, generally, then extruded through "air locks" in the nucleus wall into the cytoplasm.

The question then becomes, how is the information encoded in mRNA transferred to proteins? Another way of asking this question is, how can the information contained in a linear array of four different symbols (RNA bases) be converted into a linear array of 20 different symbols, the amino acids?

The solution to this problem revealed what is now known as the genetic code, the means by which information in the form of the DNA-RNA four-letter alphabet is transferred to the 20-letter alphabet of proteins.

The principle of the code is straightforward. A linear group of three RNA bases specifies one amino acid. For example, the group AAA specifies the amino acid lysine; the groups UUU, CCC, and GGG specify the amino acids phenylalanine, proline, and lysine, respectively. There are 64 ways to assemble the four bases into groups of three. Since there are 64 different combinations available to specify 20 different amino acids, a single amino acid can be specified by several different combinations. For example, the amino acid leucine is specified by UUA, UUG, CUU, CUC, CUA, and CUG. (See Figure 4.)

The simple correspondence of groups of three bases with particular amino acids means that the linear order of the information encoded by the DNA bases is directly reflected in the linear order of the amino acids in the protein. The linear order of the amino acids of the proteins determines the form and therefore the function of the protein. In this fashion information in DNA is transferred into cell functions.

One of the most important findings that followed the discovery of the genetic code is that the same code is used almost identically in all living systems on earth. We know of no fundamental reasons based on the laws of chemistry or physics that determine that lysine should be specified by the three nucleotides AAA. However, such is the case for all known organisms ranging from the smallest microbe to the largest whale. A major implication of the universal nature of the code is that all forms of life on earth are related by common evolution to one another. In other words, of all competing chemistries that

	U	C	A	G	
U	UUU } Phe	UCU } Ser	UAU } Tyr	UGU } Cys	U
	UUC }	UCC }	UAC }	UGC }	C
	UUA } Leu	UCA }	UAA OCHRE†	UGA OPAL†	A
	UUG }	UCG }	UAG AMBER†	UGG Trp	G
C	CUU } Leu	CCU } Pro	CAU } His	CGU } Arg	U
	CUC }	CCC }	CAC }	CGC }	C
	CUA }	CCA }	CAA } Gln	CGA }	A
	CUG }	CCG }	CAG }	CGG }	G
A	AUU } Ile	ACU } Thr	AAU } Asn	AGU } Ser	U
	AUC }	ACC }	AAC }	AGC }	C
	AUA }	ACA }	AAA } Lys	AGA } Arg	A
	AUG* Met	ACG }	AAG }	AGG }	G
G	GUU } Val	GCU } Ala	GAU } Asp	GGU } Gly	U
	GUC }	GCC }	GAC }	GGC }	C
	GUA }	GCA }	GAA } Glu	GGA }	A
	GUG* }	GCG }	GAG }	GGG }	G

Figure 4. The "key" to the genetic code. The base triplets (UUU, UUC, etc . . . .) code for amino acids (phenylalanine, etc . . . .) * means Start. † means Stop.

may have emerged in the prebiotic era only one survived. At the fundamental level of information all organisms are truly one. This conclusion both reinforces and is reinforced by the story told by the fossil record.

The discovery of the universality of the genetic code laid the foundation for contemporary biotechnology. Bits of DNA from one organism can be spliced by humans into the DNA of another organism, where the new information may be expressed faithfully in the new environment. The information stored in human DNA can be transferred to a simple bacterium or a yeast and expressed in a form similar to that in which it is expressed in human cells. Likewise, information from the DNA of microbes or plants can be inserted into the DNA of animals and expressed in the new environment.

AN EXCEPTION

There are rare exceptions to the universality of the genetic code. For example, the cells of many organisms contain small organelles called mitochondria that supply energy to the cell. Each mitochondrion can be thought of as a minute cell that contains its own DNA, RNA, and proteins. The sequence of bases in the mitochondrial RNA specify proteins according to a code that is slightly different from the code used by the rest of the cell. These differences in the DNA and RNA of mitochondria imply that the evolution of the cellular DNA and mitochondrial DNA has been independent for an extremely long time, possibly hundreds of millions of years. As cells divide, the mitochondria do too, and are passed on from mother to daughter cells. Perhaps the mitochondria are a successful symbiosis resulting from a bacterial invasion long ago.

TRANSLATION FROM RNA TO PROTEIN

The chemical means of encoding information in DNA is similar to that in RNA but different from that of proteins. The principles of chemical complementarity govern the transfer of information from DNA to RNA. Transfer of information from RNA to protein uses other principles in addition to complementarity.

Central to the process of translation of information from RNA to protein is a set of molecules collectively known as transfer RNA (tRNA). Transfer RNAs are short RNA molecules, only 72 to 80 bases long, that fold into unique shapes. (See Figure 5.) At one end (the "head") of the tRNA molecule is a group of three bases. The tRNA molecules are folded such that these three bases are exposed to the environment and available for complementary interactions with other RNA bases. The other end (the "tail") of the molecule is typically coupled to one or more amino acids. The amino acid sequence that is attached to a particular tRNA tail corresponds to the sequence of the exposed bases at the head end of the molecule. For example, if the exposed bases are UUU, which is the sequence that will recognize AAA in mRNA, then the amino acid invariably coupled to the tail of that particular transfer RNA species is lysine. There is at least one tRNA that carries each of the groups of three bases that specify an individual amino acid.

Transfer RNA recognizes groups of three nucleotides on mRNA by complementarity. The UUU bases on the head of a transfer RNA will pair only with the AAA bases of mRNA; the CCC, GGG, and UUU bases will pair only with the GGG, CCC, and AAA bases of mRNA.

The coupling of amino acids to tRNA tails is performed by a set of proteins, the coupling enzymes. There is at least one coupling enzyme for each amino acid. The coupling enzymes recognize each tRNA by the binding properties of the exposed three bases that also bind to mRNA. The tRNA molecule folds to bring the head and tail of the molecule relatively close to one another. The coupling enzymes recognize each amino acid by the size, shape, and charge of the side chains. The shape of one surface of the enzyme fits, with atomic precision, the shape of the recognized molecule. (See Figure 6.) Shape recognition and hydrogen bonding guide the specific binding of the correct tRNA to the coupling enzyme.

PUNCTUATION AND ALIGNMENT

In any code there is a need for punctuation and alignment signals that specify the point at which the message begins and ends. For the genetic code, the capital letter at the beginning of the sentence is a group of three nucleotides, the combination AUG. The AUG triplet also specifies the amino acid methionine. As a consequence, all newly made proteins start with the amino acid methionine.

There are two other groups of three nucleotides, UAA and UGA, for which there are no corresponding tRNAs. These two triplets specify the period, the termination of protein synthesis.

REGISTER

A linear code must be read in the proper register, or reading frame. There are three possible ways to read a linear code that carries information in groups of three units, depending upon where the reading starts. The translation register refers to which of the three possible groupings is actually used to make a protein. The order of the nucleotides with the AUG initiation triplet determines the order in which they will be translated.

RIBOSOME ROBOTICS

A subcellular organelle composed of about 50 proteins, called a ribosome, is responsible for the sequential reading of the messenger RNAs by the tRNAs and maintenance of the correct reading frame. It is a remarkable machine. You can picture the ribosome and its assembly-line work as follows: the ribosome halves are shaped as upper and lower molars, biting down on a long string of "dental floss" (the mRNA), beaded with base-triplet beads. The "molars" start biting at AUG on the mRNA. One side of the lower "molar" has two grooves (about where a tooth would join the gum) pointing to the upper. The groove nearest the head of the mRNA is filled with a coiled tRNA, with a base triplet at its head attached to the head-end mRNA triplet. Dangling from one of the tRNA's tail-ends, hanging from the molar, is a matched amino acid, one of a growing chain. Another tRNA binds to the adjacent groove, carrying a new amino acid. An enzyme snips off the head-end amino acids and transfers them to the tail-end one. The leading tRNA drops off, the ribosome advances one base triplet along the mRNA, making the tail-end tRNA take up the head-end position. Then a new tRNA enters the tail-end position. A long mRNA may carry 100 ribosomes or more at a time, all carrying out these steps in unison. Each ribosome terminates polymerization at UAA or UGA. (See Figure 7.) After each protein polymer is completed, the two halves of the ribosome fall apart. The initiation reaction for protein synthesis begins again when the two halves rejoin at the site of an AUG sequence along the mRNA. The energy the ribosome needs to do this work is provided through the metabolism in the cell of ATP and other molecules made from the digestion of food.

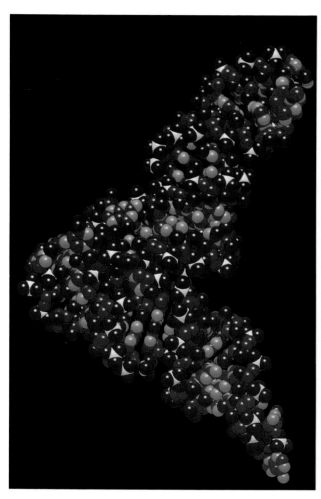

Figure 5. Computer-generated image of tRNA. The right-hand tip (head) carries three bases (blue) which are connected to mRNA by the ribosome robots, and which code for an amino acid, which will be connected to the left tip by enzymes. (Credit: Dr. Nelson Max, University of California, Lawrence Livermore Laboratory and the Department of Energy)

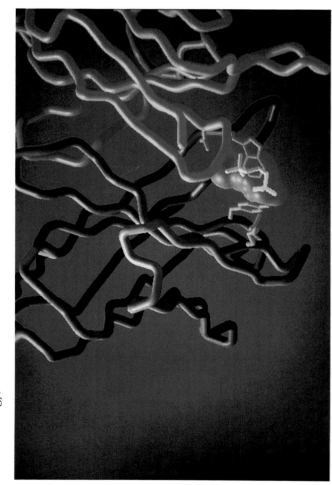

Figure 6. A small molecule antigen fits precisely into the combining site of its complementary antibody. (Credit: © Dr. Arthur J. Olson, Scripps Clinic, Department of Molecular Biology)

This microscopic ribosome assembly line makes all the varieties of proteins needed by the cell, based on the various mRNAs it reads and the variety of tRNAs it couples to.

PARADIGM SHIFTS

The discovery of the genetic code and the fundamental principles guiding protein synthesis represented a major milestone in our understanding of the natural world. However, almost as soon as the final touches had been placed on the magnificent edifice, major revisions in our thinking about how information is stored, created, and used in living systems were being made. A series of discoveries opened our eyes to the flexible nature of the information storage and transfer process. Although none of the discoveries made over the past 25 years have invalidated the fundamental principles of information transfer described above, they certainly came as surprising major variations on the central theme. These revisions to our knowledge not only involve major changes in our views of the process of information transfer—paradigm shifts—but also involve changes in our view on less important issues.

REVERSE FLOW OF INFORMATION: FROM RNA TO DNA

An hypothesis fundamental to much of the early work on information transfer was that genetic information invariably flowed from DNA to RNA and thence to protein. Therefore, the discovery that under some circumstances genetic information could be stored as RNA and then converted to DNA came as a major shock. This discovery was first made in the study of the viruses known to cause cancer in animals, the retroviruses. It was found that the genetic information of these viruses is stored as RNA. However, in a reverse of the normal flow of information, the RNA of the virus is converted into DNA when a virus invades a cell. The information in the DNA form then becomes lodged in the cellular DNA. The viral information in the cellular DNA serves to make viral RNA and the viral mRNA serves to make viral proteins. This latter half of the virus replication cycle follows the standard DNA to RNA to protein pathway. Two deadly human viruses, the AIDS virus, and a virus that causes a rare form of human leukemia, belong to the retroviruses, the name signifying that the normal information flow is reversed.

The strategy of converting information from RNA to DNA has proved to be a successful one for this family of viruses. The stable association of newly made viral DNA with cellular DNA permits viral infections to reside in cells as long as the cells remain alive. For many kinds of these viruses, infection usually doesn't kill the cell; thus, animals and untreated humans infected by retroviruses usually remain infected for life and become lifelong carriers of the virus infection.

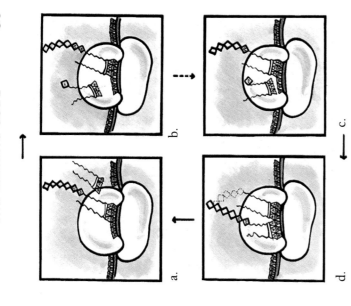

Figure 7. Ribosome robotics. (*a*) The ribosome clamps onto the mRNA molecule. A tRNA with a growing peptide chain hangs at the tail end of the ribosome. A new tRNA with one new amino acid attaches at the ribosome's head end. (*b*) The peptide chain is hung onto the new amino acid by a transfer enzyme. (*c*) The ribosome advances one base triplet along the mRNA, dragging the peptide chain and dumping the empty tRNA. (*d*) The process repeats until the ribosome comes to a "stop" signal (the triplet UAG). (Credit: Elizabeth Wen)

If the cell that is infected by the retrovirus happens to be part of the germ line (that is, cells that are destined to become either eggs or sperm cells), the infection will be passed on to the offspring and thereafter from generation to generation. This strategy of virus replication has been so successful that what we consider to be the normal DNA of many animal species has remnants of hundreds of such events. For example, as much as 2 percent of the DNA that makes up the genetic information of a mouse is a remnant of ancient retrovirus infections. The fragments are thought to be interlopers because they are not part of the normal mouse DNA and because they closely resemble sequences of known retroviruses.

In human cells, too, there are hundreds of retroviral DNA fragments inserted in the DNA. Part of what we are in genetic terms is the story of infections of our progenitors by retroviruses.

The reverse flow of genetic information is not limited to that initiated by viruses. Close study of human DNA reveals that genetic information that was once present but subsequently lost has been copied back into human DNA at new locations. In some instances, these newly created genes produce proteins that work much as the original proteins. The process of reverse flow of information from RNA to DNA occurs infrequently. However, the accumulated effects of such processes over evolutionary time spans is such that human DNA is littered with the remains of thousands of such events. These events serve to duplicate genetic information. It is very likely that by duplicating genetic information, the reverse flow of information serves to accelerate the rate of species evolution by providing spare copies of essential genes. Once a gene is duplicated, variations of either the copy or the original can occur without jeopardizing the viability of the cell. These variants of the essential genes may perform slightly different functions, permitting cells to evolve. Viewed in this context, the reverse flow of information may be a critical component of the creation of new genetic functions.

The DNA of many organisms harbors what have come to be called jumping genes. Jumping genes, also known as transposable elements, are small regions of DNA that appear to move from one site to another within the cell. Many of these mobile genetic elements act as intracellular retroviruses. First they are copied into RNA. Then the RNA copies are converted back to DNA within the original cell and inserted at a new location. Transposable genetic elements can also alter normal gene function. If the transposable element alights within the coding sequence of the gene, it may disrupt its function. If the transposable element alights between two genes it may separate their functions and alter the time and place in which such genes are expressed. The existence of such jumping genes means that no one organism that contains these genes is identical to any other.

In summary, the fundamental principles of complementarity in information transfer between DNA and RNA are not violated by the discovery of the reverse flow of information. Moreover, the reverse flow of information is fundamental to the replication of some types of viruses and may also play an important role in the evolution of novel genetic functions and of species.

RNA ENZYMES

A second shift in the biological paradigm occurred in the early 1980s. Until then proteins were thought to be the only biological molecules capable of speeding up chemical reactions. While studying the mRNA of a small multicellular organism, researchers noted that a purified RNA molecule could cut itself. Moreover, the cut always occurred at a specific site on the molecule. Proteins capable of cutting both RNA and DNA molecules at specific sites had been known for some time. In this case, however, not only did the RNA molecule cut itself, but it was RNA, not protein, doing the cutting. Further studies demonstrated that the self-cutting reaction was accompanied by a self-joining reaction. In essence the RNA snipped out a piece of itself. In the next few years similar RNA-catalyzed reactions were found to occur in other organisms, and it was shown that the cutting RNA molecules not only divided themselves but also were capable of cutting other RNA molecules, of related types that contained the same sequence of bases. One RNA "shears" was found to move from one RNA molecule to another, cutting each one in turn. The ability to carry out a series of speeded-up reactions, in this case the cutting reaction, is a classic definition of an enzyme.

Studies of RNA enzymes are still at an early stage, and the importance of RNA enzymes in much of biology still cannot be guaged accurately. However, the formation of many tRNA species has been found to require the activity of an RNA enzyme. Even at this early stage the RNA enzyme has provided a new idea for the treatment of genetic and viral disorders. It has been proposed to introduce into the cell by recombinant DNA techniques a fragment of DNA that will produce an RNA enzyme targeted to cut specific sequences. For example, RNA enzymes are now being designed to destroy the mRNA of the AIDS virus. Perhaps cells resistant to attack by the AIDS virus can be created by this means.

VARIATIONS ON A THEME

ALTERING THE INFORMATION STOREHOUSE

The notion that the information content of a cell remains fixed throughout an organism's lifetime in all cells has been revised. We now regard at least portions of the information library as being highly mobile, capable of undergoing ordered and meaningful rearrangements during the course of the development and differentiation of individual cells. The information content of cells can also be altered as a consequence of pressure from the external environment. The discovery of the semiflexible nature of the DNA storehouse has helped to shape modern ideas about evolution and about the origin of many cancers.

DNA REARRANGEMENTS

The diversity of the immune system has posed fundamental questions regarding information storage. Our bodies are capable of distinguishing at a cellular level more than one million different substances. Recognition of foreign substances is accomplished by proteins called antibodies. Each foreign substance is recognized by a different set of antibodies. According to the principles of the genetic code described so far, the existence of between one and ten million different types of proteins would imply the existence of an equal number of segments of DNA that encode the proteins. No evidence for such a massive number of antibody genes exists. The total DNA content of the human cell is too small to specify all the antibodies that are made and also specify everything else.

The solution to the problem of antibody diversity came from the discovery that the regions of DNA that specify antibody proteins are composed of multiple sets of similar DNA segments. One end of each of the regions of DNA that encode antibodies is conserved and is common to all. This is called the constant region. For some other regions there are multiple sets of each of three regions called variable (V), joining (J), and D regions. As a cell develops to produce antibodies, the DNA is rearranged so that eventually the constant region is joined to one and only one of the V, J, and D sequences. The information present in the DNA after rearrangement is colinear with the antibody protein sequence. This is a bit like a form letter on computer with one salutation and a series of similar paragraphs which can be selected to provide many different but related letters.

The combination of multiple similar units generates diversity. Further diversity in the antibody system is produced by inaccurate joining of the V, J, and D regions, leading to proteins of somewhat different composition and length. Such ordered transpositions occur in at least one other context, the production of proteins that are present on the surface of a class of immune cells called T cells (which are highly involved in AIDS).

There is an additional means by which diversity is produced. Changes in the DNA sequence may be introduced at the joining regions. Some of the changes involve the addition of nucleotides, whereas other changes involve alterations of the existing nucleotide sequence. All of these changes alter the amino acid sequence of the proteins specified by the altered DNA. The process by which such changes are introduced is not known. However, the existence of a mechanism for the introduction of what appear to be random changes into the information storage bank may ultimately force us to revise our ideas about the mechanisms that drive evolution and genetic variation and that determine the rate of evolution.

There are other examples of programmed rearrangements in the location of specific DNA fragments. In one small multicellular parasite, the organism that causes a severe disease called schistosomiasis, the main component of the outer skin of the organism changes regularly from one protein to another. The proteins differ enough from one another that antibodies to one will not recognize the others. The rate of change of the proteins is fast enough (7 days) to outpace the immune system (about 10 days). As the immune response to one surface protein begins to be made, that protein disappears and is replaced by a new one. This trick is accomplished by the sequential expression of the hundreds of multiple genes specifying the surface protein. When one of these genes is at the expression locus within the DNA, the mRNA for that protein is made and the protein is produced and placed on the cell surface. At other locales, the gene corresponding to the surface proteins is silent. A genetic program exists within the microorganism for rapidly moving segments of DNA that encode the surface proteins in and out of the expression locus.

TRANSPOSITION EVENTS AND CANCER

Transposition events in immune cells may be the starting point for some types of leukemia in which the genes that specify the antibody proteins are found to be joined to normally distant regions of the DNA. It is likely that the ordered programming of gene rearrangement goes awry in such cases, causing the wrong pieces of DNA to be joined to one another. If these genes control cell growth, their abnormal expression can begin a process that leads to cancer. In these leukemias the origin of the disease is intimately linked to the ability of cells to produce antibodies.

DNA AMPLIFICATION

The DNA of solid tumors of the muscle, stomach, and other solid tissues is grossly rearranged as compared to normal DNA. Normal human cells packaged the total DNA content into discrete units called chromosomes, each of which carries many genes. The rearrangement of the chromosomes of solid tumors is often so great that they are not recognizable as human. In addition to the multiple rearrangements, equivalent to the transposition events described above that occur in these cells, local regions of the DNA are often repeated. A region of DNA may be repeated many hundreds of times. This phenomenon is called DNA amplification.

In addition to the DNA amplification found in tumors, local regions of normal DNA may also become greatly amplified in response to external environmental pressure. For example, if normal cells are grown in the presence of gradually increasing amounts of antitumor drugs that are toxic to the cell, the regions of DNA that specify detoxifying proteins will become more numerous. Such DNA amplification occurs only in the regions that specify the drug-resistance proteins. What is normally a single gene may become amplified several hundred times. The amplified regions of DNA are passed from one generation of cells to another so long as the toxic drug is present. As soon as the drug is removed, the redundant copies of DNA begin to disappear.

The discovery that amplification of specific regions of DNA occurs in response to external stimuli provides a clue regarding the abundance of DNA amplified sequences in tumor cells. The difference between a benign and a malignant tumor is the ability of the malignant tumor to establish itself in different parts of the body and to destroy the normal tissue around it. Our current thinking is that the first change that distinguishes normal from abnormal cells is one that removes cells' normal growth restraints. A cell that is free from normal growth restraints begins to divide perpetually. Further variants then arise that give individual cells a better chance of survival. This process continues, sometimes for many years, until a fully malignant tumor is formed. The existence of multiple regions of amplified DNA probably reflects the requirement for extra copies of genes that provide specific functions needed for abnormal growth. Such genes may specify proteins that destroy surrounding tissues or that attract the blood vessels necessary for tumor growth. Systematic exploration of the nature of the amplified genes should provide a catalog of the needs of the malignant tumor cell, as each amplified region represents a response to a specific selective pressure.

The phenomenon of gene amplification also blurs the distinction between Darwinian and Lamarckian concepts of evolution. It is likely that amplification occurs when accidental gene duplications that occur infrequently are promoted by external pressure so that cells that have spontaneously duplicated the existing information will have an improved chance of survival, a typical Darwinian concept. If the cell so selected is one that yields a gamete, an egg or a sperm, the environment of the parent that gave rise to the selection of the resistant gamete cell may influence the genetic composition of the offspring, as the amplified DNA of the gamete is expected to be passed to the offspring, a Lamarckian notion.

JUNK DNA

Economy of design is the hallmark of very small organisms, such as bacteria and bacterial viruses that were the subject of extensive genetic investigations in the 1950s and 1960s. These organisms contain small amounts of DNA and for that reason are easily studied. The beginnings and ends of the regions of DNA that specify particular proteins were found to be immediately juxtaposed in these organisms, with no wasted space.

For this reason the first results of the study of human and other animal DNA provided a shock to investigators. It was found that over half the total DNA present in humans occurs in multiple short segments and does not specify any known function—"nonsense" DNA. This nonsense DNA is composed of a few different sequences that are repeated several hundred thousand times. Some of these repeated sequences have a very simple plan, such as a run of 20 to 30 dA–dT base pairs. Other more complex sequences, varying in length from 75 to 150 nucleotides, are also repeated many thousands of times. These latter sequences often appear in end-to-end arrays 50 to 100 bases long. The amount of this so-called junk DNA varies dramatically even among closely related species. For example, some species of frogs have four times as much DNA as other species, most of the difference being junk DNA. The reason for so much junk DNA in animal and human cells is a puzzle. One idea is that the junk DNA is the result of accident, but is proliferating to the maximum extent that the survival of the species will permit.

DISCONTINUOUS GENES

The biggest surprise of the 1970s was the discovery that most human and other animal genes are not continuous, but are specified by multiple regions or are interrupted by junk DNA. This discovery was made by matching the RNA known to specify a specific protein with the region of DNA from which the RNA was made. Further studies revealed that the initial mRNA copy is actually a faithful replica of the entire DNA sequence, including the nonsense regions.

However, the final message from which the protein is made is pieced together by removal of the noncoding regions; this is called splicing. Messenger RNA from which all the extra sequences have been removed is exported from the nucleus to the cytoplasm of a cell, where it encounters the ribosomes and makes proteins. The unspliced mRNA usually remains in the nucleus and is inaccessible to ribosomes.

Some genes may have only one or two junk interruptions. The extent of fragmentation of other genes is simply amazing. The gene that specifies the collagen protein, an important component of connective tissue, is specified by a sequence on mRNA that is several thousand nucleotides long. However, in the DNA these coding sequences are interrupted more than 25 times by junk DNA. These interruptions spread the gene over more than 100,000 nucleotides, or about 100 times more than the minimum amount of DNA required to specify the protein!

The reason for this striking fragmentation may be that it multiplies the power of a single gene. The number of examples is rapidly increasing in which multiple proteins are made from a single DNA region by variation in splicing of a junky primary mRNA copy. In some cases the final composition of the mRNA differs in response to external influences. In other cases differences in the coding regions included in the mRNA are dependent upon the tissue in which the RNA is made. Evidently the splicing machinery varies slightly among cell types.

Once again the immune system offers an excellent example of multiple types of proteins that can be made from a single type of pre-mRNA. One type of pre-mRNA contains enough information to make almost two complete antibody molecules. Depending upon the extent of the splicing reaction, two different proteins can be made. Both proteins have the same initial set of amino acids but end differently.

The regulation of splicing of mRNA to yield different proteins also plays a central role in the life cycle of viruses that cause human leukemia and AIDS. In these viruses, the proteins that make up the core of the virus particles are made by a full-length copy of the viral DNA. The proteins that control viral growth and are the cause of the growth abnormalities of the leukemia virus are made from the spliced forms of the viral RNA. Both the leukemia and the AIDS viruses specify proteins that control which of the two forms of RNA reach the ribosomes. An understanding of the control of this process in the leukemia and AIDS viruses may help us understand how other cells regulate this process.

TRANS-SPLICING

A portion of mRNA corresponding to one region of DNA may be joined to the mRNA made from a different region of DNA, a process called *trans*-splicing. By means of *trans*-splicing a novel protein can be made, one that does not require rearrangement of DNA. Examples of *trans*-splicing are rare, but in the schistosomiasis parasite described earlier, *trans*-splicing plays a key role in the production of mRNAs.

MESSENGER RNA EDITING

Another surprising variation in mRNA occurs in the mitochondria of the trypanosome parasite, where a certain mRNA does not correspond to the DNA sequence from which the mRNA was made. The changes occur after the RNA is made, and in one case the changes are so extensive that over 50 percent of the coding sequence is altered. The differences between the DNA and RNA sequences include removal or addition of one or more uridine residues in the mRNA. Novel start and stop signals for protein synthesis are created by these changes. The means by which these alterations occur is not known.

In the RNA of a human gene that serves an important role in liver function, a subtle change creates a new stop signal leading to production of a shortened protein. The change occurs in some but not all tissues that produce the protein.

These specific and meaningful alterations of the sequence of mRNAs are evidence that evolution has provided a means of editing the primary information content of a cell while the information is being retrieved. It is as if a computer program selectively changed the words of a stored text one out of every three times the text was printed, without changing the stored text itself. The changes would alter the meaning of the printed text—for example, the sentence "The child ran fast," might be altered to "The boy ran slowly." This is a remarkable and unexpected discovery that fundamentally alters our understanding of information storage and processing in living systems.

Yet another type of modification in RNA structure has been described. Many cells contain an enzyme that chemically alters the A residues in mRNA. Chemical alteration is accomplished by removal of one part of the structure that makes up the A base. The resulting base is called inosine (1). The base pairing properties of I are very similar to those of G—that is, it pairs preferentially with C, not with T as did the original A base. The change from an A to an I changes the coding specificity of the mRNA and weakens interactions between different parts of the same mRNA molecule.

VARIATION IN INITIATION AND TERMINATION OF MESSENGER RNAs

Variability of the site of initiation and termination of mRNA synthesis along the DNA provides additional flexibility in the use of information that is stored in the DNA. There may also be a termination failure, in which case the mRNA accumulates in the nucleus, away from the ribosomes, which are in the body of the cell. This is one means by which mRNA can be made at one time and stored for later use. In this case the signal for mobilization of the mRNA is the production of the protein that restarts the termination sequence of bases. The best-known example of storage of mRNA occurs in oocytes (eggs). Oocytes contain thousands of copies of mRNAs that are stored, to be used only when the egg is fertilized.

TRANSLATION: VARIATIONS ON A THEME. JUMPS, BUMPS, FRAMESHIFTS, AND FALSE STARTS

The most extreme example of multiple proteins produced by a single mRNA occurs in the case of the information contained in small viruses. For the small viruses there appears to be an advantage in having a small amount of genetic information code for a large number of proteins.

OVERLAPPING GENES

As described earlier, the reading register of the mRNA code is determined by the register of the initiation triplet AUG. The triplet nature of the genetic code permits a unique sequence of RNA to specify at least three different proteins, depending upon the register in which the sequence is used. Some mRNAs contain multiple AUG initiation triplets in the same sequence but in different registers. An example of the use of all three possible coding sequences of a single messenger RNA occurs in the AIDS virus. A single region of the AIDS virus mRNA is used to make a portion of the protein that makes up the outer shell of the virus, as well as two separate proteins that regulate viral growth.

FRAMESHIFTING

A shift in the register in which the code is read also occurs at specific sequences. The mRNA frameshift that occurs in the production of the proteins of the AIDS virus provides an excellent example. About 80 percent of the time, a ribosome encounters a specific sequence in the course of translating the mRNA of the AIDS virus, and it shifts the reading frame back by one nucleotide. This minus-one frameshift allows a second reading frame to be used. The second reading frame encodes a much longer protein than would be encoded if the ribosome continued in the original reading frame. Both the short and the long versions of the protein are critical for the growth of the AIDS virus.

FALSE STARTS

In most cases, one AUG sequence specifies the initiation codon. However, other AUG sequences present in the open reading frame may be used upon occasion to produce shorter versions of a protein. Once again, an excellent example of this occurs in a leukemia virus, the human T cell leukemia virus, HTLV-1. One of the proteins necessary for growth regulation has two variants, which are made at two mRNA initiation sites. The longer protein produced by initiation of protein synthesis at the beginning of the mRNA is found in the nucleus, whereas the smaller protein initiated further down the mRNA is found only in the cytoplasm. There are specific amino acids that serve to direct the longer protein to the nucleus, which are not present in the shorter protein. These two proteins differ dramatically in their effects on viral growth.

AUG is the usual initiation codon, but the sequence GUG may also serve occasionally to initiate protein synthesis, as in the mouse leukemia virus. One of the products of the leukemia virus is made in two different forms, the major form, which begins with AUG, and a less frequent longer form, which begins with GUG. The protein that contains the GUG sequence operates on the outside of the cell, whereas the shorter protein functions within the cell. The triplet ACG may also serve as an initiation codon under some circumstances.

RIBOSOME JUMPING

Surprisingly, it seems that ribosomes can jump from one part of a mRNA to another. The amino acids in a protein specified by a virus that feeds off bacteria, the T4 virus, do not represent all of the triplet nucleotides that make up its mRNA and corresponding DNA. A group of amino acids that should be present in the middle of the protein is absent. It is as if several words were deleted from a sentence—for example, "The child quickly ran and then jumped over the fence" might become "The child jumped over the fence." The absence cannot be explained by mRNA splicing, for the mRNA is intact after the protein has been made. It appears that the ribosome "jumps" from one site on the mRNA to another during the course of translation. Perhaps this jump occurs via the formation of a loop structure that conceals a portion of the mRNA from the ribosome.

TERMINATION BYPASS

Under some circumstances, the termination signals at the end of an open reading frame, the UAA and UGA triplets, are bypassed. The frequency of such bypass depends upon the sequence surrounding the termination codon. When this happens, two of the proteins are made, one longer than the other. In a virus that causes mouse leukemia, a protein that is necessary for viral growth is made only when a termination signal is bypassed.

Figure 8 (opposite). A computer-generated schematic image of a papilloma virus with surface proteins in red, RNA inside. (Credit: D. Cox, S. Meyers, E. Sandor and D. Sandin, Electronic Visualization Lab)

CONCLUSION

Our knowledge of the microverse of the cell is rapidly expanding. With this knowledge has come the ability to manipulate genetic material to our own ends. The near universal nature of the genetic code and of the mechanisms for decoding the stored information make it possible to exchange information between organisms that are separated by hundreds of millions of years of evolution. For example, information from human cells can be placed in one-celled bacteria and humanlike proteins can be made. Similarly, bacterial proteins can be made in human cells.

So powerful are these new genetic tools that it is now possible to tamper with the germ plasm of both animals and plants, to change forever the inherited traits of both. Such manipulations can change the biosphere, can change even humankind itself.

Thus, the evolution of human intelligence, a process driven by chemistry and natural selection, has given birth not just to ways of directing the process of evolution, but to ways of creating novel living entities. The use of such tools will require more intelligence and judgment than was required for their discovery.

SAMSON IN THE TEMPLE OF SCIENCE
HARRY HARRISON

ILLUSTRATION BY
JOHN COLLIER

"NO OVERTIME PAYMENTS ON THIS JOB, SAM," DR. BEN SAID. "You should have been out of here a half hour ago."

"Just want to put these away first," Sam said, taking the glass culture-envelopes out of the autoclave. He had large, thick fingers, yet his touch was light as he moved the fragile glassware, stacking it carefully on the shelf. He frowned in concentration, moving slowly, hoping that Dr. Ben would not realize how uptight he was. Almost shaking with fear. He did not want to do it: it had to be done. As he was closing the autoclave he heard the door shut behind him. He cracked his knuckles, tried to calm down, could not.

It was time. No more questions. He had been planning for days. Nothing could go wrong. No one would be in the back corridor this late. Even if he were seen he could say he was sweeping up. Don't forget the broom! Or his jacket. Now—do it.

It was his old jacket, many times patched, but it did have large pockets. Key in his right hand, broom in his left, close the lab door. No one in sight. He swept the floor slowly, humming to himself, down the hall towards the room. TERATOLOGY the sign read that had been taped to the door. And KEEP OUT. The hall was empty. One last look around—then unlock and enter, close the door. Then lean with his back against it breathing loudly in the darkness. *No time to waste*, he admonished himself. Fingers sliding down the wall to the light switch.

Turned and shuddered. He had been in here only once before to clean up the mess of a broken jar. He was sorry now that he had told Japeth about it. But he had, and now there was no turning back. He was in the room now and had to do it, had to get one of the things.

There were more of them now, two shelves of bottles and jars. Which one? It had to be one small enough to fit in his pocket. He tried not to look at the large containers, at the racked smaller jars inside of them, at the things inside the jars. But he had to. There was the one he had first noticed, floating in the transparent fluid, white flesh and tiny limbs. Eyes closed as though asleep. All of its eyes. Two heads—four eyes. He pushed aside the cover of the large container just far enough to get his hand inside. The liquid was warm. He groped for the jar, pulled it out dripping, put it into the plastic bag and slipped it into his jacket pocket.

He had to get out! Forcing down the rush of panic, Sam grabbed tight to his broom and turned the lights out. Keeping his thoughts from the monsters in the darkness behind him. Was that a sound from the hall? No, only the thud of his heart, the blood pounding in his ears. He threw the door open, stepped through and closed it behind him.

Done! He had done it. Just as he had planned. Now if only he could stop shaking it would soon be over with. Walk slowly, Sam, just as you always do. Put the broom away, check the lights, let yourself out.

"Good night Sam," someone called out, and he waved and answered back. The parking lot was almost empty when he crossed it to his lektrocycle in the open shed. The air was warm and smelled of spring; small leaves were already uncurling from the buds on the oak tree that overhung the shed. When he unlocked and opened the pannier he saw Ned's battery there. He had forgotten about it, wished that he hadn't brought it today. But his uncle had insisted. It had gone flat and he couldn't watch his TV. Get a free charge from the clinic, no point in throwing away money when Sam could get a free charge. But it was cheating and Sam didn't like it. The alligator clips touched when he took them off and he jumped at the sound of the crackling spark. He was allowed to charge his own lektrocycle here, but it didn't seem right to take advantage. A quick look around, no one in the lot. He slipped the jar from his pocket and quickly locked it into the pannier.

After he had unplugged the power cable he felt an immense sense of relief. It was done and over with. And he would never have to do anything like this again. He was straddling the cycle and buttoning his collar when Dr. Ben's car pulled out of its slot. A bright red 2015 Chevvy Thunderbolt. It had oversize batteries and could hit a hundred, do three hundred miles without recharging. It stopped close by and the window slid open.

"Can you come in an hour earlier tomorrow, Sam? The glazier will be here to replace that cracked window in the back."

"No trouble, doctor. I'll be here."

"Good. Make it up to you. Leave early on Friday."

"That's all right. . . ."

"You leave early. Remember, no overtime pay."

"If you say so."

"I do. Good night."

Sam waved after the retreating car. Twisted the rheostat and hummed out onto the road.

It was less than five miles on the highway from the Anderson-French Research Clinic to the turnoff to Sawbell Creek. That's what the sign said, although no one ever called it that. Sowbelly Crick. Mud from the unpaved road spread out darkly across the white concrete, was spattered up the post and almost obscured the sign itself. Sam slowed and turned into it, staying on the edge and out of the muddy ruts. The track turned and twisted through the bare trees following the creek that gave the valley its name. He could smell the wood smoke from the houses ahead long before they emerged from behind the trees. A single street of delapidated buildings. Built cheaply for the miners. The mine long closed, the houses gray with neglect. An outsider might have noticed this, but Sam didn't. Born and bred here, this was his home. With relatives in almost every building. Browns or Abernathys, Abernathys or Browns. He was Samson Abernathy, but all of his uncles on his father's side were Browns. People waved to him and he waved back as he rolled down the length of the street. Ned would want his battery, would be complaining by now about missing all the afternoon quiz shows. But Sam wanted to see Japeth first. Get rid of the jar and forget completely about it.

Sam pulled behind the house and leaned his cycle against the privvy, just as the door opened and Japeth came out, pulling up his suspenders.

"You got what you said you was going to git?" he asked, frowning.

"I keep my word," Sam said, drawling his words. He looked around before he opened the pannier and slipped the jar into his pocket. "Show you inside."

Only when the door was closed and the gas light lit did he take it from his pocket and place it on the table.

"May the good Lord have mercy!" Japeth said. His jaw dropped open to reveal his almost toothless gums. "It's just like you said. I wouldn't have believed it iffen I hadn't seen it with my own two eyes. An abomination in the sight of the Lord. And they done it right here in that place of evil."

"They don't do that in the clinic. Things like this happen. They sort of study this kind of thing, that's what they say."

"You defending their devil's work?" Japeth's eyes protruded from the tight flesh of his face as he leveled a shaking, scrawny finger at Sam. "You saying they didn't do this? You saying that place not a sink of Satan?"

"I ain't saying nothing," Sam said lowering his eyes and kicking at the muddy floorboards with his toe. "I just clean up there, that's all I do."

"That's all you better do. No boy from Sowbelly Crick ought to even go near that place."

"It pays good money!"

"Some things is more important than money."

"Like what? No one ever said no when they et the vittles bought with that money. Now you got that thing you can leave me alone. I did like you asked."

"For now, for now," Japeth muttered, turning the jar to catch the light and shuddering at what he saw. "An abomination."

Sam left, shuffling out with his shoulders bent, pushing the warped door shut behind him. It was growing dark and he switched on the cycle's headlight, then made his way back down the road to his home.

"I saw you go by," Uncle Ned complained. "Me just sitting here and nothing to do and you driving round for fun with my battery."

"If you was in such a hurry you could have charged it for a buck and watched soaps all day. Here it is."

"Got better use for my money." Ned gulped down the last of some of this better-use from his glass and grabbed up the battery. A moment later canned laughter filled the room: Sam went into the kitchen and sniffed happily at the smell of baking bread.

"Sure smells good, Aunt Netty."

She smiled and nodded as she put the loaf on the table. Netty didn't talk much, couldn't read either, but there was nothing wrong with her cooking. Sam took the newspaper out of his jacket pocket before he hung it behind the door. He sat at the table and skimmed the headlines.

"Says here that the First Lady, that's the President's wife, is feeling much better and there ain't no broken bones in her foot where the horse stepped on it." Netty nodded sympathetically as she shook the loaf from the pan. She had no patience for the news on TV, there was too much talk of things she didn't know or care about. It was better when Sam read from his paper. He always found something of interest.

The glazier's truck was just pulling up when he unlocked the clinic next morning. He showed them the cracked window and watched carefully while they replaced it. He signed for the repair and was cleaning up the mess they had made when Dr. Ben arrived.

"Looks a lot better."

"Be better yet when I wash those greasy fingerprints off it."

"Leave it for now. I want to see you in my office."

They have found out! was Sam's first thought. They saw the jar was missing, know that I did it. Why did I let them talk me into it?

That was stupid, he realized, and some of the panic drained away. Dr. Ben had just come in. It had to be something else. He put the broom and pan away and went down the hall to the office, knocked on the frosted glass door and went in. Dr. Ben was behind his desk lighting up a pipeful of evil-smelling tobaccoless tobacco. He nodded at the chair as he puffed the foul substance to life. Sam eased himself down and laced his hands together in his lap. From behind a green cloud of smoke Dr. Ben leafed through a file of papers.

"You remember we talked about high school?"

"Yes." Sam lowered his eyes, looked at his fingers.

"You only went six months to high school, didn't you?"

"Didn't like it."

"Your marks were pretty good."

"Don't know."

"You know. And you know that you dropped out because you were the only one in the school from Sowbelly Creek."

"Maybe."

"Surely. Don't insult my intelligence, Sam—and I won't insult yours. Your marks were first rate. I know because I have the transcript here. You should have stayed on no matter what the other students said or did."

"They didn't bother me."

"Then you should have ignored the others at home. It was that, wasn't it?"

Sam did not like to talk about this. He stared at his hands and wrung his fingers together in the continuing silence. In the end he had to answer.

"Sort of. Whenever I did my homework my uncle, you know, always found chores for me to do. Said that he didn't go to school nor anyone else he knew and maybe I was being uppity. That kind of thing. Easier to drop out of school. Particularly with this good job here."

"There are better jobs. But you need an education to get them. Would you like to go back to school?"

"Too late for that now."

"Never too late." He tapped the file with the stem of his pipe. "This is a correspondence course for high school. You could do it by mail. Right here in the clinic without taking any papers or books home. I talked to the board of directors and they like your work. Hard to find qualified people in this valley. Not the researchers of course. They line up to work here since we are doing some of the most original research in gene engineering in the country. You know what that is—don't you?"

"Not really. Has to with DNA I think."

"You think right. There are about a hundred thousand genes on the twenty-three pairs of human chromosomes. We know a good deal about them now they have all been mapped. But that is just the beginning. Embryology is an enigma and prediction difficult. There are over three thousand known genetic diseases. That is what we are working on here in the clinic. Working to correct gene-related diseases. But we need lab technicians as well as researchers. Few of them want to come this far from the city. That is why we want to train locals like yourself. Better pay—and a permanent job. Which is why the directors have agreed for you to take the time for schooling. For our benefit as well as yours. What do you say?"

"I don't exactly know. . . ."

"You will be getting more money as soon as you get a diploma, even before more training."

"It's not that."

"Then what is it?"

Sam wrung his hands together, finding his thoughts confused and hard to express. Not for the first time did Dr. Ben speak for him.

"It's your friends, isn't it? And your family. You think that you are being uppity—but that's not true. There is no reason for you not to get an education, not spend your life on welfare. Sowbelly Creek is not a bad place but they have had some bad luck. Once the mine closed they were locked into a cycle with no way out. Not only that, there is the continuing health problem. Since the turn of the century we have been able to do something about AIDS. But it is an endless war since, like all retroviruses, AIDS changes constantly. The more easily transmissable strains always win out. We fight it on three levels. Firstly with immunology, making it harder to catch. For those who do catch it we manage to increase the time before the first symptoms arrive. Finally we work constantly on methods to enable the victims to live longer. But we have not been able to wipe it out. For a number of years now it has been a genetic disease, which means effectively that everyone comes in contact with it—and the susceptible get it."

"Do you mean—everyone in Sowbelly Creek?"

"Unhappily, yes. You are one of the very few who doesn't harbor the infection. The others—well the mortality is quite high as you know. But they are being treated. Which means you should not think that they are your responsibility. You're young and you're healthy. And you have your own life to lead. You must think about yourself. And while you are thinking, try to think about this high school thing. You don't have to make your mind up now. But just promise me that you will consider it."

"Yes, I'll do that. But it's not that I don't feel grateful. It's just that there are . . . other considerations."

"Of course. We'll talk again. Perhaps next week."

Sam was glad that the new grass was high enough to cut because it would have been a bad day to handle the glassware. He rode the little electric mower, making careful turns and parallel swathes on the lawn that fronted the clinic. He did it automatically because he could think only of the new future opening ahead of him. He would no longer have to envy students he had gone to school with, who were now graduating high school. Driving cars and looking forward to college. If he worked hard he could do just as well. The smell of fresh-cut grass was in his nostrils, the spring sun warm on his shoulders. When he ate his lunch, home-baked ham on slabs of still-fresh bread, he read one of the pamphlets from the desk in the reception room. He had never bothered before—but now he wanted to know all about the clinic. Some of it was hard to follow, but he persevered.

This feeling of euphoria lasted almost all the way home, until he turned onto the unpaved road to Sowbelly Crick. This was his home and he belonged here. He did and he didn't. When he climbed off the cycle he felt his shoulders hunch as they always did. Knew that he would talk with the twang of the Crick in his voice, use the words they all knew so they wouldn't think that he was uppity and talking foreign.

"You there, Sam, you hear me," Japeth called out from across the way. "I want to see you, hear?"

Japeth waited until he was close and spoke under his voice. "Tonight at my place, nine on the clock. Use the back way."

"Sorry, but I won't be able . . ."

"You be able, Samson Abernathy, you be able. The Reverend Breakrige gonna be there and wants to see you special."

"About what?"

"You don't ask no questions, you just be there."

Sam looked worriedly at Japeth's retreating back. Breakrige made him uncomfortable. He didn't mind watching him on the county TV station, the little colored image was more amusing than frightening. He could rant and shout, call out to Jesus and lead the born again in uplifting song. But it was very different when he came to the rickety Legion Hall in the Creek. There were no more American Legion meetings there; they had buried the last World War Two veteran and even the Nam veterans were well thinned out. So the hall had become more a church for visiting preachers, and Breakrige was the most popular of them all. The Creek people shouted answers, sang with frenzy, spoke in tongues and fell unconscious when he preached. Sam, although he sang along with them, never felt caught up in their excitement and felt guilty about it. As far as he knew, Breakrige had never heard of him. He wanted to keep it that way. So why did the preacher want to see him?

After dinner he thought of all of the possibilities of escape. He could be ill or just get on his cycle and go into the city, not get back until late. They couldn't force him to be there.

Yet at nine o'clock he was knocking on Japeth's rear door. There was a rattling of the chain, unusual enough in itself since there normally wasn't a single locked door in the entire Creek. Japeth looked out through the crack, then waved him in and relocked the door. The gas lamp was turned low in the front parlor, the curtains drawn. Reverend Breakrige sat at the head of the table with a water glass of whiskey in one big hand. The two other men, sitting in silent attention, were both from the Creek.

"Is this the young man you were telling me of?" Breakrige said in that familiar husky voice.

"That's him," Japeth said. "Kin on my sister's side."

"You work at that place of evil, boy?"

"The Anderson-French Research Clinic down the road." He worked hard to keep his voice from trembling.

"The one I mean. Sinners and desecration."

"Medical research, that's what they do. Supposed to help people." Sam's voice cracked, which spoiled the effect slightly. But Breakrige was well aware of his attempt at rebellion. His eyes widened and his finger stabbed angrily at Sam.

"You sassing me, boy? You speaking back and telling me you don't know what goes on in that sink of bloody sin? They help people? They help this baby's mama when they showed him to her—they help this baby itself?"

He slammed the jar down on the table before the light, slammed it down so hard that Sam gasped, afraid it would break. So hard that the two-headed fetus inside rocked back and forth and a tiny hand drifted in a parody of a wave. The liquid in the jar was murky now, something wrong with it. What? Sam leaned closer to look, then jumped when Breakrige's voice roared in his ear.

"This so-called clinic is an abomination!" Breakrige shouted aloud, and the circle of listeners, eyes fixed on the jar, murmured agreement. "The good Lord said that if they right eye offend thee—pluck it out. That I would do. If the Lord commanded, I would pluck out my good right eye and hand it over in the name of the Lord!"

As he spoke Breakrige clutched at his eye, twisted and writhed in agony. When he took his clenched fist away his eye was screwed up and closed. He held his hand out to Sam and slowly opened it. Though he had seen Breakrige do this before, Sam almost expected to see the eye lying on the empty palm.

"When the Lord commands we do as he commands! And he tells us that this abomination must be wiped from the face of the earth. You understand, boy?"

Sam understood well enough, but could not force himself to speak. He could only nod to sign that he knew what the preacher was saying, that was all. Breakrige chose to put his own interpretation on this.

"Now you show some sense. Now you doing the right thing. This place of evil shall be scourged by fire, and yours is the blessed hand that will do the cleansing!"

"No . . ." Sam choked out.

"No!" Breakrige screeched. "You say no to me?" His open hand lashed out fast as a snake and cracked Sam's face, knocking him to the floor. Breakrige stood over him and pointed a trembling accusing finger.

"You an atheist? You a communist? You stand up for evil and against your own kinfolk? They gonna go there and you going to crawl to the police and tell on them and send them to jail? You the yellow-bellied scum gonna turn on your own kin?"

There was sudden silence as they all looked down at him. The fear welled up and Sam could not think, could only nod his head and hold his throbbing face.

"You say yes what?" Breakrige shouted bending down so his face almost touched, the smell of his bad teeth washing over Sam.

"Yes," he said, "I'll help." Whatever they wanted. Say anything to keep this frightening man at bay.

"Knew you would" Breakrige said, smiling and standing. He dropped back into his chair and took a long drink of whiskey. "Nice God-fearing boy like you ain't going back on his own folks. Now you do just as I say and there be no trouble. You got a key for that place? Now don't you lie! Japeth here told me he saw it."

"Got a key. But there is an alarm."

"Which you know how to turn off."

Sam could only nod in agreement: no way to escape that penetrating gaze.

"These good folk gonna drive you there. Gonna give you a can of coal oil and matches and and watch out for you. When you do what got to be done they gonna take you away from there. These folks in Sowbelly Creek gonna be real proud of their own boy. I heard you act uppity but I don't believe that. You one of them. And you gonna prove that this night."

Deep inside he was shouting *no, no* but not so anyone could hear. They patted him on the back and then he was in the car and moving through the night. They were all there except for Breakrige; his work was done. Quickly, too quickly, they came to the clinic, passed it and kept on going. Perhaps they had changed their minds! Any small hope was instantly taken away.

"See anyone? See any cars?"

"Nope."

"Then go back with the lights off. Pull around the back where they can't see us from the road."

There was silence when the electric motor was switched off. An owl hooted distantly.

"Go on," Japeth said. "Open it up."

They were close behind him, the coal oil gurgling in the can. He wanted to run, shout, protest. He should not be doing this—yet he was. Now he was glad of the darkness because his face was wet with tears. He did not want them to see this final humility. His fingers were numb when he fumbled out the keys.

"Open it!" Japeth whispered fiercely. "And the alarm, don't forget the alarm!"

There was no way back now. The key slid in easily, the door opened, even the alarm was easy to find by touch in the darkness. He turned it off. A box of kitchen matches was pressed into his hand, then the handle of the can.

"Do it, now. *Do it!*"

Sam shuffled down the corridor. At the turning he looked back and saw the three men outlined against the sky. This world was a prison and he could not escape. Around the corner was the room with the bottles and that was a fitting place to do it. The can gurgled and the reek of kerosene filled the air. When it was empty he stepped back and put the can down and fumbled out the matches. The can. He mustn't forget the can, they had warned him. Fingerprints. The match sputtered into bright flame and he dropped it into the dark pool at his feet.

It sputtered and went out.

His hands were shaking when he lit a second one. Held it until it was burning well. Then dropped it.

The kerosene caught in a whoosh and flames shot up to the ceiling. He grabbed up the can—then stood in paralyzed horror as the door to the bottle room slowly opened.

The foam whooshed and fluttered onto the fire which flared smokily then went out. Bright lights shown down the corridor behind him and there were shouts and the thud of running feet. Then the corridor lights came on and Sam looked on blankly as Dr. Ben Ziony turned off the fire extinguisher and set it down on the floor.

"Come into my office," he said quietly. He followed Sam's gaze. "Don't worry about it. Someone else will clean up the mess." Sam did not move until he was taken by the arm. Then he lurched forward, still numbed by the sudden turn of events. Lights were coming on all over the building now and there was the sound of a number of cars from the lot outside. Sam dropped into the chair while Dr. Ben tamped yellowish flakes into his pipe.

"I'm sorry that it had to end this way. If we could have stopped it we would have. Breakrige has been warned often enough, but he is a very stubborn man."

"You know—everything?"

"Pretty much everything. He is under close observation. We knew about the meeting tonight as soon as it was set up. We have the whole thing taped. But there was no way we could stop it from happening—or stop you from being involved. That is the thing I regret most."

"But me, I'm not important."

"Hardly. You are the most important thing in this valley, the reason why the clinic was built here. We have known about you since before you were born, and have monitored every moment of your existence since. Because you were either a threat to the entire human race—or its salvation."

Dr. Ben smiled crookedly as he dropped into his chair. "I know. It's a lot to take in at once. But there is no simple way to tell it. You remember I talked to you about AIDS being a genetic disease now. Your mother had it before you were born, and she was treated by a researcher who used the people in this valley as guinea pigs. I won't tell you his name but I will tell you that, since there is no longer a death penalty in this country, he will die in jail. He was a monster who placed himself above all others, who thought himself superior to all others. And before he was caught he treated her—and you. He took bone marrow cells and infected them with a modified retrovirus that carried a human gene. Your mother died when you were born so we will never know what would have happened with her. But you lived—and you do not have AIDS. The altered gene structure prevented the disease from developing."

"Then this doctor who made the cure—what was his crime? I don't think that I understand."

"His crime was modifying a virus to affect a human gene," he said grimly. "A virus that could have possibly gotten out of control, that might possibly have destroyed the entire human race. This is a fear that has haunted gene research from the very beginning, the reason for all the laws and controls on this kind of research. But what this doctor did was modify the retrovirus so that it could reproduce itself only a fixed number of times, with a terminal sequence that chopped off one gene each time it replicated. It was danger-ous—but it worked. If it had not, this retrovirus could have spread, changed—I dread to think of the consequences. But this meant that your life has been monitored steadily, your health has been under constant scrutiny. We tried to arrange it so that you would lead as normal a life as possible. I hope that you have. The rest of Sowbelly Creek is chronically ill. You are not. We did our best. . . ."

"I can't go back there now," Sam said. His voice was empty, all emotion spent.

"I know." Dr. Ben was embarrassed, tried to hide it behind a cloud of smoke, could not. "It was a choice we had to make. We could have placed you in an orphanage. But frankly, your health and those around you were easier to keep track of here. And we had to think about your future—and mankind's future. If your genes were permanently modified with a degree of immunity to AIDS, this would be of utmost importance. Your genes might control the very future of the species."

"Do you mean that you wanted me to go around scr . . . impregnating every girl I could find?"

"Please! Let us not be vulgar. There are . . . scientific ways of assuring entrance into the gene pool. But that is still in the future. For your entire life your health has been under constant scrutiny. We tried to arrange it so that you would lead as normal a life as possible. I hope that you have. The rest of Sowbelly Creek is chronically ill. You are not. We did our best. . . ."

Sam realized the import of these words and his voice was ice cold when he spoke again. "Yes, I see now. The experiment that saved my life was too important to ignore or neglect. This doctor, who will die in jail, made a valuable discovery despite the danger of his methods. And I am sure that you have all profited by it. If not—why it is obvious that all of Sowbelly Creek would have been sterilized. Would we all have ended up in bottles like those in the other room?!"

"Don't be too quick to judge, Sam. After all—it was you who killed the baby in the bottle."

"What are you saying? It was dead, a preserved specimen. . . ."

"Quite the opposite. Your friend Breakrige had it completely wrong when he talked about the baby's mother and how she felt. We do not experiment with deformed babies—we try to prevent their birth. That wasn't a baby but a collection of nonviable cells. That fetus was a few weeks old, the egg that it grew from taken from a woman killed in a car accident, the sperm from a frozen bank. We need to experiment with human cells to prevent natural birth deformities. Congress and the medical profession have drawn up strict rules about this, needed rules in this area where medicine and morals meet. The doctor who experimented with your genes was immoral because he threatened the entire human race to satisfy his ego. Breakrige is immoral because he knows nothing of science, cares even less, and stands in the way of any progress in ending killer diseases."

Sam found it hard to think clearly; the world as he knew it had changed, would never be the same again.

"But—what is going to happen to me now? What is my future to be like? Am I to go forth and be fertile? World stud? You have taken away my past—so tell me what my future is to be like."

Dr. Ben clasped his hands before him, looked down with a great sadness. "That will be up to you. Under the circumstances I think the right thing was done. You have had your childhood, family and friendships. That is probably finished now. I doubt if you will be very welcome back in Sowbelly Crick, not with Breakrige and the rest facing trial. I'm afraid that your childhood is over. But you know that you are always welcome here. . . ."

"Am I? As an experimental animal? Supplier of AIDS-free sperm?"

Dr. Ben looked up, a great sadness in his eyes, shook his head no. There was no other answer forthcoming. There was no going back on what had happened. The past was immutable, the future unknown. Sam waited in silence for an answer that would never come. In the end he rose and left. The door closed behind him with a firm and final sound.

THE MOLECULAR WORLD

ESSAY BY
WILLIAM M. GELBART

SPECULATION BY
POUL ANDERSON

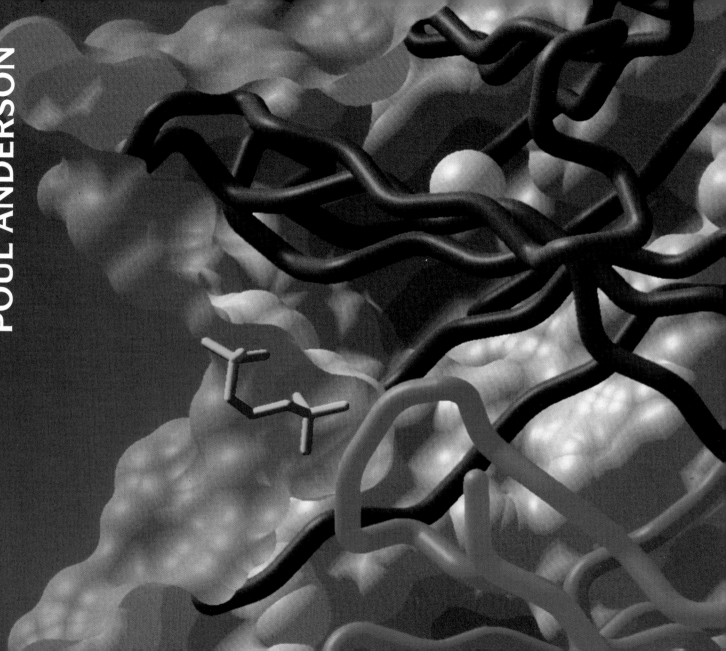

THE WORLD OF MOLECULES

WILLIAM M. GELBART
UCLA

THE IDEA OF THE MOLECULE

FEW PEOPLE REALIZE HOW THE FRENCH REVOLUTION—whose bicentennial the world is presently commemorating—is dramatically intertwined with the birth of the notion of molecules.

The great chemist Antoine Lavoisier, for example, probably contributed more than anyone to the early understanding of pure substances as aggregates of molecular building blocks. He was guillotined in the Reign of Terror. Similarly, Joseph Proust, a French chemistry professor in Madrid, was the first to distinguish between mixtures and chemical compounds and to state, coincidentally in 1789, that the latter are always found with the same composition. ("A compound is a substance to which Nature assigns fixed ratios.") His laboratory was pillaged two decades later by a French army siege. Of course, Lavoisier did not lose his life, or Proust his laboratory, because of any conflict between science and politics. And yet it is no accident that their ideas had such great impact on chemistry and physics at this juncture in history.

Today, "believing in" molecules is something we take for granted as an integral part of our modern worldview, just as we accept, from the time we are schoolchildren, that the earth goes around the sun, that energy is conserved, and so on. And yet, few of us (including scientists!) take the time to question these "facts" or "laws" and to wonder how it might have been unnatural—even inconceivable—for skeptical thinkers to arrive at these conclusions. How, then, did people first come to "believe in" molecules?

As in other breakthroughs in science, the process occurred in many steps, with frustrating ups and downs and fits and starts. But surely Lavoisier's and Proust's observations concerning the constant composition of chemical compounds were crucial. Specifically, a series of careful weighings involving the definite proportions of elements in pure substances suggested compellingly in the late 1700s that compounds consisted of fixed molecular building blocks. These observations laid the fertile field in which the British chemist John Dalton was to plant the atomic theory only a few years later.

Dalton's idea, which had been incubating irregularly since the time of the Greeks, was so simple that "at first sight it is not illuminating," as a modern scientist has noted. It asserted that the chemical elements are each made up of indivisible units—*atoms*—which are unalterable: all atoms of a given element are identical—for example, each has the same weight (Figures 1a-b). It follows that chemical compounds—formed by reaction of their constituent elements—must always involve whole numbers of atoms in fixed proportion, thereby explaining all the observations of Lavoisier, Proust, and others.

It is surely an impressive fact that these theories and experiments were reconciled so clearly and correctly without the benefit of anyone having ever directly *seen* a molecule! Similarly, many of the laws of organic synthesis and electrochemistry were developed in the midnineteenth century, long before electrons were discovered as the "stuff" of cathode rays by J. J. Thomson in 1897. Chemistry was indeed a rather comprehensive and sophisticated discipline many years before Rutherford, Bohr, and Lewis had worked out the first modern ideas concerning atomic structure and rules of combination in the early part of this century.

A key *physical* idea that significantly enhanced the molecular "picture" of matter was the kinetic theory formulated by Maxwell and Boltzmann in the late 1800s. They imagined the molecules in gases to undergo repetitive billiard-ball-like collisions with one another and with the walls of their container. For a given temperature and volume, the pressure exerted against the walls was shown to be proportional to the number of molecules (weight of gas). In the case of liquids, the particles were argued to undergo a persistent jiggling motion in the space spared them by their neighbors. The French physicist Perrin first related this phenomenon (now referred to as "Brownian motion") to the microscopic observation (by the Scottish botanist Brown) of the rattling motion of a suspended piece of pollen in water: it was being buffeted about by the too-small-to-be-seen water molecules, much as a sailboat in a stormy harbor appears to an observer from afar.

In this essay we offer the reader a brief tour of the "world of molecules." All of us grow up taking the existence of molecules for granted—but how much do we (you!) know about their different shapes and sizes, the forces that hold them together, their characteristic motions and reactions, and the ways in which they might be designed and engineered to make new materials? We shall proceed through these questions one by one, adding as we go along to our understanding and feeling for the idea of "molecule."

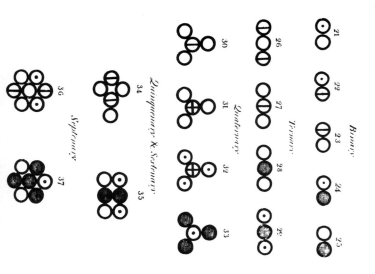

Figure 1a. Dalton's representations of atoms and molecules. This simple but elegant notation, with only slight modifications, is still used today, as in figure 1b. (Source: John Dalton, in *A System of Chemical Philosophy*, Part 1., 1842)

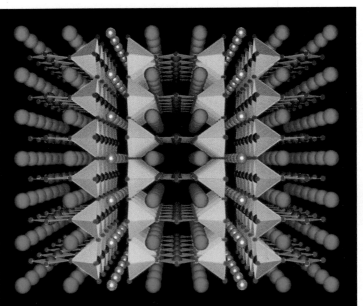

1b. Computer-generated image of the molecular arrangement of copper-barrium-yttrium high temperature superconductor. (Photo credit: courtesy of IBM)

THE MOLECULAR ZOO

Let's take an excursion through the fantastic "zoo" of molecular species. Most of us are familiar and even comfortable with the world of small molecules, ones containing just a few atoms. Most notably, we drink H_2O (water), breathe O_2 (oxygen), and are poisoned by CO (carbon monoxide). But we are even more sophisticated than that: we read in the papers about how CO_2 (carbon dioxide) clouds contribute to the "greenhouse" warming of our planet, how CF_3CCl_3 (and other freons) depletes the atmosphere's O_3 (ozone) layer, and how $NaHCO_3$ (sodium bicarbonate) helps soothe a bee sting (or is that just an old wives' tale?).

We are also accustomed to dealing with extremely large molecules. Just as prehistoric periods are commonly referred to by their prevailing working materials—for example, the Stone Age, Bronze Age, and so on—so our contemporary era is aptly described as the "age of plastics." It is certainly a fact that this image is notorious for negative connotations: a wood desk enjoys decidedly more prestige than a plastic one; plastic parts in a machine are considered cheap, and so on. And yet in making these superficial judgments we often fail to consider seriously the incredibly positive impact of plastic. In fact, anyone who has spent time in a hospital intensive care unit or confronted the challenge of fabricating lightweight and high-stress materials is likely to appreciate the dramatic achievements facilitated by these super-big-molecule compounds. Perhaps most familiar of all are the many synthetic fibers (nylon, Dacron, polyester, and others) that now dominate the clothing market.

What is it that makes plastics so special in their physical and chemical properties, and how can we picture and understand them on a molecular level? Consider a polyethylene container, for example. As you read these words, you conjure up easily the translucent, flexible material which makes up our refrigerator boxes and spray bottles. But do you realize that polyethylene is a pure substance, with a chemical composition as simple as that of the most elementary hydrocarbon (i.e., hydrogen- and carbon-containing compound)? Propane (C_3H_8) and butane (C_4H_{10}) are familiar *gases* used for heating: they are the first two members in the series $CH_3(CH_2)_nCH_3$, with $n = 1, 2, 3, \ldots$. These are "string" compounds:

$$\begin{array}{l} H\,H\,H\,H\,H\quad\ H \\ H\,C\,C\,C\,C\,C\ldots CH \\ H\,H\,H\,H\,H\quad\ H \end{array}$$

String compounds consist of $n+2$ carbons and $2n+6$ hydrogens. Octane, with $n=6$, is already a qualitatively different substance—a *liquid* at room temperature—which we pump into our cars (along with bits of lead and other things) at service stations. For n in the range 10–15 the corresponding hydrocarbons have still another character: they are the waxlike paraffins that we burn as candles or apply as sliding-wood-door lubricants. Most dramatic of all, however, are the properties of the very-large-n "strings," the polyethylene compounds (with n on the order of thousands and larger).

Polyethylene is just one example of a *polymer* (from the Greek *poly*, meaning "many," and *meros*, meaning "part"). Depending on the "mer"—that is, on the basic unit repeated along the long string—one finds different properties for the polymer. Even apparently small changes in the basic unit result in very new features for the polymer: $-CH_2CH_2-$, as already discussed, gives polyethylene; $-CH_2CHCl-$ gives PVC (replacing metal for most exterior piping), $-CH_2-CHCN-$ gives Orlon, $-CF_2CF_2-$ gives Teflon, and so on. In many other important instances the polymers are not simple "strings," but are highly branched and/or cross-linked. These more complicated spatial organizations significantly affect the observed properties. But the main distinguishing quality of polymers derives from the fact that they always involve extremely long chains of chemically bound units. As a consequence, the molecules are highly entangled, with distinctly desirable attributes of weight, stability, elasticity, and so on.

More spectacular still than Teflon and PVC are the naturally occurring, biological polymers, most famous of which are the nucleic acids, such as RNA and DNA. Cellulose, for example, the earth's most abundant organic compound, is a linear polymer of sugar rings with a total molecular weight comparable to that of typical polyethylenes and synthetic fibers. It is nature's own lightweight, high-strength, building material, forming the main structural element in plant cell walls. DNA, which is discussed elsewhere in this book, is a double helix of linear polymers, each strand consisting of up to one million molecular groupings. (Each of these groups involves a weakly basic nitrogen-containing ring compound, a five-carbon sugar, and phosphoric acid.) These strands are in turn linked to one another in an extraordinarily special way—the particular sequence of the four basic groupings in one completely determines the ordering of units in the other. It is this special order, of course, that constitutes the unique genetic information carried by DNA.

Replication of DNA during cell reproduction, and *transcription* of its specific instructions for protein synthesis, which are the absolutely fundamental processes of biology, are discussed in detail elsewhere in this book. Here we simply stress the sense in which, as polymer chains, DNA represents an important example of molecular organization into large aggregates. The remarkable ordering and extraordinary complexity of its chemically bound units, and the special role played by *enzyme* molecules in promoting its reactions in vivo, account for why biology is not simply a straightforward extension of organic chemistry and polymer science. Rather, it involves a myriad of ongoing technical and conceptual challenges to the ultimate reductionist notion that living organisms can be fully understood in terms of chemical structures and reactions.

CHEMICAL BONDS

The idea represented by the term "chemically bound," which is mentioned above, has implicitly underlain all of our discussion so far. Understanding of how atoms join together to form molecules really became possible only in the early part of this century, after subatomic particles were discovered and the quantum mechanical picture of electron charge "clouds" had been developed. Previously, in the late 1800s, organic chemists had already figured out many empirical rules concerning the combining number—or "valency"—of atoms. For example, sulphur sometimes reacts with two hydrogens (H_2S) and other times with additional species (H_2SO_4). But a systematic basis for the periodic properties of the elements and for the wide range of their combining rules required the quantum theory. To understand the electrostatic (ionic) binding in sodium chloride (NaCl) between the charged species Na^+ and Cl^- is relatively straightforward: opposite charges attract each other. (Here the + and − superscripts refer to the fact that the otherwise neutral atoms have one too few and one too many electrons, respectively. An atom is generally electrically neutral because the positive charge of its nucleus is balanced by its full complement of negatively charged electrons.) But what about the ("covalent") binding between two neutral (and even identical) atoms, as in H_2, O_2, and H_2O? Here the quantum theory serves to explain how electrons are "smeared out" around their nucleus and how they can be "shared" between one or more atoms that are sufficiently close. This very special "sharing" constitutes the chemical bond that causes certain groupings of atoms to be more stable in their combined than in their separated form.

In most of the familiar molecular compounds, the chemical bond is indeed so strong that it is "broken" only under exceptional circumstances. The oxygen (O_2) molecule, for example, involves two oxygen atoms as close as 1 angstrom (Å)—a 10 billionth of a centimeter—with an energy which is about 4 electronvolts (eV) lower than that of two isolated (separated) O's. Four eV is 100 times the typical energy available to a small molecule as a result of its thermal motion at normal temperatures. That means the O_2 molecules can (and do!) collide with each other many times without being able to acquire enough energy to break their bond. To succeed in breaking the bond we need to either raise the temperature drastically, so that the average energy of collision is sufficiently high, pass a strong electric discharge through the sample, thereby exciting and "ripping out" the shared electrons, or shine light having sufficiently a short wavelength so that photons of large enough energy are absorbed by the molecules to dissociate them.

It is interesting to note that some molecules are highly stable—insofar as the binding energy of their atoms is concerned—but also highly *reactive* in the sense that they combine readily with other chemical species to form still more stably bound aggregates. A common example is that of the hydroxyl radical OH, whose atoms are bound as strongly as those in O_2, but which reacts extremely fast with a hydrogen atom (H) to form H_2O. (As a result of the OH species' "living" such a short time, it is very difficult to "catch" and "observe" it.) The reason for this exceptional reactivity is the same as that which underlies the strength of chemical bonding: each atom tends to share a certain number of electrons with other atoms because the shared state has lower energy. The quantum theory of atomic structure provides specifically that H and O atoms should share one and two electrons, respectively (i.e., have "valencies" of 1 and 2). Accordingly, H_2 involves a single bond, and O_2 a double bond; similarly, for H and O to satisfy their valency requirements, OH must combine with H to form HOH (H_2O!). "Radicals" such as OH, then, are examples of electrically *neutral* molecules that are highly reactive because they lack an electron. *Charged* species such as H_2O^+ are also very short-lived, for the same reason. Both these classes of molecules play an important role in atmospheric and radiation chemistries, and many clever tricks and state-of-the-art technologies are necessary to study them.

Finally, we mention a special kind of bond, the investigation of which has become possible only in the past few years. Consider again the O_2 and H_2 molecules: each is stable because all the electrons that need to be shared are shared. That is why we do not normally see gaseous oxygen or hydrogen in any form other than diatomic (O_2, H_2). However, stable molecules do attract each other weakly because of very subtle forces known as dispersional forces, or van der Waals forces (after the Dutch physicist who first suggested them). But the resulting binding energy—at most a few tenths of an electron-volt—is too small to withstand the disruptive effect of normal thermal motion. To see bound aggregates of O_2 or H_2, then, we would have to find a way to cool the molecules to very low temperatures *without* causing their condensation (from gas) to the liquid or solid state. This is just what is achieved by forcing these gases to expand quickly (at supersonic speeds) out of a nozzle into a vacuum. (See Figure 6.) In this way chemists have recently been able to study increasingly large complexes of stable molecules (e.g., successively larger clusters of benzene molecules). These experiments offer the exciting possibility of investigating the evolution of properties from small to big aggregates and to understand on a microscopic level the fundamental differences between rarefied and condensed states of matter.

Throughout the discussion above we have been referring, both directly and indirectly, to molecules as clearly identifiable collections of nuclei and electrons. So before going on to describe further their chemical (reactive) and physical properties, let's digress a bit and talk more explicitly about the structure of molecules and how we study the characteristic motions of the electrons and nuclei that comprise them.

MOLECULAR STRUCTURE AND MOTIONS

Imagine again a simple diatomic molecule such as H_2 (it is, in fact, the simplest neutral—uncharged—molecule). It consists of two hydrogen atoms—each composed of one proton (the nucleus) and one electron—"bound" together in the sense that the electrons are optimally shared. "Optimally shared" means that the negatively charged electrons, "smeared out" between the positively charged protons, do the best job possible of overcoming the otherwise repulsive electrostatic force between the nuclei. As a result the two atoms are bound together strongly at a distance of about 1 Å, requiring the absorption of a great deal of energy if we want to break them apart. So what happens if we shine light on an H_2 molecule and allow the electrons to absorb energy? Suppose the light is "white"—that is, it contains *all* wavelengths of electromagnetic radiation. (Sunlight is a familiar example of light that is "white" over the range of wavelengths from the infrared through the visible and ultraviolet.) The fantastic thing is that we find only a very few wavelengths absorbed by the electrons: the rest of the light passes through the molecules as if they weren't there!

What's going on? It turns out that, according to the laws of quantum mechanics, the bound electrons are able to have only certain, specifically discretized energies as they move throughout the molecule. Thus, if they are to absorb energy from the incident light, it must be in one of the special amounts corresponding to the difference between some pair of allowed values. Each particular energy difference is associated in turn with a unique wavelength in the sense that only light with that wavelength can excite (via absorption) the molecule from the lower energy value to the higher. Most of H_2's electronic absorption, for example, takes place in the ultraviolet: the same is true for most other small molecules, including the notable example of ozone, O_3 (which is why we must be careful not to further deplete its supply in our atmosphere—less ozone implies less absorption of ultraviolet wavelengths and hence more sunburn and skin cancer). By studying these absorption frequencies and intensities in detail, we have learned a great deal about the characteristic motions of electrons in a wide variety of molecular species.

Just as the laws of quantum mechanics require that *electronic* excitation energies be discretized, they also imply that the allowed energies of *nuclear* motions in molecules can only take on special values. What are the possible ways, for example, that the two nuclei in H_2 can move? One involves simple *vibrational* motion along their line of centers. This motion is very much like that which you would see if you pulled down the weighing pan of a grocer's scale and then let go. The big difference is that, in the case of the scale, all amplitudes of vibration would be possible, whereas for vibrating nuclei only certain ("quantized") energies are allowed. The characteristic energy differences between allowed molecular vibrations turn out to be about 10 times smaller than those associated with the electronic excitations mentioned above. Accordingly, the frequencies of absorbed electromagnetic radiation are also 10 times smaller, lying in the infrared rather than the visible or ultraviolet range. Finally, we mention that a diatomic molecule like H_2 can also undergo *rotational* motion, tumbling end-over-end with different angular frequencies. Yes—you guessed it—the corresponding energies are also quantized, with differences which are from 10 to 100 times smaller than those for vibration (thereby involving characteristic frequencies in the microwave region). Again, from a careful study of these vibrational and rotational spectra, much has been learned about the springlike forces and separation distances (bond lengths) between nuclei.

In polyatomic molecules, consisting of several nuclei bound together chemically, all of the above considerations still apply, except for some interesting technical and conceptual complications. Of special interest is the theoretical problem of describing vibrational motion in many-atom molecules which have absorbed a lot of energy. In the diatomic case everything is simple because there is only one way in which the nuclei can vibrate: as we put in successively more energy the two atoms just oscillate increasingly vigorously along their line of centers—eventually, when the absorbed energy exceeds the bond strength, the two nuclei fly apart and the molecule is dissociated. But in the polyatomic case, there is a large number of ways in which the vibrational energy can be realized. For low enough energies the excitation tends to "stay put" in the particular bonds ("springs") where it is initially placed. At higher energies, however, it begins to quickly spread out chaotically over all of the bonds; ultimately, for strong enough excitations, the molecule ends up breaking in some way. Figuring out how vibrational energy is redistributed over the springs of a polyatomic molecule, and how it eventually results in dissociation, remains one of the unsolved problems in physical chemistry.

CHEMICAL REACTIONS

The breaking apart of molecules by the absorption of large amounts of vibrational energy is only one of the many ways in which chemical reactions can occur. In the case described above, the reaction is *photo* induced in the sense that light (from, say, a strong infrared laser) is used to bring about the excitation. High-energy collisions with other molecules or with electrons can also be effective in breaking the bonds between atoms. And, of course, direct chemical reaction involves the breaking of "old" bonds and the formation of "new" ones, as in the familiar example of $2H_2 + O_2 \rightarrow 2H_2O$. No "external" energy source (such as incident light or bombarding particles) is necessary in these cases. Chemistry involves the study of nothing less than all of these reaction possibilities, under all conceivable conditions of temperature, pressure, external fields, and state of the immediate environment (e.g., gas, liquid, or solid).

Perhaps the simplest environment for studying chemical reactions is that of the gas phase. Here a molecule can be imagined to undergo at most one collision (with other molecules) at a time, especially at low pressure. In the air around us, for example, at normal room temperature and atmospheric pressure, a typical oxygen or nitrogen molecule (the major components of "air") moves for as long as a billionth of a second in between collisions. This may sound like a very short time, but you must realize that the speed of a typical molecule is such that it moves thousands of molecular diameters between encounters with other molecules. So it is effectively isolated over distances that are large compared to its size. This means that we can think about a chemical reaction between oxygen (O_2) and nitrogen (N_2) molecules in terms of individual, separated collisions between pairs. In a liquid, on the other hand, because of the high density of particles, each molecule is in continual contact with *several* neighbors. That is, the molecules never have a chance to move without undergoing many collisions, very much like a rush-hour commuter on a crowded subway platform.

Even in the dilute gas phase, it turns out that it is not possible to study individual collisions unless one goes to a great deal of experimental effort. Consider, for example, a glass bulb containing the room-temperature and atmosphere-pressure sample of air that we've just discussed. It's true that the bimolecular collisions are isolated, with each molecule moving a large distance (relative to its size) between successive encounters. But in any one second there are as many as 10^{27} (trillions of trillions) pair encounters in each cubic centimeter of gas! So any simple measurement we make of the reaction kinetics will necessarily involve an average over huge numbers of bimolecular collisions. If we want to know, for example, how a reaction rate depends on the relative velocity of the colliding pair or on the initial amount of "internal" (e.g., vibrational) energy in each of the partners, this averaging washes out all hope.

In the last two to three decades ingenious new experimental methods have gotten around this problem by providing the means to study bimolecular reaction kinetics on a single-collision basis. Techniques have been devised for directly colliding beams of different kinds of molecules in an evacuated chamber and then measuring the amounts of the reaction products, as well as their velocities. Moreover, the speeds of the molecules in the beams can be controlled, along with their vibrational and rotational energies and even their orientation.

In a real sense, then, we can carry out a chemical reaction on a single-collision level, in distinct contrast to the classic "bulb" case where rate measurements necessarily involve averaging over a broad range of internal energies and orientations and very different relative velocities. And by breaking up the reaction probabilities into their specific dependencies on each of these molecular degrees of freedom, we are indeed performing the ultimate experiment of chemical kinetics, learning on a microscopic level how energy is transferred and bonds broken and formed.

In a dense gas or a liquid, on the other hand, we are *not* interested in studying reactions on this same detailed level. Rather, the relevant challenge is to determine the effect of the environment on the course of any particular bimolecular process. Imagine, for example, that we shine light on a diatomic molecule (e.g., iodine—I_2) that has been dissolved in a simple liquid solvent. If the iodine were in the low-pressure gas phase, it would simply separate into two atoms after absorbing sufficiently high frequency ultraviolet radiation: the "spring" we spoke of earlier would break as a consequence of the influx of so much excitation energy. Dissolved in a liquid solvent, however, the iodine atoms run into a "cage" of solvent molecules as soon as they have moved an angstrom or two apart. Rebounding back into each other, they might even recombine (reform their bond) if enough energy has been lost in their collisions with the solvent. By studying the fraction that recombine, for different frequencies of exciting light and for a range of solvent temperatures (i.e., average molecular speeds), a great deal can be learned about the dynamics of "cages" in liquids. An even more significant effect of the solvent arises in liquids whose structure is somehow incompatible with that of the solute. In the important case of proteins in water, the conformation and internal motions of the dissolved macromolecules are often significantly distorted by the local packing demands of the surrounding water molecules; accordingly, the protein may have a very different size, shape, and kinetics, depending upon the detailed nature of the aqueous solution. Similarly, by carrying out reactions of various kinds in solids and probing them on short enough time scales, we can monitor the special nature of correlated (many-molecule) structural and energy relaxation processes in systems with long-range positional order.

On solid *surfaces* the typical bonding types and characteristic dynamics of adsorbed molecules are dramatically different from those in dilute gases or condensed bulk phases. Recently it has become possible to cleave essentially perfect crystals (i.e., lattice arrangements of atoms or molecules with virtually no defects) and to prepare "clean," "smooth" surfaces of them. "Clean" means that the region above the freshly "sliced" solid is evacuated to such a degree that too few chemical species are present above it to become adsorbed in any significant number. "Smooth" describes the fact that the surface consists of a neat plane of long-range-ordered molecules, except for imperfections such as "steps" and "clumps" which involve only a few molecules at a time: the surface

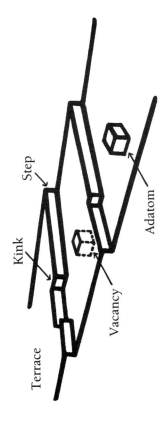

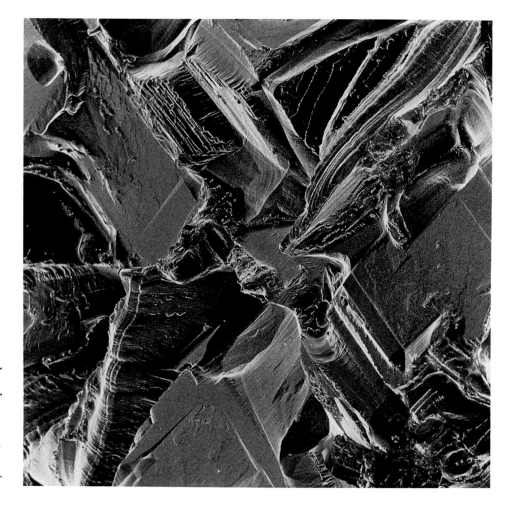

Figure 2a (top). Schematic representation of a cleanly cleaved crystal surface, with ledges, kinks and other types of imperfections. 2b (*bottom*). SEM image of sea salt crystals, with step imperfections. (Photo credit: © David Scharf, 1986)

is *rough* only on the scale of angstroms. (See Figures 2a-b.) Nevertheless, it is possible to directly determine the structures of such imperfections by several different experimental techniques, including electron tunneling microscopy, which is described elsewhere in this book. Furthermore, these "defects"—which are largely unavoidable "facts of life" characterizing the cleanest and smoothest surfaces—play a dominant role in controlling the dynamics of reactions on surfaces, largely through the local electric fields to which they give rise. In particular they comprise the "active sites" at which chemistry occurs preferentially in the case of reactions that are significantly enhanced by the presence of a solid surface. Many industrially important processes (e.g., ammonia synthesis and conversion of hydrocarbon chains to ring compounds) are believed to involve this kind of *catalysis*, in which the surface imperfections promote the reaction without themselves being chemically transformed.

Perhaps the most exotic molecular environment of all is that which obtains in the interstellar medium. Recall from our earlier discussion that an air molecule at atmospheric pressure and room temperature typically undergoes as many as one billion collisions per sec. Even under the best evacuation conditions presently realizable, a molecule still can't move for more than about one second before colliding with others; in fact, it collides first with the container walls at these very low pressures. In the interstellar medium, however, molecules are such rare commodities that this "mean free time" becomes as long as one million seconds! The fact that they are isolated from collisions for as long as several months has many curious consequences for their relaxation dynamics. For example, whenever a molecule manages to become electronically excited via absorption of ultraviolet radiation from hot stars—and this happens only once every few weeks!—there is no way for it to get rid of this excess energy except by emission of light. By contrast, under "normal" pressure conditions, the electronic excitation—after being converted internally into vibrational and rotational energy of the nuclei—is dissipated as heat through collision. Thus, the "molecular landscape" of the interstellar medium emerges as a kind of wasteland in which chemical species are so rare that they do not have the chance to encounter one another in an excited state. Nevertheless, our observation of them—in particular, the identification of certain compounds but not others—provides many important clues into the origins and evolution of the universe, the birth of the stars and planets, and perhaps the origin of life. (See Figure 3.)

MAKING NEW MOLECULES AND MATERIALS

In concentrating on a few kinds of molecules and molecular behaviors, we have of course neglected to mention many other important examples. We cannot close, however, without devoting some brief attention to the synthesis of new

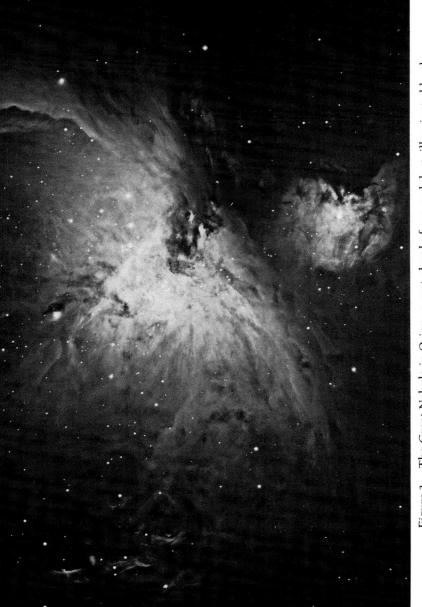

Figure 3. The Great Nebula in Orion, a vast cloud of gas and dust, illuminated by the high energy radiation of hot stars, which causes hydrogen to fluoresce red and oxygen to fluoresce green. In the dust clouds, complex organic molecules are sheltered from the ultraviolet. (Photo credit: David Malin, © Anglo-Australian Observatory Board, 1981)

molecular species and new molecular materials. These provide important motivation for much of the earlier-described work on molecular structure and dynamics. After all, the more we understand about how a naturally occurring molecule is formed and held together, the better we can make it ourselves in the laboratory.

Before starting with illustrations we should first clear up a widespread and unfortunate misunderstanding concerning the presumed differences between "natural" and "synthetic" substances. "Organic" farmers and "health food" suppliers often tell us, for example, that their products contain no "chemicals"; hence, a storefront sign boasts that "our baked goods are made without chemicals," and a roadside billboard asserts, "Chemicals belong in test tubes, not in bodies—drink milk"! What they are really saying is that naturally occurring rather than laboratory-synthesized compounds (chemicals!) are to be found in their bread and milk. Similarly, the organic farmer is careful to use as ammonia-containing compounds only those that are part of manure and other "natural" fertilizer material. The mistaken assumptions in all these cases are that laboratory-made compounds are different from their naturally occurring counterparts, and that the former are necessarily bad for us whereas the latter are necessarily good.

From our earlier discussion we know that a molecule is nothing more or less than a chemically bound group of certain elements that always involves the same numbers and configuration of its constituent atoms. Let's also be clear about the fact that a "chemical" is just a pure compound with a specific composition—that is, a molecule! Furthermore, a molecule is the same in every way regardless of whether it is synthesized in the laboratory or found in nature. Clearly, the harm or good of a particular substance has nothing to do with how we might make it or find it (trace contaminants excepted).

One important class of chemical syntheses is motivated by the desire to make certain compounds for less money than it costs to extract them from natural products or processes (or to generate more of substances which would otherwise become "extinct"). In the case of methane (CH_4) for example, it has been found that the reaction $3H_2 + CO \rightarrow CH_4 + H_2O$ can be made to run very efficiently if it is carried out in the presence of metal supports, such as nickel or cobalt. A much more complicated example, from the chemical reaction point of view, is provided by the laboratory synthesis of, say, vitamin B_{12}: dozens of successive synthetic reactions—each more ingenious then the next—are necessary to arrive at the final product. Even more important, perhaps, is the fact that one can also make in the laboratory various substances that do not naturally occur in our world.

A beautiful set of such examples is provided by the series of organic molecules that have recently been synthesized to act as "guests" for special "host" compounds, fitting into them selectively as part of biochemical reaction pathways. Indeed the key idea here is to develop highly structured molecular complexes that can mimic those in living organisms. Thus, "hosts" are the synthetic counterparts to the receptor sites of enzymes, genes, and antibodies, while "guests" correspond to inhibitors, drugs, and antigens. Not only can the binding of guest by host be made very strong, but it can also be engineered to be extremely selective. Consider, for example, the complex shown in Figure 4, in which a lithium ion is bound by a "spherand" consisting of benzene rings with oxygen atom substituents. The host-guest association tendency of such a complex turns out to be 10 billion times greater for sodium than for potassium ions! Similarly, highly effective hosts have been designed for larger ions, such as the citrates and phosphates, and have been shown to exert in this way a great influence on biological metabolism. Furthermore, the guest species need not be charged and are observed to form strong complexes in both water (aqueous) and organic solutions.

More generally, chemists are working hard to design new drugs and pharmaceuticals that will do a better job than their naturally occurring counterparts. In this context it is important to realize that, in addition to novel laboratory synthetic techniques, large-scale computer calculations have also begun to make significant contributions to drug design. Consider, for example, the fact that several classes of anticancer drugs are believed to "work" through their specific interactions with DNA. In particular, their effectiveness is hypothesized to correlate with the extent to which they bind to special sites in the double helix (e.g., slipping in between neighboring base pairs). To optimize the anticancer activity of such compounds, then, supercomputers are currently being used to determine the geometry and the strength of their binding to DNA. (See Figure 5.) Quantum chemical calculation of these binding forces have already suggested many synthetic modifications of the drug agents.

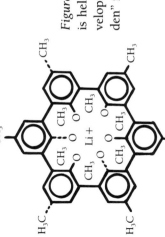

Figure 4. A lithium atom missing one electron is held in thrall by the electric charge of the enveloping rings of benzene. The metal ion is "hidden" from other chemical reactants.

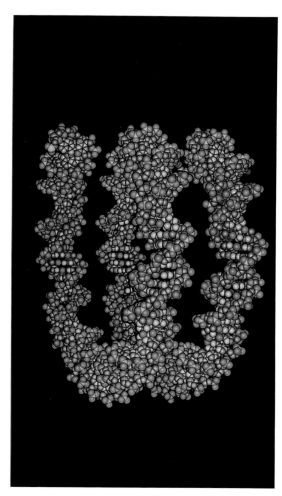

Figure 5. Computer-generated image of part of a DNA double helix, which is shown coiled as it would be in the nucleus of a cell. (Credit: Dr. Nelson Max, University of California, Lawrence Livermore Laboratory and the Department of Energy)

Finally, we say a few words about the synthesis of materials, as opposed to molecules. The most famous example is one that we mentioned earlier—namely, that of plastics and fibers. Here one first synthesizes the molecule and then processes it into various convenient forms (e.g., plastic sheets and fibers). The processing in these cases often involves the use of specific additives, which are chosen to enhance desired properties, such as flexibility, strength, color-fastness, and so on. (As in our above discussion of natural and synthetic food-stuffs, we remind ourselves that chemical "additives" are not necessarily bad for us.) In other cases it is found that blends of polymeric molecules can produce materials that incorporate the good features of each of their constituents at the same time that they show wholly new characteristics.

An analogous situation arises in the case of liquid crystals. A liquid crystal is a liquid whose (usually) rod-shaped molecules tend to point along the same direction. In an "ordinary" liquid, on the other hand, the molecules are not aligned. (When a liquid crystal is warmed up above a certain temperature, it "melts" to an "ordinary" liquid.) Because of their preferred orientation, liquid crystals have special light-polarization properties that make them extremely useful as optical display devices. Synthesis of new rod-shaped molecules, and preparation of novel mixtures of such species, permits us to design liquid crys-tal materials with convenient thermal and electric-field responses. Indeed, the displays on wristwatches, pocket calculators, and briefcase computers rely upon the fact that samples can be found that can respond to small voltages over a wide range at about room temperature.

An even more exotic kind of liquid crystal arises in the case of concentrated solutions of surfactant molecules in water. A surfactant is a molecule that is "hermaphroditic": one end of it is, generally, a long hydrocarbon chain ("tail"), essentially insoluble in water; the other end (the "head") is ionic (i.e., nega-tively or positively charged) or dipolar, so that it is easily incorporated in water. Consequently, above trace concentrations, the surfactant molecules dissolve in aqueous solutions *as aggregates*—the water is shielded by the "surface" of heads from the "interior" of tails. When the aggregates are sufficiently rodlike and their concentration high enough, they align to show liquid crystal properties, much as individual molecules do in the simpler one-component example dis-cussed in the preceding paragraph. More generally, the surfactant molecules in water can form many other structures. Upon addition of significant amounts of oil, for example, the aggregates "swell" to form emulsion drops: this is the mechanism whereby grease and other organic residues are solubilized by deter-gent and soap (and may yet account for cost-effective ways of recovering trapped oil from underground reservoirs). The basic idea is that the surfactant allows for oil to be dispersed in water without direct contact between these otherwise unmixable species. More interesting still are the vesicle structures, which are formed when, say, phospholipid surfactant molecules like the leci-thins are dissolved in water. These aggregates resemble closely the actual mem-

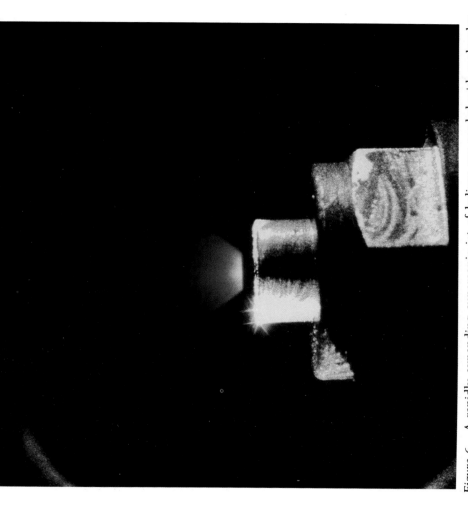

Figure 6. A rapidly expanding supersonic jet of helium gas seeded with molecular iodine fluoresces under laser illumination, allowing study of single molecule and very low energy state interactions. (Photo credit: Donald H. Levy, The James Franck Institute, The University of Chicago)

branes of living cells and have already been used extensively in the development of highly sophisticated in vivo drug delivery systems. Finally we mention a very different kind of surfactant structure—namely, the single-layer system—where the "heads" are adsorbed on a solid (metal or glass) support, with the "tails" forming a chemically inert surface just above. These films serve a variety of purposes in recently emerging electronics and computer technologies, making possible many novel processes involving optical signal modulation, chemical sensing, and integrated circuit devices.

The goal of this essay has been to "raise the molecular consciousness" of the reader, in the hope that she or he will *never again look at the world around us without seeing molecules everywhere.* In addition, readers are encouraged to be intrigued by the wondrous fact that many of the macroscopic (physical and chemical) properties of matter have already been explained in terms of what individual molecules are doing on a microscopic level. Still other features are not yet understood and await the development of more ingenious experiments and more comprehensive theories on how molecules interact in their wide variety of types and in the full spectrum of the many states of matter.

DEATH WISH
POUL ANDERSON
ILLUSTRATION BY PAMELA LEE

THE CELL IS A SEA WHERE MOLECULES DRIFT ON THERMAL tides. In the abyss the great double helices lie waiting. Their electrons leap in quantum response to random approaches. That flotsam which cannot bind, recoils. Fields lay hold of that which fits. Piece by piece, they link it together. The DNA becomes the matrix of itself and of the code borne away by the RNA to the ribosomes. There the RNA in its turn, as blindly and as ineluctably, controls the growth of the proteins that form and rule the living entity. Seldom does this flux go awry. Almost always, it brings each last atom into the exact place that the configurations themselves have ordained.

A while after nightfall, George Lanthier believed he was ready. If he waited longer, he might lose his resolution. The means of getting it back were on hand, but he wanted no more of such things. Enough that the wine he had taken glowed softly through his veins.

Mendelssohn's Violin Concerto sighed around him. Everywhere around him; the singing microcrystals pervaded the walls. Anita had loved the piece, but she had never heard it like this. Lanthier half wished she had—her life ended too soon—and half wished for the old, inadequate two-speaker system they had listened to together. But that was pure sentimentalism. He probably shouldn't have ordered the music at all.

Certainly he would not call up the illusion of her, full size and three dimensional, smiling as he remembered and speaking in the voice he knew. It had been a mistake having the computer recreate her, changing and changing everything about the image according to his uttered corrections, interpolating where memory failed him until he saw what she must have been when he married her. The photograph taken not in her youth but in her old age was as much as he could bear tonight. He made as if to kiss it, but drew back and only stroked fingers across.

They touched the envelope that lay on the table, addressed to Joanie, and for an instant trembled. He was going to play a bad trick on her. He could only hope that in time she would understand. A few firm words on paper were better than a live-recorded message, and of course a direct call would have been out of the question.

Lanthier drew a breath, squared his shoulders, and picked up the thing that waited beside the envelope. The west wall opened for him and he went forth into the night.

He limped a bit, weariness dragged at him, small aches nibbled here and there. The latest of his successive organic restorations had, like its predecessors, worked less than perfectly. That was five years ago. Manuel said total rejuvenation was now possible and would become standard clinical practice. Lanthier had decided not to wait. A wholly youthful and healthy body might change his mind for him.

Air was cool, tinged with a little pungency from the pine forest that reared on the far side of a crumbling abandoned highway. Grass glimmered dewy along the path he took. Gravel scrunched underfoot. That sound changed to thuds and clacks when he came onto the stones that covered the beach. They shone with a wetness somehow as hard as the feel of them through his shoes. He smelled salt and kelp, odors equally ancient, and felt he drew strength from them. He was returning to primeval things.

The ocean before him no longer was among them. Surf still tumbled and boomed, pale white, and the wrinkled vastness beyond it ran westward around the curve of the world. Most of it, though, heaved dark beneath mats of non-algae, growing foodstuff or he knew not what else, which made doubly bright a school of grazers that cruised by, taking pure metals from the water for human use and to breed more of their kind. He did glimpse a whale afar. Wildlife was coming back in abundance—but managed, monitored, modified to fit the wholly controlled planet.

Lanthier looked behind him and from side to side. He saw no other person. Cabins were everywhere around; fifteen billion people could live in prosperity but rarely in solitude. (However, these dwellings all nestled among trees designed to be tall after one year and screen them off.) His vision caught merely a few window gleams, and his wish was fulfilled; he had the strand to himself. He did not want to carry out his purpose within walls.

Not that he really had open sky, he thought. When Joanie and Manuel offered him the place of his own that they had come to realize he needed, he chose the Washington coast partly because clouds or rain or fog often closed it in. He could imagine it as once he knew it, not an engineered dream within his head but an unchanged reality. Tonight heaven stood naked. A shimmer, not aurora but luminescence from atmosphere-regulating processes high aloft, overran it. Two orbiting solar energy collectors dazzled any glance that strayed near. Three or four stars barely shone through, if you knew where to seek them.

The moon rose behind the woods, nearly full. Sudden brilliance flooded. The shield was blanketed in clouds, a featureless white save where winds roiled them into swirls or opened a gap for water beneath to flash. It was like a small second sun. For a moment Lanthier was half blinded.

Sight recovered. He did not want it to. His purpose congealed. He brought the pistol up. Its kiss was cold on his temple. Then, for no reason clear to himself, he lowered it, pressed the mouth against his breast. The heart is a chancy target, he knew, but he had loaded in an expanding magnum bullet. "Good-bye," he whispered, which was meaningless, and, "I'm sorry," which was as awkward as his grip on butt and trigger. He fired.

In their uncountable numbers and their multitudinous varieties, the pseudo-bacteria are at work. Where industry once savaged the land, some turn organic poisons into harmless vapors or sequester toxic metals. Some produce fertile soil from desert sand and stone. Some convert the fused, volatilized bodies of comets, deliberately crashed into the moon, to breathable air and pure water. Some tunnel microscopically toward the very cores of planets in quest of minerals or knowledge. Some brew food, drink, medicine. Some hound down and devour those organisms of disease that pseudoviruses cannot more readily destroy. Some enter into symbioses such as evolution would never have brought forth, with consequences unknown in nature. And more, and more. They do it because they are so made; they cannot do otherwise. Call them, if you will, not life but micromachines.

Helen Murasaki, special investigator for the World Security Command, happened to be in a sheriff's station when the call came. Were total information in the databases, she need never have visited the area, unless on a vacation trip back to the scenes of her childhood. As it was, she must prowl about, look hard and immediately into anything suspicious, and above all talk with people. One of them might provide her a clue.

Local officers on night duty were apt to be relaxed, able to let their minds wander freely. First she must put them at ease. That took some doing, as formidable as her status and as possibly terrifying as her mission were. But the folkways quickly came back to her. This was old-established tourist country, yet remained rural, conservative, close knit. Gossip was a favorite pastime.

Behind the desk, Bill Swenson leaned back in his creaky, antique swivel chair and said thoughtfully, "No, I guarantee you Sam Rice isn't up to anything. He does put in for a lot of data and sends after fancy stuff, but it's just that he likes to tinker with plants on that play farm of his. I've been there more'n once, sociable-like, and—"

The phone chimed. He straightened and pressed ACCEPT. A man's head and shoulders appeared above the set. He looked white, shaken. Sweat trickled down his cheeks. "Sheriff's department, Hoquiam station," Swenson said.

"B-b-ben Lewis," the caller identified himself. "At Kalaloch. We got a dead man here. Shot."

Swenson grew taut. Murasaki felt the same surge in her own muscles, quelled it, sat with the feline alertness that had been trained into her. "Details, please," the deputy said.

"I was stepping out for a stroll—family's rented a cabin for the summer—I heard what sounded like a shot, went to look—Moon so bright I couldn't miss him. Lying on the rocks with his chest blown open. Pistol under his hand, nine millimeter, I'd say. Shot himself, I guess." Lewis gulped. "Oh, God, his face! I think I'd better get a memory scrub."

"Don't quit on me. What'd you do?"

"Hauled him to my cabin. Yelled at the kids to go into a back room and close the door. Wouldn't have them see this. Wife helped me. We emptied the freezer and put him in." Self-congratulation flickered. "Moved fast. Can't be too much brain damage."

Swenson glared. "You fool! Don't you know water expands when it freezes? Could do harm to his cells they don't know how to repair—yet, anyway. Pull him out again. Keep his head *cool*, packed in ice. We'll have an emergency unit there, pronto. What's your address code?"

When he had that, the deputy switched the phone off and punched for what he required. An alert bell shrilled. He stood up. "I'm riding along," he said. "Sorry, Captain. We'll continue later, okay?"

Murasaki rose likewise. "Oh, I'm coming too," she replied.

He stared. "Huh? Look, I admit suicide is damn near unheard of anymore, but if it is somehow a murder—"

"I'm interested in everything unusual, remember? Murder's also becoming rare throughout the United States and Canada. And that makes it the more menacing when it happens." At his inquiring glance: "Think. A person who feels violent impulses and does not seek medication has to have something fundamentally wrong with him. And in the U.S., at least, the government cannot constitutionally compel every individual to be tested. So far."

"Car's ready," said an intercom voice. They went out. Two men with paramedic training sat in the main compartment amidst the apparatus. Swenson and Murasaki got in front. He set for the destination. The big teardrop whirred to speed altitude and lined out. The starlike lights of other vehicles darted across the sky as their computers caught the police signal and veered well aside.

Light off the clouded moon dwindled the glitter of the town. Radiance washed over the high roof of that Victorian mansion called Hoquiam Castle. A few things endured, Murasaki thought fleetingly. Treated as it had been, the wood in that relic and its furnishings would never decay. Ironic; the era had believed itself so solid, so unchangeable except for steady progress toward its own perfection.

"Do you think this, uh, incident might have something to do with—what you're looking for?" Swenson asked.

"Probably not," Murasaki answered. "But it's the first thing I've encountered that has no safe, easy explanation. I can't afford to ignore it."

"Maybe there's nothing here for you to find. Maybe you're just chasing after rumors that don't mean a thing," Swenson shivered. "Christ, I hope so."

"Do you think I don't? Frankly, my superiors strongly suspected from the first that the whole matter is baseless. No terrorists concocting something dreadful, no clandestine experiment too dangerous to be allowed. That's why the Command's trying to keep it hushed up. A panic could actually kill people. Which may be the reason the hints were started. A fanatic group's idea of how to make a social point, or a lunatic's idea of a joke. Whatever the truth may be, we want to nail the parties responsible."

Moonlight pouring in the canopy made trenches of shadow where Swenson grimaced. "And you can't even suppose it is a hoax, can you? Not till you're absolutely sure."

Murasaki nodded. "The margin's too thin. Everybody remembers the Russian disaster. Ten million dead, fifty million refugees, half a million square kilometers of rich land devastated and not yet fully reclaimed, a decade afterward." They did not remember how narrowly the blue slime had been kept from engulfing the entire terrestrial biosphere; that remained top secret. "They don't generally think about the little accidents that could have been much worse if not handled in time, or the computer power required to work out adequate safeguards for every new undertaking. Nearly always, self-reproducing nanoprocesses cannot continue under outside conditions, as the law demands. But 'nearly always' isn't good enough for us to relax; and sometimes the law is deliberately violated."

"Yeah, I guess we've got a lot more dangerous world than people realize." Murasaki shrugged. "Perhaps no more than it used to be. Depends on who and where you are." Across the years there came back to her, she once more a small girl shocked and puzzled, the sight of her father crying. He'd kept her from seeing the documentary he had just witnessed, on Africa. The continent of contentment, the travel brochures called it today.

Countryside unrolled below the car, moon-drenched white. She recognized a complex of buildings sprawling low and sleek among meadows: a factory. Inspecting it had held a special poignancy for her, because it occupied the site of one of her parents' orchards. Theirs might have been the last outfit in the state raising apples commercially. It paid less and less, what with a new taste sensation on the market practically every week, until in the end they must sell out and retire; but they had loved their trees.

Although their lengths be measured in nanometers (billionths of a meter; hundredths of a wavelength of visible light), the directing molecules are giants. Nothing less than a computer made on the same scale could have devised their labyrinthine complexities and overseen the compounding of them. Now, though, they are complete, and in their own realm sovereign. They form and dispatch messenger molecules that bear their coded directives to the assembly structures. Within the chemical bath, atom joins to atom, each precisely in its rightful place. Between dawn and dusk of a working day, an engine takes shape. The crystals being perfect, the lightweight material of it is as strong as natural law permits. Incorporating intricate circuits, it will vary its pattern of fuel consumption so as to constantly run at the highest possible efficiency; and it will break down any pollutants that appear before they can escape it. In other tanks, other molecules copy themselves. Like a living thing, the factory breeds.

Project Heimdall had suffered an accident. A meteoroid struck a spacecraft servicing the Web, with sufficient force to penetrate the hull. That was not serious; the vessel was an unmanned robotic job, discharging fresh raw material at a growth node on the outer edge, and was already healing itself. However, its controls temporarily deranged, it had blundered into the mesh. Several hundred kilometers' worth of strands were torn and tangled.

This too was self-repairable. But those processes required close monitoring. In a state of nature, wounded live tissue often ends scarred or otherwise altered. The project could not let that happen to the Web. The slightest imperfection might cause loss or, worse, distortion of some whisper from a far corner of the universe.

Laden with instruments, Manuel Silvela glided carefully, carefully along a frame cable. A battery-powered motor drew him; jet exhaust could have contaminated the ongoing chemistry. His spacesuit posed no such hazard—totally sealed, recycling every molecule that went through him, yet hampering no more than would one additional layer of skin. Indeed, the microservos and sensory amplifiers in the glove sections heightened the powers of his hands so greatly that they always felt numb for a while after he'd gone back to base.

He kept his attention on the readouts of the instruments, displayed before his eyes in the helmet. Peripherally, he could not help staying aware of splendor. The sun was at his back, tiny, its light astream over silvery threads and cords subtly interwoven. Stars shone between them and everywhere else, brilliant, unwinking. They well-nigh crowded the blackness out of heaven. The

Milky Way foamed argent across a silence in which breath and heartbeat fluttered loud. Jupiter stood like a pale golden lamp; he could make out three of the Galilean moons. He could not really see the far end of the Web. The processes that were consuming a large asteroid had already spun it over more than two million kilometers.

And I, Silvela thought at the back of his mind, I am helping this glory come into being.

An alarm buzz stabbed him. He halted the tow motor and hung weightless. The displays vanished; the cosmos overwhelmed his vision.

"Manuel?" he heard. "Heinrich here. Message for you from Earth. I think you'd better return straight to base and respond. I'm sending Chu to relieve you. Do you want the message right away?"

"Yes. Yes, please," Silvela mumbled. If it was urgent—when the laser beam took twenty minutes or more to carry it—

His wife's voice wavered in his ears. "Manuel, this is Joan. Dad's shot himself. They're not sure yet if they recovered him in time. I— Don't fret about me, darling. I'll be all right. I know you can't get back fast." In a rush: "And I want you to stick with the job, finish your hitch. But . . . if we could talk—time lag doesn't matter, if I could just see your face and hear you—"

"Por supuesto, querida," he heard himself say, uselessly before he had reached the main communicator. "¡Ay, damnación! ¿Por qué, por qué?"

"I'm terribly sorry, Manuel," Heinrich Rohm ventured. "You can have leave as soon as—"

Silvela shook his head, blindly. "No, thank you. I won't risk compromising the project. She agrees. It matters too much. I may ask the medic for a worry killer till we see how this is going to go."

At his feet, the superconductors of the Web thrilled to the pulses of the universe. Project Heimdall was humbly named. The watchman of the Norse gods could only see to the ends of the earth, only hear the grass grow. With ever more vast capabilities, the web mapped planets light-years off. It traced energies from the beginnings of time out at the rim of space. Nearer home, it followed probes hurtling away from the Solar System, and caught messages passing between star and star. When humanity began to understand and respond to those—soon, now, soon—it would enter into the fellowship of the galaxy.

The computer is the size of your fist. Most of that volume consists of channels for cooling fluid, and pumping this through at the necessary rate requires somewhat more equipment. Connecting wires within the computer also add bulk. The units that they link scarcely do. Each consists of a molecule. When working, it springs to and fro between certain isomeric states. In that respect, the system harks back to the nineteenth century, Babbage's calculating engine and such other mechanical devices as came for a while into practical use. But a nanomachine moves through a nanodistance, at atomic rates of acceleration. Thus the speed of these units exceeds that of an electronic chip by orders of magnitude. Conjoined in numbers comparable to the number of cells in a human brain, they engender about a million times the information-processing capacity of that brain. Thanks to molecular self-replication, computers like this are available, cheaply, in unlimited quantities. They can direct the most complex and delicate actions that humans can imagine for them; and they can carry imagination to lengths that are beyond human comprehension. Their analytical potency makes laboratory experimentation, if not altogether obsolete, secondary; and they design the experiments and wield the instruments. Set to research and development, they can do a million years' worth – old style – in a single twelvemonth.

Joan Lanthier Silvela lived in Idaho. A full-figure phone image showed Helen Murasaki a tall blond woman who moved lithely. Perhaps she played a lot of tennis. Behind her was a glimpse of a room in a house that was kept alive to grow and change. A window opened on a mountain peak whose snows were flushed with dawnlight.

"I'm sorry to disturb you at such a time, and this early an hour," Murasaki apologized.

"I've been awake since the news came," Silvela answered. "A distraction is welcome." She managed a smile. "If you were here in person, I'd give you breakfast."

"You won't enjoy my conversation."

Silvela shrugged. "I understand. The police need to know. I've taken both my antifatigant and my stress easer."

Murasaki forbore to mention what police force she belonged to. "The last I heard, the prognosis for your father was favorable."

"As far as physical recovery goes." Medication or no, Silvela's lips twisted. "But what made him do it? Will that go away?"

"Let's see if we can't guess our way toward an answer," said Murasaki in her softest voice. "I do have some knowledge of . . . violence."

"He was not a violent man. *Is* not," Silvela declared harshly. "An old soldier, true, but always a gentleman, always full of love."

"Tell me about him, please."

Silvela half turned to stare out at mountain and sky. "What can I say? He was born in, um-m, 1950; yes, last year we celebrated his hundred and twenty-first birthday. Career army officer, served in three wars but never talked much about them, retired with rank of colonel, went into management—an electronics firm—but retired altogether when he saw it becoming hopelessly antiquated. He was restless then, traveled a great deal, moved often, till at last my husband and I helped him establish himself at Kalaloch. He kept in touch with us and a few others. We thought he was reasonably happy."

"Wasn't he married?"

Silvela shook her head. "His first wife, my mother, died in 2027. A horrible accident, no sense in preservation, everything that was her would be gone." Silvela drew breath. "He remarried, and I think had occasional liaisons afterward, but nothing lasted. He sort of grinned once, and said he was too set in his ways for anybody modern."

"I gather you were his only child?"

Silvela nodded.

"You've taken treatment remarkably well," Murasaki added in an attempt at friendliness.

Silvela rattled a laugh. "For a woman of eighty-seven, I look pretty good? Well, doubtless heredity helps. Dad also responded satisfactorily to each new rehabilitative treatment as it became available. And now, it seems, before long we'll have total rejuvenation."

"May I ask if he, well, if he has grandchildren?"

Silvela had calmed again. "Three, by my previous marriages. But they've gone their separate ways. Pleasant, well meaning, we hear from them at Christmas and so forth. Distant acquaintances. What else can we expect?"

"Nothing, usually," Murasaki sighed. "I hate to pry, but I'd also like to ask about you and your present husband."

"You could get it out of the public database anyway," Silvela's words emerged flat. "He's in nanotech, currently working on the Heimdall Web. I'm in what they call creative data interpretation, but that's on the way out. After I'm really back in the prime of life, I hope to return to ballet dancing—till, I assume, we have synthetic dancers too graceful for me to compete with." Defiance: "And, yes, Manuel is thirty-three years old. What difference does that make anymore?"

"None, of course. Your business. As an individual, I like the movement today to revive a concept of privacy. But as a police officer—" Murasaki hardened. "I must know whether there was anything criminal involved in your father's death."

"No, damn you!" broke past the drugs. Then: "I'm sorry. Overwrought. But no, it's impossible. He absolutely wasn't that kind of man. Ask him yourself, if you must."

"I don't expect I'll have to," Murasaki murmured. "This looks more and more like a purely personal matter." She hoped that would prove right, for Silvela's sake, and Lanthier's, and the world's.

The dead man lies, carefully shrouded, in a bath of liquid nitrogen. The blood has been drawn from him and his body perfused with a material that will not swell, as it freezes, and do further harm. At the hospital he is taken forth, drained, connected to machines that provide surrogates for what he has lost. Specialized molecules enter, proliferate, perform their manyfold tasks. By their resonances shall you know what is left and what is gone. The signs are auspicious. Some brain damage has occurred, but not sufficient to expunge memory, habit, all those traces we call personality. They are functions of the nervous system as a whole. Pseudomicrobes go in, designed to eat deteriorated tissue, then decompose and be flushed away. The molecules that follow them join with the DNA to read out specification for the replacement structures that other molecules will cause to form where they are needed. Cells of brain, heart, lungs, bone, muscle, skin, blood repair themselves or develop anew. While it is busy, the chemistry executes various improvements that medical science has lately made possible. The body will be better, closer to true and enduring youthfulness, than it was before. The machines restart its organs and, on a continuously controlled schedule, withdraw from it.

—*though he were dead, yet shall he live.* There remain those who consider this blasphemy.

George Lanthier was conscious for three days before the doctors let him have visitors. He was strong enough physically, could anticipate full recovery in a week, but they wanted to know his mental state. Beneath the iron calm he maintained, the equilibrium might be precarious; they had scarcely any experience with suicide. Finally they yielded to his daughter's insistence.

He was in bed reading when she entered his room, reading not text on a screen but an old printed book brought from his cabin at his request. She recognized the *Meditations* of Marcus Aurelius, recalled that she had never looked at it herself, and wondered if he was the last man who ever did or ever would.

The room was private, airy, sunny. On this uncommonly clear day its view ranged over the towers of Seattle to Mount Rainier. Sight of that whiteness afloat in heaven made her feel as if somehow she were coming home.

He glanced up at her footfall and, slowly, smiled. Her heart stumbled. "Hi, Dad," she whispered into the stillness.

"Hello, Joanie," he replied in a level tone. "How are you?"

"Okay myself, but—but—" She stopped at the bedside and groped for his hand. Tears blurred the sight of him. "You."

He sighed. "I'm sorry about distressing you, darling. But didn't you see my note?" She felt him stiffen. "Did you not think I knew what I was doing?"

She caught her breath. "You wouldn't try again!"

"I believed I had explained myself," he told her starkly.

"I'm afraid I, I couldn't quite understand. Your language was so, oh, so formal." Even the close: "Know that I love you, and losing you is the single thing I regret. Have it well. Your father."

He shook his head. "That may have been a mistake," he allowed. "My hope was to explain things in a logical way, make you see that nothing was your fault and you need feel no guilt. But to be sure, the issues are emotional."

She gripped his hand hard, leaned close above him, and exclaimed, "Right. Right. And you are not rational, Dad. Yes, the world is changing, faster and faster. It always was, but now molecular technology— Nobody knows what's ahead. Nobody can even make a sensible guess. But is that a reason to bow out? I never imagined you were a quitter."

With a flash of anger, he replied, "I am not. I simply found I cannot cope with things any longer. I cannot learn fast enough."

She straightened as if to command him. "You can if you want. Start by learning how to let a computer help you learn."

He gentled. "It'll be obsolete in two years, extinct in five. But never mind. What I really can't do is change fast enough. I'm no coward, I'm not afraid of what may happen to me, but I see this razor's edge we're living on and I think of the children and that's too much to take."

"We aren't doomed, you know."

"Maybe not. Except that in another century or less, if we survive, we won't be anything we'd recognize today."

"We'll still be ourselves, Dad. You and I and everybody. No boundary on how long we'll live, what we'll do and discover and . . . become."

He stared from her, off into the sky. By day it wasn't very greatly changed from what he and all the former generations of mankind had known. "I tried," he said. "I tried my damnedest to adapt."

She bit her lip and nodded.

"But I couldn't," he went on. "I was useless, a pensioner, almost a charity case. At last you and Manuel, in your kindly way, found me the nearest thing possible to a haven. An enclave. Peace, serenity, a dwindling remnant of what was once eternal. None of us foresaw that it'd give me too much time. Time to think, time to remember, time to feel everything that is forever lost, that doesn't mean anything to anybody these days—except me, and I could feel it slipping away from me too, I was losing it. Eventually I decided to go where your mother is, Joanie."

"Which is nowhere," she retorted low.

"I suppose so." He looked back at her, and pride returned to him. "Didn't I have a right to steer my own course? Don't I? It was a perfectly sane decision." She braced herself to blurt, "Was it? Then why didn't you blow your brains out? That would've been permanent."

He flinched for the first time. "I, well, I didn't want to leave you that sight—"

"Are you sure? Didn't you, down inside, mean to leave yourself some small chance?"

His mouth tightened. "Let's be honest. I haven't any. I'm not whining. It's just the fact."

"It is not! You know about psychomedications. Keep yourself cheerful and optimistic."

"Chemical consolations," he gibed.

"Would you refuse an anesthetic if you broke your arm?" she counterattacked.

"That's your attitude."

"It can be yours."

"If I choose. Nobody can compel me. I thank the God I don't believe in that we still have a Bill of Rights in this country; and I prefer not to be around when it's repealed."

"I think it'll merely become irrelevant." She turned her manner mild, reasonable. "Besides, mood drugs are a stopgap. I've been talking at length with Dr. Horn. She's retrieved the preliminary data for me. In a few years, maybe very few, they'll have the means to reprogram the nervous system. They can turn you into a person who can and does cope, participate, look forward to a life that may be a million years long."

"That person would not be me."

"Why not? Think about it. Oh, Dad, please."

He saw her fight not to weep, and held out his arms, and she came to him. After she had gone, he set himself to thinking about it.

Author's note: This story is not a science fantasy, but a fairly conservative extrapolation of present-day fact. The best discussion of nanotechnology to date is by K. Eric Drexler, *Engines of Creation* (New York: Anchor Press/Doubleday, 1986). He is not responsible for any mistakes or misinterpretations I may have made.

THE NUCLEAR WORLD

ESSAY BY
PHILIP MORRISON
WITH
WILLIAM R. ALSCHULER
SPECULATION BY
PAUL PREUSS

THE NUCLEAR WORLD

PHILIP MORRISON

MASSACHUSETTS INSTITUTE OF TECHNOLOGY

WITH WILLIAM R. ALSCHULER

THE ANALYSIS OF MATTER

THE ANALYSIS OF MATTER AND SPECULATION ABOUT ITS fundamental nature is an old, old human activity. No one knows how or when it started, but almost everyone has heard of the four elements of the Greeks, the foundation of Aristotelian and post-Aristotelian philosophy. They were earth, air, fire and water, and they were very intelligently chosen. The philosophers did not literally mean those four materials; rather, the words described properties. Today we would say earthiness, wateriness, fiery quality, and airy quality; a fifth element, the ether, was conceived of as a mysterious and pervasive quintessence. Using these elements, philosophers were able to explain quite a bit about the natural world. Consider the question, what is a metal? A metal will melt, unlike a rock, at ordinary fiery temperatures, so it has a watery quality; perhaps a metal is a combination of earth and water. It is a sophisticated idea to look for commonality in things, and that is what the idea of a few fundamental properties attempts to do.

In many cultures, there is a completely different tradition, one far more sophisticated yet entirely inarticulate and unrecorded (except in the works themselves): the artisan's tradition. If you look at goldwork from Ur of the Chaldees (easily 4,000 years old), the outstanding quality, workmanship and understanding of the material are evident and are the equal of anything since. Gold (like copper and silver) occurs naturally in rocks in native form; it is clearly metallic, distinctive in color, lustrous, and malleable. It was probably learned by accident, and then checked by careful experiment, that slow heating would melt and further purify these metals until a point was reached where their properties did not change; they were pure. Artisans also found that metals from any source finally acted in just the same way, always ending up in the same state. The ancients found that a combination of two metals, an alloy, could be made in the fire and that, though "impure," an alloy had interesting new properties as to polish, malleability, and so on. Artisans wished to give away or sell their wares, so they had an incentive to standardize the metals with regard to weight and volume. Soon they found weight more reliable. Craftsmen developed thereby a reasonably clear idea of relative density. The first recorded measures of density (in relation to buoyancy) are credited to Archimedes in Greece about 450 BC. He could check the composition of an alloy of gold and silver by measuring its weight loss in water. That is a quite sophisticated idea, which must have had a long tradition behind it.

The artisans' tradition was preserved and passed on through apprenticeship (largely undocumented, since the artisan class did not write history); it yielded a clear idea of pure materials. At some point, that idea combined with the philosophical idea of the elements to give the idea of the pure elements. For example, there was gold and there was iron; gold could not be made out of iron except by a magician. No artisan could do that, though there were alchemists who claimed to, by various secret heatings and chemicals. Such transformations have become possible in the twentieth century by entirely different methods.

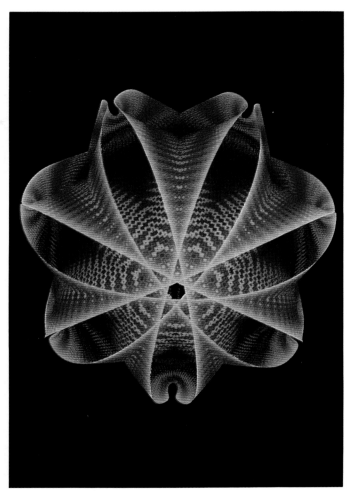

Figure 1. Computer generated image suggesting the complexity of nuclei. (Credit: © James T. Hoffman)

The philosophical idea of the atom as an indivisible constituent of all matter did not relink with the idea of a pure element until the fifteenth century, even though it had been expounded by Democritus in Greece in the fifth century BC. By the time of the Renaissance many had begun to believe this notion; most significantly, Isaac Newton believed it. I think Newton was attracted to it because of his tremendous success with the idea that massive bodies act as the summation of tiny attracting particles. Once you have the idea of gravitation being universal it is no great leap to say, "If this works for the planets and the sun, it works for tiny particles of matter; that is what holds them together." (We know now that electromagnetism is responsible for holding bricks and people together.) Furthermore, he had great success with his new differential and integral calculus, in which the ideas of infinitely small particles and summations of small steps to yield definite bounded results play large roles. However, he still conceived of atoms as things having sharp points and hooks; this did not take him very far.

The seventeenth century brought the beginnings of modern chemistry. Almost everyone has had a certain experience having to do with chemistry: burning food. No matter what you burn, if it is edible, it turns black—except for water and salt. They prove the rule. Water is indispensable for life, yet it is not a nutrient; nor is salt. Everything else we eat is carbonaceous and chars to black carbon. This observation was combined with the artisans' observations that many distinct ores could be heated to produce the same pure substances. Foods contain mainly carbon and water (which comes off as vapor when heated): fundamental things that hang together. That is the idea of the elements. But how one answered the question of whether there were atoms was still a matter of philosophical taste.

Fire and light were still included among the elements. Chemistry as a science trailed astronomy and celestial mechanics by a hundred years. Robert Boyle's treatise on chemistry is much less sophisticated than his friend Newton's *Principia Mathematica*. By the time of the French Revolution, Antoine Lavoisier (who was beheaded at an early age) had published a list of the elements that included many metals, sulphur (which occurs in native form near volcanoes—the ancient brimstone), and about 20 others. There were some mistakes—compounds we now know as oxides of metals, which the chemists of that era couldn't reduce to elements with their techniques—but not many. Weighing a substance on a balance was still the fundamental way to measure purity. Oxygen was not listed, although Lavoisier and his contemporaries noted its presence in the air. They finally realized that when a substance burns, its weight increases: oxygen goes in. Sometimes—as for mercury—you can easily bake it out again.

A pure element is made of like particles that weigh something definite—a direct result of the nature of the atom and the atomic nucleus. We now say (to get a bit ahead of ourselves) that the nucleus is what is characteristic of every element, whereas the electrons that tag along weigh very little. Electrons can also be found nearly everywhere in more or less liberated form though often still held within matter. When it was discovered early in the nineteenth century that electric currents (transferring electrons) had chemical consequences, the new electrochemical separations allowed sodium, potassium, and other elements to be isolated as pure metals. Worldwide mineral collections were established and analyzed; organic compounds were analyzed, and chemistry and the list of elements both grew.

The old discovery of strong acids led to a multitude of new reactions and new compounds, to the observation that some reactions release heat, and to the idea that compounds are combinations of elements in definite ratios, which could be confirmed by the simple technique of careful weighing. The electrolysis of water using early batteries demonstrated the regular appearance of two lines of bubbles; oxygen collects at one electrode and hydrogen at the other. When combined, oxygen will always burn two volumes of hydrogen to become water, never one or three. Of course, the actual measurement is something like 2.00 plus or minus .004, but that suggests exactly 2, which in turn suggests the precise combination of atoms.

Electrolysis had another important result. It showed that a given amount of electric charge always released the same mass of an element, or simple multiples of that mass. This indicated both that atoms made up the molecules of compounds and that electricity was probably atomistic. The notion of the electron as a discrete particle received experimental support only after 1890.

Thus, separations and weighings led directly to these remarkably simple ratios. By 1810 John Dalton had seriously considered how atoms would work, showing that if they had fundamental fixed masses the weight results were beautifully explained. He also began to draw molecular diagrams more or less as we draw them still, small balls of conventional colors for various atoms, and lines as bonds to connect them. (See "The World of Molecules," by William M. Gelbart.) Twenty years later chemists began to believe in this model, though no one had seen a single atom or molecule or had any idea how big they were. After 50 years they found, through experiments on the bonds, that atoms combined in three-dimensional space, a result now beautifully confirmed visually in the electron microscopes and by X-ray analysis of the structure of crystals. Methane, a fundamental organic compound, is a tetrahedron. Yet the various three-dimensional combinations of chlorine with methane are compounds with differing properties that nevertheless weigh the same and must therefore have the same number of atoms. Their differences result from the fact that they are put together differently in space. Chemists thus came to believe in atoms as real objects in three dimensions, whose size was unknown but, clearly, very small.

In the second half of the nineteenth century, Dmitry Mendeleyev arranged the elements in a table, in groups with common properties (he was not the first to suggest the possibility), doing such a beautiful job that he could predict the existence of missing elements and the nature of their oxides, sulphates, solubility, color, and so on, simply by reasoning from the properties of the elements above and below the empty places in the table. Some believed that the table implied the existence of a subatomic structure, based largely on the unit atomic mass of hydrogen, which they thought might be added to heavy atoms to yield other elements, but there was no real evidence for such transmutation of elements.

In the 1860s, James Clerk Maxwell gave a complete theory of light as electromagnetism, and connected the idea of charges to the idea of their fields, static or traveling in space. In other work he showed that gas pressure is the result of the random motions of gas particles in space, and thereby he greatly reinforced the idea of atoms as fundamental, particlelike constituents. Gas-discharge experiments using vacuum techniques showed that positive and negative charges were liberated in gas breakdown. Atoms must contain negative electrons and something positively charged in an equal amount, also very small in size, so that atoms were electrically neutral in their normal state.

Now we are near the turn of the century, and the state of theory and experiment changes incredibly rapidly. In just 20 years the model of the atom went from the classical one of a charged fluid, to that of the quantum and relativistic atom, in which the orbiting particles have a wave nature as well as particle properties, and matter can be converted into energy.

SCATTERING EXPERIMENTS AND
THE DISCOVERY OF THE NUCLEUS

About 1900, J. J. Thomson devised a model of the atom in which the electrons were distributed like little plums throughout a big "pudding" of positive charge. This satisfied the requirement for the electrical neutrality of the atom (positive canceled negative) and correctly assumed that electric forces held the atom together. But it was proved wrong in a classic experiment by Ernest Rutherford, the prototype for almost all later experiments on subatomic particles and forces. However, a description of Rutherford's experiment requires some background.

In 1896 X rays were discovered and, unlike light, were found to be highly penetrating, even through metal. Yet they were shown to be electromagnetic waves, like light. Within a few months of the publication of the discovery of X rays, the Curies discovered that atoms, which had been thought immutable, disintegrated naturally in rare elements. In this process of disintegration, called radioactivity, energetic and penetrating fragments, like X rays, were given off. The atoms that disintegrated turned out to be chemically identical to stable atoms, and therefore must have the same electric charge, and yet they were unstable. (The term soon invented for these unstable atoms was *isotope*; isotopes of a particular atom all sit at the same place in the periodic table.) Isotopes can be characterized by their radioactivity rate (their average lifetime), and by the types of radiation they emit (alpha, beta, or gamma rays). If a radio isotope sits in a bottle for a while, eventually enough decays would occur that something chemically different from the pure chemical present at the start would be found.

In 1911, Rutherford and his assistants Ernest Marsden and Hans Geiger started their famous experiment to investigate atomic structure. They used a radioactive source to fire alpha particles (now known to consist of two protons and two neutrons—i.e., helium nuclei) at a very thin gold foil. The idea for doing that came from the discovery of the penetrating power of X rays. It had been observed that X rays—and alphas too—would be stopped more easily by metal foils than by paper of the same weight; so metal must be a substantial barrier on a subatomic scale. Rutherford observed where the particles were scattered by watching for the flashes of light created when they struck a screen of fluorescent mineral. Most went straight ahead, unaffected. Some flashes were seen at small angles, but Rutherford was astonished to find that a few were scattered at angles greater than 90 degrees; they had been scattered backward! (These events were so rare that it took hours of constant visual observation, sitting in a darkened room with radioactive sample, microscope, gold foil, and screen, to spot a few of them. To get decent statistics they counted a hundred thousand events! The experiment was carefully done: Rutherford had two people count together, to catch what one person would have missed while blinking! Eventually they figured out how to use automatic electrical counters.)

Rutherford knew the alpha particles were positively charged and thus repelled by other positive charges, so the simplest explanation of the backward scattering was that most of the atom's mass was positive, but concentrated in a tiny volume at the atomic center, the nucleus. To get a picture of this model, imagine a covered pool table on which a few billiard balls are anchored to the table. If a large number of cue balls are shot along the table, most will pass straight through, some will be deflected to the corners and sides, and a very few will come straight back. These last must be the ones that hit the anchored balls dead center. You can't see this happen because of the cover (in the case of atoms, you can't see because they're too small), but it must be so. Physical laws governing the behavior of objects in the mechanics of simple collisions are fully known, so Rutherford was able to write an equation that predicted these extraordinary results.

RADIOACTIVITY, FUSION, NEUTRONS, AND QUANTUM MECHANICS

Years before he discovered the nucleus, Rutherford had realized that radioactive decay was a measurable constant for each species of radioactive atom. Such an internal clock could be used to date rocks, which was immensely useful to geologists. Radioactivity was so sensational that radioactive spring water (Vichy, for example) was considered healthful. As late as 1960 I drank some fine Italian spring water labeled "contains healthful radioactive minerals." People (including Marie Curie) who long handled radioactives such as radium, or who used X-ray tubes, developed serious lesions on their hands, and the danger began to be recognized.

Early on, it was seen that the decay of pure samples of radium steadily gave off heat. The ejected fragments must fly out with a lot of energy. By 1915 the attempt was made to make new elements by striking known ones with alpha particles. To see the results you needed a way to view individual atomic events. Charles Wilson's invention of the cloud chamber in 1910 improved on the fluorescent screen.

Cosmic rays, which are high-energy rays from outer space, were easily seen with the cloud chamber. That they were extraterrestrial was soon proved by comparing counting rates at sea level, on mountains, and in balloons at high altitudes. That they are subatomic particles and not lightlike gamma rays was not settled until the 1930s; Bruno Rossi and Luis Alvarez showed they must be charged because they are deflected by the earth's magnetic field. In 1947 it was shown that cosmic rays were made up of various kinds of nuclei. In manned balloon experiments conducted high in the stratosphere by Frank Oppenheimer and by Helmut Bradt and Bernard Peters (see Figure 2), the experimenters detected protons (hydrogen nuclei) and helium and carbon nuclei—all ordinary matter, but accelerated to very high energies. This range of elements suggested that cosmic rays were "cooked" in the stars and were not of primordial "cosmological" origin. (For further discussion, see "Inner Space/Outer Space," by Edward W. Kolb.)

This notion of elemental stellar cookery had occurred to Rutherford when he made new elements in the 1920s, because stellar interiors were the only places in the universe that were hot enough to do that and gave out a lot of energy. He also argued that other sources of energy would not keep the sun shining long enough. (If the sun were solid wood, burning with oxygen, it would last 10,000 years. If it were a gas heated merely by its own gravitational contraction, it would shine for tens of millions of years. Lord Kelvin, who was very influential, took the latter position, and at a famous meeting Rutherford argued diplomatically that the geologic record, which could be dated using the

Figure 2. A particle shower generated by the impact of a high energy cosmic ray. The secondaries penetrate lead sheets in a balloon-borne cloud chamber. (Photo credit: Lawrence Livermore Laboratory, University of California)

radioactive decay clock, as well as the fossil record, required the sun to have been shining with its current luminosity for billions of years.) The nuclear reactions that provide this long-term energy supply fuse hydrogen nuclei into helium. Contrary to a widespread impression, the sun's energy reactions are not very vigorous. A person produces more heat per gram per second by his or her metabolism than the sun does by fusion. But the sun has a very large volume, so it produces a lot of energy and its surface is quite hot.

For a short while it was thought that radioactivity might provide the sun's energy, but this idea was dropped when it was realized that not enough radioactive elements (uranium, radium, and so on), exist on the sun. There had to be another type of nuclear reaction, and in the 1920s Arthur Eddington proposed that fusion might work. He guessed that the high temperature of the sun's interior would impart a high-enough velocity to the nuclei that, in collisions, they could overcome their natural electrical repulsion and somehow stick together.

In 1932 a strong clue about that nuclear glue turned up when James Chadwick discovered the neutron, the other fundamental, but electrically neutral, nuclear particle. Neutrons stick to protons and themselves because of a very-short-range force called the *strong force*. The strong force is much stronger than the protons' mutual electromagnetic repulsion, within its very small sphere of influence.

At about the same time, George Gamow was able to show theoretically that a piece of a large nucleus (say uranium) could, with a small probability, tunnel through the strong-force barrier and appear on the outside of the nucleus. This phenomenon is key to understanding the fusion process in stars, because even at the temperatures of stellar interiors the electric repulsion between protons is too strong to overcome, but tunneling allows a slight chance for protons to meet and undergo fusion.

With this theoretical step experimenters were able to begin gathering data on the inherent efficiency of the many possible collisions by which protons can fuse into heavier nuclei. These collision efficiencies are called cross-sections, and they are listed now in tables of fundamental physical data. With this data, people could estimate the fusion reaction rates to be expected inside stars. Eventually, Hans Bethe showed how a several-step reaction could produce helium from hydrogen, or from hydrogen, carbon, nitrogen and oxygen.

Also in the 1930s the first particle accelerators were built, which gave experimenters control over their subatomic projectiles, instead of having to depend on radioactive sources, and allowed them to investigate reaction rates for collisions at ever-higher energies and with ever-larger target nuclei. This trend toward bigger machines continues today, and the great majority of discoveries about nuclei and the large array of subatomic particles were made with such machines. (See "An Experiment in High-Energy Physics," by Leon M. Lederman.)

REACTORS, THE BOMB, AND ACCELERATORS

In the late 1930s I was a graduate student and war was in the air. People criticized the physics profession for living in an ivory tower. I answered that my work on the nuclear physics of solar energy was most relevant, because someday we humans would release energy the same way. I was thinking of fusion, as was everyone else. But you couldn't do that in the laboratory (even now, after a lot of hard work, break-even fusion in the lab is still in the future). Fusion was not the short route to nuclear energy.

In the early 1930s Leo Szilard patented the idea of a neutron-fed chain reaction, in which a neutron splits an atom which releases two neutrons, and another neutron, which can then split the next atom. I was ignorant of this at the time, but everyone realized its implications with a bang when Niels Bohr, the great quantum physicist, visited Princeton and New York in January 1939 and reported Fritz Strassman's and Otto Hahn's experiment that showed that radium changed to barium when bombarded with neutrons. Otto Frisch and Hahn's former student Lise Meitner, who had fled the Nazis and gone to Sweden, almost simultaneously showed that each fission event released *two or more* neutrons. It was then immediately clear that a self-sustaining chain reaction was possible. Within a month my group of graduate students had devised a blackboard atomic bomb. It was all wrong in detail—but the broad ideas were there.

This is one of a few ideas I call "latent discoveries." They should have been made earlier because the understanding and apparatus to do so were distributed all over the world. The first was X rays. The week that Wilhelm Roentgen's paper on X rays came out, they were produced in Colorado, Dartmouth, Pennsylvania, Chicago, New York, Japan, even Siberia! Fission was the same way. The week we heard of the explanation from Meitner the results were reproduced in Berkeley, Columbia, Japan, and Germany. I went down to the lab the day after the colloquium (in Berkeley) and equipment had already been modified to disclose fission. (The arrival of high-temperature superconductors in 1987 is reminiscent of that.)

I was still working on my thesis under J. Robert Oppenheimer. I wrote a popular article for the *Saturday Evening Post* in 1940, to make a little money, and it covered fission, nuclear weapons, and nuclear reactors. It was rejected.

After the war, of course, we had demonstrated and used the bomb and built working fission reactors, and there was a lot more money for physics and more experience with large science projects. New particle accelerators were built to create subatomic collisions and do scattering experiments at higher and higher energies. Many new short-lived radioactive isotopes were created (we now know of more than 2,000), and these are still being investigated. And of course the new accelerators eventually allowed the observation of many new particles, to the point that the collection became known as the particle zoo. The picture became so complicated that it was unsatisfactory. In the 1970s, it was brilliantly unified, with the recognition of quarks, which are the constituents of many of these particles, including mesons and nucleons.

Free quarks will probably never be observed, but many scattering experiments that bounce electrons off protons or neutrons show that there are three quarks inside each nucleon, and that each quark can occupy various energy states.

There are other properties associated with nucleons, and like electric charge these come in only discrete amounts, as predicted by quantum mechanics. These include spin and isotopic spin. But one of the major properties of nucleons is not predicted: their masses. Are quarks (and the leptons: electrons, neutrinos, and so on) the truly fundamental particles of matter? Even if they are, some still more complete theory will be needed to predict their masses and to show why just these particles exist.

THE NATURAL HISTORY OF ATOMS

Where did the elements originate? We get clues to this question by examining the natural abundances of the elements in various locations. In the second half of the 1800s, as mentioned above, chemists began to analyze rocks from all over the world. They found that the earth is made up mainly of silicon, oxygen, aluminum, magnesium, and iron, with traces of other metals plus carbon, and with a lot of hydrogen bound up in water and in fossil fuels.

At almost the same time, the techniques of optical spectroscopy were developed and were soon used to examine the abundances of elements in the sun and other stars. For a while, the gross differences between the spectrum of the sun and that of hotter blue stars were thought to mean that the hot stars were composed mostly of hydrogen and helium, while the sun was earthlike and rich in metals. Spectral analysis became quantitative in the 1920s, as quantum theory was elaborated to explain atomic structure, the spectral signatures of the elements, and the influence of temperature and pressure on spectral features. Cecelia Payne Gaposchkin, who first made spectral analysis quantitative, was able to show that stars were mostly hydrogen, with a bit of helium. The gross differences among stellar spectra were in fact due to the different surface temperatures and pressures of different stars, not to differing recipes (see Figures 3a-b).

Optical spectroscopy is still astronomy's most powerful analytical tool. Almost all the stars, the gas nebulas both cold and hot, the giant planets in our solar system, and other galaxies, too, are made of 90 percent hydrogen, 8 percent helium, and 2 percent or so trace elements (by number of atoms). Of course, for us the "trace elements" are very important: without locally abundant carbon and oxygen we would not exist, and without silicon and iron the earth would be a completely different place!

The observed differences in abundances—the earth, moon, and inner planets are rocky and metallic, while everything else is mostly hydrogen gas—clearly suggest that planetary formation processes differentiated the earth with regard to the original, cosmological abundances. Thus on the cosmic scale, nuclear processes must have operated to form the elements seen everywhere among the stars.

In 1957 Geoffrey Burbidge, Margaret Burbidge, William Fowler, and Fred Hoyle wrote a famous and still classic summary in which they used early computer models of stellar interiors, along with a huge compilation of fundamental nuclear reaction data (both observed in the lab and predicted by theory), to predict the evolution of stars and the production of the heavier elements. They were able to explain almost all the observed abundances, including those of some of the rarest heavy elements, by the operation of successive stages of fusion inside the stars, building on hydrogen and helium. For some of the

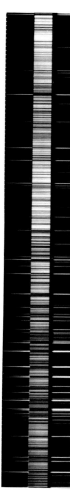

Figure 3a. Spectrum of the sun (center band), showing absorption lines due mostly to iron and other metals. Bright lines are lab comparison spectrum. (Photo credit: Hansen Planetarium and Hale Observatories)

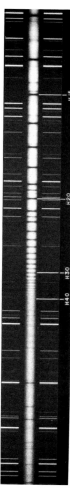

3b. Spectrum of a hot star, showing strong lines of hydrogen, and few metals. (Photo credit: Hansen Planetarium and Hale Observatories)

elements hardest to make or easiest to destroy, the processes depended on the supernova explosions of stars more massive than the sun. A few years earlier George Gamow had tried to predict the abundance by using a cosmic explosion, what we now call the universal "big bang," and not the stars, as the source of energy and density to power all the reactions. Gamow's work, however, could not go beyond the two elements hydrogen and helium; the stars have to do the rest. (Hoyle at one time explained the creation of hydrogen by a mysterious process of continuous creation, which would have required the creation of just one hydrogen atom per cubic centimeter per quadrillion years to maintain a constant density in the face of the observed expansion of the universe.)

It turned out that the really tough elements to explain were the rare light elements lithium, berylium, and boron, which lie between helium and carbon (both very stable) and are easily broken down at low stellar temperatures into helium. They are observed to be very rare cosmically, though they have been chemically concentrated and are found rather easily on the earth's surface. These elements are at very low levels in the stars. (We think that in cosmic rays they are found largely as the breakdown products of collisions between cosmic rays and interstellar gas.) Since these three elements "burn" so easily, we have to answer the question, How is it that they are visible at all in the stars? Why are they not all gone, since they are constantly burned? Where did they originate?

The best answer seems to be that they also were mainly produced early on in the hot, dense universe. In fact, predicting the abundances of helium, lithium, berylium, and boron is one of the best ways of choosing a model of early conditions and the evolution of the expanding universe. So our present idea of the origins of the elements is that the elementary particles were present in space as a whole. These then reacted to form the bulk of hydrogen, helium, and the minor constituents, lithium, beryllium, and boron. The heavier elements came later from the first generation(s) of cookery within the stars. (There are, of course, other good reasons to believe in an early hot universe, the strongest being the observed universal microwave black body radiation, a relic of the white-hot times.) The stellar cookery is still in operation, especially powerful in supernovae.

THE STABILITY OF NUCLEI

Nuclei with an even number of protons are much more numerous than those with an odd number. Therefore, the evens must be more stable; the nuclear forces that hold together the protons favor pairing nucleons off. The helium nucleus (alpha particle), with its pair of protons and pair of neutrons, is one of the most stable of all. Other nuclei, which can be viewed as being made up of linked alphas, such as carbon (three heliums) and oxygen (four heliums), are also very stable. (Various other alpha combinations are even more stable, up to 14 alphas (nickel-56), which decays to the most abundant of heavier nuclei (iron-56), which is slightly more stable.)

Beyond iron, nuclei are less stable again, and we find more and more neutrons per proton. The heaviest elements are unstable over geological times so they are naturally radioactive. (See Figure 4). The reason for this lies primarily in the nature of the strong force and the electromagnetic force. The proton-proton electrostatic repulsion is effective at any distance, while the strong force attracts only over very short distances. It really can attract only the nearest layer or two of nucleons. The neutrons act as proton glue; more neutrons per proton are needed to hold the protons in the nucleus in the face of the increasingly strong electrical repulsion within the larger nuclei. The protons feel the repulsion of all the other protons, and this eventually (in the largest nuclei) overwhelms the attraction of the nearest and second-nearest neutrons and protons, and the nuclei tend to split spontaneously: fission! The probability depends on the detailed nuclear structure—we now say, on the interactions of stability the quarks and gluons which make up mesons and nucleons. (See "Quarks and Beyond," by Alvaro De Rújula.)

The ultimate abundances of the various nuclei on earth are the product of the rules of nuclear stability, the events of the big bang, early universe stellar cookery, the cool formation of the solar system, the early solar wind, the evaporation of the light elements from the inner planets because of solar heat, and the complex processes in earth's rocks, including tectonics and geochemistry. Life on earth is made of the stuff of stars; in fact, we could be said to be made of solar clinker!

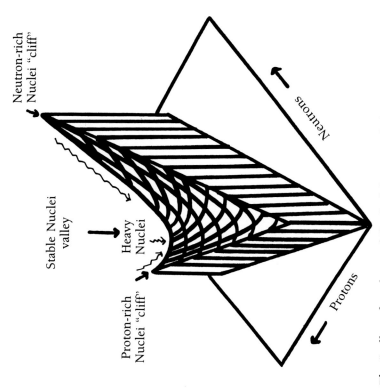

Figure 4. The "valley of nuclear stability" of the natural elements and their isotopes. Unstable nuclei decay (wavy arrows) to stable nuclei which lie at the valley bottom.

NATURAL REACTORS

One of the remarkable facts of the geologic past is that natural fission reactors once could occur. Fifteen years ago the French discovered in a large uranium mine in Gabon that the ratio of costly uranium-235 (U-235) to cheap U-238 (a number they routinely check to be constant to four decimal places), varied in a few runs by several tenths of a percent. Careful study led them to a few spots in the mine where the depletion of U-235 was about 50 percent. Each volume of depleted ore was about as big as a living room. That same rock was found also to be full of uranium fission products, in ratios very distinctly due to fission and nothing else. It is clear that the fission products are the result of a neutron-driven chain reaction. (In fact, this possibility had been predicted by an American chemist, though no one paid attention at the time.)

U-235 is an odd neutron/even proton isotope and thus less stable than U-238, which is even/even. It thus has a much shorter half-life, though still a couple of billion years. Over geologic time, most of the original U-238 remains, but less of the easily fissionable U-235. To make reactors and especially bombs, the natural uranium must at present be enriched with U-235. But two billion years ago in Gabon the uranium was 4 percent U-235, and it hadn't decayed yet; it was reactor-grade. The uranium was in a concentration of nearly-pure uranium oxides mixed with quartz sand in a pool of fresh water. Its natural radioactivity made enough neutrons to set off a chain reaction in the U-235 that heated the water (which acted to slow the neutrons and further promote the chain reaction). Some water boiled off, and the reaction slowed. Then the water cooled and the chain reaction recommenced. This cycle repeated itself until the concentration of U-235 dropped below critical. It all probably simmered like a big tea kettle for 100,000 years, putting out 100 kilowatts or so.

CONFIRMATION OF SUPERNOVA COOKERY

We have received a recent, serendipitous, and amazing confirmation of the principles of supernova cookery of the heavy elements. It came in the form of a pulse of neutrinos and then of cobalt gamma rays from the supernova observed in 1987 in the Large Magellanic Cloud. Neutrinos are a product of the normal fusion reactions of the sun and other stars, but many more are created in a supernova explosion (see Figure 5).

In a wonderful experiment, Raymond Davis and co-workers have been looking for "normal" solar neutrinos using a detector of 100,000 gallons of the cleaning fluid trichlorethylene. It is predicted that we exist in a solar (and universal) rain of neutrinos that are neutral, are nearly or completely massless, and interact with almost nothing. The least energetic type of solar neutrinos occasionally will interact with a chlorine atom in the cleaning fluid and convert it to radioactive argon. The tank is swept by bubbling helium through it, and the collected argon is measured by decay counters. Five or six decays per month were expected, based on standard solar models and known fusion reaction rates. The apparatus is set up at the bottom of a deep gold mine in South Dakota, to reduce the background interference of cosmic rays. Davis was surprised to find only two decays per month. This may seem like a modest difference, but it isn't, and it has led to a questioning of the standard solar model, as well as many wild ideas—for example, that the sun's interior spins rapidly or contains a black hole or is variable in output, or even that the theory of relativity is wrong. The latest suggestion, which I credit more, is that neutrinos oscillate between two different forms both of almost-zero mass as they pass

Figure 5 (opposite). The exploding star, supernova SN 1987A (the bright star above center), appeared near the Tarantula Nebula, in the LMC, about 160,000 light years from our galaxy. Neutrinos from the explosion were detected on earth. (Photo credit: the European Southern Observatory)

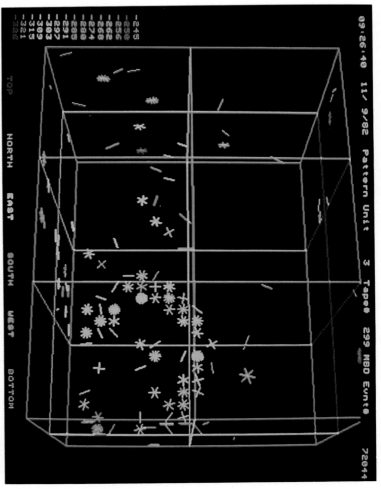

Figure 6. Computer-generated image of a cosmic ray neutrino event, caught in the Irvine-Michigan-Brookhaven detector, which is buried in a mine near Cleveland. (Photo credit: © David Parker/Science Photo Library)

through matter and that one of those forms is not detected by the Davis experiment. So our understanding of solar fusion and its waste neutrinos is a bit up in the air right now (or underground?). (See Figure 5.)

The much more exotic supernova seems to be better understood. New experiments are being set up to look for high-energy solar neutrinos, which should be more numerous and produced from more fundamental reactions than the unusual ones detected by Davis. It was some of this very equipment, still being tested, that saw the neutrino pulse of the 1987 supernova. The fact that the neutrinos were observed in one brief "flash" of some 10 seconds also puts a limit on the neutrino mass, since massy neutrinos would have been given various velocities in the explosion and thus would have had a spread in arrival times, which was not observed.

THE USES OF NUCLEI

Rocks, especially igneous ones, contain uranium and other radioactives and their daughter products. Helium is always found with uranium, which is a hint that something is going on, because helium is otherwise a rare gas, unreactive, forming no others, and not at all chemically like uranium. We know the half-life of uranium, so by measuring the ratio of radioactive uranium (or another radioactive element) to its decay product, the absolute age of the rock can be determined. This technique of radioactive dating has revolutionized geology. It was used to date lunar rocks brought to earth and has been extended, through W. F. Libby's discovery of carbon-14 dating, to organic materials. That work has improved our understanding of the chronology of prehistoric human cultures as far back as 100,000 years. A beautiful, though not universally useful technique, etches natural glass (like obsidian) with uranium traces, to reveal microscopic pits, which can be counted. The glass is then irradiated by a standard source of known activity, and the pits are recounted. The ratio of the two counts, along with the glass composition, gives the age. This single method can work for Victorian glass 100 years old or for a glassy meteoritic inclusion one billion years old!

Radioisotopes find wide use as tracers in chemical and biochemical reactions and as monitors of biological pathways, because their chemical properties are almost identical to those of stable atoms, yet they are visible because of their radioactivity. Chemical properties are mainly affected by electrostatic forces and hardly at all by differences in spin or mass, which alone are affected by the number of neutrons. (The big exception is hydrogen; its isotopes—deuterium and tritium—are dissimilar chemically, for the relative difference in mass is very large.)

Of course radioactive isotopes are also used in cancer therapies to kill tumors by penetrating bombardment. This treatment, though widely used, has serious side effects.

The bulk use of radioactive elements generates radioactive waste. Handling this requires great care, and the question of how, ultimately, it should be disposed of is still controversial. I believe the problem is solvable: the French, Swedes, and Australians glassify the waste, contain it, put it into secure dry holes, and keep watch. This is not cheap, but it is feasible and seems safe.

THE FRONTIERS OF RESEARCH

One of the most interesting areas of current work is the study of reactions produced by the collision of heavy nuclei. There are hints of unexpected reaction products, new particles, and new states of matter.

Neutrino mass and stability are important topics of active research. Our understanding of the sun and stars and of the future of the universe may be affected by the results.

Stellar astronomers and cosmologists continue to improve upon our explanations for the observed abundances and the origins of the elements. A hint of the complexities, which include the birth of the light elements after helium and of some of the heavy elements, was given above. Observations and theories in this field interact strongly and many puzzles remain.

MOST OF THE UNIVERSE MAY NOT BE NUCLEI

I am currently most excited by the possibility that all the nuclear information surveyed above may apply to only 10 percent of the matter in the universe! A number of strong lines of evidence, including the motions of stars near the sun in our galaxy, the orbits of stars in other galaxies, and the motions of clusters and superclusters of galaxies strongly suggest the presence of much matter that doesn't shine at all in any observed wavelength and yet exerts a strong gravitational influence on the mass we can see.

It is quite exciting to think when we look up at the sky, that most of what is out there might not be hydrogen, iron, or any of the ordinary things, but something we have no name for or, at best, a name that hardly anybody has heard!

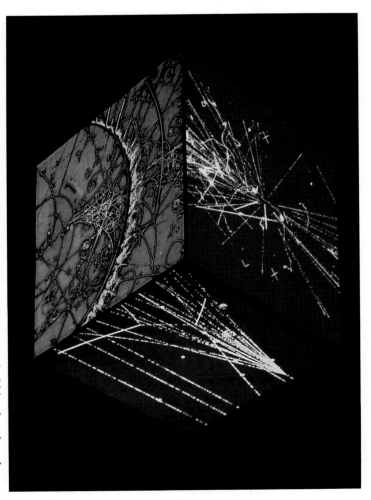

Figure 7. Computer-enhanced images of particle collisions in bubble chamber detectors. (Photo credit: CERN)

HALF-LIFE
PAUL PREUSS
ILLUSTRATION BY
KEVIN JOHNSON

THE OPEN WINDOW IS A BRIGHT RECTANGLE OF SUNSHINE, filled with scintillating disks of green—at this distance my worm-out eyes will no longer resolve the leaves of the poplars, stirring in the summer air.

Beyond the trees, the Alps are a smudge of blue streaked with white; flecks of white, trembling randomly upward through the cobalt sky, detach themselves from the greater white that is the crown of Mont Blanc. Could I focus on these specks I would surely see them for what they are, small live things, cabbage butterflies. But cataracts and crude operations have almost destroyed my sight, and I imagine the fluttering specks not as butterflies but as bits of my soul, leaving me, fragment by fragment.

"Madame . . ."

I feel the doctor's fingers against my cheek and turn to let him remove the thermometer from my dry mouth. He takes it off somewhere into the shadows and studies it in silence. When I stretch numb fingers to him, he surrenders the instrument without protest.

I raise my head and fumble for my thick-lensed glasses, fishing them up by the cord around my neck. With the glass tube of the thermometer at just the right distance, I manage to focus on its scale.

"Thirty-nine degrees." Is that pitiful whisper my own voice? "It's lower." My head falls back against the pillow, my hand drops to the stiff sheets, and I suppose the thermometer rolls away. The doctor retrieves it before it falls to the floor. I am too tired to be ashamed.

"A good sign, Mé." Eve is sitting close to the bed, almost leaning on it, as she has taken to doing these last few days; her need to reassure me is urgent. "The fever has broken. You're going to be better now."

173

"It was not the medicines," I say, for I want no more of these ignorant and painful attempts to cure me. My eyes seek the radiant window. "It was the pure air, the altitude. . . ."

"Yes. It was a good idea for us to get out of Paris, wasn't it?" My daughter reaches to take my hand; I picture what I cannot see clearly, her dark, solemn features, her glossy brown hair pulled back. Her face is an echo of mine when I was her age, her darkness a sort of negative of my paleness, and I think—not only because her darkness is Pierre's—she is more beautiful than I was.

My once-bright hair is now sparse and white and so fine I cannot control it; my face is wrinkled, my mouth still set in the straight line that formed there, without my realizing it, when I left childhood behind—but now deeply bracketed by creases. How stern I must seem! I fix my daughter with that frightening, that demanding stare; a question plagues me. "Was it done with radium or mesothorium?"

"I . . . I don't . . ."

It comes back. "The decay product of the emanation. My mind must be wandering." The more important question recurs. "When are they returning from Stockholm? They promised to see me."

"Who promised, sweet?"

"Irène and Fred. Fred made a very provocative speech." I try to mimic my son-in-law, but my thin voice does no justice to his baritone: "'We are entitled to think that scientists, building up or shattering elements at will, will be able to bring about transmutations of an explosive type.' Where is the evidence to support such a statement?"

Eve has no answer and clearly thinks I am raving. She reaches for my hand, but I irritably withdraw it. "It was printed in all the newspapers," I grumble.

The point, of course, is not that Fred *has* no evidence for these specula-tions, but that he and Irène have not presented the evidence to *me*.

"I'm afraid I have not seen the reports," Eve whispers.

"Well, well, then, Eve . . ." I have never exhibited the slightest favoritism between my daughters, but I suspect that in the midst of her love, Eve—the musician, the writer—resents me for not telling her how to conduct her life so as to please me better. Irène never needed to be told.

Why am I suddenly so weary, so cold? I sense Eve gently lifting the thick glasses from my closed eyes. She does not realize that they weigh nothing.

The door opens and I hear Dr. Lowys's brisk tread leaving the room, fol-lowed a moment later by Eve's light footsteps. Relieved of their presence, I allow my eyes to reopen. The massed leaves outside my window cast their shadows against the white enameled wall, gathering and organizing themselves like dark figures on a cinema screen, tentative and jerky. . . .

Horseshoes clatter on the cobbles. Iron tires screech. A gruff voice mumbles: "This Curie's place? We got a consignment from the station."

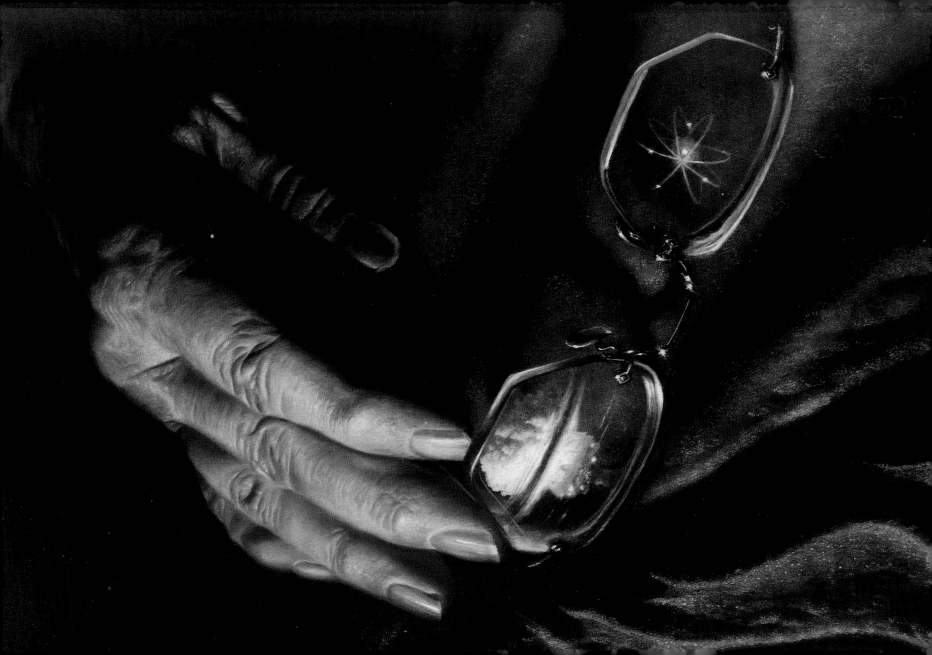

"Pierre," I call out joyously. "It has arrived—come see!" I sweep the flyaway hair from my eyes; the laboratory smock flaps behind my long black skirts as I dash into the paved courtyard, slick with dew in the weak Parisian sunlight. Workmen are already pulling the heavy sacks from the back of the coal wagon, piling them on the cobblestones.

Dear rough-bearded, close-cropped Pierre emerges from the shed that serves us both as laboratory and stands with hands clasped behind him, observing the unloading of the sacks with a proprietary air—or thinking of something else altogether, as he so often is.

Pierre and I have been married for three years. He is older than me, certainly wiser; he and his brother were making discoveries of fundamental importance while I was still self-exiled to Poland's sugar-beet plains, working as a governess and hoarding my rubles to send my sister to medical school. But my constitution is hardier than his, this rugged-looking Frenchman of mine, and it is my choice to do the heavy work.

And my ideas have managed to capture his imagination; he has married his researches as well as his person to mine, and science consumes our lives. Our newborn Irène is necessarily in the care of her nurse and her loving grandfather, Pierre's father, for most hours of the day. The sad set of her mouth is already fixed, earlier than was my own.

The heap of sacks in the courtyard rapidly grows into a miniature mountain of pitchblende, the ore already processed to remove the uranium metal, which is useful in ceramic glazes. But in these sacks of worthless residues, miniscule amounts of other elements remain, or so we are determined to prove: we have named them polonium and radium, and they surpass uranium in their power to charge the air and make shadows on sealed photographic plates—the property to which I have applied the term *radioactivity*. The challenge is to isolate our new elements chemically, in order to establish their actual existence.

Unable to restrain my enthusiasm for this stuff which has cost us so much of our meager earnings in freight charges, I take a knife from one of the workmen and slash into the sackcloth. Soft brown earth spills onto the paving stones. I plunge my hands into the rich dirt and scoop it up in my fingers; the loamy soil is mixed with pine needles from Bohemia, from the mines of St. Joachimsthal.

It is the first day of a labor that will consume my strength for four years. . . .

Eve follows the doctor down the hall of the sanatorium. In her mother's room she has seen what she has seen, and she knows what she has to do; ahead she hears familiar voices: the doctor's polite murmur, and the smooth, assured baritone that could only be that of her brother-in-law.

"We arrived last night," Frédéric is saying. "Would it be convenient to see her now?"

"I'm Dr. Lowys," says the doctor. "And you are the Professors Joliot-Curie . . .?"

As Eve comes into the waiting room Frédéric turns to her, mildly surprised. He is a tall, thin-faced, clean-shaven man; Eve thinks his looks worthy of a cinema star; he is as handsome as Chevalier. The sight of him with Irène stirs vague excitement, edged with coppery resentment. She avoids his glance, looking past him instead to the wall calendar behind him. July 1934. It occurs to her—rather inanely, she reflects—that the weather could not be more glorious.

Clutching her notebook, she pushes herself forward again, moving toward her older sister—Irène is as dark and beautiful as she, with an even more solemn expression—and they embrace, quickly and efficiently.

"Pardon us, please," says Frédéric, turning back to the doctor with some embarrassment; he is not the sort to forget the social amenities. "Under the circumstances . . ."

"Of course. Madame Curie was just speaking of the two of you. You have been in Stockholm?"

"Stockholm?" Frédéric looks at Eve with a quizzical expression. "What's this about Stockholm?"

"Mé is confused," Eve tells him. "She was quoting a speech you supposedly made—something about the destructive power of the elements. As if you were accepting the Nobel Prize."

"She was remembering Pé's Nobel speech," Irène says.

"No," says Eve, "I think she dreamed that her hopes for the two of you had come true."

"Well, certainly we share those hopes," says Frédéric. "What do you say, doctor? Is she . . .?"

"If you would like, you may just step in and look at her—but please don't disturb her rest."

Irène turns implacable eyes upon the doctor; one who did not know her as well as Eve would assume that the grief that shone from them was for her mother's sake, but Irène has worn this expression of loss since early childhood. "She is dying, then."

The doctor nods. "It cannot be long. Her temperature is falling rapidly."

"But she does not know, and she must not be allowed to suspect," Eve says vehemently. "If we were all to gather suddenly at her bedside, she would realize . . ."

"Eve, we will not waken her," Frédéric says firmly.

They enter the sickroom. Eve promptly resumes her chair at her mother's bedside, watching them.

Frédéric stands in the sunny room watching Marie's labored sleep. Tears pool in his eyes. His natural warmth—Eve can feel it—makes him want to go to her, to this woman who has been his beloved teacher, the founder and chief of the institute where he has worked all his professional life. He wants to take her frail body in his arms.

Fred tenses to move, but Irène's hand on his arm restrains him. "Remember our promise." Her expression is inscrutable. They stay a moment longer, watching Marie in silence; then Irène tugs at Frédéric's sleeve and they creep silently out of the room.

Eve, watching them go, releases a tiny sigh and returns her burning attention to the motionless shape of her mother on the bed.

The shadows on my wall shift and coalesce. It is night. I take Pierre's hand as we stand alone in the empty shed. On all sides, on every shelf and tabletop, bottles and test tubes glow with blue luminescence.

Those four years, those tons of residue—when the weather was good, we processed it outside, in the cramped courtyard of our makeshift laboratory. When the weather was bad, we breathed the fumes indoors, under the leaking glass roof. In all seasons, in all weathers, I shoveled and carried and poured, stirring the boiling caldrons with an iron rod as tall as I.

When the crude ore separations were complete, we patiently coaxed the metallic salts to precipitate, working on the rude pine benches, using the glassware and electrical apparatus we had made for ourselves. Eventually we obtained enough of the pure chloride—a few tenths of a gram laboriously separated from each ton of brown dirt—for the chemical proof that radium is indeed the new element we have claimed.

I squeeze his hand.

"Pierre, do you remember saying you hoped that when we found radium, it would have a lovely color?"

"I got more than I hoped for, certainly." His dark eyes sparkle in the glow-worm darkness. "These are like fairy lights."

"Also useful lights! With a little of the salt, I have been able to read in darkness with perfect ease."

Pierre never condescends to me, but he laughs now. "It will not replace gas or electricity, I think—in all this time we have made less than a gram of it."

We know that the concentrated salts of radium glow with more than visible light. The glass vessels in which the chloride is stored turn a lovely purple. The cotton wadding in which these vessels rest eventually crumbles to powder. Radium burns the flesh without heat, as our colleague Becquerel and I discovered accidentally—an effect Pierre established somewhat more methodically, giving himself a festering wound on the arm which did not heal for weeks.

The physicians tell us that this intense radiation penetrates deep into the body, and that dense tumors absorb more of the radiation than ordinary healthy tissue. These discoveries, we are delighted to learn, suggest new treatments for disease.

Our friends urge us to patent our methods for radium extraction. We agree that we could not do such a thing; the benefits of science are not to be diluted by the quest for profit. . . .

Frédéric and Irène stand in the sanatorium's sunny anteroom, where Eve has introduced them—at their insistence—to the distinguished specialist from Geneva. The man stands nervously by, his coat already over his arm and his bag already in hand.

"The first thing I did was to review the blood assays," he is explaining, "and I found that the count of white corpuscles and of red alike were falling rapidly."

"What could that mean?" Frédéric asks.

"I reassured madame that it was not the previously diagnosed gallstones, as she seemed to fear, and that we would perform no unnecessary surgery."

"Very well, then," Irène says impatiently. "And your diagnosis?"

He pauses to hum a little, deep in his throat, before he announces, "Pernicious anemia in its extreme form. I instituted what means of treatment were available, but as you see I was called too late. Much too late. I'm afraid I must now excuse myself. Sir. Madame." The doctor moves jerkily toward the door. "My taxi . . ."

Eve does not fail to note Irène's skeptical eyebrow, raised as she watches the doctor depart.

Nor does Frédéric. He shakes his head at Irène. "A physician of his stature, a patient of hers . . . one can hardly blame him for his discomfort."

Irène stares at the potted palm in the corner of the room, then studies the geometric pattern of the faded Shiraz carpet on the floor. She turns her dark stare upon her younger sister. "So. We are barred from her room."

Eve flushes. "Mé clings to the belief that she has a passing fever. If she sees us all lined up like mourners . . ."

"Eve has reason, I think," Frédéric says, insinuating himself solemnly into the sisters' broken argument.

Irène nods once, sharply. "Well, Fred . . . do you have the proofs of the paper with you?"

"Yes. They are in my case."

"Shall we look at them?" she suggests. "While we are waiting?"

"If we can take a walk outside first. I must have a cigarette if you expect me to get any thinking done."

They leave Eve standing in the anteroom, her cheeks rosy with apprehension. She turns slowly and walks toward the sickroom, where time and her mother dream entwined dreams.

•

•   •

Pierre's voice reaches me, muffled and far away. "Will I see you at the laboratory?"

"Too much to do today." I am upstairs, feeding Eve, planning how I will do all today's necessary errands. "Don't get wet."

Pierre slams the door behind him and hurries out into the blustery weather.

April is wet this year, 1906. . . .

He walks beside the rain-swept Seine, toward the university.

Lunch with the science faculty in the rue Danton—the subject is laboratory safety—then a futile trip to his publisher, closed down by a strike . . . now he is heading toward the river again, toward the laboratory, unexpectedly early, with the prospect of a good afternoon's work ahead of him. The rue Dauphine is crowded with traffic, its sidewalks too narrow for umbrella-carrying pedestrians to pass without jostling, and there is danger of receiving an umbrella's ribend in the eye. Pierre steps off the curb, following a horse-drawn cab. The rain comes down harder; the surface of the street, freshly paved with asphalt, is black and slick. The blind black enclosure of the high cab prevents him from seeing ahead. Why is the driver dawdling?

I am with Pierre, hovering a little above his shoulder, and I can see what he cannot, the iron-tired freight wagon loaded to the top with bundles of clothing, which has just entered the crowded street, crossing the quai from the Pont Neuf, drawn by two young and windy horses.

Lost in thought, daydreaming again, Pierre forgets where he is—I try to scream, to warn him, but no sound emerges from the airy O of my mouth—as impatiently he steps out from behind the slow cab and collides with the oncoming team of horses. His umbrella flies from his grip. He clutches at the harness of the nearest horse to prevent himself from falling, but the steaming beast rears up, startled, and Pierre's feet slip on the wet pavement. As he falls the onlookers shout with horror, giving voice to my voiceless agony. The wagon driver hauls back on the reins with all his strength, but the horses are wild with fear, for the street has erupted in panicked cries.

The horses clatter over Pierre, past him. He lies in the middle of their path, untouched by their iron-shod hooves. The front wheels of the wagon grind into the pavement on either side of him. He lies still, safe. Seconds more . . . There is to be no miracle. The left rear wheel rolls over his head, crushes his skull into sixteen fragments, spatters his brain in the gutter. Already my despairing consciousness has wheeled away into the low-lying clouds—

—back to our home, to await the arrival of his body at my door. . . .

This body now on the bench is muddy like his; its head is a mass of blood-soaked bandages like his, but ten years have passed since I held Pierre's crushed head in my arms, and this is a boy in uniform, still barely alive.

I arrange the X-ray source and check the current from the van's generator. A Irène, eighteen years old—intransigent, darkly beautiful—holds the plates.

surgeon stands by, his long apron painted with blood like a corner butcher's, red on brown from ankle to chest. In a few minutes the images of the shell fragments will appear on the developed photographic negatives, sharp and black; knowing where to cut, the surgeon will cut with somewhat more precision than he is accustomed to.

The young men are dying in the indescribable muck of Verdun and the Somme, dying by the tens of thousands, by the hundreds of thousands, eventually by the millions. Of the French alone, nearly two million men will be counted dead or will have vanished into the liquefied earth by this war's end.

I have established two hundred radiological stations. My radiological corps numbers twenty mobile X-ray vans, including the Renault I drive myself. In Paris I supervise the preparation of ampules of radium emanation and train others in their use as a radiation source. X rays were not my speciality, but in the interests of the wounded I have learned what I need to know.

This form of radiation too will save lives. I will see to it.

"I irradiate the target with alpha rays from the source." It is Fred's voice, speaking to Irène as he leans over the table—

—but he is not here, he could not be here, we have not met him yet. "The Geiger counter is crackling like crazy," he says, and indeed there is a sound like frying sausage—"but when I take the source away from the target . . ."

The frying continues. "The counter ought to stop," says Irène. "The target is still emitting."

I am somewhere halfway between myself and darkness, with no sense of where I am in space, but I have a sudden conviction of where I am in time. It is less than a year ago from now, the fall of 1933. I watch as my daughter and son-in-law bend to their experimental equipment: a polonium source, an aluminum foil target, an ionization chamber. . . .

"I'll do it again," he says. "Mark the time."

Irène looks at her watch and listens endless minutes until the Geiger counter's clicks drop off, becoming indistinguishable from the normal background level. "Perhaps a few seconds over ten minutes."

"It's been just that every time," he says. "It falls off as a succession of half-lives."

"Then so it must be."

"But by what sequence? None of the known isotopes . . ."

"If the aluminum is capturing the alpha particle, then immediately emitting a neutron . . ."

"Then decaying to . . .?"

The answer would be a new isotope of phosphorus, but she does not say it. "What if something's wrong with the counters?" she says instead, abruptly ending the speculation.

He does not argue with her. "Gentner's a specialist, let's have him verify that the instruments are in working order." Fred straightens his shoulders, backing away from the equipment with reluctance. He smiles his dark-eyed smile. "For now, let's be off—to deal with that damned dinner. For the sake of the institute, of course."

"Don't pretend to be so glum, Fred." My daughter grants him as much of a smile as she can manage. "You are as much a socializer as a scientist."

"I prefer to think of myself as a socialist," he says happily, shrugging off his laboratory coat.

They are soon gone, leaving me, and the place is dark, except for the glowing bottles and tubes....

This is not the shed, long since torn down. This is the Radium Institute of the University of Paris, at number 1 rue Pierre Curie; the Curie name is carved in stone over the entrance. There are trees in the courtyard; the rooms have high ceilings and smooth white plastered walls, and the basic equipment of a good chemistry laboratory is to be found here. This is the place I have built in Pierre's name.

Fred and Irène know what they have found, but they will not permit themselves to believe it. Not yet. They have been too often humiliated—that *annus mirabilis* of physics, 1932, held no wonders for them. They had discovered the positron but failed to realize it; an American had claimed the prize. They had discovered the neutron but failed to realize it; an Englishman had claimed the prize. But this time ...

When they return from their dinner party, there is a note on the bench from Gentner: "The Geiger-Müller counters are in good working order."

To see the look on Fred's face is as good as reading his firm English prose in *Nature* for the first time, when he announces their triumph to the British, to the Americans, to the world: "Our latest experiments have shown a very striking fact: when an aluminum foil is irradiated on a polonium preparation, the emission of positrons does not cease immediately when the active preparation is removed. The foil remains radioactive and the emission of radiation decays exponentially as for an ordinary radio-element....

"The transmutation ... has given birth to new radio-elements...."

This time they will not fail to claim the prize....

Satisfied, I allow myself to open my eyes. Eve looks up from her ink-smudged notebook and leans forward, willing herself not to intrude, but listening for any word that I might have for her.

From the lawn the voices of Fred and Irène float through the open window, distant and indistinct, and I catch the pungent odor of Turkish tobacco. Eve suppresses a spasm of ill temper. What if Frédéric and Irène disturb me with their distant conversation, she is thinking. What if I smell his cigarette? What will she do about that? Eve can hardly slam the window shut or shout at them to be quiet. What will she do about her sister and brother-in-law? What will she do about her love and jealousy?

No matter; my eyes are closing again. Eve goes back to her writing. She believes that I am asleep, but I am not. Instead, my consciousness has worked some slack in its mooring; I seem to be able to take up a stance quite apart from my own body. The thought neither thrills me nor disturbs me; it is a thing to be observed.

I am looking down upon my wasted self lying on the high white bed in the sunny white room. Beside the bed, my weary younger daughter, hunched over her notebook, is at work on the biography of Madame Professor Marie Sklodowska Curie. She cannot become an extension of her mother, as Irène did, yet with her skill with words she hopes to fix my life on the page. I see the repetitious phrases she has copied into her notebook, as distant from me but as sharp as images seen through a reversed telescope; they are inscriptions from the letters she and Irène wrote to me as children: "Darling Mé," "My Sweet darling," "Sweet Mé. . . ."

On the floor nearby rests a pair of soft, ankle-high Navaho moccasins—my most comfortable footgear, given to me when I visited the Grand Canyon. Outside the window, Fred is still talking—he is so much better at it than the rest of us—and I can hear him quite distinctly:

". . . I will never forget the expression of intense joy which came over her when Irène and I showed her the first artificially radioactive element in a little glass tube. I can still see her taking in her fingers (which were already burnt with radium) this little tube containing the radioactive compound—as yet one in which the activity was very weak. To verify what we had told her she held it near a Geiger-Müller counter, and she could hear the rate meter giving off a great many clicks. . . ."

I swiftly rejoin myself, reminded of an important matter. "Eve! The paragraphing of the chapters ought to be done all alike."

Eve looks up, startled. "What, Mé?"

I have frightened her, but never mind. "The paragraphs about artificial elements were added so late. I worry that . . ."

"Please don't worry," Eve says, soothing me. "It will be a fine edition."

"Yes, yes." My voice hardly troubles the air. "See to it." I know she will see to it; it is the sort of thing she cares for. So I dart off, clear out the window, to hear what Fred is going on about—

". . . As Madame Curie put it, it was like a return to the glorious days of the old laboratory. This was doubtless the last great satisfaction of her life. . . ."

Fred too! Well, I did say that about the glorious old days, but Fred is too bold! As if there were to be no more great satisfactions in this life. As if I am to be spoken of only in the past tense.

Is it in irritation, then, that I fly on toward the snows of Mont Blanc, as fitfully as one of the little white butterflies that tumble through the summer air, leaving Fred to stroll and smoke his cigarette and pontificate?

I am caught on an updraft and mount swiftly higher. Soon the air grows cold and thin, and still I soar. Down there, the cold is creeping up the shriveled limbs that no longer contain me; even my numb fingers, normally insensitive to temperature, feel the cold.

I have the unsettling sensation that the Earth is rearranging itself, down below.

I can see nothing distinct, but my senses are far from numb. There is a tang in the air, tantalizing, familiar—the scent of sagebrush. I know it from that interminable train ride through the American west, across the furred plains and through the skeletal mountains.

A voice comes to me in the darkness, booming and harsh, stripped of its resonant frequencies by crude electronics. At first I am reminded of the excruciating speeches I sat through on my American tours; are any people more lavish than the Americans in their public displays of affection? Even their president, who was among the worst . . .

But this voice, rolling in echoing waves as if across vast open spaces, has nothing to say. It only counts.

Three. Two. One. . . .

A thing boils out of the fragrant dark, an obscene bubble devouring the endless sage flats with its savage glare, flaring across the distant dry mountains. I hear the strangest sound I could have imagined coming out of the darkness: the cheers and hearty laughter of men, a mob of them, watching this excrescence of light.

I feel a great wind and a flush of heat across my cheeks. My butterfly consciousness goes tumbling on the bosom of the wind.

Afterimages are playing inside my eyelids in negative rainbows; meanwhile the joyous shouts become louder, a triumphant chorus mounting like the final movement of Beethoven's Ninth Symphony—

—becoming strident now, sour now, until the voices are no longer joyous, until they have become infused with a quality of questioning, and then of horrid certainty, of agony and terror.

All around, splotches of black liquid are falling. The slick wet pavement of the rue Dauphine which tilted from under Pierre's desperate feet has turned to a bubbling mass of asphalt. People are fleeing along the melting boulevards, toward the boiling river. I have been in this landscape before, this tumble of rubble lit by the candelabra of burning trees; I have looked out upon the no-man's-land of the western front. But this population—these outstretched arms, these uplifted faces—these people are orientals.

Images flicker in front of me like a grainy silent film. I linger on a shadow-picture etched on a granite porch—the image of a whole body, sitting there when it must have been taken by the very thing that took its picture. Then the hot wind takes me.

Through the rolling clouds I hear the denatured metallic voice again: *Three. Two. One. . . . .*

A horror of light, bursting upward through layers of cloud, streaking outward along thin cloud layers, discoloring the surface of the ocean.

Three. Two. One. . . . .

An ocean heaving itself toward heaven but failing to escape the earth, falling back in a million Niagaras upon the hole in itself that was a coral island.

Tri. Dva. Adin. . . . .

A frozen steppe vaporizing in a concussion as of a ravening comet, falling upon the Earth.

Surely these are terrible natural disasters. . . . .

Three. Two. One.

"I don't want it! I want to be let alone," cries the feeble old woman on the bed.

Dr. Lowys, the narcotic needle poised in his manicured fingers, looks at Eve.

Her fingers are ink smudged from her scribbling. "Do as she wishes," she whispers.

The doctor lowers the needle. "You should know . . . ," he begins softly.

"I know." Eve abandons her book and gathers her mother's hand into both her own.

The doctor moves to the far side of the bed, reaches out, and takes the stiff and calloused fingers of the old woman who lies there, the old woman who refuses to see the inevitable.

Outside, barred from the room by the fierce solicitude of her younger sister, Irène waits with Frédéric, talking physics.

The death watch goes on for sixteen hours. Only when the sun strikes the high peaks of the Alps does Marie's heart stop beating.

"Madame Pierre Curie died at Sancellemoz on July 4, 1934. The disease was an aplastic pernicious anemia of rapid, feverish development. The bone marrow did not react, probably because it had been injured by a long accumulation of radiations."

She was sixty-six. The true name of her disease was leukemia.

Not until the following year, 1935, were Irène and Frédéric Joliot-Curie awarded the Nobel Prize in chemistry, "for synthesizing new radioactive elements."

In 1956, at the age of fifty-nine, Irène died of leukemia.

In 1958, at the age of fifty-eight, Frédéric died following internal hemorrhaging of uncertain etiology.

In 1906, at the age of forty-six, Pierre Curie died in a street accident. In 1988, as these words are written, Eve Curie is alive and active in various good causes.

In the nature of things, as specified by quantum mechanics, one cannot predict the lifetime of an individual atom. For the radioactive elements, however, one can specify a half-life: the time required, on the average, for half a given population of atoms to decay to another element, or elements—its daughters—by the emission of some collection of alpha particles, electrons, gamma rays, neutrons, positrons, neutrinos, antineutrinos, and so on. Half-lives, mere averages, have been measured with great precision.

The half-life of the most stable isotope of uranium, a naturally occurring element, is four and a half billion years.

The half-life of the most stable isotope of thorium, a naturally occurring element, is fourteen billion years.

The half-life of the most stable isotope of polonium, a naturally occurring element, is 138 days.

The half-life of the most stable isotope of radium, a naturally occurring element, is 1,620 years.

The half-life of the most stable isotope of radon, or "emanation," a naturally occurring element, is three days, nineteen hours, and forty-eight minutes.

The half-life of phosphorus 30, the first known artificially radioactive isotope, is three minutes and fifteen seconds.

The half-life of plutonium 239, the first artificially prepared fissile isotope, is 24,360 years.

The half-life of the human species varies by era and culture; consult appropriate actuarial tables.

The half-life of planets is undetermined; the experimental sample is too small.

THE ELECTRON

ESSAY BY
GERALD FEINBERG

SPECULATION BY
ROBERT SILVERBERG

THE ELECTRON
GERALD FEINBERG
COLUMBIA UNIVERSITY

ELECTRONS WERE THE FIRST SUBATOMIC PARTICLES TO BE discovered and are the particles with the greatest influence on what happens both in everyday life and in much of the universe.

Although we do not yet understand why electrons have all of the properties that they do, by assigning precise numerical values to a few of these properties we can account for an immense variety of the phenomena of nature that were once incomprehensible. This scientific progress was once succinctly summarized by the British theoretical physicist Paul Dirac, who, in an article about equations that describe the way electrons behave in atoms, remarked that these equations accounted for "all of chemistry and most of physics."

As we have learned more about the properties of electrons we have been able to invent new technologies that utilize their properties. In addition to the familiar array of consumer electronic products, these practical embodiments of our knowledge of electrons include such scientifically important devices as electron microscopes, which allow for the visualization of objects such as viruses that are too small to be seen with optical microscopes.

HOW ELECTRONS WERE DISCOVERED

The first clear recognition that electrons exist came from observations that were done in the late nineteenth century of electric discharges through gases. In these experiments, a large voltage difference is maintained between the ends of a long tube, similar to the bulb in a neon sign, which contains a gas at very low pressure (Figure 1). In many conditions, a stream of light is observed traveling from the low voltage end, known as the cathode, to the high voltage

Figure 1. A low-pressure gas, excited by collisions with energetic electrons traveling through the tube, emits light as the atoms relax to low-energy states, as in a neon sign. (Photo credit: Science Photo Library)

end. Experiments on these cathode rays, especially by the British physicist Joseph Thomson, showed that it was not a form of light that moved across the tube. Instead the moving objects are a stream of charged particles, which can be deflected by the application of electric or magnetic forces. The light is a byproduct, produced when the moving charges hit atoms in the gas and lose some of their energy. Thomson's experiments showed that the cathode ray particles all carry negative charge, that the ratio of the charge to the particle mass was always the same, and that this ratio was much greater than that for charged atoms.

These results conclusively showed that the cathode ray particles, or electrons, as they came to be known after a suggestion by the Irish physicist George Stoney, were a new type of matter. Furthermore, the fact that the same type of negative particles was observed whatever the gas in the tube or the material of the cathode strongly suggested that electrons are a constituent of all types of matter.

The model that was rapidly accepted was that ordinarily matter contains positive charges in addition to the negative electrons, and that the two are held together by electric attraction. In the conditions of a discharge tube some electrons are stripped from the positive charges and appear as isolated objects, until they can enter into other atoms, where their charge is neutralized.

Since electrons are much lighter than the positive charges in matter, which we now know are concentrated in a heavy central nucleus, the electrons respond more readily to the action of external forces, such as a collision between atoms, or the impact of light on the atom. Because of this, most of the things that atoms do involve changes in the configuration of their electrons, rather than in the nucleus.

THE PROPERTIES OF ELECTRONS

Electrons are in many ways like the structureless point particles studied in physics textbooks. No experiments have ever been done which suggest that electrons have any definite size or are made of yet other objects. This is different from what we know about such other subatomic particles as protons, which do behave as if they have a definite extension in space and are now thought to be made of simpler objects known as quarks. (See "Quarks and Beyond," by Alvaro De Rújula.) Yet while electrons do not have a finite size they all have a few simple properties that determine their behavior and that of objects containing them, such as atoms. Three basic properties derive from these three and so are not considered fundamental. Still other properties, such as the recently measured "weak charge," determine how electrons interact with other subatomic particles.

The mass of electrons, which is a measure of how easily their motion can be changed by the application of forces, is small in comparison with the mass of ordinary objects and even in comparison with that of other subatomic particles. It would take more than 10^{30} electrons to add up to a mass of one kilogram. Actually, one kilogram of ordinary matter has many fewer electrons than that, because ordinary neutral matter also contains protons and neutrons, which are much more massive than electrons. A proton has 1,836 times as much mass as an electron, and a neutron slightly more mass than a proton. The mass of the electron is the smallest of all the subatomic particles known to have mass. (A few types of particles, such as photons, have zero mass. It has also been conjectured that neutrinos have nonzero masses even smaller than that of electrons, but this has not yet been established.)

Electrons get their name from their property of electric charge. It is because they have a negative electric charge that electrons are able to produce electric and magnetic forces, and to respond to such forces produced by other objects. The charge of an electron is approximately 1.6×10^{-19} coulomb, the amount of charge corresponding to the flow of one ampere of current for one second.

The charge on single electrons was first measured accurately by the American physicist Robert Millikan.

Unlike masses, which so far as we know can take on any value, the electric charges of particles found in nature can take on only certain values, which are all integer multiples of a unit charge. For a long time, this unit charge was thought to be that of electrons. However, recently physicists have come to believe that the smallest charge is that carried by some of the quarks, which is one-third that of an electron. The reason for this relation among the charges of otherwise different particles, or "quantization of charge" as it is called by physicists, is not entirely known, although it may be connected to the existence of yet undiscovered magnetic monopoles (isolated "north" or "south" magnetic particles).

The third basic property of electrons, spin, involves a novel type of motion. An electron, like any other particle, can move through space. If an electron moves in a closed orbit, as electrons do in atoms, then one aspect of its motion is described by a property known as orbital angular momentum, which is related to how quickly the electron completes one orbit. In Newtonian physics, the angular momentum of an object could have any value. However, an important postulate made by the Danish physicist Niels Bohr in 1913, known as the "quantization of angular momentum," assumed that the orbital angular momentum of any electron is always an integer multiple of a unit of angular momentum. The unit is h/2π, where h is known as Planck's constant (Max Planck derived this constant from an investigation of the continuous spectra of hot objects). This assumption, later proven by direct observation, allowed Bohr to understand many features of atomic spectra that had previously been puzzling to scientists, including the precise wavelengths of light emitted by hydrogen atoms.

It was soon recognized that Bohr's conclusion about electrons applied to the orbital angular momentum of all objects. But because Planck's constant is a very small number on the scale of everyday objects, this fact does not play any role in everyday life. Only on the atomic or subatomic scale, where angular momenta are in any case expected to be comparable to Bohr's unit, does the quantization of angular momentum restrict what could otherwise happen.

Several years later two Dutch physicists, George Uhlenbeck and Samuel Goudsmit, realized that in order to understand the details of how light was emitted by complex atoms with an odd number of electrons, such as sodium, it was necessary to assume that electrons had another type of angular momentum in addition to orbital angular momentum. They called this new quantity spin angular momentum, in analogy with the motion of a top about its axis. The main difference between electron spin and orbital angular momentum is that spin always has a magnitude of h/4π, or half the unit of orbital angular momentum. It was later found that other particles, including protons and neutrons, also carried the same amount of spin angular momentum as electrons.

A peculiarity of both types of angular momentum is that if a magnetic force is exerted on the electron, the angular momentum can align itself only at one of a small number of angles with respect to the direction of the magnetic force, whereas according to Newtonian physics, any angle would be possible. (Think of a spinning top, which, apparently, can tip at any angle.) In the case of electron spin the alignment can be either parallel or opposite to the magnetic direction. This is a consequence of quantum mechanics (Figures 2a and b).

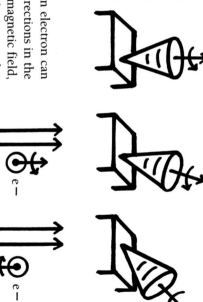

Figure 2a. The rotational axis of a spinning top appears to take any orientation in space in the Earth's gravitational field, and can spin at any speed.

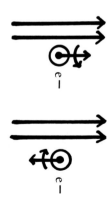

2b. The rotational axis of an electron can only orient in two discreet directions in the electric field of an atom or a magnetic field, and can have speeds of only discreet multiples of Planck's constant, because of quantum effects.

HOW ELECTRONS BEHAVE

When electrons were discovered, it was imagined that they would follow the physical laws then known, those of Newtonian mechanics. But these laws were soon found to be wholly inadequate to describe the actual behavior of electrons. The first indication of this came around 1905, when it was discovered that for electrons moving at near the speed of light, such as those produced in the radioactive decay process known as beta decay, the mass seemed to increase as the speed increased, whereas according to Newtonian mechanics it should remain constant. Providentially, Einstein's special theory of relativity, which had just been invented, implies that just such an increase should occur. One consequence of this is that electrons cannot be made to travel at the speed of light or at higher speeds, a prediction borne out by many observations since that time.

A much more profound change in our understanding of the laws that govern the behavior of electrons grew out of Bohr's theory, and was ultimately expressed in a new description of nature known as quantum mechanics, which applies not only to electrons, but everywhere on the atomic and subatomic scale. Two consequences of quantum mechanics, the quantization of the magnitude of angular momentum and the fact that angular momentum in a magnetic field can only point in certain directions, have already been mentioned. Another consequence is that in atoms, the energy of electrons and the average distance of the electron from the nucleus can only take on certain values. For example, there is a minimum energy level for electrons in each type of atom that is ultimately responsible for the stability of atoms and for the fact that under ordinary conditions, all atoms with the same number of electrons have similar properties, which some nineteenth-century physicists attributed to divine providence.

Bohr's theory and quantum mechanics also changed our notion of how electrons carry out one of their main activities, the emission of light. According to Maxwell's electromagnetic equations and Newtonian mechanics, an electron is expected to emit light whenever a force acts on it, so that it is accelerated. This remains true in quantum mechanics for unbound electrons. However, an electron in an atom, on which the electric force of the nucleus acts, does not emit radiation so long as it remains in its lowest energy level. Only when the energy level changes is light emitted.

The discrete energies of electrons in atoms show up when the atom emits light, because the frequency of the light emitted is always equal to the difference of the energies that the electrons have before and after the light comes out, divided by Planck's constant. If these energies could differ by an arbitrary amount, as they could according to Newtonian physics, then each type of atom could emit light of any frequency, instead of the discrete spectral lines that are observed. (See Figure 2, in "The Nuclear World.")

This quantization of energies also applies to electrons under the influence of a magnetic force. Here it is the two spin directions that have different energy. This difference can be measured by observing the frequency of radiation, in this case microwaves, needed to make the electron jump from one spin direction to the other. This technique, known as ESR (electron spin resonance), invented by the physicists Felix Bloch and Edward Purcell, is closely related to that applied in the magnetic resonance imaging devices that are now used in medicine.

Another consequence of quantum mechanics is that electrons sometimes exhibit wave properties similar to those of light. An electron moving through space with a definite speed will behave like a wave with a definite wavelength, inversely proportional to the speed. For an electron that has moved through a voltage difference of two hundred volts, the wavelength is about one tenth of a nanometer, about the size of an atom. Such electron waves can be reflected and refracted and can form images as do light waves, but the much smaller wavelengths of electrons compared to visible light means that images can be made of correspondingly smaller objects (Figure 3). This wave behavior of electrons is taken advantage of in the construction of electron microscopes.

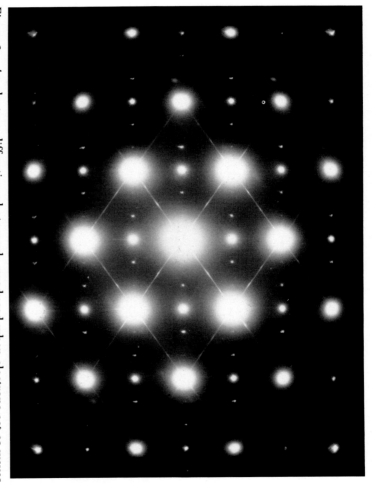

Figure 3. An electron diffraction photograph, produced when electrons act as waves as they travel through a crystal with an interatomic spacing of a few atomic diameters. Compare to Figure 3, Chapter 3, made by X rays. (Photo credit: Kenneth S. Vecchio, University of California, San Diego)

Another purely quantum mechanical aspect of electron behavior is indirectly connected with their spin. In 1925, the German physicist Wolfgang Pauli realized that the observed details of atomic structure suggested that no two electrons in an atom could simultaneously have the same energy, the same orbital angular momentum, and the same spin direction. This result, which has come to be known as the exclusion principle, is actually even more general. No two electrons in the universe can be the same with respect both to their motion through space and their spin direction. In spite of the apparent correlation that it enforces between the behavior of widely separated particles, the exclusion principle places no additional restriction on electrons that are located more than a few atomic diameters apart in space, since their condition is very different anyway just because they are far apart. But it plays a fundamental role in determining the behavior of electrons in the same atom. For example, the exclusion principle implies that in a lithium atom, the third electron must have a higher energy than the other two. This leads to the result that lithium easily loses electrons to other atoms, making it highly active chemically. The exclusion principle is also responsible for the fact that solids are relatively impenetrable, because electrons in one atom cannot enter into the regions of space already occupied by electrons in other atoms.

The exclusion principle plays an important role in the collapsed astronomical objects called white dwarfs, the evolutionary endpoints of stars of one solar mass. Most of the electrons in a white dwarf are not in atoms, but instead move freely as do the molecules of a gas. Since no two electrons can have the same spin and motion, some of the electrons must be moving at much higher speeds than they would if the exclusion principle did not apply. This results in an outward pressure that resists the tendency of gravity to make the star collapse still further.

In order for the exclusion principle to apply to electrons, it is necessary that the basic properties of mass and charge for any two electrons should be identical. Otherwise, for example, two electrons that began with different spins could over a period of time evolve so that they had the same spin.

The exclusion principle turns out to apply to groups of any particles, such as protons and neutrons, whose spin is the same as that of electrons ($h/4\pi$). Particles whose spin is zero, or twice that of the electron, do not satisfy the exclusion principle. Instead, two of such particles are more likely to be found with the same values of motion and spin than with different values. This difference in the behavior of particles whose spin is an integer multiple of $h/2\pi$ from those whose spin is a half integer multiple is one of the important consequences of the standard description of subatomic particles known as quantum field theory.

In the early 1930s it was discovered that electrons and their antiparticles, positrons, could be created together when sufficient energy was available in the form of radiation, and such pairs could annihilate into radiation (Figure 4). Positrons have the same mass and spin as electrons, and equal but opposite electric charge. In one such creation process, when two photons moving in opposite directions collide, each with energy slightly more than the energy of an electron at rest, there is a substantial probability that the photons will disappear and an electron and positron appear in their place. In the reverse annihilation process, an electron and positron come together and disappear, with two photons being formed. Both processes are explained by a theoretical description of electrons, invented by Paul Dirac, which combines the principles of special relativity and quantum mechanics.

WHERE ELECTRONS ARE FOUND

The British astrophysicist Arthur Eddington once wrote that he knew exactly how many electrons there were in the universe. The number he gave, 2^{256} (10^{77}), is about equal to the number that we now believe exist. However, there is no theoretical justification for Eddington's exact value. In fact, the number of electrons in the universe is constantly changing. For example, something like a trillion electrons and positrons are created each second in the earth by the impact of high-energy cosmic rays.

molecules. Also familiar to us are the collections of many atoms and molecules that are bound together into solid bodies by the same electrical forces that hold together individual atoms. These different types of objects provide distinct environments that bring out different aspects of the behavior of the electrons that they contain.

The behavior of electrons within a specific type of atom is the result of the interplay of several factors: electric forces among the electrons and between the electrons and the nucleus, the inertial motion of the electrons, and the exclusion principle, which forbids the electrons from crowding together near the nucleus. The result of this interplay is a standard configuration, the so-called ground state, for an atom containing a specified number of electrons. In this ground state the electrons are usually at a distance of about 10^{-10} meters from the nucleus, although quantum mechanics does not permit that distance to be precisely determined. The familiar properties of individual types of atom, such as the fact that helium is an unreactive gas, are really properties of the ground states of the atoms.

Normally, atomic electrons will remain placidly in their ground state, hardly affected by outside influences. However, there are some exceptions to this situation. If light of sufficiently short wavelength impinges on an atom, it may excite one of the electrons to a higher energy level within the atom, or remove it from the atom completely, leaving behind a positive ion. This process is known as photoionization. The electron that is set free will wander through its material environment until it finds an atom with which it can combine. The electron then loses its extra energy, for example by emitting a photon, and again becomes a contented member of an atomic family.

Another circumstance in which atomic electrons may be radically disturbed occurs when an atom of a suitable type approaches near to the atom in which the electrons reside. For example, if an isolated sodium atom is approached by a chlorine atom, one of the sodium electrons is likely to desert its atom, jumping to the chlorine atom. Because of the electrical attraction between the positive and negative ions formed in this way the rest of the sodium atom follows in the wake of the electron, leading to a tightly bound combination of the two atoms, the sodium chloride molecule (salt). In sodium chloride, each of the electrons is closely associated with one or the other of the nuclei. In other molecules, especially the organic molecules containing carbon, many of the electrons are shared between the nuclei, and undergo motions that take them sometimes near one nucleus, sometimes near the other. It is such mobility of electrons, a consequence of their small mass, that allows the immense variety of chemical reactions that we observe to take place.

When many atoms are near each other, still another type of environment for electrons can be formed. A large number of sodium atoms can arrange themselves into a regular latticelike structure, known as a crystal. Such crystals can be thought of as giant molecules, whose subunits, the individual atoms, arrange themselves into a regular geometric pattern, which in the case of sodium is a cube. These simple patterns repeat over and over in the solid. In metallic crystals, the nuclei, with some electrons attached to them, remain in place at specific locations in the lattice. The rest of the electrons move freely through the lattice, as if they formed a gas in a container. It is these electrons that are responsible for such characteristic properties of metals as the conduction of heat and electricity. Just as for the electrons in a single atom, the detailed behavior of the free electrons in a metallic crystal is strongly influenced by the exclusion principle. For example, the gas of electrons in a metal does not conduct electricity nearly as well as it would if the exclusion principle did not apply to electrons.

THE USES OF ELECTRONS

The characteristic technology of our time is electronics, the application of specific properties of electrons to perform definite tasks. Television and the computer are but two examples of electronic devices that are central to late-twentieth-century life. While the detailed operation of such devices involves many distinct principles and effects, a few of them are basic. One of these is the mutual interaction of light and electrons, which allows information to be transferred back and forth between them. Another is the responsiveness of electrons to applied electric and magnetic forces, which allows them to be easily guided into specified paths. To see how the principles of quantum mechanics apply in the construction of a useful device, let us examine the physical principles behind a computer. The aim of this discussion is not to give a detailed description of the device, but to show how the properties of electrons make its operation possible.

The computer is based on technology that applies the behavior of electrons in a type of solid known as a semiconductor. Semiconductors are materials, such as silicon, whose electronic properties are intermediate between those of metallic conductors, which have many free electrons to conduct electricity, and insulators such as rubber, which have essentially no free electrons. The physical property that is characteristic of both insulators and semiconductors is the existence of a gap between two ranges of energy, or energy bands, that are quantum mechanically allowed for the unattached electrons. Because of this gap, in a pure semiconductor at absolute zero temperature, there are no electrons in the upper band. The electrons in the lower band cannot conduct electricity, because that band is completely filled, and the exclusion principle forbids those electrons from moving in the way required to conduct. Therefore a pure semiconductor at absolute zero acts like an insulator. Several different effects allow semiconductors to conduct electricity anyway. In what are called intrinsic semiconductors, the gap is very small. As a result, when the temperature is above absolute zero, a few of the electrons have their energy raised by random collisions enough so that they are in the upper band, and can conduct electricity. Other types of semiconductors are made by "doping," that is, by introducing impurity atoms at precisely defined places in the crystal. In the n-type semiconductor, these impurities liberate new electrons. Since the lower energy band is already filled with electrons, the exclusion principle requires that the extra electrons have energies in the upper conduction band. These impurity generated electrons can increase the conductivity by a huge factor. It is also possible for certain impurities to decrease the number of electrons in their neighborhood. These missing electrons are taken from the previously filled lower band, leaving vacancies there. This produces concentrations with an effective positive charge, known as "holes." The holes can also conduct electricity, although in the opposite direction from what an electron would do. Semiconductors that are doped to give positive hole conduction are called p-type.

The different types of semiconductor can be combined to produce a wide variety of devices to regulate and amplify the flow of electricity. The most important and versatile of these devices is the transistor, invented at Bell Laboratories in 1947. There are many types of transistors with various functions, but most of them operate by combining layers of n-type and p-type semiconductors. For example, a transistor amplifier can be made from a sandwich of three layers of semiconductor in the form n-p-n, or p-n-p. (See Figure 5.) Current can flow easily in one direction, but not in the other. By varying a small voltage applied to the central layer, large currents can be made to flow between the outer layers. Transistors can be made much smaller than previously used electronic devices, such as vacuum tubes, and they do not require any heating of their working elements. These properties are obviously crucial for computers, where speed of operation is of the greatest importance. Today, hundreds of thousands of transistors can be produced on a dime-sized chip (Figure 6). This technology is the key to cheap personal computers. The shrinkage in scale will continue as it becomes possible to produce ever smaller layers and etch smaller lines.

Superconductivity, another physical phenomenon that is based on the quantum properties of electrons, holds great promise for future technological applications. It was observed in 1911 that some metals lose all of their electrical resistance when they are cooled to low temperatures. The temperature at which this happens for a specific substance is called the critical temperature (T_c). Until 1987, the highest known value of T_c was less than 30 degrees above absolute zero, which limited the prospective technological applications of superconductivity. (It is very expensive to keep materials that cold.) However, in 1987, it was found that new compounds that are more ceramic than metallic are superconductors at temperatures up to 120 degrees above absolute zero. It is possible that some yet undiscovered materials are superconductors at room

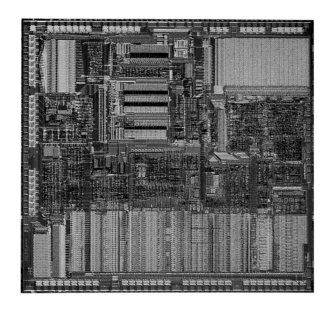

Figure 5 (left). Computer image of a single-transistor semiconductor sandwich on a chip substrate. (Photo credit: IBM) *Figure 6 (right)*. Enlarged image of a microprocessor chip with more than 100,000 transistors and other components. (Photo credit: Intel Corporation)

temperatures. These discoveries of high-temperature superconductors have raised new hopes for technological applications, such as very powerful magnets, magnetically levitated vehicles, and effective storage and transmission of electrical energy. However, they have also raised new questions for our understanding of superconductivity.

The previously known superconductors with low T_c were successfully understood, beginning in the late 1950s, through a description known as the BCS theory, after the initials of its originators, John Bardeen, Leon Cooper, and John Schrieffer. In BCS superconductors, an important role is played by bound pairs of electrons. The force that holds these electrons together can be thought of as arising from the exchange between them of particles called phonons, in analogy to the exchange of photons that can bind opposite electric charges into atoms. However, the phonons are not really particles in their own right, but rather are quantized excitations of the crystal lattice. The paired electrons in a superconductor always have opposite spin and equal but opposite velocity. When the temperature is below T_c some of the electrons in the superconductor form such pairs. It is these paired electrons that carry the persistent currents that characterize superconductors. Many properties of superconductors follow from the fact that there is a gap between the lowest energy level of the superconductor and excited levels in which some of the pairs are broken apart. For example, such excited levels must be occupied in order for a current of pairs to dissipate. Since this excitation takes more energy than is available in the superconductor at low temperature, once a current is set up, it persists indefinitely.

It is not yet clear whether phonon binding of electron pairs also applies to the high-T_c superconductors. In addition to their much higher value of T_c, these involve a different class of materials, usually containing a rare earth element, together with copper and oxygen. Furthermore, some of the characteristic properties of BCS superconductors, such as a dependence of T_c on the mass of the nucleus, may not be present in these materials. However, there is evidence that electron pairs are involved in high-T_c superconductivity as well. Many mutually conflicting theories have been put forward to explain high-T_c superconductivity, but none has yet demonstrated any clear-cut superiority. It is too early to tell what novelties these materials will reveal about how electrons can behave in a complex environment.

WHAT WE DON'T KNOW ABOUT ELECTRONS

Our present theoretical description of electrons has proven capable of accounting for almost everything that we observe about them. This is especially true of the theory known as quantum electrodynamics, or more familiarly as QED. That theory is essentially a union of quantum mechanics and special relativity theory applied to the combination of electrons and light. Using QED, physicists have calculated such quantities as the magnetic forces produced by isolated electrons and the wavelengths of light emitted by hydrogen atoms, and these calculations have agreed with what is observed to precisions of one part in a billion.

Nevertheless, there remain questions about electrons that are not answered by existing physical theories. Some of these questions refer to electrons themselves. For example, we would like to know whether electrons are really structureless or whether, like protons, they are composed of yet simpler objects. We do know that if electrons have a structure, this manifests itself only over sizes of 10^{-18} meter or less, much smaller than the size of a proton.

Other questions concern the relation between electrons and the many other known types of subatomic particles. Why, for example, is the electron's mass so much smaller than that of the other particles? And why, in contrast, do all particles, whatever their mass and other properties, have electric charges that are simply related to one another? Such questions are not answered by the theories that are now accepted by physicists. Of course, other theories have been put forth that do attempt to answer them, such as the so-called grand unified theories that attempt to relate the properties of electrons and quarks. But no such theory has yet been found that both answers existing questions and predicts new phenomena that have been observed in the laboratory. So the search for a theory that will take us beyond what we presently know about electrons goes on. That search will build on the wealth of information that we have discovered about those most significant of subatomic particles in the century since they were first recognized.

CHIP RUNNER
ROBERT SILVERBERG
ILLUSTRATION BY
RALPH McQUARRIE

HE WAS FIFTEEN AND LOOKED ABOUT NINETY, AND A FRAIL ninety at that. I knew his mother and his father, separately—they were Silicon Valley people, divorced, very important in their respective companies—and separately they had asked me to try to work with him. His skin was blue-gray and tight, drawn cruelly close over the jutting bones of his face. His eyes were gray too, and huge, and they lay deep within their sockets. His arms were like sticks. His thin lips were set in an angry grimace.

The chart before me on my desk told me that he was five feet eight inches tall and weighed 71 pounds. He was in his third year at one of the best private schools in the Palo Alto district. His IQ was 161. He crackled with intelligence and intensity. That was a novelty for me right at the outset. Most of my patients are depressed, withdrawn, uncertain of themselves, elusive, shy: virtual zombies. He wasn't anything like that. There would be other surprises ahead.

"So you're planning to go into the hardware end of the computer industry, your parents tell me," I began. The usual let's-build-a-relationship procedure.

He blew it away instantly with a single sour glare. "Is that your standard opening? 'Tell me all about your favorite hobby, my boy'? If you don't mind I'd rather skip all the bullshit, doctor, and then we can both get out of here faster. You're supposed to ask me about my eating habits."

It amazed me to see him taking control of the session this way within the first thirty seconds. I marveled at how different he was from most of the others, the poor sad wispy creatures who force me to fish for every word.

"Actually I do enjoy talking about the latest developments in the world of computers, too," I said, still working hard at being genial.

"But my guess is you don't talk about them very often, or you wouldn't call it 'the hardware end.' Or 'the computer industry.' We don't use mundo phrases like those anymore." His high thin voice sizzled with barely suppressed rage. "Come on, doctor. Let's get right down to it. You think I'm anorexic, don't you?"

"Well—"

"I know about anorexia. It's a mental disease of girls, a vanity thing. They starve themselves because they want to look beautiful and they can't bring themselves to realize that they're not too fat. Vanity isn't the issue for me. And I'm not a girl, doctor. Even you ought to be able to see that right away."

"Timothy—"

"I want to let you know right out front that I don't have an eating disorder and I don't belong in a shrink's office. I know exactly what I'm doing all the time. The only reason I came today is to get my mother off my back, because she's taken it into her head that I'm trying to starve myself to death. She said I had to come here and see you. So I'm here. All right?"

"All right," I said, and stood up. I am a tall man, deep chested, very broad through the shoulders. I can loom when necessary. A flicker of fear crossed Timothy's face, which was the effect I wanted to produce. When it's appropriate for the therapist to assert authority, simpleminded methods are often the most effective. "Let's talk about eating, Timothy. What did you have for lunch today?"

He shrugged. "A piece of bread. Some lettuce."

"That's all?"

"A glass of water."

"And for breakfast?"

"I don't eat breakfast."

"But you'll have a substantial dinner, won't you?"

"Maybe some fish. Maybe not. I think food is pretty gross."

I nodded. "Could you operate your computer with the power turned off, Timothy?"

"Isn't that a pretty condescending sort of question, doctor?"

"I suppose it is. Okay, I'll be more direct. Do you think you can run your body without giving it any fuel?"

"My body runs just fine," he said, with a defiant edge.

"Does it? What sports do you play?"

"Sports?" It might have been a Martian word.

"You know, the normal weight for someone of your age and height ought to be—"

"There's nothing normal about me, doctor. Why should my weight be any more normal than the rest of me?"

"It was until last year, apparently. Then you stopped eating. Your family is worried about you, you know."

"I'll be okay," he said sullenly.

"You want to stay healthy, don't you?"

He stared at me for a long chilly moment. There was something close to hatred in his eyes, or so I imagined.

"What I want is to disappear," he said.

That night I dreamed I was disappearing. I stood naked and alone on a slab of gray metal in the middle of a vast empty plain under a sinister coppery sky and I began steadily to shrink. There is often some carryover from the office to a therapist's own unconscious life: we call it countertransference. I grew smaller and smaller. Pores appeared on the surface of the metal slab and widened into jagged craters, and then into great crevices and gullies. A cloud of luminous dust shimmered about my head. Grains of sand, specks, mere motes, now took on the aspect of immense boulders. Down I drifted, gliding into the darkness of a fathomless chasm. Creatures I had not noticed before hovered about me, astonishing monsters, hairy, many legged. They made menacing gestures, but I slipped away, downward, downward, and they were gone. The air was alive now with vibrating particles, inanimate, furious, that danced in frantic zigzag patterns, veering wildly past me, now and again crashing into me, knocking my breath from me, sending me ricocheting for what seemed like miles. I was floating, spinning, tumbling with no control. Pulsating waves of blinding light pounded me. I was falling into the infinitely small, and there was no halting my descent. I would shrink and shrink and shrink until I slipped through the realm of matter entirely and was lost. A mob of contemptuous glowing things—electrons and protons, maybe, but how could I tell? —crowded close around me, emitting fizzy sparks that seemed to me like jeers and laughter. They told me to keep moving along, to get myself out of their kingdom, or I would meet a terrible death. "To see a world in a grain of sand," Blake wrote. Yes. And Eliot wrote, "I will show you fear in a handful of dust." I went on downward, and downward still. And then I awoke gasping, drenched in sweat, terrified, alone.

Normally the patient is uncommunicative. You interview parents, siblings, teachers, friends, anyone who might provide a clue or an opening wedge. Anorexia is a life-threatening matter. The patients—girls, almost always, or young women in their twenties—have lost all sense of normal body-image and feel none of the food-deprivation prompts that a normal body gives its owner. Food is the enemy. Food must be resisted. They eat only when forced to, and then as little as possible. They are unaware that they are frighteningly gaunt. Strip them and put them in front of a mirror and they will pinch their sagging empty skin to show you imaginary fatty bulges. Sometimes the process of self-skeletonization is impossible to halt, even by therapy. When it reaches a certain point the degree of organic damage becomes irreversible and the death spiral begins.

"He was always tremendously bright," Timothy's mother said. She was fifty, a striking woman, trim, elegant, almost radiant, vice president for finance at one of the biggest Valley companies. I knew her in that familiarly involuted California way: her current husband used to be married to my first wife. "A genius, his teachers all said. But strange, you know? Moody. Dreamy. I used to think he was on drugs, though of course none of the kids do that anymore." Timothy was her only child by her first marriage. "It scares me to death to watch him wasting away like that. When I see him I want to take him and shake him and force ice cream down his throat, pasta, milkshakes, anything. And then I want to hold him, and I want to cry."

"You'd think he'd be starting to shave by now," his father said. Technical man, working on nanoengineering projects at the Stanford AI lab. We often played racquetball together. "I was. You too, probably. I got a look at him in the shower, three or four months ago. Hasn't even reached puberty yet. Fifteen and not a hair on him. It's the starvation, isn't it? It's retarding his physical development, right?"

"I keep trying to get him to like eat something, anything," his stepbrother Mick said. "He lives with us, you know, on the weekends, and most of the time he's downstairs playing with his computers, but sometimes I can get him to go out with us, and we buy like a chili dog for him, or, you know, a burrito, and he goes, 'Thank you, thank you,' and pretends to eat it, but then he throws it away when he thinks we're not looking. He is so weird, you know? And scary. You look at him with those ribs and all and he's like something out of a horror movie."

"What I want is to disappear," Timothy said.

He came every Tuesday and Thursday for one-hour sessions. There was at the beginning an undertone of hostility and suspicion to everything he said. I asked him, in my layman way, a few things about the latest developments in computers, and he answered me in monosyllables at first, not at all bothering to hide his disdain for my ignorance and my innocence. But now and again some question of mine would catch his interest and he would forget to be irritated, and reply at length, going on and on into realms I could not even pretend to understand. Trying to find things of that sort to ask him seemed my best avenue of approach. But of course I knew I was unlikely to achieve anything of therapeutic value if we simply talked about computers for the whole hour.

He was very guarded, as was only to be expected, when I would bring the conversation around to the topic of eating. He made it clear that his eating habits were his own business and he would rather not discuss them with me,

or anyone. Yet there was an aggressive glow on his face whenever we spoke of the way he ate that called Kafka's hunger artist to my mind: he seemed proud of his achievements in starvation, even eager to be admired for his skill at shunning food.

Too much directness in the early stages of therapy is generally counterproductive where anorexia is the problem. The patient loves her syndrome and resists any therapeutic approach that might deprive her of it. Timothy and I talked mainly of his studies, his classmates, his stepbrothers. Progress was slow, circuitous, agonizing. What was most agonizing was my realization that I didn't have much time. According to the report from his school physician he was already running at dangerously low levels, bones weakening, muscles degenerating, electrolyte balance cockeyed, hormonal systems in disarray. The necessary treatment before long would be hospitalization, not psychotherapy, and it might almost be too late even for that.

He was aware that he was wasting away and in danger. He didn't seem to care.

I let him see that I wasn't going to force anything on him. So far as I was concerned, I told him, he was basically free to starve himself to death if that was what he was really after. But as a psychologist whose role it is to help people, I said, I had some scientific interest in finding out what made him tick—not particularly for his sake, but for the sake of other patients who might be more interested in being helped. He could relate to that. His facial expressions changed. He became less hostile. It was the fifth session now, and I sensed that his armor might be ready to crack. He was starting to think of me not as a member of the enemy but as a neutral observer, a dispassionate investigator. The next step was to make him see me as an ally. You and me, Timothy, standing together against them. I told him a few things about myself, my childhood, my troubled adolescence: little nuggets of confidence, offered by way of trade.

"When you disappear," I said finally, "where is it that you want to go?"

The moment was ripe and the breakthrough went beyond my highest expectations.

"You know what a microchip is?" he asked.

"Sure."

"I go down into them."

Not I *want* to go down into them. But I *do* go down into them.

"Tell me about that," I said.

"The only way you can understand the nature of reality," he said, "is to take a close look at it. To really and truly take a look, you know? Here we have these fantastic chips, a whole processing unit smaller than your little toenail with fifty times the data-handling capacity of the old mainframes. What goes on inside them? I mean, what *really* goes on? I go into them and I look. It's like a trance, you know? You sharpen your concentration and you sharpen it and sharpen it and then you're moving downward, inward, deeper and deeper." He laughed harshly. "You think this is all mystical ca-ca, don't you? Half of you thinks I'm just a crazy kid mouthing off, and the other half thinks here's a kid who's smart as hell, feeding you a line of malarkey to keep you away from the real topic. Right, doctor? Right?"

"I had a dream a couple of weeks ago about shrinking down into the infinitely small," I said. "A nightmare, really. But a fascinating one. Fascinating and frightening both. I went all the way down to the molecular level, past grains of sand, past bacteria, down to electrons and protons, or what I suppose were electrons and protons."

"What was the light like, where you were?"

"Blinding. It came in pulsing waves."

"What color?"

"Every color all at once," I said.

He stared at me. "No shit!"

"Is that the way it looks for you?"

"Yes. No." He shifted uneasily. "How can I tell if you saw what I saw? But it's a stream of colors, yes. Pulsing. And—all the colors at once, yes, that's how you could describe it—"

"Tell me more."

"More what?"

"When you go downward—tell me what it's like, Timothy."

He gave me his lofty look, his pedagogic look. "You know how small a chip is? A MOSFET, say?"

"MOSFET?"

"Metal-oxide-silicon field-effect-transistor," he said. "The newest ones have a minimum feature size of about a micrometer. Ten to the minus sixth meters. That's a millionth of a meter, all right? Small. It isn't down there on the molecular level, no. You could fit 200 amoebas into a MOSFET channel one micrometer long. Okay? Okay? Or a whole army of viruses. But it's still plenty small. That's where I go. And run, down the corridors of the chips, with electrons whizzing by me all the time. Of course I can't see them. Even a lot smaller, you can't see electrons, you can only compute the probabilities of their paths. But you can feel them. I can feel them. And I run among them, everywhere, through the corridors, through the channels, past the gates, past the open spaces in the lattice. Getting to know the territory. Feeling at home in it."

"What's an electron like, when you feel it?"

"You dreamed it, you said. You tell me."

"Sparks," I said. "Something fizzy, going by in a blur."

"You read about that somewhere, in one of your journals?"

"It's what I saw," I said. "What I felt, when I had that dream."

"But that's it! That's it exactly!" He was perspiring. His face was flushed.

His hands were trembling. His whole body was ablaze with a metabolic fervor I had not previously seen in him. He looked like a skeleton who had just trotted off a basketball court after a hard game. He leaned toward me and said, looking suddenly vulnerable in a way that he had never allowed himself to seem with me before: "Are you sure it was only a dream? Or do you go there too?"

Kafka had the right idea. What the anorexic wants is to demonstrate a supreme ability. "Look," she says. "I am a special person. I have an extraordinary gift. I am capable of exerting total control over my body. By refusing food I take command of my destiny. I display supreme force of will. Can you achieve that sort of discipline? Can you even begin to understand it? Of course you can't. But I can." The issue isn't really one of worrying about being too fat. That's just a superficial problem. The real issue is one of exhibiting strength of purpose, of proving that you can accomplish something remarkable, of showing the world what a superior person you really are. So what we're dealing with isn't merely a perversely extreme form of dieting. The deeper issue is one of gaining control—over your body, over your life, even over the physical world itself.

He began to look healthier. There was some color in his cheeks now, and he seemed more relaxed, less twitchy. I had the feeling that he was putting on a little weight, although the medical reports I was getting from his school physician didn't confirm that in any significant way—some weeks he'd be up a pound or two, some weeks down, and there was never any net gain. His mother reported that he went through periods when he appeared to be showing a little interest in food, but these were usually followed by periods of rigorous fasting or at best his typical sort of reluctant nibbling. There was nothing in any of this that I could find tremendously encouraging, but I had the definite feeling that I was starting to reach him, that I was beginning to win him back from the brink.

Timothy said, "I have to be weightless in order to get there. I mean, literally weightless. Where I am now, it's only a beginning. I need to lose all the rest."

"Only a beginning," I said, appalled, and jotted a few quick notes.

"I've attained takeoff capability. But I can never get far enough. I run into a barrier on the way down, just as I'm entering the truly structural regions of the chip."

"Yet you do get right into the interior of the chip."

"Into it, yes. But I don't attain the real understanding that I'm after. Perhaps the problem's in the chip itself, not in me. Maybe if I tried a quantum-well chip instead of a MOSFET I'd get where I want to go, but they aren't ready yet, or if they are I don't have any way of getting my hands on one. I want to ride the probability waves, do you see? I want to be small enough to grab hold of an electron and stay with it as it zooms through the lattice." His eyes were blazing. "Try talking about this stuff with my brother. Or anyone. The ones who don't understand think I'm crazy. So do the ones who do."

"You can talk here, Timothy."

"The chip, the integrated circuit—what we're really talking about is transistors, microscopic ones, maybe a billion of them arranged side by side. Silicon or germanium, doped with impurities like boron, arsenic, sometimes other things. On one side are the N-type charge carriers, and the P-type ones are on the other, with an insulating layer between; and when the voltage comes through the gate, the electrons migrate to the P-type side, because it's positively charged, and the holes, the zones of positive charge, go to the N-type side. So your basic logic circuit—" He paused. "You following this?"

"More or less. Tell me about what you feel as you start to go downward into a chip."

It begins, he said, with a rush, an upward surge of almost ecstatic force: he is not descending but floating. The floor falls away beneath him as he dwindles. Then comes the intensifying of perception, dust motes quivering and twinkling in what had a moment before seemed nothing but empty air, and the light taking on strange new refractions and shimmerings. The solid world begins to alter. Familiar shapes—the table, a chair, the computer before him—vanish as he comes closer to their essence. What he sees now is detailed structure, the intricacy of surfaces: no longer a forest, only trees. Everything is texture and there is no solidity. Wood and metal become strands and webs and mazes. Canyons yawn. Abysses open. He goes inward, drifting, tossed like a feather on the molecular breeze.

It is no simple journey. The world grows grainy. He fights his way through a dust storm of swirling granules of oxygen and nitrogen, an invisible blizzard battering him at every step. Ahead lies the chip he seeks, a magnificent thing, a gleaming radiant Valhalla. He begins to run toward it, heedless of obstacles. Giant rainbows sweep the sky: dizzying floods of pure color, hammering down with a force capable of deflecting the wandering atoms. And then—then—

The chip stands before him like some temple of Zeus rising on the Athenian plain. Giant glowing columns—yawning gateways—dark beckoning corridors—hidden sanctuaries, beyond access, beyond comprehension. It glimmers with light of many colors. A strange swelling music fills the air. He feels like an explorer taking the first stumbling steps into a lost world. And he is still shrinking. The intricacies of the chip swell, surging like metal fungi filling with water after a rain: they spring higher and higher, darkening the sky, concealing it entirely. Another level downward and he is barely large enough to manage the passage across the threshold, but he does, and enters. Here he can move freely. He is in a strange canyon whose silvery walls, riven with vast fissures, rise farther than he can see. He runs. He runs. He has infinite energy; his legs move like springs. Behind him the gates open, close, open, close. Rivers of torrential current surge through, lifting him, carrying him along. He senses, does not see, the vibrating of the atoms of silicon or boron; he senses, does not see, the electrons and the not-electrons flooding past, streaming toward the sides, positive or negative, to which they are inexorably drawn.

But there is more. He runs on and on and on. There is infinitely more, a world within this world, a world that lies at his feet and mocks him with its inaccessibility. It swirls before him, a whirlpool, a maelstrom. He would throw himself into it if he could, but some invisible barrier keeps him from it. This is as far as he can go. This is as much as he can achieve. He yearns to reach out as an electron goes careening past, and pluck it from its path, and stare into its heart. He wants to step inside the atoms and breathe the mysterious air within their boundaries. He longs to look upon their hidden nuclei. He hungers for the sight of mesons, quarks, neutrinos. There is more, always more, an unending series of worlds within worlds, and he is huge, he is impossibly clumsy, he is a lurching reeling mountainous titan, incapable of penetrating beyond this point—

So far, and no farther—
No farther—

He looked up at me from the far side of the desk. Sweat was streaming down his face and his light shirt was clinging to his skin. That sallow cadaverous look was gone from him entirely. He looked transfigured, aflame, throbbing with life: more alive than anyone I had ever seen, or so it seemed to me in that moment. There was a Faustian fire in his look, a world-swallowing urgency. Magellan must have looked that way sometimes, or Newton, or Galileo. And then in a moment more it was gone, and all I saw before me was a miserable scrawny boy, shrunken, feeble, pitifully frail.

I went to talk to a physicist I knew, a friend of Timothy's father who did advanced research at the university. I said nothing about Timothy to him.

"What's a quantum well?" I asked him.

He looked puzzled. "Where'd you hear of those?"

"Someone I know. But I couldn't follow much of what he was saying."

"Extremely small switching device," he said. "Experimental, maybe five, ten years away. Less if we're very lucky. The idea is that you use two different semiconductive materials in a single crystal lattice, a superlattice, something like a three-dimensional checkerboard. Electrons tunneling between squares could be made to perform digital operations at tremendous speeds."

"And how small would this thing be, compared with the sort of transistors they have on chips now?"

"It would be down in the nanometer range," he told me. "That's a billionth of a meter. Smaller than a virus. Getting right down there close to the theoretical limits for semiconductivity. Any smaller and you'll be measuring things in angstroms."

"Angstroms?"

"One ten-billionth of a meter. We measure the diameter of atoms in angstrom units."

"Ah," I said. "All right. Can I ask you something else?"

He looked amused, patient, tolerant.

"Does anyone know much about what an electron looks like?"

"*Looks* like?"

"Its physical appearance. I mean, has any sort of work been done on examining them, maybe even photographing them—"

"You know about the Uncertainty Principle?" he asked.

"Well—not much, really—"

"Electrons are very damned tiny. They've got a mass of—ah—about nine times ten to the minus twenty-eighth grams. We need light in order to see, in any sense of the word. We see by receiving light radiated by an object, or by hitting it with light and getting a reflection. The smallest unit of light we can use, which is the photon, has such a long wavelength that it would completely hide an electron from view, so to speak. And we can't use radiation of shorter wavelength—gammas, let's say, or X rays—for making our measurements, either, because the shorter the wavelength the greater the energy, and so a gamma ray would simply kick any electron we were going to inspect to hell and gone. So we can't see electrons. The very act of determining their position imparts new velocity to them, which alters their position. The best we can do by way of examining electrons is make an enlightened guess, a probabilistic determination, of where they are and how fast they're moving. In a very rough way that's what we mean by the Uncertainty Principle."

"You mean, in order to look at an electron in the eye, you'd virtually have to be the size of an electron yourself? Or even smaller?"

He gave me a strange look. "I suppose that question makes sense," he said. "And I suppose I could answer yes to it. But what the hell are we talking about, now?"

I dreamed again that night: a feverish, disjointed dream of gigantic grotesque creatures shining with a fluorescent glow against a sky blacker than any night. They had claws, tentacles, eyes by the dozens. Their swollen asymmetrical bodies were bristling with thick red hairs. Some were clad in thick armor, others were equipped with ugly shining spikes that jutted in rows of ten or twenty from their quivering skins. They were pursuing me through the airless void. Wherever I ran there were more of them, crowding close. Behind them I saw the walls of the cosmos beginning to shiver and flow. The sky itself was dancing. Color was breaking through the blackness: eddying bands of every hue, interwoven like great chains. I ran, and I ran, and I ran, but there were monsters on every side, and no escape.

Timothy missed an appointment. For some days now he had been growing more distant, often simply sitting silently, staring at me for the whole hour out of some hermetic sphere of unapproachability. That struck me as nothing more than predictable passive-aggressive resistance, but when he failed to show up at all I was startled: such blatant rebellion wasn't his expectable mode. Some new therapeutic strategies seemed in order: more direct intervention, with me playing the role of a gruff, loving older brother, or perhaps family therapy, or some meetings with his teachers and even classmates. Despite his recent aloofness I still felt I could get to him in time. But this business of skipping appointments was unacceptable. I phoned his mother the next day, only to learn that he was in the hospital; and after my last patient of the morning I drove across town to see him. The attending physician, a chunky-faced resident, turned frosty when I told him that I was Timothy's therapist, that I had been treating him for anorexia. I didn't need to be telepathic to know that he was thinking, *You didn't do much of a job with him, did you?* "His parents are with him now," he told me. "Let me find out if they want you to go in. It looks pretty bad."

Actually they were all there, parents, stepparents, the various children by the various second marriages. Timothy seemed to be no more than a waxen doll. They had brought him books, tapes, even a laptop computer, but everything was pushed to the corners of the bed. The shrunken figure in the middle barely raised the level of the coverlet a few inches. They had him on an IV unit, and a whole webwork of other lines and cables ran to him from the array of medical machines surrounding him. His eyes were open, but he seemed to be staring into some other world, perhaps that same world of rampaging bacteria and quivering molecules that had haunted my sleep a few nights before. He seemed perhaps to be smiling.

"He collapsed at school," his mother whispered.

"In the computer lab, no less," said his father, with a nervous ratcheting laugh. "He was last conscious about two hours ago, but he wasn't talking coherently."

"He wants to go inside his computer," one of the little boys said. "That's crazy, isn't it?" He might have been seven.

"Timothy's going to die, Timothy's going to die," chanted somebody's daughter, about seven.

"Christopher! Bree! Shhh, both of you!" said about three of the various parents, all at once.

I said, "Has he started to respond to the IV?"

"They don't think so. It's not at all good," his mother said. "He's right on the edge. He lost three pounds this week. We thought he was eating, but he must have been sliding the food into his pocket, or something like that." She shook her head. "You can't be a policeman."

Her eyes were cold. So were her husband's, and even those of the stepparents. Telling me, *This is your fault, we counted on you to make him stop starving himself.* What could I say? You can only heal the ones you can reach. Timothy had been determined to keep himself beyond my grasp. Still, I felt the keenness of their reproachful anger, and it hurt.

"I've seen worse cases than this come back under medical treatment," I told them. "They'll build up his strength until he's capable of talking with me again. And then I'm certain I'll be able to lick this thing. I was just beginning to break through his defenses when—when he—"

Sure. It costs no more to give them a little optimism. I gave them what I could: experience with other cases of severe food deprivation, positive results following a severe crisis of this nature, et cetera, et cetera, the man of science dipping into his reservoir of experience. They all began to brighten as I spoke. They even managed to convince themselves that a little color was coming into Timothy's cheeks, that he was stirring, that he might soon be regaining consciousness as the machinery surrounding him pumped the nutrients into him that he had so conscientiously forbidden himself to have.

"Look," this one said, or that one. "Look how he's moving his hands! Look how he's breathing. It's better, isn't it!"

I actually began to believe it myself.

But then I heard his dry thin voice echoing in the caverns of my mind. *I can never get far enough. I have to be weightless in order to get there. Where I am now, it's only a beginning. I need to lose all the rest.*

I want to disappear.

That night, a third dream, vivid, precise, concrete. I was falling and running at the same time, my legs pistoning like those of a marathon runner in the twenty-sixth mile, while simultaneously I dropped in free fall through airless dark toward the silver-black surface of some distant world. And fell and fell and fell, in utter weightlessness, and hit the surface easily and kept on running, moving not forward but downward, the atoms of the ground parting for me as I ran. I became smaller as I descended, and smaller yet, and even smaller, until I was a mere phantom, a running ghost, the bodiless idea of myself. And still I went downward toward the dazzling heart of things, shorn now of all impediments of the flesh.

I phoned the hospital the next morning. Timothy had died a little after dawn.

•   •

•

Did I fail with him? Well, then, I failed. But I think no one could possibly have succeeded. He went where he wanted to go; and so great was the force of his will that any attempts at impeding him must have seemed to him like the mere buzzings of insects, meaningless, insignificant.

So now his purpose is achieved. He has shed his useless husk. He has gone on, floating, running, descending: downward, inward, toward the core, where knowledge is absolute and uncertainty is unknown. He is running among the shining electrons, now. He is down there among the angstrom units at last.

PARTICLE PHYSICS

ESSAY BY
LEON M. LEDERMAN

SPECULATION BY
ROBERT L. FORWARD

SPECULATION BY
CONNIE WILLIS

AN EXPERIMENT IN HIGH-ENERGY PHYSICS

LEON M. LEDERMAN

FERMI NATIONAL ACCELERATOR LABORATORY

Cast of Characters

Name	Symbol	Mass (in energy units)
electron	$e^{\pm}$	0.5 MeV
muon	$\mu^{\pm}$	100 MeV
electron neutrino	ν_e	less than 15 eV
muon neutrino	ν_e	less than 200 KeV
photon	γ	zero
proton	p^{+}	1,000 MeV
antiproton	$\bar{p}$	1,000 MeV
pion	$\pi^{\pm}$	150 MeV

THERE ISN'T MUCH TO STOP THE WINDS THAT SWEEP ACROSS the snow-covered Illinois prairie in midwinter. In a 7,000-acre tract of converted cornfields, about 30 miles west of Chicago, sits the Fermi National Accelerator Laboratory. The dominating structure is a 16-story high rise sweeping upward from the flat, flat land, somewhat like a Dürer drawing of hands held in prayer. Other than this, a nondescript cluster of small buildings stands out sharply in the snow, reflecting curious light from a three a.m. sky. The accelerator, buried 30 feet underground, is running. The Computer Center, on the eighth floor of the high rise, is brightly lit, and lights shine from the small windows of the scattered huts where researchers sit and monitor their experiments. The underground high-energy beam from the accelerator sends streams of protons out to the various targets, so precisely controlled that two miles from the exit point of the ring, the directed stream of protons impacts precisely on a razor-thin target, hour after hour.

The director is on his rounds. It is bitterly cold this night and the graduate student in charge, one Drasko by name, on shift in the neutrino hut, is fully dressed, anorak over blue jeans, seated on an electric heater and typing into his modem with gloves on. He has obviously been awake for at least 30 hours, unshaven, red eyed. Drasko had been called back in, just after coming home from his last shift, to repair some electronic modules that only he understands. One repair led to another and, lo, it was time to go on shift again.

Added to Drasko's troubles is this unexpected visit from the laboratory director.

"Yes, the experiment is working well," says Drasko.

The drafty and poorly heated hut is crammed with electronics. Thick multiwire cables lead from the racks of electronics 300 feet down and over to where the action is taking place: in a huge vault, a large particle detector weighing over 1,000 tons is being bombarded with neutrinos, those most elusive of particles. Much has been learned about these particles since their discovery in 1961 at the Brookhaven Laboratory on Long Island. They emerge from the spontaneous disintegration of another subnuclear particle, the pi meson, or pion. (See Figure 1.) Protons from the Fermi accelerator barrel into a small piece of tungsten at an energy of 800 billion electron-volts (800 GeV). At this energy, the Einsteinian relation makes the protons weigh 800 times their normal mass when at rest. In the violent collision, much of the energy carried in by the proton, E=mc² (Energy = mass × velocity of light squared), is converted to pions, kaons, and other massive subnuclear debris. The entire barrage pours forward in a narrow cone defined by the motion of the incident proton. A long flight path of some thousand yards is allowed—distance is time, and in the time taken to cross this space (even at 99 percent of the speed of light), about 10 percent of the pions disintegrate; they undergo a spontaneous reaction:

$$\pi \rightarrow \mu + \nu_\mu$$

These hieroglyphics (physicists often use Greek letters as shorthand) mean that a pion converts to a muon and a muon-type neutrino. The newly born particles follow in the path of the pion and smash into a thick wall of buried steel, steel salvaged from a retired battleship and arranged to make a wall 500 yards thick. The undecayed pions interact with atomic nuclei in the wall and eventually expire, as do the kaons and other strongly interacting particles. The muons are tougher, but eventually they dissipate all their energy and succumb to the steel fortress.

But the neutrinos, which bear zero electric charge and are not subject to the strong force, can penetrate the steel wall. (See Figure 2.) (For further discussion, see "The Forces of Nature," by Sheldon Lee Glashow.) On the other side of the wall is Drasko's detector. If neutrinos can easily penetrate the 500-yard-thick wall, they can as easily pass through the detector. However, the total number of neutrinos generated by the intense proton beam is enormous, so

Figure 1. A pion (π) disintegrates in about 2.5 × 10⁻⁸ secs into a charged muon (μ) and a neutral, massless neutrino (ν_μ). (Credit: Leon M. Lederman)

some small probability exists for a collision to take place between a neutrino and the nuclei of the massive detector.

Drasko's time trip: As an undergraduate Drasko had done the numbers in a thought experiment. A high-energy neutrino would have a 50 percent probability of interacting (i.e., striking a nucleus) if the steel wall had a thickness of about 100 million miles (i.e., the distance from the earth to the sun!). So thick a detector would clearly be very costly, but there could be a way out. If you insist on seeing one collision and there are two neutrinos, you need only half the thickness. If there are 100 million neutrinos per second you need about 100 millionth as thick a detector, so an affordable detector can be constructed. In the Fermi experiment, there are enough neutrinos to give Drasko and his colleagues on the experiment about one neutrino collision in their detector every second. When these high-energy neutrinos collide with nuclei, they generate muons and other nuclear particles (e.g., pions). The products of collisions are the main observables in high-energy physics research.

Why are collisions so instructive? "Lets count the ways," quipped one of Drasko's graduate student colleagues on the experiment. For one, by studying how one particle deviates from its path under the influence of another particle, one can elucidate the nature of the force between the two particles. It was via scattering experiments that Ernest Rutherford discovered the existence of nuclei.

Who could forget the drama of that experiment? The issue was how the heavy material of the nucleus was distributed. Most physicists thought the matter was spread out over the entire volume of the atom. Rutherford shot his alpha particles at a very thin layer of gold and, much to his astonishment, he found alpha particles bouncing backward. It was as if one had shot a cannon ball into a bale of feathers and the ball had bounced backward. The alpha particles must have encountered something very small, dense, and massive. Detailed studies of how the alphas scattered led to the conclusion that almost the entire mass of the atom resided in a "core" of volume less than a trillionth the volume of the atom. Rutherford had discovered the nucleus. Since that time, the pattern of scattered particles has given physicists an increasingly fine picture of the structure of matter in the nucleus and of the forces between the particle probe and nuclear constituents.

Collisions also permit the conversion of kinetic energy to mass energy and therefore the creation of new particles. This takes place in accordance with the same Einstein relation, $E = mc^2$, already noted. The discovery of a "zoo" of new and totally unexpected particles in the 1950s laid the foundation for a new perception of the subnuclear world and the basis for the Standard Model of Particle Physics, that concise statement that everything in the world is made of six quarks and six leptons subject to the influence of the four forces of nature.

Figure 2. A 1,000-ton electronic neutrino detector sits behind a 500-yard-thick steel filter which passes only neutrinos, produced from pion decays at the Fermilab proton accelerator. (Photo credit: Fermilab National Accelerator Laboratory)

The correct choice of collision partners, energy, and observational detail are the decisions out of which Nobel Prizes are fashioned.

The director's time trip: Boy, do I remember those funny neutrino numbers! We worked them out at Columbia in 1959 for the first time and decided that 10 tons of aluminum would be enough to detect the high-energy neutrinos that the Brookhaven accelerator, then the highest energy in the world, could produce. We struggled with everything. How intense a neutrino beam could we get? How could we aim the beam properly? How close to the machine could we place shielding? Where could we get thousands of tons of steel? And most violently we argued about the detector. How could we build something as massive as 10 tons and yet so well subdivided that we could see the details of collisions?

What drove us?

Theorists were baffled at the refusal of certain reactions to take place. This refusal violated the "totalitarian rule" of physics: Anything that isn't forbidden is compulsory! But the forbiddenness was inexplicable in the simple world of one neutrino. One way out was to propose that there were two kinds of neutrinos. The director recalled his colleague T. D. Lee's explanation, written with crystalline logic on his Columbia office blackboard

$$\mu \rightarrow e + photon$$

In words, a muon should be able to disintegrate into an electron and a photon. Yet experiment says the process seems to be forbidden. Experimenters at the NEVIS labs at Columbia have been trying for years to see the reaction without success. The maximum rate is at least ten thousand times smaller than expected. Why do we believe this reaction *must take place?* Because it can go in two stages:

Stage 1: $\mu \rightarrow e + \nu + \bar{\nu}$

(This stage 1 reaction is well known and well measured; over 99 percent of all muons decay this way: in words, a muon decays into an electron and a neutrino and an antineutrino.)

(The neutrino and its antiparticle, which were generated in stage 1, annihilate into photons.)

Lee emphasized that both reactions are well understood and that the quantum uncertainty principle allows them to take place almost simultaneously, so that the net result is just the reaction that does not show up in the experiment. This is a crisis.

What is the way out? Lee speculated: "Suppose stage 1 produces not a neutrino and its antiparticle but two different kinds of neutrinos? One can belong to the electron family, the other to the muon family.

"The two-neutrino hypothesis would imply that in all weak interactions, the muon is always associated with its own neutrino, and the electron with its neutrino. To verify that this is what nature is really like would be a tremendous contribution. In that case, for a positive muon decay, stage 1 becomes:

Stage 2: $\nu + \bar{\nu} \rightarrow$ photon

$$\mu^+ \rightarrow e^+ + \nu_e + \bar{\nu}_\mu$$

This states that a positively charged muon gives rise to a positive electron (positron), an electron-neutrino, and an anti-muon-neutrino. Then stage 2 cannot take place and the failure of a muon to decay into an electron and photon is understood theoretically." Lee then faced the future director and said: "You've got to do the neutrino experiment!"

This puzzle was in a sense the final straw; it pushed us to seriously consider detecting these rather spooky particles. A neutrino is unique in that it reacts only by virtue of the weak force. This makes reactions very rare (e.g., a mean path length for collision of 100 million miles of steel!). But each reaction would be pure gold, giving us a chance to study weak forces at high energy. There was ample motivation to take chances. But the proposal met with lots of resistance.

The Brookhaven accelerator was brand-new and the proprietors were clearly upset when the Columbia scientists proposed to stack 1,000 tons of rusty armor plate, salvaged from the battleship *Missouri*, near their shiny new accelerator. The shield was to screen out all particles but neutrinos. The challenge was to build a massive detector into which one could "see" and determine that a neutrino had indeed produced a reaction. The solution was the newly invented spark chamber: a series of flat metal plates held at high voltage and separated by half-inch gaps filled with neon gas. If a particle passed through the gap, an electric discharge along the path of the particle would render the track visible, to be photographed by fast cameras. (See Figure 3.) The director remembered the frenzy of work—three professors, two visiting scientists, and

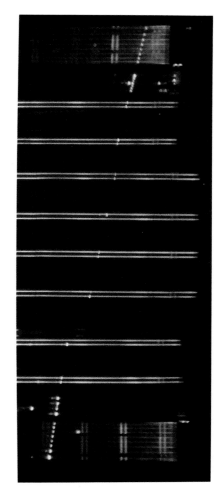

Figure 3. Captive lightning: the path of a high-energy subatomic particle crosses the metal plates of a gas-filled spark chamber at the Saturne accelerator, near Paris. (Photo credit: William R. Alschuler)

two graduate students aided by some undergraduates worked 16 hours a day, seven days a week, for months to ready the experiment.

"How many times did I look just like Drasko," the director muses.

The run began in February 1961 and by June some 50 neutrino events—clear, clean, unmistakable—had been recorded. The result: proof of the existence of two types of neutrinos, one belonging to the electron class, the other to the muon class. The proof lay in the fact that whereas the detector was in a beam that was almost pure in neutrinos arising from pion decay ($\pi \rightarrow \mu + \nu$), these neutrinos almost always gave rise to muons when they collided with nuclei, *and* they never gave rise to electrons. The only conclusion: neutrinos born with muons remember that they are muon-type. Using the language of today, the director thought, we had discovered "flavor" (i.e., the existence of two neutrinos of different flavor).

The neutrino research also started a quantitative study of the weak interactions—"Those were the days," sighed the director. "Seven guys could mount an experiment, run it, and analyze the data in less than a year, and here are Drasko and his 30 friends working for four years. . . ."

In the years since the discovery of the muon-type neutrino, neutrino physics has become a cottage industry, with experiments at Brookhaven, Fermilab, in Geneva at the great European Center for Nuclear Research (CERN), and in the Soviet Union's Protvino Laboratory, called Serpukhov. Much has been learned about the neutrino, one of the basic ingredients in the Standard Model. The neutrino has also been used as a probe of the nuclear domain; some of the most precise information on the arrangement of quarks inside the proton has come from neutrino scattering.

The neat idea of modern scattering experiments is that the collisions of interest are highly inelastic (called "deeply inelastic scattering," or DIS) and are viewed most profitably from the point of view of the quantum theory applied to the force fields. In this picture, the neutrino arrives near the proton or neutron of the nucleus and sends out a ghostly W particle—ghostly because there is no way to detect it directly; the whole picture works because it explains so much data. The W particle is the carrier of the weak force.

In leaving the neutrino, the W (positively or negatively charged) changes it into a muon (negative or positive) and proceeds to seek out a quark. The lucky quark swallows the W and takes off with a large energy increment. The experimentalist actually knows only that he directed an energetic neutrino into the reaction; he measures a muon coming out in a new direction with decreased energy, and he also sees the nuclear debris characteristic of highly inelastic collisions. But the accumulation of tens of thousands, even millions, of such events *requires* the theoretical interpretation given above, and then the analysis yields a rich harvest of information on how the quark was moving just prior to the neutrino invasion and on the detailed nature of the force between neutrinos and quarks.

Drasko's experiment is one of the more sophisticated studies of the properties of neutrinos. The director had brushed up before his three a.m. visit. Particle physics now recognizes three types of neutrinos. One belongs to the electron family, an e-neutrino (v_e), one is the mu-neutrino (v_μ), and the most exotic is the tau-neutrino (v_τ), related to the tau-lepton, discovered at the Stanford machine in 1976. They are the neutral members of the three families of quarks and leptons that are the Standard Model's basic particles. A crucial issue has to do with the masses of neutrinos. Experiments indicate that the masses are extremely small, much less than the mass of the electron. The v_e is found to be less than a twenty-thousandth of the electron's mass (i.e., less than 15 eV). The masses of the other two neutrinos, if they have any, are also quite small. Can they all be zero? A lot of theorists insist that neutrinos must have zero mass, zero being an elegant number. Experimenters want to check.

How do you weigh a neutrino? Drasko's professor had devised a very sensitive and ingenious method. It depended on the phenomenon called neutrino oscillations. Suppose that both the muon neutrino and the electron neutrino have mass and that the muon neutrino is slightly the heavier of the two. Theory says that one result would be the curious wave-particle quantum phenomenon of particle mixing. Quantum uncertainties permit the description of neutrinos both as waves and as particles. The minuteness of the neutrinos' mass and the similarity of their properties permit the waves of the two neutrinos to mix so intimately that one neutrino can change into the other. It turns out that a v_μ can turn into a v_e and, in time, back into a v_μ. The laws of quantum theory permit oscillations only if the neutrinos have nonzero mass, and the oscillations depend on the mass difference of the neutrinos.

One facet of the apparent spookiness of quantum theory is that the "empty" space around a particle such as a neutrino is actually filled with the transient and ghostlike presences of other particles that are connected, however slightly, with the initial neutrino. The oscillation process implies that one of these ghosts has a nonzero probability of materializing and, in effect, changing places with the original neutrino.

The idea of oscillations was first proposed by the Italian experimentalist Bruno Pontecorvo while he was working in the Soviet Union in 1967. The question of whether neutrinos have mass is currently a very lively subject since the mass of the neutrino and the phenomenon of particle mixing are issues in the quest for a grand unification in particle physics.

Also, if neutrinos have mass, they are crucial candidates for the dark matter that, astrophysicists insist, fills the universe and accounts for over 90 percent of its mass.

Astrophysicists, who have established the big bang theory of the expanding universe, have calculated that there are enough neutrinos in the universe that if one of the three varieties had a mass of more than 20 eV, this accumulation would add enough gravitational mass to account for the dark matter and enough to slow the expansion of the universe. A significantly higher mass could lead to a closed universe—that is, a reversal of the expansion and the beginning of a gravitational compression leading eventually to the Big Squeeze. The question of the electron neutrino's mass had the benefit of much attention, since one can produce these neutrinos with radioactive sources. Most such experiments were on tabletop equipment and failed to detect any mass. A very careful Soviet experiment, based upon the decay of the radioisotope tritium, strongly indicated that the neutrino has a nonzero mass. However, the most sensitive measurement came from a surprising source, the supernova 1987A, which radiated fantastic quantities of energy throughout space, including prodigious numbers of electron neutrinos. If they had masses and all were liberated at the same instant, then their different energies would have given rise to different velocities and thus a spread in arrival times, as well as a delay in arrival compared to X rays and gamma rays traveling at the speed of light. A few neutrinos were detected on earth, and calculations based on their arrival times gave an extremely small value for the upper limit of the electron neutrino's mass. Thus the oscillation experiment focused on the muon-neutrino and the result was of tremendous import to cosmology and to our understanding of the fate of the universe.

The neutrinos are emitted during a brief period in the agonies of the collapsing star, a period of several seconds. They race the light of the explosion and, 160,000 years later cross the finish line, detection on the planet Earth. Any mass that the neutrinos carry slows them down. If their velocity is slower than that of light by as little as one part in a million, they will arrive months later, so great is the distance traveled. But the astronomers know that the cosmic race was much closer than that, that the arrival of light and neutrinos was closer than a few hours apart. Simple arithmetic converts this to a limit on how much mass the neutrino can have.

Meanwhile, back at the freezing electronics hut and the three a.m. conversation of graduate student Drasko and his laboratory director, the director is saying, "We have set up a beam which should be almost pure ν_μ, neutrinos belonging to the muon class. You have two 500-ton detectors, separated by 500 yards. As I understand it, the first detector should very largely see only interactions characteristic of ν_μ:

$$\nu_\mu + nucleus \rightarrow \mu + nuclear\ debris$$

That is, the muon-neutrino gives rise to a muon in the course of its collision with the nucleus.

"However, if there is mass in the neutrino system, by the time the beam arrives at the second detector, some ν_μ's should have oscillated into ν_e's and you should see events like

$$\nu_e + nucleus \rightarrow e + nuclear\ debris.$$

"Your detectors can easily tell a muon from an electron, and any sign of electrons implies the presence of ν_e's and is proof of mass. The number of ν_e's compared to ν_μ's gives some information on the mass difference and therefore on the order of magnitude of the mass of the heavier neutrino."

Drasko is torn between fatigue, his need to concentrate on the apparatus, and his need to show respect for the director.

"That's correct, sir. The beam has been very steady for the past week and events are coming in nicely." A whistle sounds, causing Drasko to jump. "Excuse me, I've got to change tapes."

The data arrives at the electronics racks in the form of electrical pulses from several thousand transmitting sensors, capable of detecting the passage of particles by the energy deposited in the sensitive gas layers of the spark chamber detector.

The pulses are received by the data acquisition system, are filtered to remove noise, and then are digitized (i.e., converted to digital information—a series of zeros and ones in accordance with a code that transforms the information carried by the electrical pulses into a form more conducive to computer manipulation). The data is predigested by the electronics, mostly home built, in the neutrino hut. Some of the data is rejected as "garbage" and some of it is prepared for writing to magnetic tape for further analysis on the large computer located on the eighth floor of the Fermilab high rise.

A portion of the data is analyzed by a minicomputer in the hut so that the physicist on shift can verify that all the components of the complex detector are working well.

The director glances around the crowded electronics shack. It is a continuous miracle that a series of magnetically aligned domains on a reel of plastic-based tape (magtape) can contain, in the form of an almost infinite train of zeros and ones, information of mind-boggling variety. One tape can contain the record of President Reagan's address to the nation, another can give the lifetime of the B-meson. What even this jaded physicist-turned-administrator could never get over was the process of converting these "zeros and ones" into knowledge so abstract and so remote from the human condition as the collisions of neutrinos with up and down quarks in the nuclear proton.

"How long have you been on this experiment, Drasko?" asks the director.

"Well, I worked on the design concept during my apprenticeship four years ago. After passing my prelims I started full-time two years ago. If the machine doesn't break down and we finish the data collection phase in the next six months, then I can get the data completely analyzed in two years. I should be able to write it all up and get my Ph.D. in less than three years from now."

Drasko pours coffee from a blackened pot into a plastic cup. "Want some coffee? Boy, it's cold in here!" Drasko surveys the flashing lights and oscilloscope traces. A printer begins to produce summaries of the various channels of information that arrive in the hut from the underground detector.

"How do you tell the difference between muons and electrons?" asks the director. "That's crucial to the experiment, isn't it?"

"Sure is, but we made absolutely certain we could do it. We put a portion of our detector in a beam of electrons two years ago, and the test beam's results convinced us that we had to make the plates of the detector thinner. Muons are easy, they pass through many meters of steel and it is quite simple to identify them. They leave nice tracks and do very little in the steel.

"It is the electrons that are harder. Typically, a high-energy electron will create a shower of electrons and photons in a few centimeters of iron. When charged particles are deflected from straight lines, they 'shake off' some of the cloud of ghost photons that accompanies them. Since the low-mass electrons are easily deflected, they radiate lots of photons. These in turn readily convert to electron-positron pairs, each of which radiates photons, and pretty soon there are a few hundred particles in the shower. If the plates of the detector (separated by layers of gas in which the number of tracks is measured electronically) are too thick, the entire shower can be confined to a few inert plates and would not be evident.

"After some debate, we finally decided on half-inch plates. This cost more, but science isn't cheap, and we were relieved when the lab approved our plan and set the engineers to work on the design and procurement.

"A half-inch plate detector was cobbled together and was again tested for six months in the electron and muon beams before we really went into production. We needed 5,000 plates, each weighing almost one-third of a ton. Meanwhile we built the electronics in the university, together with our collaborators at Columbia and CalTech."

At this point, the director says, "Okay, I see how you detect the muons and the electrons, but I still have a lot of questions. How do you know you are looking at neutrino events? Can anything fool you, any background events? Suppose the muon from the ν_μ reaction escapes the detector? Can some of the nuclear debris include particles that look like electrons in that they also give rise to showers? If the muon left the detector *and* a nuclear particle born in the collision looks like an electron, you count a ν_e when there was no such thing."

Drasko, while thinking, surveys the graphics display on which his minicomputer presents sample events. Everything seems smooth, events flash on and then clear, and new events flash on. In most of the events, the long muon track is clearly evident. Pions, kaons, and other particles all collide with nuclei after passing through several plates. He sips his coffee.

"Well, we've thought of all those things and even a few other problems. But we may have missed something, so that's why we set the experiment up in two separate locations along the neutrino line. (See Figure 4.) We've looked at about 10,000 neutrino events taken two months ago in detector 1. Just as you say, most of them had one clear, long muon track. The remainder are mostly 'neutral current events, events where the ν_μ stays a ν_μ after bouncing off the nucleus. Drasko writes on a small chalkboard:

$$\nu_\mu + \text{nucleus} \rightarrow \nu_\mu + \text{nuclear debris}$$

We of course don't detect the outgoing ν_μ, but the nuclear breakup is detected. We saw that about five percent of these had a possible muon track, but perhaps too short to prove it. Anyway there are only a tiny number of cases in which we are not sure we have a muon *and* have anything that we'd say could be an electron-induced shower. Most of these are probably pi zero mesons that decay into photons that make showers. Of these "phony showers," about 10 events out of our total sample looked like our calibration events taken in the electron test beam. Incidentally, sir, in those events that have muons, we see the same background. This is a powerful independent check and sets an experimental limit to our background. If there is no oscillation effect we should see roughly 10 suspicious electronlike events out of thousands of clear $\nu_\mu \rightarrow \mu$ events in detector 2. Our sensitivity to oscillations, then, is that there have to be at least 50 clear electrons in the second detector. If we see them, we've got it!"

The director suppresses a smile—the enthusiasm that makes Drasko's fatigue seem to vanish is familiar.

"How many physicists are in your collaboration?"

"There are about 30, with eight graduate students."

The director looks at his watch. He wants to stop at one more experiment before calling it quits.

"Well, thanks for the information and the coffee. What time is your relief?"

Drasko is already reading the printed output and entering information in the large logbook. He looks up, now the very picture of death warmed over.

"Oh, about seven—then I'm going to sleep for a week, except that I have to take the tapes to the Computer Center on my way home . . ."

As the director walks out he takes a last look at the scene. Some few miles away, in a large control room, a half dozen technicians are operating the accelerator and all its components. Particles start their route in a Cockcroft-Walton electrostatic machine, which pushes the protons up to 700,000 electron-volts (700 KeV). The protons then enter a linear accelerator (linac) whose radiofrequency cavities carry the protons on an electromagnetic wave, a 500-foot ride to 200 million electron-volts (MeV). The next transfer is to the booster ring— which whirls the protons up to 8 GeV. Transfer time! The particles enter the "old main ring," a ring four miles in circumference that the protons transit 50,000 times a second, gaining a few million volts on each turn. At 150 GeV, the protons are fed by magnetic guides into the superconducting tevatron, sitting 20 inches below the main ring. Here, final acceleration to 800 GeV takes place. (See Figure 5.)

The controls for all the accelerators are located in the main control room, where thousands of pressures, temperatures, voltages, and currents are read by computers and compared with preset values. Graphic displays in multicolor consoles inform the operators of the state of things.

And the entire organization, backed by a personnel office, a purchasing department, a U.S. Department of Energy managing office with the pipeline to the money—all of this vast enterprise—all exists to provide young Drasko with his protons so that he can weigh neutrinos.

The director shakes his head and, as he leaves, he experiences a vivid fantasy, so vivid that he stands still outside the hut, impervious to the fierce wind. And this is the fantasy:

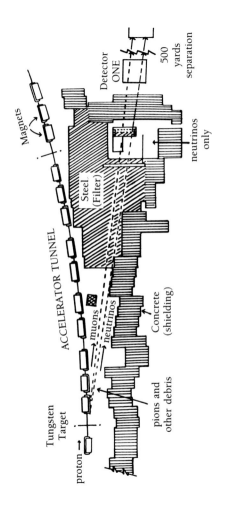

Figure 4. Bird's-eye view of the edge of the Tevatron, showing the accelerator magnets, collision target, the spray of collision products, shielding, filters, and particle detectors.

Figure 5. A view down the tunnel of the Tevatron accelerator. The "old" main magnets (blue) are above, the Tevatron 800 GeV magnets (orange) below. (Photo credit: Fermilab National Accelerator)

Drasko reads his computer output, and suddenly his fatigue and discomfort vanish. Something in the pattern of numbers catches his attention. "*Can't be. . . .*"

He types rapidly, asking for a check and for additional events to be summed up. He waits a few minutes and the printer begins to clack. There it is again, and very clear—the same characteristic shower pattern he had seen over and over again in the test beam—not one or two events, but 50 or 60—almost no muons. Drasko feels a new kind of chill, his breathing becomes heavy, his hands shake and he knows.

He, one person out of the planet's teeming billions, he alone, sitting in a small hut at four o'clock in the bitterly cold morning, on a converted cornfield in the heartland of the nation, he alone has come into a profound new knowledge. Neutrinos oscillate, the muon neutrino is massive, at least 30 or 40 electron-volts, enough to account for the dark matter, enough to close the universe. He alone knows the fate of the universe in its unimaginably distant future.

In the director's fantasy is mixed the vividly remembered passion of lonely discovery, the envy and sadness and yet also the "winning out," that boundless joy that science brings on these rare occasions.

The director steps away from Drasko's hut and heads his car for the photon laboratory, where there is a known difficulty with the apparatus. The professor in charge was covering up, but at four a.m., only graduate students are on shift, and they have not yet learned to lie.

He looks back at the neutrino hut: "It *could* happen that way!" (It hasn't: the neutrino's mass is still unknown.)

Note: Some poetic license has been taken with the characters and with Fermilab experiment E-701, but these were for the sake of simplification and do not violate the essential physics of the research.

A MATTER
MOST STRANGE
DR. ROBERT L. FORWARD

ILLUSTRATION BY
JOHN COLLIER

MATT KNEW THERE WAS TROUBLE AHEAD.

He had been summoned to the office of the Director of Brookhaven National Laboratory. Director Stevens normally never bothered to talk to the visiting scientists that came to use his facility except perhaps at parties. Matt stared at the picture on the opposite wall of the reception room. It showed Leon Lederman, Melvin Schwartz, and Jack Steinberger at Brookhaven in 1961, shortly after they had proved that there were two kinds of neutrinos.

"Those were the days," Matt thought, soothing his anxiety by stroking his neat professor-style beard, flecked with strands of prematurely gray hair.

The secretary finally ushered him in, and Calvin Stevens introduced him to Congressman James Deal, the Chairman of the House Science, Space, and Technology Committee, and Secretary of Energy "Billy" Hurley, President Peterson's "hatchet man" at the Department of Energy.

"Professor Shaw is Principal Investigator of the 'S-Drop Experiment,'" said Director Stevens. "It's an attempt to find evidence for a new state of matter called 'strange' matter."

"'Strange' matter?" Billy Hurley looked at Matt.

Matt started the set speech he used to explain his experiment to lay people. "All massive particles, like the protons and neutrons that make up the atoms in your body, are in turn made up of more basic particles, called quarks. Quarks come in six different types, labeled 'up,' 'down,' 'strange,' 'charm,' 'top,' and 'bottom.' A proton can be imagined as a bag containing two 'up' quarks and one 'down' quark, while a neutron is one 'up' and two 'down' quarks. All known particles can be represented by some combination of two or three quarks. Quarks have never been seen individually. They always seem to come in 'bags' of two or three.

"If you get enough quarks together at one time, however," Matt continued, "say, 50 or more, *and* some of them are strange quarks, then you can form large bags, or drops, of a new type of matter, called strange matter. The purpose of our experiment is to slam the heaviest ions Brookhaven can accelerate into a heavy metal target, and search the resulting debris for S-drops—drops of strange matter."

"What are the chances of success?" asked Billy, critically.

"It's hard to say," Matt replied. "Although the theory suggests that large drops of strange matter should be stable, the smaller drops we can produce at Brookhaven may only be marginally stable. Then, there is the problem of identifying the few S-drops produced among all the other particles coming from the target."

"What is the probability of success?" Billy persisted. "Give me a number." Matt couldn't force himself to lie. "Less than one percent," he finally admitted.

Billy leaned back. He didn't like this job Peterson had asked him to do—but at least he wouldn't feel bad about cancelling this marginal experiment. "Tell him the bad news, Cal," he said.

Director Stevens squirmed. "By the direction of President Peterson, Brookhaven National Laboratory is to be closed down at the end of this fiscal year," he said.

"What?"

"Can you get your experiment completed by September thirtieth?" continued the Director. "If not, you might as well shut it down right now."

"Every cent saved means that much more for the scientists trying to complete the Superconducting Super-Collider," said Congressman Deal.

"Peterson's budget for 1998 has zero dollars in it for the SSC," explained Secretary Hurley. "He is determined to balance the budget—and he isn't going to do it by stripping the ragged shirts off the backs of the poor. I've consulted with the chief scientist types at the Department. They all agree that real breakthroughs in high energy physics come only from those machines at the highest energy—and in the USA, that machine is the SSC. To save the SSC, the rest of the machines have to go."

"But there is good science going on at those smaller machines," protested Matt.

"'Gap-filler' science," said Chairman Deal, almost sneering. "We've got poor who need our help to make it through these belt-tightening times. We can't afford a welfare program for second-rate scientists."

Matt winced internally, but held his temper. "It's not me or the other scientists I'm worried about," he said. "The people who will get hurt will be the graduate students. I've got two who are counting on my experiment to get their Ph.D.'s."

"They had better change their majors to something more practical," said

Billy. "By next year, the only place that will need particle physicists will be the SSC. Unless, of course, they go to work for the Department of Defense. The Air Force will be turning most of the particle accelerators into antimatter factories."

Calvin brought the discussion back. "Can you get your experiment done in time?" he persisted.

"We were planning on three months of beam time to produce conclusive results," replied Matt. "But we can make do with one month if we have to." He thought for a while. "If we work 24-hour days, we can get the experiment ready a month before the end of the fiscal year." He got up abruptly. "You give me no other choice, so I'd better get busy," he said, and left without shaking hands.

Working day and night, Matt and his two graduate students, Wu Yong-Shi and Patti Morrison, struggled to get their experiment operational. Yong-Shi was the computer and software whiz, while Patti was the electronics and hardware expert.

One evening, Matt dropped in unexpectedly at the experimental building after midnight. The downstairs control room was empty. He went upstairs—no one in the offices or the lounge. Then he heard voices and a powerful electric motor echoing through the long corridor that led from the control building to the experiment floor proper. He checked the indicators above the door to the corridor. The beam was off and the radiation monitors were green. He made his way through the narrow walkway to the top of the wall of concrete blocks that shielded the control room from the experimental area. The gate on top of the meter-thick wall was open, and someone had taken the safety key down into the experimental area. The voices were clearer now. He descended the circular staircase that spiraled down the other side of the six-meter-high wall, and walked through the zig-zag portal into the experimental area.

"Patti!!! What the *hell* are you doing!" Matt roared. His voice echoed back from the 20-meter-high ceiling of the gigantic metal shed that covered the experimental area. Wu Yong-Shi and some people that Matt recognized as Patti's friends were trying to look inconspicuous in the far corner.

High above, hanging from the overhead crane, was a 40-ton block of dense concrete—one meter wide, two meters tall, and three meters long. Standing on top of the block, one hand holding the steel suspension cable and the other holding the crane controls, was a thin young woman with long, bushy red-brown hair pulled back into a pony-tail. She was dressed in faded blue jeans, scruffy fluorescent-red jogging shoes, and a bulky white sweatshirt that said, "North Pole University."

"Oh! Hi, Professor Shaw," said Patti down from above. "I was hoping to have this done before morning."

"When I *usually* show up," said Matt, disapprovingly.

Patti's eyes dropped, her shoulders hunched forward, and she seemed to shrink, as she went into her "mooching" pose.

"What are you up to?" Matt asked again, sternly.

"Well . . ." started Patti. "The other experiments in the hall had to stop because they couldn't be finished before the shutdown. So, instead of having our experiment crowded into the small area we were originally allocated, I was just rearranging things to take advantage of the extra room."

"There's *got* to be more to it than that," replied Matt, still frowning. "All we need for the first phase of the experiment is the target for the heavy ion beam to collide with, the bending magnet to separate out the S-drops, and the time-of-flight detector that shows the particle is really an S-drop. They fit into our area just fine."

"But since there is more room," said Patti. "We can bring in our equipment for the second phase—where we capture the S-drops."

"*If* the S-drops exist," reminded Matt. "Remember, first we have to prove they exist. Second, we try to capture them and grow them large enough that they are stable."

"But we have only one month of beam time," said Patti. "I was just trying to make the most of it."

"Well . . ." Mat hesitated.

"It's our last chance!" persisted Patti.

"Let's see what you have in mind," said Matt, giving in.

"I'll meet you on top of the right shield wall." She started to lower herself. Matt found a ladder and climbed to the top of the thick wall that shielded one experiment from another.

"The block I was lifting came from the wall at the end of our area, right behind the beam dump," said Patti, pointing as they walked along. "Instead of throwing the S-drops away in the beam dump, I was planning to take them through a hole in the wall into the next area. There I was going to set up the decelerator, the holding ring, and the storage bottle."

"There is certainly room for them there," Matt admitted, stroking his beard. "And the equipment is just waiting for us in the storage annex," said Patti, eagerly.

The crane was soon busy. The remaining blocks in the wall were removed, opening up a hole. Yong-Shi set up a laser beam that passed through the center of the S-drop detector and simulated the path that the S-drops would take. The red beam went through the break in the wall, six feet above the floor, and passed down the length of the adjoining area.

Soon Patti was flying back again. This time she was balanced on a ten-meter-long segment of the S-drop decelerator. It was a particle accelerator that had been redesigned to run backwards. As Patti slowly lowered the thick cylinder with its banks of rf generators hanging off the sides, the others pushed and pulled on the ends until the laser beam threaded through the five-centimeter bore of the long tube. The support feet were lowered to the floor, and Patti went flying off to get the next section, while final adjustments were made on

"She's light-years ahead of me in intelligence and talent. All I can do is make money."

"That takes talent, too," said Matt.

"All it takes is a pleasant personality and a convincing line to sell stock," said Charles. "I hope my line has been convincing enough for Patti." He looked at his watch. "The Tokyo exchange just opened," he said. "I'd better keep on top of the first few hours. Tell Patti I'll be back before eleven thirty." He went out the door.

Matt went to the control console. The main screen had slowly growing bars showing the amount of data collected. The "S-drops" column was blank. Up in the right corner was an engineering display monitoring the high voltage supplies to the gamma ray counters. The indicator for counter eight was erratically shifting from a green OK to a yellow LOW. Suddenly it changed to a steady green.

"Did that work?" echoed Patti's voice from the crawlway.

"Yes!" yelled Matt. Patti reappeared and soon was back down on the floor. She shivered lightly as she put on her faded jeans and Einstein sweatshirt.

Patti took over the control console while Matt went upstairs to his little office to plow through his grant paperwork. A little after eleven, he came back down. Patti was sitting back in the chair, bare feet up on the console, looking at a small object.

"Any 'strangers' show up?" Matt asked.

"Afraid not," said Patti. She tapped a key with a big toe and the screen changed. She put the object on her finger, and Matt realized it was a ring, a huge diamond solitaire.

"That's some rock you have there," Matt said admiringly.

"Charlie gave it to me last night," said Patti. "And asked me to marry him—again." She patted her rounded tummy. "I guess he wants to make me an honest woman."

"Oh!" Matt said, flustered. "I thought you were gaining . . ."

"Weight?" Patti giggled. "You might say that. Except that I expect to lose it all in five months." She suddenly turned pensive. "I'm normally very careful. But I got careless during that depressing period right after the bottom fell out of particle physics. I sometimes wonder if it was really carelessness or just Mother Nature playing tricks on me with my own hormones. I thought seriously about having an abortion—you can't be a post-doc and raise kids at the same time—but I kept putting it off." She looked at the clock display on the screen. "Almost time for Charlie to come." She tapped her big toe on the keyboard again and the tape drive across the room started to rewind. She bent over, slipped on her shoes, and stood up.

Matt went to the tape drive and removed the reel of tape. He walked over to Patti.

"Here's your Ph.D. thesis," he said, handing it to her.

Patti took the reel that symbolized ten years of her life. Four grinding years getting her B.S. in Physics at CCNY, another four grinding years getting her Masters and passing the Ph.D. qualifying exams at SUNY-Stony Brook, and two years with Matt Shaw designing, building, and operating this experiment. But the grind wasn't over. It would take the good part of another year to turn the null data on that tape into an acceptable thesis. And when she was done and had received her doctorate, it would have been for nothing. She had sent out literally hundreds of job applications all over the world, and had received not one positive response. No one wanted another average female particle physicist when there were hundreds of men and women, some better than she was, clamoring for the few post-doc positions left open in the field.

She shrugged, tossed the reel of tape into a nearby trash can, mooched over to her work desk, and started stuffing her backpack with her personal belongings.

"Patti!" exclaimed Matt.

"I'm tired," said Patti in a discouraged tone. "I quit."

Matt fished the reel of tape from the trash and took it over to her. "You can't quit now," he said. "You've almost got your Ph.D.! Think of your future. Think of your career!"

The door opened and Charles walked in. Patti perked up and greeted him with a big kiss. Supporting herself by holding onto his arm, she turned to face her Professor.

"My future is with Charlie," she said. She patted her tummy. "I'm going to make a career of being a wife and a mommy . . ." A defiant look came on her face, "A damn good wife and mommy," she added. "With Charlie I'll be happy and wanted and loved. Which is more than I can expect from a life as a scientist." She grabbed her backpack. "Goodbye, Professor Shaw." They left, leaving Matt still holding the reel of tape.

Dejected, Matt returned to the console and collapsed in the chair. He looked at the screen clock. "2327 TUE 30 SEP 1997," it said.

"Only thirty-three minutes left. Then the beam goes off . . . forever," said Matt to himself. He leaned back in the large comfortable chair and let his tired eyes close.

The early morning sun sent a bright shaft of light through a window and woke Matt up. It was 6 A.M. He had fallen asleep, and the beam had been off for six hours. There was a voice coming from upstairs—it had an urgent tone, but whatever was being said was being repeated in an automatic manner. Puzzled, he made his way up the stairs. There, on a shelf, was a small television monitor sitting on top of a video recorder. It was repeating a scene from *Star Trek*, Yong-Shi's favorite television program. The picture showed Mr. Spock speaking over the intercom.

"Intruder Alert! Intruder Alert! We have a stranger on the lower deck."

Matt went quickly down the corridor, let himself through the safety gate, and clambered quickly down the circular staircase. Slowly he entered the experimental area, a radiation monitor held out in front of him.

The first experimental area was quiet. As he moved through the breech in the shield wall into the second experimental area and started to walk down the long length of the decelerator tube, the ticks from the radiation monitor became more active. The needle was still in the green area, however, so he continued on. As he approached the holding ring, the needle on the monitor dial began to creep into the yellow area. The radiation was especially intense near the segment of the chamber that contained the liquid deuterium.

Matt activated the auxiliary control console in one corner. The bars on the screen indicated no data had been lost while he was asleep—but most importantly, the column labeled "S-drops" was no longer empty. Sometime in the last few minutes of beam operation, a drop of strange matter had been formed. For the last six hours it had been circulating around in the holding ring, feeding on the liquid deuterium, growing fatter and heavier.

"I'd better get it out of there before it gets too heavy and flies out of the holding ring!" said Matt. Holding his breath, he activated the switching circuit. If everything had worked correctly, the heavy drop of strange matter should have been transferred from the holding ring into the storage bottle. Grabbing the radiation monitor, Matt ran back. The gamma radiation from the holding ring was gone. He went over to the storage bottle and waved the monitor around it. Nothing. Had he lost it?

But S-drops only gave off radiation when they were being fed. He ran back to the auxiliary console and turned on the gun that shot deuterium atoms across the center of the storage bottle. Instantly, the four gamma ray detectors surrounding the bottle started to indicate cascades of low-energy gamma rays as the neutrons in the deuterium penetrated the drop of strange matter and became one with it. He called up a computer routine that calculated the total amount of energy being emitted in gamma rays for every neutron swallowed. "Over three percent!" exclaimed Matt. "Three percent of the mass of the neutron is being converted into energy! That's better than fusion energy! And Billy Hurley thought that new physics only came from the highest energy machines."

He turned off the deuterium gun, and the drop of strange matter stopped emitting gamma rays. "Best of all, there is no residual radioactivity when you turn it off," he gloated. "And when it gets too big, you just hit it hard with a large, high-speed nucleus, and you can break it into *two* S-drops and start up another power plant."

"How big *did* it grow during those six hours, anyway?" he asked himself. He pulled down another routine that used the electromagnetic fields in the storage bottle as a "spring" to weigh the S-drop.

"Over a trillion times heavier than a uranium nucleus!" he exclaimed. "It's almost big enough to see!" They had a borehole telescope for inspecting the inside of beam lines. He found it and took it to the storage bottle. It took a long time to arrange the floodlights and the telescope just right. Then, a final twist of the focus knob brought a tiny speck of silver into view.

"There it is," Matt whispered. A thrill ran through his body. "A Nobel Prize for me . . . instant Ph.D.'s for Patti and Yong-Shi . . . and perhaps salvation for Brookhaven, its researchers, and all the other 'second-rate' facilities in the country. But best of all, it's a new source of radiation-free nuclear power for the world . . ."

Nuclear fusion had once promised to be free of residual radioactivity, but secondary reactions had made fusion reactors almost as dangerously radioactive as fission reactors. Would there be something about strange matter energy conversion that would negate its advantages?

Then, from the back of his mind came the memory of an article he had read on "strange stars". According to the article, if a single drop of strange matter fell into a neutron star, the whole star would turn into an ultradense ball of strange matter. Yet, according to the same theorists, nothing like that should happen with normal matter. Since a drop of strange matter has a cloud of electrons around it, it would interact with normal matter in much the same way as a normal atom, which also has a cloud of electrons around it. The electron clouds would act as barriers to keep the strange matter from getting to the protons and the neutrons in the nuclei of the normal matter.

"But suppose . . ." Matt muttered to himself, "that the strange matter drop were allowed to get too large—like almost happened to me—and it got too heavy to hold and fell down into the Earth. Would the S-drop go all the way to the center of the Earth? And are the pressures at the center of the Earth high enough to crush the clouds of electrons shielding the strange matter and allow it to eat up the Earth?"

He didn't know the answer. And even after the theorists had repeated their calculations and showed that even large drops of strange matter would not eat up the Earth—could you be *sure* their calculations were correct?

"I am the only one that knows we were successful," Matt said to himself softly, right hand stroking his beard as he pondered. "I could break up this S-drop into smaller ones that would evaporate away into harmless alpha particles, and no one would be the wiser. Yong-Shi would still get his Ph.D., Patti would get what she wants, and no one else would bother to try the same experiment if I reported a failure."

He paused to sigh deeply. His mind churned over the positive and negative options.

"Is the world ready for this?" he asked himself.
"What shall I do?"

AT THE RIALTO
CONNIE WILLIS
ILLUSTRATION BY
DARREL ANDERSON

Seriousness of mind was a prerequisite for understanding Newtonian physics. I am not convinced it is not a handicap in understanding quantum theory.

—Excerpt from Dr. Gedanken's
keynote address to the
1988 International Congress
of Quantum Physicists Annual
Meeting, Hollywood, California

I GOT TO HOLLYWOOD AROUND ONE-THIRTY AND STARTED trying to check into the Rialto.

"Sorry, we don't have any rooms," the girl behind the desk said. "We're all booked up with some science thing."

"I'm with the science thing," I said. "Dr. Ruth Baringer. I reserved a double."

"There are a bunch of Republicans here, too, and a tour group from Finland. They told me when I started work here that they got all these movie people, but the only one so far was that guy who played the friend of that other guy in that one movie. You're not a movie person, are you?"

"No," I said. "I'm with the science thing. Dr. Ruth Baringer."

"My name's Tiffany," she said. "I'm not actually a hotel clerk at all. I'm just working here to pay for my transcendental posture lessons. I'm really a model/actress."

"I'm a quantum physicist," I said, trying to get things back on track. "The name is Ruth Baringer."

She messed with the computer for a minute. "I don't show a reservation for you."

"Maybe it's in Dr. Mendoza's name. I'm sharing a room with her."

She messed with the computer some more. "I don't show a reservation for her either. Are you sure you don't want the Disneyland Hotel? A lot of people get the two confused."

"I want the Rialto," I said, rummaging through my bag for my notebook. "I have a confirmation number. W37420."

She typed it in. "Are you Dr. Gedanken?" she asked.

243

"Excuse me," an elderly man said.

"I'll be right with you," Tiffany told him. "How long do you plan to stay with us, Dr. Gedanken?" she asked me.

"Excuse me," the man said, sounding desperate. He had bushy white hair and a dazed expression, as if he had just been through a horrific experience or had been trying to check into the Rialto.

He wasn't wearing any socks. I wondered if *he* was Dr. Gedanken. Dr. Gedanken was the main reason I'd decided to come to the meeting. I had missed his lecture on wave-particle duality last year, but I had read the text of it in the *ICQP Journal*, and it had actually seemed to make sense, which is more than you can say for most of quantum theory. He was giving the keynote address this year, and I was determined to hear it.

It wasn't Dr. Gedanken. "My name is Dr. Whedbee," the elderly man said. "You gave me the wrong room."

"All our rooms are pretty much the same," Tiffany said. "Except for how many beds they have in them and stuff."

"My room has a *person* in it!" he said. "Dr. Sleeth. From the University of Texas at Austin. She was changing her clothes." His hair seemed to get wilder as he spoke. "She thought I was a serial killer."

"And your name is Dr. Whedbee?" Tiffany asked, fooling with the computer again. "I don't show a reservation for you."

Dr. Whedbee began to cry. Tiffany got out a paper towel, wiped off the counter, and turned back to me. "May I help you?" she said.

Thursday, 7:30-9 p.m. *Opening Ceremonies.* Dr. Halvard Onofrio, University of Maryland at College Park, will speak on the topic, "Doubts Surrounding the Heisenberg Uncertainty Principle." Ballroom.

I finally got my room at five, after Tiffany went off duty. Till then I sat around the lobby with Dr. Whedbee, listening to Abey Fields complain about Hollywood.

"What's wrong with Racine?" he said. "Why do we always have to go to these exotic places, like Hollywood? And St. Louis last year wasn't much better. The Institut Henri Poincaré people kept going off to see the arch and Busch Stadium."

"Speaking of St. Louis," Dr. Takumi said, "have you seen David yet?"

"No," I said.

"Oh, really?" she said. "Last year at the annual meeting you two were practically inseparable. Moonlight riverboat rides and all."

"What's on the programming tonight?" I said to Abey.

"David was just here," Dr. Takumi said. "He said to tell you he was going out to look at the stars in the sidewalk."

"That's exactly what I'm talking about," Abey said. "Riverboat rides and movie stars. What do those things have to do with quantum theory? Racine would have been an appropriate setting for a group of physicists. Not like this . . . this . . . do you realize we're practically across the street from Grauman's Chinese Theatre? And Hollywood Boulevard's where all those gangs hang out. If they catch you wearing red or blue, they'll—"

He stopped. "Is that Dr. Gedanken?" he asked, staring at the front desk.

I turned and looked. A short roundish man with a mustache was trying to check in. "No," I said. "That's Dr. Onofrio."

"Oh, yes," Abey said, consulting his program book. "He's speaking tonight at the opening ceremonies. On the Heisenberg uncertainty principle. Are you going?"

"I'm not sure," I said, which was supposed to be a joke, but Abey didn't laugh.

"I must meet Dr. Gedanken. He's just gotten funding for a new project."

I wondered what Dr. Gedanken's new project was—I would have loved to work with him.

"I'm hoping he'll come to my workshop on the wonderful world of quantum physics," Abey said, still watching the desk. Amazingly enough, Dr. Onofrio seemed to have gotten a key and was heading for the elevators. "I think his project has something to do with understanding quantum theory."

Well, that let me out. I didn't understand quantum theory at all. I sometimes had a sneaking suspicion nobody else did either, including Abey Fields, and that they just weren't willing to admit it.

I mean, an electron is a particle except it acts like a wave. In fact, a neutron acts like two waves and interferes with itself (or each other), and you can't really measure any of this stuff properly because of the Heisenberg uncertainty principle, and that isn't the worst of it. When you set up a Josephson junction to figure out what rules the electrons obey, they sneak past the barrier to the other side, and they don't seem to care much about the limits of the speed of light either, and Schrödinger's cat is neither alive nor dead till you open the box, and it all makes about as much sense as Tiffany's calling me Dr. Gedanken.

Which reminded me, I had promised to call Darlene and give her our room number. I didn't have a room number, but if I waited much longer, she'd have left. She was flying to Denver to speak at C.U. and then coming on to Hollywood sometime tomorrow morning. I interrupted Abey in the middle of his telling me how beautiful Cleveland was in the winter and went to call her.

"I don't have a room yet," I said when she answered. "Should I leave a message on your answering machine or do you want to give me your number in Denver?"

"Never mind all that," Darlene said. "Have you seen David yet?"

·   ·   ·

To illustrate the problems of the concept of wave function, Dr. Schrödinger imagines a cat being put into a box with a piece of uranium, a bottle of poison gas, and a Geiger counter. If a uranium nucleus disintegrates while the cat is in the box, it will release radiation which will set off the Geiger counter and break the bottle of poison gas. It is impossible in quantum theory to predict whether a uranium nucleus will disintegrate while the cat is in the box, and only possible to calculate uranium's probable half-life; therefore, the cat is neither alive nor dead until we open the box.

From "The Wonderful World of Quantum Physics,"
a seminar presented at the ICQP Annual Meeting
by A. Fields, PhD, University of Nebraska at Wahoo

I completely forgot to warn Darlene about Tiffany, the model-slash-actress.

"What do you mean you're trying to avoid David?" she had asked me at least three times. "Why would you do a stupid thing like that?"

Because in St. Louis I ended up on a riverboat in the moonlight and didn't make it back until the conference was over.

"Because I want to attend the programming," I said the third time around, "not a wax museum. I am a middle-aged woman."

"And David is a middle-aged man who, I might add, is absolutely charming."

"Charm is for quarks," I said and hung up, feeling smug until I remembered I hadn't told her about Tiffany. I went back to the front desk, thinking maybe Dr. Onofrio's success signaled a change. Tiffany asked, "May I help you?" and left me standing there.

After a while I gave up and went back to the red and gold sofas.

"David was here again," Dr. Takumi said. "He said to tell you he was going to the wax museum."

"There are no wax museums in Racine," Abey said.

"What's the programming for tonight?" I said, taking Abey's program away from him.

"There's a mixer at six-thirty and the opening ceremonies in the ballroom and then some seminars." I read the descriptions of the seminars. There was one on the Josephson junction. Electrons were able to somehow tunnel through an insulated barrier even though they didn't have the required energy. Maybe I could somehow get a room without checking in.

"If we were in Racine," Abey said, looking at his watch, "we'd already be checked in and on our way to dinner."

Dr. Onofrio emerged from the elevator, still carrying his bags. He came over and sank down on the sofa next to Abey.

"Did they give you a room with a seminaked woman in it?" Dr. Whedbee asked.

"I don't know," Dr. Onofrio said. "I couldn't find it." He looked sadly at the key. "They gave me 1282, but the room numbers go only up to seventy-five."

"I think I'll attend the seminar on chaos," I said.

The most serious difficulty quantum theory faces today is not the inherent limitation of measurement capability or the EPR paradox. It is the lack of a paradigm. Quantum theory has no working model, no metaphor that properly defines it.

— Excerpt from Dr. Gedanken's keynote address

I got to my room at six, after a brief skirmish with the bellboy-slash-actor, who couldn't remember where he'd stored my suitcase, and unpacked. My clothes, which had been permanent press all the way from MIT, underwent a complete wave function collapse the moment I opened my suitcase, and came out looking like Schrödinger's almost-dead cat.

By the time I had called housekeeping for an iron, taken a bath, given up on the iron, and steamed a dress in the shower, I had missed the "Mixer with Munchies" and was half an hour late for Dr. Onofrio's opening remarks.

I opened the door to the ballroom as quietly as I could and slid inside. I had hoped they would be late getting started, but a man I didn't recognize was already introducing the speaker. " —and an inspiration to all of us in the field."

I dived for the nearest chair and sat down.

"Hi," David said. "I've been looking all over for you. Where were you?"

"Not at the wax museum," I whispered.

"You should have been," he whispered back. "It was great. They had John Wayne, Elvis, and Tiffany the model-slash-actress with the brain of a pea-slash-amoeba."

"Shh," I said.

" —the person we've all been waiting to hear, Dr. Ringgit Dinari."

"What happened to Dr. Onofrio?" I asked.

"Shhh," David said.

Dr. Dinari looked a lot like Dr. Onofrio. She was short, roundish, and mustached, and was wearing a rainbow-striped caftan. "I will be your guide this evening into a strange new world," she said, "a world where all that you thought you knew, all common sense, all accepted wisdom, must be discarded. A world where all the rules have changed and it sometimes seems there are no rules at all."

She sounded just like Dr. Onofrio, too. He had given this same speech two years ago in Cincinnati. I wondered if he had undergone some strange transformation during his search for room 1282 and was now a woman.

"Before I go any farther," Dr. Dinari said, "how many of you have already channeled?"

•   •   •

Newtonian physics had as its model the machine. The metaphor of the machine, with its interrelated parts, its gears and wheels, its causes and effects, was what made it possible to think about Newtonian physics.

Excerpt from Dr. Gedanken's keynote address

"*You knew* we were in the wrong place," I hissed at David when we got out to the lobby.

When we stood up to leave, Dr. Dinari had extended her pudgy hand in its rainbow-striped sleeve and called out in a voice a lot like Charlton Heston's, "O Unbelievers! Leave not, for here only is reality!"

"Actually, channeling would explain a lot," David said, grinning.

"If the opening remarks aren't in the ballroom, where are they?"

"Beats me," he said. "Want to go see the Capitol Records building? It's shaped like a stack of records."

"I want to go to the opening remarks."

"The beacon on top blinks out Hollywood in Morse code."

I went over to the front desk.

"Can I help you?" the clerk behind the desk said. "My name is Natalie, and I'm an—"

"Where is the ICQP meeting this evening?" I said.

"They're in the ballroom."

"I'll bet you didn't have any dinner," David said. "I'll buy you an ice cream cone. There's this great place that has the ice cream cone Ryan O'Neal bought for Tatum in *Paper Moon*."

"A channeler's in the ballroom," I told Natalie. "I'm looking for the ICQP." She fiddled with the computer. "I'm sorry. I don't show a reservation for them."

"How about Grauman's Chinese?" David said. "You want reality? You want Charlton Heston? You want to see quantum theory in action?" He grabbed my hands. "Come with me," he said seriously.

In St. Louis I had suffered a wave function collapse a lot like what had happened to my clothes when I opened the suitcase. I had ended up on a riverboat halfway to New Orleans that time. It happened again, and the next thing I knew I was walking around the courtyard of Grauman's Chinese, eating an ice cream cone and trying to fit my feet in Myrna Loy's footprints.

She must have been a midget or had her feet bound as a child. So, apparently, had Debbie Reynolds, Dorothy Lamour, and Wallace Beery. The only footprints I came close to fitting were Donald Duck's.

"I see this as a map of the microcosm," David said, sweeping his hand over the slightly irregular pavement of printed and signed cement squares. "See, there are all these tracks. We know something's been here, and the prints are pretty much the same, only every once in a while you've got this," he knelt

down and pointed at the print of John Wayne's clenched fist, "and over here," he walked toward the box office and pointed to the print of Betty Grable's leg, "and we can figure out the signatures, but what is this reference to 'Sid' that keeps popping up? And what does this mean?"

He pointed at Red Skelton's square. It said, "Thanks Sid We Dood It."

"You keep thinking you've found a pattern," David said, crossing over to the other side, "but Van Johnson's square is kind of sandwiched in here at an angle between Esther Williams and Cantinflas, and who the hell is May Robson? And why are all these squares over here empty?"

He had managed to maneuver me over behind the display of Academy Award winners. It was an accordionlike wrought-iron screen. I was in the fold between 1944 and 1945.

"And as if that isn't enough, you suddenly realize you're standing in the courtyard. You're not even in the theater."

"And that's what you think is happening in quantum theory?" I said weakly. I was backed up into Bing Crosby, who had won for Best Actor in *Going My Way.* "You think we're not in the theater yet?"

"I think we know as much about quantum theory as we can figure out about May Robson from her footprints," he said, putting his hand up to Ingrid Bergman's cheek (Best Actress, *Gaslight*) and blocking my escape. "I don't think we understand anything *about* quantum theory, not tunneling, not complementarity." He leaned toward me. "Not passion."

The best movie of 1945 was *Lost Weekend.* "Dr. Gedanken understands it," I said, disentangling myself from the Academy Award winners and David. "Did you know he's putting together a new research team for a big project on understanding quantum theory?"

"Yes," David said. "Want to see a movie?"

"There's a seminar on chaos at nine," I said, stepping over the Marx Brothers. "I have to get back."

"If it's chaos you want, you should stay right here," he said, stopping to look at Irene Dunne's handprints. "We could see the movie and then go have dinner. There's this place near Hollywood and Vine that has the mashed potatoes Richard Dreyfuss made into Devil's Tower in *Close Encounters.*"

"I want to meet Dr. Gedanken," I said, making it safely to the sidewalk. I looked back at David. He had gone back to the other side of the courtyard and was looking at Roy Rogers' signature.

"Are you kidding? He doesn't understand it any better than we do."

"Well, at least he's trying."

"So am I. The problem is, how can one neutron interfere with itself, and why are there only two of Trigger's hoofprints here?"

"It's eight fifty-five," I said. "I am going to the chaos seminar."

"If you can find it," he said, getting down on one knee to look at the signature.

"I'll find it," I said grimly. He stood up and grinned at me, his hands in his pockets. "It's a great movie," he said.

It was happening again. I turned and practically ran across the street.

"*Benji IX* is showing," he shouted after me. "He accidentally exchanges bodies with a Siamese cat."

Thursday, 9–10 P.M. "The Science of Chaos." I. Durcheinander, University of Leipzig. A seminar on the structure of chaos. Principles of chaos will be discussed, including the Butterfly Effect, fractals, and insolid billowing. Ballroom.

I couldn't find the chaos seminar. The Clara Bow Room, where it was supposed to be, was empty. A meeting of vegetarians was next door in the Fatty Arbuckle Room, and all the other conference rooms were locked. The chandeler was still in the ballroom. "Come!" she commanded when I opened the door. "Understanding awaits!" I went upstairs to bed.

I had forgotten to call Darlene. She would have left for Denver already, but I called her answering machine and told it the room number in case she picked up her messages. In the morning I would have to tell the front desk to give her a key. I went to bed.

I didn't sleep well. The air conditioner went off during the night, which meant I didn't have to steam my suit when I got up the next morning. I got dressed and went downstairs. The programming started at nine with Abey Fields' Wonderful World workshop in the Mary Pickford Room, a breakfast buffet in the ballroom, and a slide presentation on "Delayed Choice Experiments" in Cecil B. DeMille A on the mezzanine level.

The breakfast buffet sounded wonderful, even though it always turns out to be urn coffee and donuts. I hadn't had anything but an ice cream cone since noon the day before, but if David were around, he would be somewhere close to the food, and I wanted to steer clear of him. Last night it had been Grauman's Chinese. Today I was likely to end up at Knotts' Berry Farm. I wasn't going to let that happen, even if he was charming.

It was pitch-dark inside Cecil B. DeMille A. Even the slide on the screen up front appeared to be black. "As you can see," Dr. Lvov said, "the laser pulse is already in motion before the experimenter sets up the wave or particle detector." He clicked to the next slide, which was dark gray. "We used a Mach-Zender interferometer with two mirrors and a particle detector. For the first series of tries we allowed the experimenter to decide which apparatus he would use by whatever method he wished. For the second series, we used that most primitive of randomizers——"

He clicked again, to a white slide with black polka dots that gave off enough light for me to be able to spot an empty chair on the aisle ten rows up. I hurried to get to it before the slide changed, and sat down.

"—a pair of dice. Alley's experiments had shown us that when the particle detector was in place, the light was detected as a particle, and when the wave detector was in place, the light showed wavelike behavior, no matter when the choice of apparatus was made."

"Hi," David said. "You've missed five black slides, two gray ones, and a white with black polka dots."

"Shh," I said.

"In our two series, we hoped to ascertain whether the consciousness of the decision affected the outcome." Dr. Lvov clicked to another black slide. "As you can see, the graph shows no effective difference between the tries in which the experimenter chose the detection apparatus and those in which the apparatus was randomly chosen."

"You want to go get some breakfast?" David whispered.

"I already ate," I whispered back, and waited for my stomach to growl and give me away. It did.

"There's a great place down near Hollywood and Vine that has the waffles Katharine Hepburn made for Spencer Tracy in *Woman of the Year*."

"Shh," I said.

"And after breakfast, we could go to Frederick's of Hollywood and see the bra museum."

"Will you please be quiet? I can't hear."

"Or see," he said, but he subsided more or less for the remaining ninety-two black, gray, and polka-dotted slides.

Dr. Lvov turned on the lights and blinked smilingly at the audience. "Consciousness had no discernible effect on the results of the experiment. As one of my lab assistants put it, 'The little devil knows what you're going to do before you know it yourself.'"

This was apparently supposed to be a joke, but I didn't think it was very funny. I opened my program and tried to find something to go to that David wouldn't be caught dead at.

"Are you two going to breakfast?" Dr. Thibodeaux asked.

"Yes," David said.

"No," I said.

"Dr. Hotard and I wished to eat somewhere that is *vraiment* Hollywood."

"David knows just the place," I said. "He's been telling me about this great place where they have the grapefruit James Cagney shoved in Mae Clark's face in *Public Enemy*."

Dr. Hotard hurried up, carrying a camera and four guidebooks. "And then perhaps you would show us Grauman's Chinese Theatre," he asked David.

"Of course he will," I said. "I'm sorry I can't go with you, but I promised Dr. Verikovsky I'd be at his lecture on Boolean logic. And after Grauman's Chinese, David can take you to the bra museum at Frederick's of Hollywood."

"And the Brown Derby?" Thibodeaux asked. "I have heard it is shaped like a *chapeau*."

They dragged him off. I watched till they were safely out of the lobby and then ducked upstairs and into Dr. Whedbee's lecture on information theory. Dr. Whedbee wasn't there.

"He went to find an overhead projector," Dr. Takumi said. She had half a donut on a paper plate in one hand and a styrofoam cup in the other.

"Did you get that at the breakfast brunch?" I asked.

"Yes. It was the last one. And they ran out of coffee right after I got there. You weren't in Abey Fields's thing, were you?" She set the coffee cup down and took a bite of the donut.

"No," I said, wondering if I should try to take her by surprise or just wrestle the donut away from her.

"You didn't miss anything. He raved the whole time about how we should have had the meeting in Racine." She popped the last piece of donut in her mouth. "Have you seen David yet?"

Friday, 9–10 P.M. "The Eureka Experiment: A Slide Presentation." J. Lvov, Eureka College. Descriptions, results, and conclusions of Lvov's delayed conscious/randomed choice experiments. Cecil B. DeMille A.

Dr. Whedbee eventually came in carrying an overhead projector, the cord trailing behind him. He plugged it in. The light didn't go on.

"Here," Dr. Takumi said, handing me her plate and cup. "I have one of these at Caltech. It needs its fractal basin boundaries adjusted." She whacked the side of the projector.

There weren't even any crumbs left of the donut. There was about a millimeter of coffee in the bottom of the cup. I was about to stoop to new depths when she hit it again. The light came on. "I learned that in the chaos seminar last night," she said, grabbing the cup away from me and draining it. "You should have been there. The ballroom was packed."

"I believe I'm ready to begin," Dr. Whedbee said. Dr. Takumi and I sat down. "Information is the transmission of meaning," Dr. Whedbee said. He wrote "meaning" or possibly "information" on the screen with a green Magic Marker. "When information is randomized, meaning cannot be transmitted, and we have a state of entropy." He wrote it under "meaning" with a red Magic Marker. His handwriting appeared to be completely illegible.

"States of entropy vary from low entropy, such as the mild static on your car radio, to high entropy, a state of complete disorder, of randomness and confusion, in which no information at all is being communicated."

Oh, my God, I thought. I forgot to tell the hotel about Darlene. The next time Dr. Whedbee bent over to inscribe hieroglyphics on the screen, I sneaked out and went down to the desk, hoping Tiffany hadn't come on duty yet. She had.

"May I help you?" she asked.

"I'm in room 663," I said. "I'm sharing a room with Dr. Darlene Mendoza. She's coming in this morning, and she'll be needing a key."

"For what?" Tiffany said.

"To get into the room. I may be in one of the lectures when she gets here."

"Why doesn't she have a key?"

"Because she isn't here yet."

"I thought you said she was sharing a room with you."

"She will be sharing a room with me. Room 663. Her name is Darlene Mendoza."

"And your name?" she asked, hands poised over the computer.

"Ruth Baringer."

"We don't show a reservation for you."

We have made impressive advances in quantum physics in the ninety years since Planck's constant, but they have by and large been advances in technology, not theory. We can only make advances in theory when we have a model we can visualize.

Excerpt from Dr. Gedanken's keynote address

I high-entropied with Tiffany for a while on the subjects of my not having a reservation and the air conditioning and then switched back suddenly to the problem of Darlene's key, in the hope of catching her off-guard. It worked about as well as Alley's delayed choice experiments.

In the middle of my attempting to explain that Darlene was not the air conditioning repairman, Abey Fields came up.

"Have you seen Dr. Gedanken?"

I shook my head.

"I was sure he'd come to my Wonderful World workshop, but he didn't, and the hotel says they can't find his reservation," he said, scanning the lobby. "I found out what his new project is, incidentally, and I'd be perfect for it. He's going to find a paradigm for quantum theory. Is that him?" he said, pointing at an elderly man getting in the elevator.

"I think that's Dr. Whedbee," I said, but he had already sprinted across the lobby to the elevator.

He nearly made it. The elevator slid to a close just as he got there. He pushed the elevator button several times to make the door open again, and when that didn't work, tried to readjust its fractal basin boundaries. I turned back to the desk.

"May I help you?" Tiffany said.

"You may," I said. "My roommate, Darlene Mendoza, will be arriving some time this morning. She's a producer. She's here to cast the female lead in a new movie starring Robert Redford and Harrison Ford. When she gets here, give her her key. And fix the air conditioning."

"Yes, ma'am," she said.

The Josephson junction is designed so that electrons must obtain additional energy to surmount the energy barrier. It was found, however, that some electrons simply tunnel, as Heinz Pagel put it, "right through the wall."
From "The Wonderful World of Quantum Physics," A. Fields, UNW

Abey had stopped banging on the elevator button and was trying to pry the elevator doors apart. I went out the side door and up to Hollywood Boulevard. David's restaurant was near Hollywood and Vine. I turned the other direction, toward Grauman's Chinese, and ducked into the first restaurant I saw.

"I'm Stephanie," the waitress said. "How many are there in your party?"

There was no one remotely in my vicinity. "Are you an actress-slash-model?" I asked her.

"Yes," she said. "I'm working here part-time to pay for my holistic hairstyling lessons."

"There's one of me," I said, holding up my forefinger to make it perfectly clear. "I want a table away from the window."

She led me to a table in front of the window, handed me a menu the size of the macrocosm, and put another one down across from me. "Our breakfast specials today are papaya stuffed with salmonberries and nasturtium/radicchio salad with a balsamic vinaigrette. I'll take your order when your other party arrives."

I stood the extra menu up so it hid me from the window, opened the other one, and read the breakfast entrees. They all seemed to have cilantro or lemongrass in their names. I wondered if "radicchio" could possibly be Californian for "donut."

"Hi," David said, grabbing the standing-up menu and sitting down. "The sea urchin pâté looks good."

I was actually glad to see him. "How did you get here?" I asked.

"Tunneling," he said. "What exactly is extra-virgin olive oil?"

"I wanted a donut," I said pitifully.

He took my menu away from me, laid it on the table, and stood up. "There's a great place next door that's got the donut Clark Gable taught Claudette Colbert how to dunk in *It Happened One Night*."

The great place was probably out in Long Beach someplace, but I was too weak with hunger to resist him. I stood up. Stephanie hurried over.

"Will there be anything else?" she asked.

"We're leaving," David said.

"Okay, then," she said, tearing a check off her pad and slapping it down on the table. "I hope you enjoyed your breakfast."

Finding such a paradigm is difficult, if not impossible. Due to Planck's constant the world we see is largely dominated by Newtonian mechanics. Particles are particles, waves are waves, and objects do not suddenly vanish through walls and reappear on the other side. It is only on the subatomic level that quantum effects dominate.

Excerpt from Dr. Gedanken's keynote address

The restaurant was next door to Grauman's Chinese, which made me a little nervous, but it had eggs and bacon and toast and orange juice and coffee. And donuts.

"I thought you were having breakfast with Dr. Thibodeaux and Dr. Hotard," I said, dunking one in my coffee. "What happened to them?"

"They went to Forest Lawn. Dr. Hotard wanted to see the church where Ronald Reagan got married."

"He got married at Forest Lawn?"

He took a bite of my donut. "In the Wee Kirk of the Heather. Did you know Forest Lawn's got the World's Largest Oil Painting Incorporating a Religious Theme?"

"So why didn't you go with them?"

"And miss the movie?" He grabbed both my hands across the table. "There's a matinee at two o'clock. Come with me."

I could feel things starting to collapse. "I have to get back," I said, trying to disentangle my hands. "There's a panel on the EPR paradox at two o'clock."

"There's another showing at five. And one at eight."

"Dr. Gedanken's giving the keynote address at eight."

"You know what the problem is?" he said, still holding onto my hands. "The problem is, it isn't really Grauman's Chinese Theatre, it's Mann's, so Sid isn't even around to ask. Like, why do some pairs like Joanne Woodward and Paul Newman share the same square and other pairs don't? Like Ginger Rogers and Fred Astaire?"

"You know what the problem is?" I said, wrenching my hands free. "The problem is you don't take anything seriously. This is a conference, but you don't care anything about the programming or hearing Dr. Gedanken speak or trying to understand quantum theory!" I fumbled in my purse for some money for the check.

"I thought that was what we were talking about," David said, sounding surprised. "The problem is, where do those lion statues that guard the door fit in? And what about all those empty spaces?"

Friday, 2–3 P.M. *Panel Discussion on the EPR Paradox.* I. Takumi, moderator, R. Iverson, L. S. Ping. A discussion of the latest research on singlet-state correlations, including nonlocal influences, the Calcutta proposal, and passion. Keystone Kops Room.

I went up to my room as soon as I got back to the Rialto to see if Darlene was there yet. She wasn't and when I tried to call the desk, the phone wouldn't work. I went back down to the registration desk. There was no one there. I waited fifteen minutes and then went into the panel on the EPR paradox.

"The Einstein-Podolsky-Rosen paradox cannot be reconciled with quantum theory," Dr. Takumi was saying. "I don't care what the experiments seem to indicate. Two electrons at opposite ends of the universe can't affect each other simultaneously without destroying the entire theory of the space-time continuum."

She was right. Even if it were possible to find a model of quantum theory, what about the EPR paradox? If an experimenter measured one of a pair of electrons that had originally collided, it changed the cross-correlation of the other instantaneously, even if the electrons were light years apart. It was as if they were eternally linked by that one collision, sharing the same square forever, even if they were on opposite sides of the universe.

"If the electrons *communicated* instantaneously, I'd agree with you," Dr. Iverson said, "but they don't, they simply influence each other. Dr. Shimony defined this influence in his paper on passion, and my experiment clearly—"

I thought of David leaning over me between the best pictures of 1944 and 1945, saying, "I think we know as much about quantum theory as we do about May Robson from her footprints."

"You can't explain it away by inventing new terms," Dr. Takumi said.

"I completely disagree," Dr. Ping said. "Passion at a distance is not just an invented term. It's a demonstrated phenomenon."

It certainly is, I thought, thinking about David taking the macrocosmic menu out of the window and saying, "The sea urchin pâté looks good." It didn't matter where the electron went after the collision. Even if it went in the opposite direction from Hollywood and Vine, even if it stood a menu in the window to hide it, the other electron would still come and rescue it from the radicchio and buy it a donut.

"A demonstrated phenomenon!" Dr. Takumi said. "Ha!" She banged her moderator's gavel for emphasis.

"Are you saying passion doesn't exist?" Dr. Ping said, getting very red in the face.

"I'm saying one measly experiment is hardly a demonstrated phenomenon."

"One measly experiment! I spent five years on this project!" Dr. Iverson said, shaking his fist at her. "I'll show you passion at a distance!" Dr. Takumi, and

"Try it, and I'll adjust your fractal basin boundaries!" Dr. Takumi said, and hit him over the head with the gavel.

Yet finding a paradigm is not impossible. Newtonian physics is not a machine. It simply shares some of the attributes of a machine. We must find a model somewhere in the visible world that shares the often bizarre attributes of quantum physics. Such a model, unlikely as it sounds, surely exists somewhere, and it is up to us to find it.

Excerpt from Dr. Gedanken's keynote address

I went up to my room before the police came. Darlene still wasn't there, and the phone and air conditioning still weren't working. I was really beginning to get worried. I walked up to Grauman's Chinese to find David, but he wasn't there. Dr. Whedbee and Dr. Sleeth were behind the Academy Award Winners folding screen.

"You haven't seen David, have you?" I asked.

Dr. Whedbee removed his hand from Norma Shearer's cheek.

"He left," Dr. Sleeth said, disentangling herself from the Best Movie of 1929–30.

"He said he was going out to Forest lawn," Dr. Whedbee said, trying to smooth down his bushy white hair.

"Have you seen Dr. Mendoza? She was supposed to get in this morning."

They hadn't seen her, and neither had Drs. Hotard and Thibodeaux, who stopped me in the lobby and showed me a postcard of Aimee Semple McPherson's tomb. Tiffany had gone off duty. Natalie couldn't find my reservation. I went back up to the room to wait, thinking Darlene might call.

The air conditioning still wasn't fixed. I fanned myself with a Hollywood brochure and then opened it up and read it. There was a map of the courtyard of Grauman's Chinese on the back cover. Deborah Kerr and Yul Brynner didn't have a square together either, and Katharine Hepburn and Spencer Tracy weren't even on the map. She made him waffles in *Woman of the Year*, and they hadn't even given them a square. I wondered if Tiffany the model-slash-actress had been in charge of assigning the cement. I could see her looking blankly at Spencer Tracy and saying, "I don't show a reservation for you."

What exactly was a model-slash-actress? Did it mean she was a model *or* an actress or a model *and* an actress? She certainly wasn't a hotel clerk. Maybe electrons were the Tiffanys of the microcosm, and that explained their wave-slash-particle duality. Maybe they weren't really electrons at all. Maybe they were just working part-time at being electrons to pay for their singlet-state lessons.

Darlene still hadn't called by seven o'clock. I stopped fanning myself and tried to open a window. It wouldn't budge. The problem was, nobody knew anything about quantum theory. All we had to go on were a few colliding electrons that nobody could see and that couldn't be measured properly because of the Heisenberg uncertainty principle. And there was chaos to consider, and entropy, and all those empty spaces. We didn't even know who May Robson was.

At seven-thirty the phone rang. It was Darlene.

"What happened?" I said. "Where are you?"

"At the Beverly Wilshire."

"In Beverly Hills?"

"Yes. It's a long story. When I got to the Rialto, the hotel clerk I think her name was Tiffany, told me you weren't there. She said they were booked solid with some science thing and had had to send the overflow to other hotels. She said you were at the Beverly Wilshire in Room 1027. How's David?"

"Impossible," I said. "He's spent the whole conference looking at Deanna Durbin's footprints at Grauman's Chinese Theatre and trying to talk me into going to the movies."

"And are you going?"

"I can't. Dr. Gedanken's giving the keynote address in half an hour."

"He is?" Darlene said, sounding surprised. "Just a minute." There was a silence, and then she came back on and said, "I think you should go to the movies. David's one of the last two charming men in the universe."

"But he doesn't take quantum theory seriously. Dr. Gedanken is hiring a research team to design a paradigm, and David keeps talking about the beacon on top of the Capitol Records Building."

"You know, he may be onto something there. I mean, seriousness was all right for Newtonian physics, but maybe quantum theory needs a different approach. Sid says——"

"Sid?"

"This guy who's taking me to the movies tonight. It's a long story. Tiffany gave me the wrong room number, and I walked in on this guy in his underwear. He's a quantum physicist. He was supposed to be staying at the Rialto, but Tiffany couldn't find his reservation."

The major implication of wave/particle duality is that an electron has no precise location. It exists in a superposition of probable locations. Only when the experimenter observes the electron does it "collapse" into a location.
The Wonderful World of Quantum Physics,
A. Fields, UNW

Forest Lawn closed at five o'clock. I looked it up in the Hollywood brochure after Darlene hung up. There was no telling where he might have gone: the Brown Derby or the La Brea Tar Pits or some great place near Hollywood and Vine that had the alfalfa sprouts John Hurt ate right before his chest exploded in *Alien*.

At least I knew where Dr. Gedanken was. I changed my clothes and got in the elevator, thinking about wave/particle duality and fractals and high entropy states and delayed-choice experiments. The problem was, where could you find a paradigm that would make it possible to visualize quantum theory when you had to include Josephson junctions and passion and all those empty spaces? It wasn't possible. You had to have more to work with than a few footprints and the impression of Betty Grable's leg.

The elevator door opened, and Abey Fields pounced on me. "I've been looking all over for you," he said. "You haven't seen Dr. Gedanken, have you?"

"Isn't he in the ballroom?"

"No," he said. "He's already fifteen minutes late, and nobody's seen him. You have to sign this," he said, shoving a clipboard at me.

"What is it?"

"It's a petition." He grabbed it back from me. "We the undersigned demand that annual meetings of the International Congress of Quantum Physicists henceforth be held in appropriate locations.' Like Racine," he added, shoving the clipboard at me again. "Unlike Hollywood."

Hollywood.

"Are you aware it took the average ICQP delegate two hours and thirty-six minutes to check in? They even sent some of the delegates to a hotel in Glendale."

"And Beverly Hills," I said absently. Hollywood. Bra museums and the Marx Brothers and gangs that would kill you if you wore red or blue and Tiffany/Stephanie and the World's Largest Oil Painting Incorporating a Religious Theme.

"Beverly Hills," Abey muttered, pulling an automatic pencil out of his pocket protector and writing a note to himself. "I'm presenting the petition during Dr. Gedanken's speech. Well, go on, sign it," he said, handing me the pencil. "Unless you want the annual meeting to be here at the Rialto next year." I handed the clipboard back to him. "I think from now on the annual meeting might be here every year," I said, and took off running for Grauman's Chinese.

When we have the paradigm, one that embraces both the logical and the nonsensical aspects of quantum theory, we will be able to look past the colliding electrons and the mathematics and see the microcosm in all its astonishing beauty.

Except from Dr. Gedanken's keynote address

"I want a ticket to *Benji IX*," I told the girl at the box office. Her name tag said, "Welcome to Hollywood. My name is Kimberly."

"Which theater?" she said.

"Grauman's Chinese," I said, thinking, This is no time for a high entropy state.

"Which theater?"

I looked up at the marquee. *Benji IX* was showing in all three theaters, the huge main theater and the two smaller ones on either side. "They're doing audience-reaction surveys," Kimberly said. "Each theater has a different ending."

"Which one's in the main theater?"

"I don't know. I just work here part-time to pay for my organic breathing lessons."

"Do you have any dice?" I asked, and then realized I was going about this all wrong. This was quantum theory, not Newtonian. It didn't matter which theater I chose or which seat I sat down in. This was a delayed-choice experiment and David was already in flight.

"The one with the happy ending," I said.

"Center theater," she said.

I walked past the stone lions and into the lobby. Rhonda Fleming and some Chinese wax figures were sitting inside a glass case next to the door to the restrooms. There was a huge painted screen behind the concessions stand. I bought a box of Raisinets, a tub of popcorn, and a box of jujubes and went inside the theater.

It was bigger than I had imagined. Rows and rows of empty red chairs curved between the huge pillars and up to the red curtains where the screen must be. The walls were covered with intricate drawings. I stood there, holding my jujubes and Raisinets and popcorn, staring at the chandelier overhead. It was an elaborate gold sunburst surrounded by silver dragons. I had never imagined it was anything like this.

The lights went down, and the red curtains opened, revealing an inner curtain like a veil across the screen. I went down the dark aisle and sat in one of the seats. "Hi," I said, and handed the Raisinets to David.

"Where have you been?" he said. "The movie's about to start."

"I know," I said. I leaned across him and handed Darlene her popcorn and Dr. Gedanken his jujubes. "I was working on the paradigm for quantum theory."

"And?" Dr. Gedanken said, opening jujubes.

"And you're both wrong," I said. "It isn't Grauman's Chinese. It isn't movies either, Dr. Gedanken."

"Sid," Dr. Gedanken said. "If we're all going to be on the same research team, I think we should use first names."

"If it isn't Grauman's Chinese or the movies, what is it?" Darlene asked, eating popcorn.

"It's Hollywood."

"Hollywood," Dr. Gedanken said thoughtfully.

"Hollywood," I said. "Stars in the sidewalk and buildings that look like stacks of records and hats, and radicchio and audience surveys and bra museums. And the movies. And Grauman's Chinese."

"And the Rialto," David said.

"Especially the Rialto."

"And the ICQP," Dr. Gedanken said.

I thought about Dr. Lvov's black and gray slides and the disappearing chaos seminar and Dr. Whedbee writing "meaning" or possibly "information" on the overhead projector. "And the ICQP," I said.

"Did Dr. Takumi really hit Dr. Iverson over the head with a gavel?" Darlene asked.

"Shh," David said. "I think the movie's starting." He took hold of my hand. Darlene settled back with her popcorn, and Dr. Gedanken put his feet up on the chair in front of him. The inner curtain opened, and the screen lit up.

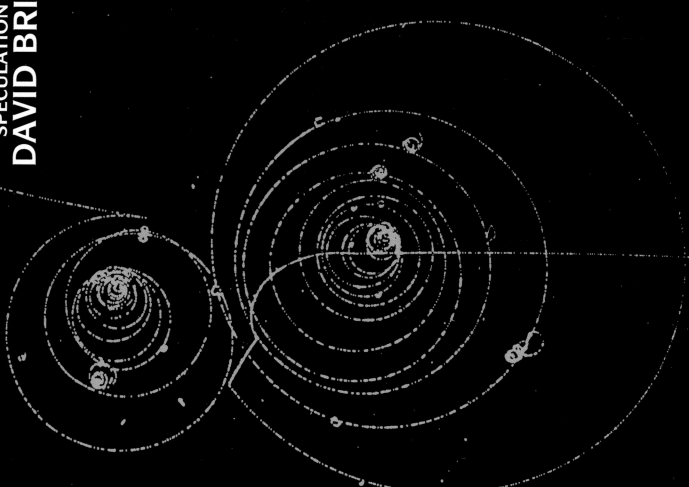

QUARKS

ESSAY BY
ALVARO DE RÚJULA
SPECULATION BY
DAVID BRIN

QUARKS AND BEYOND
ALVARO DE RÚJULA
CERN

IMAGINE YOU WERE AN ALIEN BEING FROM ANOTHER WORLD, disembarking in our neighborhood for the very first time. You would immediately notice that our universe is made of more or less complicated "particles" of different sizes, held together by various forces.

The largest known "particles" are galaxies and "clusters" of galaxies, made of billions to trillions of stars. Around at least one of those stars, and presumably most others, there are planets and their satellites. All of these large objects are held together by the force of gravity, whose use to you at this very moment is to allow you to sit down. Experts on these largest of particles, in order of their decreasing size, are called cosmologists, astrophysicists, and astronomers.

On at least one planet, but no doubt on many others, there are living creatures. The forces holding these living "particles" together are gregarious and sexual instincts, useful for maintaining and steering the evolution of the different species, but not the main concern of most scientists. Experts on the interactions between these living beings are variously called sociologists, biologists, and taxi drivers.

Were you to probe inside the previously mentioned objects at a microscopic scale, you would find that they are made of molecules, such as the water molecule. Molecules are made of atoms; the helium atom, for example, consists of two negatively charged electrons orbiting around a doubly charged nucleus. Molecules and atoms are stabilized by electromagnetic forces between their charged constituents. These forces are responsible for the variety of the natural world at our scale, for chemistry, for life, for the telephone bill, and so forth. Experts on these subjects are variously called atomic physicists, chemists, and plumbers.

264

Once upon a time atoms were thought to be the "elementary" particles: those having no smaller parts. But scores of different atoms exist in nature. "Had the Lord Almighty consulted me upon creation, I would have recommended something simpler," commented Alfonso X the Wise, King of Castilla and Leon, when confronted with the world as it appeared to an educated thirteenth-century man. The stable constituents of matter that we believe at the moment to be elementary are much fewer than the different types of atoms: King Alfonso may rest in peace. This apparent simplicity will be challenged in the closing paragraphs of this essay, when we consider the unstable universes "parallel" to ours.

Electrons are believed to be elementary, but atomic nuclei are not: they are made of protons and neutrons. These are also composites of two types of smaller objects: "up" quarks and "down" quarks. Quarks, much like the proverbial men of the Grand Old Duke of York, are neither up nor down, at least in the ordinary sense. Up quarks have a charge $+2/3$: "upward" of down quarks, whose charge is $-1/3$. Once scientists preferred to baptise newly found objects with pretentious Greek names; now we borrow from everyday language, a fashion whose effects are always confusing and often sophomoric. Quarks are held together in protons or neutrons by the "chromodynamic" force (pretentious), more congenially known as "color" (confusing) or "glue" (guess what). After years of bewilderment and intense study, I have discovered what, in the grand scheme of things, the main purpose of the chromodynamic force is: to justify my salary.

All that is needed to construct any material object, from the simplest atom to the most delicious wine, are u's, d's and e's: up quarks, down quarks, and electrons. But if we want to let the sun and natural radioactivity work the way they do, a fourth particle type is needed: neutrinos (v), as well as a fourth force, the weak force. No experiment to date has been able to reveal a substructure inside either electrons, neutrinos or quarks: they are all candidate "elementary particles." There is nothing much that today's scientists can establish about objects smaller than these or larger than the largest we have just described.

Elementary particles are simple in at least two respects: two of a kind are absolutely identical, and the list of their properties is extraordinarily short. Electrons, poor little things, have only four basic properties: mass, electric charge, weak charge, and spin. The mass and the electric and weak charges dictate the way electrons interact with gravity and with the electromagnetic and weak forces. The spin describes how they "rotate about themselves" or behave under rotations. Neutrinos are even simpler than electrons: they have no electric charge and presumably no mass. Quarks have only one more property than electrons: "color"; the artist's conception in Figure 1 incommensurately exaggerates the details of their structure. Quark color, you will have guessed, has nothing to do with ordinary color, it is a new type of charge responsible for the extraordinary behavior of quarks.

To each of the particle types we have mentioned (u, d, e and v), there corresponds an antiparticle, denoted with a bar over the particle's symbol ($\bar{u}$, $\bar{d}$, $\bar{e}$, $\bar{v}$). Antiparticles have the same mass and spin as the corresponding particle, but opposite charges. When brought into close enough contact, a particle-antiparticle pair "annihilates": it transforms itself into lighter particles. That is simply the nature of antimatter. Opposite electrical charges attract: for a little while, before they self-destroy, an e and an $\bar{e}$ (a positron) bind together into a neutral [$e\bar{e}$] system. Quarks and antiquarks behave in the same manner, but compared to that of the [$e\bar{e}$] compounds, quark binding is much stronger: this is the first hint that quarks carry a new type of charge, called "color." Like charges repel, and should one try to get two or three electrons to stick together, the attempt would fail miserably. But, lo, not two, but *three* quarks (or three antiquarks) do stick together, and with as much might as a quark-antiquark pair; the "color" charge responsible for this peculiar treble-homophilic behavior must be not only stronger, but also much more interesting than the more conventional electrical charge. Protons and neutrons are the only long-lived examples of quark triplets; the proton is made of two u's and one d, the neutron is made of two or three electrons to stick together, the other way around: $p = [uud]$, $n = [udd]$. Other quark triplets, such as [uuu] and [ddd], also exist, but are short-lived (they decay into lighter particles). The existing quark-antiquark pairs and quark triplets are shown in Figure 1. There is nothing striking about quark-antiquark compounds, but the three-quark systems have mysterious properties, besides their very existence. To name just one example, [uuu] exists only with its three quarks spinning in one direction, while [uud] exists not only that way but also as a proton, wherein one of the quarks spins counter to the other two. Why?

The hydrogen atom, [pe] in our notation, and the [$e\bar{e}$] system we just discussed are bound by the electromagnetic attraction between the opposite charges of their constituents, and so they are neutral: their total charge is zero—all this to bend your eye with obvious, repetitive, and well-known facts. A particle and an antiparticle have opposite charges; if quarks carry a "color" charge, a quark-antiquark pair will also be bound by an attractive "color" force, before the pair decays into lighter objects. To continue down the tautological path, these bound quark-antiquark systems have a zero total color charge, they are "color neutral." And now for the surprise: it turns out that the correct theory of quarks, the one explaining their peculiar and more normal whims, is found by imposing the condition that sets of three quarks also be "color neutral," even sets of three identical quarks, such as [uuu] or [ddd]. This sounds ridiculous, for "if in some units the quark color charge is 1, then the charge of three quarks will be $1 + 1 + 1 = 3$, you idiot," I can hear you say. Nope. But the hat trick is a little tricky, requiring a separate, slightly more highfalutin paragraph.

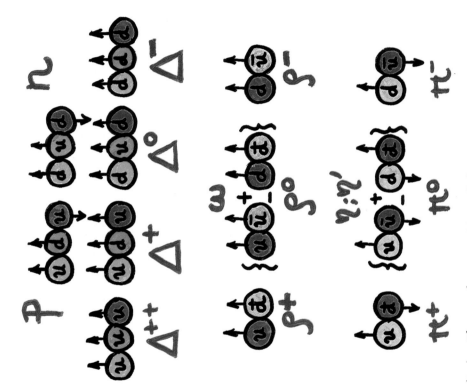

Figure 1a. (*top*). The quark composition of the proton (p), and neutron (n). *1b* (*bottom*). *Various mesons.* (Credit: Alvaro De Rújula)

Figure 2. The quarks come with various new properties: up and down, color, etc. . . . . (Credit: Alvaro De Rújula)

Let each type of quark, u or d, exist in three different colors of your choice, or my choice. There are thus a red, a blue, and a green up quark (u_R, u_B, u_G), all identical but for their "color charges." Ditto for the downs (d_R, d_B, d_G). The hat trick is to have the color charges add up, not like ordinary numbers, but like arrows. Much as one can draw three arrows "adding up to zero" (think of superimposing them on the sides of a triangle), one can think of the three colors as directions in an abstract three-dimensional space, and have the red, blue, and green quarks in a proton add up to zero color, much as the colors of the rainbow add up to white. One more sentence for the mathematically sophisticated reader who despises excessive poetic licence (everybody else abstain). The quark-color "arrows" are three-dimensional complex vectors spanning the fundamental representation of SU(3), the "3" is the number of quarks in a proton; their totally antisymmetric colorless combination allows for the existence of three-fermion states with parallel spins, such as [uuu]; and the "complex" is to make quarks and antiquarks, or protons and antiprotons, be as different as they happen to be. (Aah! I can hear most of you say.)

Quark color, and the peculiar but mathematically explicit rules for adding up colors to make color-neutral objects, are sufficient to explain which quark-antiquark or three-quark combinations are allowed or forbidden. But there is more to color than the successful explanation of who is supposed to be or not to be. To proceed, let us endow the color charges with the same properties that the electrical charge has in quantum electrodynamics (QED), the theory of electromagnetic interactions between electrically charged particles. To put it bluntly, we take an older and very successful theory and try to imitate it blindly, giving the new theory, just in case it is right, a resounding name, quantum chromodynamics (QCD). In QED the interactions between charges are "mediated" by the exchange of "photons." Photons are also elementary particles: they are the particles of light. In an interaction between electrons, such as that in Figure 3, a photon is emitted by one of the electrons and absorbed by the other. The crucial rules of the theory are embedded in the precise description of what happens at the point at which the electrically charged particle emits or absorbs a photon. These rules can be derived from a deep and mysterious principle called "gauge invariance," but they boil down to the statement that the emission or absorption is the simplest possible one. In QCD the interactions between quarks are mediated by the exchange of "gluons," as in Figure 3(b). Photons are electrically neutral, but gluons are not color neutral. When an electron emits a photon, as in Figure 3(a), it stays an electron with the same charge: the neutral photon carries away no charge. But a red quark may become green, as in Figure 3(b), by the emission of a "red-antigreen" gluon: gluons are "colored": they carry color charges. This implies that gluons themselves "couple" to gluons: they may emit and absorb gluons, as in Figure 3(c). Photons are neutral and do not couple to photons: there is no QED analog to Figure

3(c). This minor difference makes all the difference between the behavior of electrons and that of quarks. The interaction energy of an [$e\bar{e}$] pair decreases with the distance between the electron and its antiparticle. But the same is not true of a quark-antiquark or three-quark system. This brings us to the weird subject of "quark confinement."

We have repeatedly said that a proton, $p = [uud]$, is made of three quarks. If it has these three parts, what would be more natural than to take it apart? But no collision experiment, no matter how high its energy, has ever succeeded in breaking a proton down into its separate pieces or in dismembering any other particle allegedly made of quarks and/or antiquarks. Neither has anybody succeeded in finding a single, "liberated" quark in nature, though thorough searches have been made in all sorts of materials, including oysters. (The individuals responsible for this particular search were not crooks trying to get

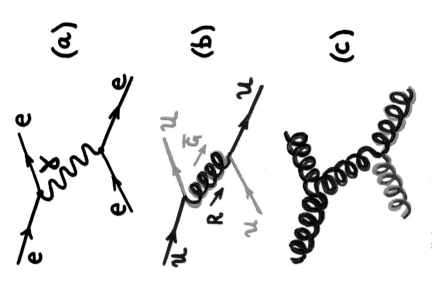

Figure 3a. (*top*). Electrons collide via exchange of virtual photons (wavy line). *3b* (*center*). Quarks interact by exchanging gluons (curly line) and may change color in the process. *3c* (*bottom*). Gluons interact with themselves, unlike photons. (Credit: Alvaro De Rújula)

many delicious free dinners out of the science-funding agencies, but wise people who realized that oysters filter many times their weight of water every day, and in so doing accumulate all sorts of substances with rare properties. Nothing would have a rarer chemistry than a liberated quark or quark compound with a fractional, as opposed to integer or zero, electric charge.) We haven't held a quark in our hand or seen one in a real picture (unlike Figure 1). Why do we think that quarks are more real than UFOs or Nessie are?

They teach you in kindergarten that an atom of hydrogen is made of a proton and an electron, and this for two reasons. First, this "model" successfully accounts for the properties of all the states of hydrogen, which correspond to the different ways its two constituents can vibrate and spin about each other. This "proof" that $H = |pe|$ is 99.9 percent convincing. Second, you can shoot an electron, a photon, and whatnot hard enough into hydrogen to break it into its constituent pieces, separate them as much as you like, and measure their properties. This adds the remaining tenth of a percent; now you *really know* that $H = |pe|$. We know that protons, neutrons, and scores of other (unstable) particles are made of quarks because of the equivalent of the first reason, but that's all. The success of the quark model in explaining the properties of all the particles in Figure 1 and more suffices to convince us of the reality of quarks, even if we believe that we will never hold the ultimate smoking gun: a picture of a naked quark.

What happens when you actually try to kick a quark out of a proton? This may be done, for instance, by shining very energetic photons onto it, as in Figure 4(a). The photons couple to the electric charge of the quarks and may be absorbed by one of them. The struck quark recoils with the original photon's momentum, while the others lag behind. One might expect that the result of the stretching of Figure 4(b), for a sufficiently energetic kick, would be a breakdown of the proton into a quark and the rest. Not so. Superman can jump out of the Earth's attraction or break hydrogen with the photons of his X-ray vision, but he would not succeed in getting an isolated quark out of a proton, no matter how enormous his might might be. The energy stored in the attractive interaction between a proton and an electron decreases with the distance between the objects that attract each other: the further away they are, the smaller the energy required to break their bond. However, because they are colored, the gluons responsible for the attractive binding of quarks produce precisely the opposite effect (the proof of this fact from the basic principles of QCD is not yet polished to everybody's satisfaction). The energy in the interaction between the quarks in a proton *increases* with the distance between them, as if they were attached by a piece of string or a rubber band. With the energy of a charging bull you can stretch a proton, as in Figure 4(b), to a size of about two feet. But much before you reach this point there is enough energy in the interaction between the distant quarks to produce a quark-antiquark pair (remember $E = mc^2$: the interaction energy can be traded for the mass of the newly created particles). The "string" that glues the quarks breaks, but the ruptured ends cover themselves with either a quark or an antiquark, like the beheaded neck of a mythical dragon whose freshly cut head would immediately grow back into place. Figure 4(c) shows, and its caption explains, as a particular case the net result of our efforts to "photodisintegrate" a proton: what you get out of the photon-proton collision is a neutron [udd] and an [$u\bar{d}$], called a charged pion. You could also get a proton and a neutral pion, or innumerable other things, *but never an isolated quark*. So much for Superman.

The alien being that you are (for the purposes of reading this chapter) has by now reached the conclusion that our universe is made of clusters that are made of galaxies that are ensembles of stars, planets and satellites, and that, as

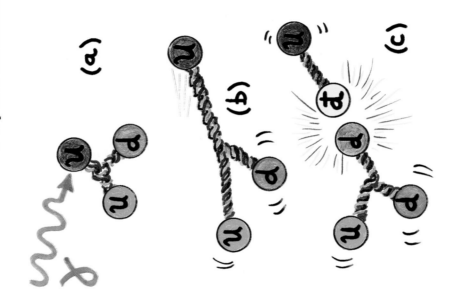

Figure 4a (top). A high energy photon strikes a proton (u,u,d). 4b (*center*). The glue force strengthens as the quarks separate. 4c (*bottom*). The excess force in the quark bond produces a quark, anti-quark pair, resulting in a neutron and a pion but no free quarks. (Credit: Alvaro De Rújula)

everybody on our planet knows, our natural satellite is made of cheese, which, like everything else, is made of molecules that are made of atoms that are made of apparently structureless electrons and a nucleus of protons and neutrons, which are made of quarks (gasp!). But that is not all there is. The basic process behind the natural radioactive decay of some atomic nuclei is the spontaneous decay of a down quark into a lighter up quark, an electron and an antineutrino: $d \Rightarrow ue\bar{\nu}$. So the list of the constituents of matter and their debris is short: u, d, e and ν, with the understanding that each quark can be "painted" in three different colors and that you may add everybody's antiparticles. Electrons and neutrinos are very similar but for the fact that the latter are neutral. They are collectively dubbed "leptons," from the Greek word for "light in weight." At the time when you landed on our planet (now), there is no evidence that either quarks or leptons have a substructure; nor is there proof of the contrary. But in the past we have always found smaller and smaller building blocks as our technology has allowed us to dig deeper and deeper into things. So we may fear that this will happen once again, forcing us back to the drawing board. But affairs may have taken an unexpected turn.

Instead of going yet another step into the guts of things and finding that quarks (u, d) and leptons (e,ν) have smaller parts, we seem to have taken a sideways alley in our quest for the fundamental constituents of matter. For reasons to become clear (typical wishful thinking), we call the ensemble (u, d, e, ν) of good old quarks and leptons the "first family." Totally unexpectedly, there happen to exist fake copies of these building blocks of matter. These newcomers are also organized in some kind of imitation families: to each member of the first family there is a cousin with identical properties, except for weight and average lifetime. Other than for the extra neutrinos, whose masses have proved too small to measure, the extra particles are "fat," in the sense of being more massive than the corresponding members of the first family. Once more with the exception of the neutrino, the extra particles are unstable: they decay into the lighter particles in very tiny fractions of a second, appearing to have no redeeming value.

We have known for about fifty years that there exists a particle called a "muon" (μ) that is the second family's cousin of the electron. All of its basic properties are identical to those of the electron, except that the muon is some 200 times heavier. After decades of acquaintance with this intruder into the restricted club of allegedly elementary particles, we do not yet know "who ordered it." Muons last an average of 2.2 millionths of a second before they decay into an electron, a neutrino, and an antineutrino ($\mu \Rightarrow e\nu_\mu\bar{\nu}_e$). These ν and $\bar{\nu}$ are not a particle and its own antiparticle. One of them is a member of the second family: the "muon neutrino" (ν_μ). The other is the antiparticle of the first family neutrino: the "electron neutrino" (ν_e), whose surname is now needed to distinguish it from its cousin ν_μ, to whom I just introduced you. The parlance of physicists is often confusing and sometimes blatantly bizarre: the couple (μ, ν_μ) are called the leptons of the second generation, even though "lepton" means "light" and the muon is a heavy electron: no respect here for the language of the Greek forefathers of science.

"Cosmic rays" are high-energy protons and other particles raining upon us from the sky; their origin and mechanisms of acceleration are obscure and debated. Cosmic ray collisions with atoms in the atmosphere often produce muons and other short-lived particles. But more often than not, the study of unstable particles requires their production in collisions of artificially accelerated electrons, positrons, protons, and antiprotons. Many unstable particles have first been found in cosmic ray "showers," to be subsequently "established" in laboratory accelerator experiments. No exception to this rule are most of the quarks we have not yet met.

Quarks are fancier than leptons, and that is also true of the quark members of the second family. The first to be found was the "strange" quark (s) of Figure 5. This quark was discovered, in a sense, before quarks were discovered. The point is that quarks are never caught naked, but always disguised as a quark triplet or quark-antiquark pair. "Strange" particles containing strange quarks were discovered experimentally much before the concept of quarks was introduced, and the fact that nobody expected or understood these particles is blatantly reflected in their name. The strange quark is heavier but otherwise basically identical to its first family cousin, the d quark. It too is unstable and decays in various ways: $s \Rightarrow u e \bar{\nu}_e$, $s \Rightarrow u \bar{u} d$, etc.

Yes, you are right! The second family also contains a heavy imitation up quark, called the "charmed" quark (c). This makes the second family a foursome (c, s, μ, ν_μ), much like the first (u, d, e, ν_e). As in previous cases, the robust but attractive figure of Figure 6 may not be the most literal rendering of a charmed quark. Unlike the other members of its family, this particular

Figure 5 (*left*).   The strange quark. *Figure 6* (*right*).   The charmed quark. (Credit: Alvaro De Rújula)

Figure 7 (above). A "charmed" proton counterpart. (Credit: Alvaro De Rújula) *Figure 8 (opposite).* Computer image of higher dimension fractal space projected into 3-D space, with a 2-D slice. Suggests the behavior of fundamental particles in our space may depend on their properties in higher order spaces. (Photo credit: IBM)

particle was predicted on very solid theoretical grounds and its discovery was eagerly expected, but believe it or not, only by the overwhelming minority of physicists. The point is not that most of the physics community is made up of dummies, but that things were not always as crystal clear as they appear to you at this very moment(??). One of the literal meanings of "charm" is "a device to avert evil," and charmed quarks were indeed invented to evade disaster: their existence was required to cure some serious inconsistencies of what we all (now) know (and very few knew then) is the correct theory of electromagnetic and weak interactions. By an irony of history, the first particle ever produced that contained a charmed quark was a [c$\bar{c}$] pair. Its charm was very discreet: the properties of the charmed quark were excellently veiled by its companion antiparticle. The first truly charmed particle to be found was the charmed counterpart of a proton, wherein one of the proton's up quarks is replaced by a charmed one [uud] ⇒ [ucd]. This particle is the subject of Figure 7, featuring its constituent quarks as well as the glue that glues them. Not even this discovery sufficed to convince everybody of the existence of charmed quarks. It took an extra year or two of experimental effort (and lobbying by the tenants of

truth) to find large samples of several other particles containing a single charmed quark and to settle for good the issue of its existence. For a while there were four forces of nature, four leptons, and the four tricolored quarks. In spite of repeated reports in the scandalous press, there is at present no ship-shape evidence for the existence of more than four forces, but leptons and quarks definitely continue to proliferate.

It is downhill from here onward, both in terms of the surprise value of other recently discovered particles and in terms of the poetry of their names. Yes, there is a third family of quarks and leptons. Yes, they are heavier than their corresponding first and second family cousins; perhaps with the excep-tion of neutrinos, whose masses we do not know. The leptons of the third family are called the "tau" and the "tau-neutrino" (τ, ν_τ). The τ weighs more than 3,470 electrons; to call a τ a "lepton" is an accepted etymological mon-strosity. The third family quarks are called "top" and "bottom" (t, b). With names like that they cannot be "artistically" interpreted into a figure, as the preceding quarks were, lest censorship strike. The present evidence for the existence of ν_τ is indirect but convincing. The top quark, whose existence is demanded by theory, still remains to be found, in spite of occasional press announcements of its "discovery." (It appears to be too massive to be effectively produced in the accelerators at our disposal, owing to their "modest" energy and funding.) To summarize, here is a list of the three known families and of their membership:

Neutrinos are the only members of the second and third families for which we know of a hypothetically "useful" role in nature. The simplest and most successful cosmological models require that the mass of the universe be some 10 times bigger than what we can account for in the form of ordinary matter: stars, planets, and interstellar gas and dust. The remaining 90 percent of the stuff of the universe is called the "dark mass." If sufficiently long-lived, and if their masses are conveniently chosen, neutrinos could be what the dark mass of the universe is made of. They would be practically impossible to detect, except via their collective gravitational pull. If all these speculations are right, the second and third generation quarks came here just for the ride: they are useful only inasmuch as their inevitable(?) neutrino brothers are.

We do not know for a fact that the fundamental laws of nature must be simple or that the fundamental constituents of matter should be few. Nor do we know that all natural objects must have a "good reason" to exist and have properties that are understandable in terms of simple rules. Yet all of these prejudices are part of the scientist's credo. One reason is the considerable suc-cess that this search for simplicity has had in the past: we are able to explain an enormous number of natural phenomena in terms of a very few basic concepts and rules. But at the moment, when we list the present candidate fundamental constituents of matter, we must admit that their numbers and properties are contrary to the physicist's credo, for we may ask:

Why do particles occur in families of two colorless leptons and two tri-colored quarks?

What determines the number of quarks and leptons? We are acquainted with what would seem a few too many. Are there even more?

What dictates the apparently random value of the different quark and lepton masses, the most mysterious property distinguishing one particle from another?

Why do the constituents of matter come in families, only the first of which is (anthropocentrically) useful? Or in other words, are the almost identical but unstable replicas of the stuff of matter, these evanescent universes parallel to ours, just a random caprice of nature?

All these questions share a single answer: we do not know.

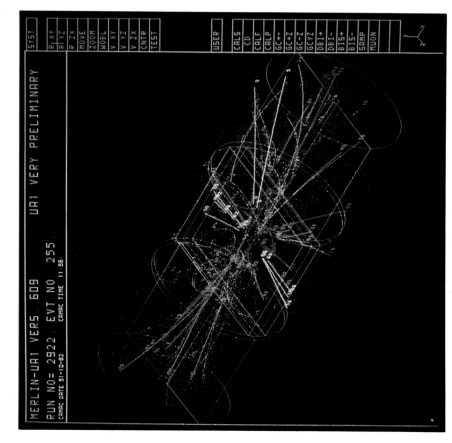

Figure 9. Computer-generated image of a collision at high energy in the CERN accelerator. (Photo credit: CERN)

AMBIGUITY

DAVID BRIN

ILLUSTRATION BY MICHAEL CARROLL

1.

BACK IN SCHOOL, STAN GOLDMAN AND HIS FELLOW STUDENTS used to play a game of make-believe.

"How long do you think it would take Isaac Newton to solve this homework set?" they would ask each other. Or, "If Einstein were alive today, do you think he'd bother with graduate school?"

It was the same sort of lazy, get-nowhere argument debate he'd heard his musician friends debate on occasion—"What d'you figure Mozart would make of our stuff," they'd pose over bottles of beer, "if we could snatch him out of his own time and bring him up to the 1990s? Would he freak out and call it damned noise? Or would he catch on, wear mirror shades, and cut an album right away?"

At that point, Stan used to cut in. "Which Mozart do you mean? The disciplined craftsman of the biographies? Or the brash rebel of Amadeus?"

The composers and players seemed puzzled by his non sequitur. "Why, the real one, of course."

Their reply convinced him that, for all their closeness, for all their well-acknowledged affinity, physicists and musicians would never fundamentally understand each other.

Oh, I see. The real one . . . of course . . .

But what is reality?

Through a thick portal of fused quartz, mediated by a series of three hundred field-reinforced half-mirrors, Stan now watched the essence of nothingness. Suspended within a sealed vacuum, a potential singularity spun and danced in nonexistence.

In other words, the chamber was empty.

Soon though, potentiality would be turned into reality. The virtual would become actual. Twisted space would spill out light. Tortured vacuum would briefly give forth matter.

The improbable would happen. Or at least that was the general idea.

Stan Goldman watched and waited, patiently.

Until the end of his life, Albert Einstein struggled against the implications of quantum mechanics. He had helped invent the new physics. It bore his imprint as fully as Dirac's or Heisenberg's or Bohr's. And yet, like Max Planck, he had always felt uncomfortable with its implications, insisting that the Copenhagen rules had to be only crude approximations of the *real* patterns governing the world. In much the same way as Newton's laws had proved to be rude, tinker-toy versions of geometrodynamics, so Einstein hoped to find order controlling apparent chaos.

Underneath the dreadful quantum ambiguity, he felt there had to be the signature of a Designer.

Only the design eluded Einstein. Its elegant precision fled before the experimentalists, who prodded first at atoms, then nuclei, and at last the so-called fundamental particles. Always, the deeper they probed, the fuzzier grew the mesh of creation.

To a later generation of physicists, in fact, ambiguity was no enemy. Rather it became a tool. It was the law.

Stan pictured Nature as a whimsical goddess. She seemed to be saying, *Look at me from afar, and you may pretend that there are rules, that here there is cause and there effect. But remember, if you wish this solace, you must keep back and squint!*

If, on the other hand, you dare to approach—should you examine my garments' warp and woof—then be prepared for what you'll find. And don't say I did not warn you.

"Don't say I didn't warn you," Stan Goldman whispered to himself, watching the blackness reflected to him by three hundred mirrors.

"You ready down there, Stan?"

Alex Lustig's voice carried down the companionway. He and the others were in the control center, but Stan had volunteered to keep watch here by the peephole. It was a vital job, but one requiring none of the quickness of the younger physicists . . . in other words, just right for an old codger like himself.

"I'm ready as I'll ever be, Alex," he called back.

"Good. Your timer should begin running . . . now!"

True to Alex's word, the display to Stan's left began counting down in whirling milliseconds.

He wiped his palms on his dungarees and wondered why he felt so nervous. After all, he had participated before in the manufacture of bizarre objects. In his youth, at CERN, it had been a zoo of subatomic particles, wrought out of searing heat at the target end of the great accelerator. Even then, the names used by physicists told you more about the scientists' personalities than the creatures they were studying.

He recalled graffiti on the wall of the men's room in Geneva.

Question: What do you get when you mix a charmed red quark with a strange one that's green, and a third that's true blue?

Underneath were scrawled answers, in various hands and as many languages:

I don't know, but to hold them together you'll need a gluon with attitude!
It sounds like what they served in the cafeteria, today.
Speaking of which, anyone here know the flavor of beauty?
Doesn't it depend on who's on top, and who's on the bottom?
I'm getting a hadron just thinking about it.
Hey! What boson thought of this question, anyway?
Yeah. There's a guy who ought to be lepton!

Stan smiled, remembering good times. They had been hunters, he and the others, chasing down and capturing specimens of elusive species. Since those days he had helped expand the bestiary until the shape and pattern and theory of everything had begun to become clear.

Gravitons and gravitinos. Magnetic monopoles and photinos. With grand unification came power . . . the power to mix and match and use nature's ambiguity to create somethingness out of nothingness.

As a youth he never would have imagined that he would someday use singularities—micro–black holes—using them as *circuit elements*, just as blithely as an electrical engineer strung together inductors and resistors. But now it was relatively commonplace. Young fellows such as Alex seemed to take it all in stride.

To Stan Goldman, it all still felt quite weird.

"Three minutes, Stan!"

"I can read a clock face!" he shouted back trying, for appearance sake, to sound more irritated than he really was. In truth, he had lost track of the time. His mind now moved at a tangent to that flow . . . nearly but not quite parallel to the event cone of the objective world.

We're told that subjectivity, the old enemy of science, becomes a friend and ally down at the level of the quantum. For some say it is the observer who causes the probability wave to collapse. It is the observer who ultimately takes note of the fall of an electron from its shell, as well as the sparrow in the forest. Without the observer, not only is a falling tree without sound, but it is a concept without meaning.

Of late Stan had been wondering ever more about that. Nature, even down to the level of the lowliest quark, seemed to be performing . . . as if for an audience. Arguments raged between adherents of the strong and weak anthropic principles, over whether observers were *required* by the universe, or merely *convenient* to it. But no one, any longer, contended that the audience did not matter.

So much, then, for the debate over what Newton would say if he were snatched out of his time and brought to the present. His clockwork world was as alien to Stan's as that of a tribal shaman. In some ways, the shaman actually had it hands down over prissy old Isaac. At least, Stan imagined, the shaman would probably make better company at a party.

"One minute! Keep your eye on—"

Alex's voice cut off suddenly as automatic timers sent the crash doors hissing shut. Stan shook himself, hauling his mind back, making an earnest effort to concentrate.

It would have been different were there something for him to *do*. But everything was sequenced, even data collection. Later, they would pore over it all and argue. For now, he had only to watch. To observe . . . .

Before man, who performed this role for the universe?

Well, there appears to be no requirement that the observer be conscious, so animals might have served quite well as Nature's audience, without having to be self-aware. And on other worlds, creatures might have existed long before life spilled forth in Earth's gray seas. It isn't necessary that every event, every rock fall, every quantum of light, be appreciated, only that some of it, somewhere, come to the attention of somebody who notices and cares.

"But then," Stan debated himself aloud, "who noticed or cared at the beginning? Before the planets? Before the stars? Who was there in the precreation nothing, to watch the vacuum fluctuation of all time? The one that turned into the Big Bang?"

In his thoughts, Stan answered his own question.

If the universe needs at least one observer in order to exist. Then that is the one compelling argument for the necessity of God.

The counter reached zero. Beneath it, the panel of fused quartz remained black.

Nevertheless. Stan knew something was happening. Deep in the bowels of the chamber, the energy state of raw vacuum was being forced to change.

Uncertainty. That was the lever. Take a cubical box of space with six sides, X centimeters on a side. Does it contain a proton? If so, there is a limit to how much you can know about that proton with any certainty.

You cannot know the proton's momentum more precisely than a given value without destroying your chance of knowing *where* the proton is. Or if you find a way to zoom in on the box until the proton's location is incredibly exact, then your knowledge of its speed and direction plummets to zero.

Another linked pair of values is energy and time. You may think you know how little energy the box contains. (In a vacuum it tends toward zero.) But what about fluctuations? What if bits of matter and energy and antimatter were to suddenly appear and then disappear again? Then the average would still be the same.

Within the chamber, modern trickery was using this loophole to pry at nature's wall, forcing Nothing, reluctantly, to become Something.

He glanced at the mass gauge. It sped up the scale rapidly. Femtograms, picograms, nanograms of matter coalesced in a space too small to measure. Micrograms, milligrams . . . each newly born hadron pair shimmered briefly for a moment too narrow to notice.

Particle and antiparticle tried to flee; they tried to annihilate. But before they could cancel out again, each was drawn instead into a trap of folded space, sucked into a narrow funnel of gravity—a speck much smaller than a proton, with no more personality than a smudge of blackness. The hole continued siphoning these ephemeral creations into its maw.

The singularity began to take on serious weight.

The mass gauge whirled. Kilograms converted into tonnes. Tonnes into kilotons. Boulders, hillocks, mountains poured forth, a torrent flowing into the greedy mouth.

When Stan was young they had taught him—you weren't supposed to be able to make something from nothing.

But nature did allow you to *borrow*.

Alex Lustig's machine borrowed from the vacuum and instantly paid it all to the singularity. That was the secret. Any bank will loan you a million bucks, so long as you want it for only a microsecond.

Megatonnes, gigatonnes . . . Stan had participated in the construction of holes before, singularities more complex and elegant than this one. But never had anyone attempted anything so drastic, so mammoth and momentous.

The pace accelerated.

Something shifted in the sinuses behind his eyes. That warning came moments before the gravimeters began singing a melody of alarm . . . full seconds in advance of the first creaking sounds coming from the reinforced metal walls.

Come on, Alex. You promised me this would not run away.

They had come to this lab, on a distant asteroid, on the off chance that something might go wrong. But Stan wondered how much good that would do if their meddling managed to tear a rent in the fabric of Everything.

There were stories of how some of the scientists on the Manhattan Project had shared this fear . . . that the demon they were releasing was no mere monster—no thing that could be caged and used, for well or ill—but an instant conflagration, something uncontrollable.

What if—they had asked—what if the chain reaction does *not* stay restricted to the plutonium, but spreads to iron, to silicon and oxygen. On paper, the idea was absurd. But no one knew for sure until the flash of Trinity, when the first atomic test went off as planned and then, also according to expectation, the fireball died back into little more than a glittering cloud and a terrible stench.

There were those who witnessed the first explosion and sighed with *relief*, that they had *only* invented a bomb.

Now Stan felt that same dread return. What if this process today somehow took off on its own? What if there came a point when the singularity no longer needed Lustig's machine to yank matter out of vacuum? What if the effect carried on and on, with its own momentum?

This time, we might have gone too far.

He felt them now. The tides. And in the quartz window, mediated by three hundred half mirrors, a ghost took shape. It was microscopic, but the colors it shone with were as none he had ever seen before.

The mass scale spun. Stan felt the awful attraction of the thing. Any moment now it was going to reach out and drag down the walls. In a flash, he, the station, the planetoid, would be enfolded into that pinpoint. And even then would it stop?

"Alex!" He shouted as the tides stretched his skin taut. His viscera began migrating toward his throat. Uselessly he braced his feet. "Dammit, you—"

Stan blinked. And his next breath would not come. Time felt suspended.

Then he knew.

It was gone.

Goosebumps shivered in the tidal wake. He looked at the mass gauge. It read zero.

One moment it had been there, the next it had vanished.

Alex Lustig's voice echoed over the intercom. Stan could sense the satisfaction in his voice.

"Right on schedule. Time for a beer. You were about to say something, Stan?"

He searched his memory and somewhere found the trick to breathing again. Stan let out a shuddering sigh.

"I . . ." He tried to lick his lips, but could not wet them. Hoarsely, he tried again.

"I was saying that you had better have something up there stronger than beer to drink. Because I need it."

2.

They tested the chamber in every way imaginable, but there was nothing there. Nothing at all.

For a time, it had contained the mass of a small planet. The black hole had been palpable. Real. Now it was gone.

"They say a gravitational singularity is a tunnel to another place," Stan mused.

"Some people think so." Alex Lustig nodded agreeably. He sat across the table, sharing with Stan the darkened lounge. It was strewn with debris from the celebration. But now the two of them were alone, looking through the impact glass onto the starry panorama of the Outer Belt.

"In practice, such tunnels probably are useless. No one will ever use one for transportation, for instance."

"That's not what I meant." Stan shook his head. He poured another shot of whiskey. "I mean, how do we know that hole we created hasn't popped into space somewhere else, perhaps to become a hazard for some other poor bastards?"

Alex shook his head. He looked amused.

"That's not how it works, Stan. The singularity we made today was special. We caused it to grow too fast . . . past the threshold where our universe could contain it. We're used to envisioning a black hole—even a micro–black hole—as something like a *funnel*, a deep pit in the fabric of space. But in this case, that fabric rebounded, folded over, sealed over the breach. The hole is simply *gone*, Stan."

"I know that." Stan felt tired and bleary, but he'd be damned if he'd let this young hotshot patronize him. "I know all causality links with our universe have been severed. There is no connection with the thing anymore.

"But still I wonder. Where did it *go?*"

There was a momentary silence. Then Alex replied.

"That's the wrong question, Stan. A better way of putting it would be—what has the singularity we made *become?*"

Stan turned to look at his colleague. Alex's mood had changed again. The young genius now had that look in his eyes again—the philosophical one.

"What do you mean?" Stan asked.

"I mean that the hole and all the mass we poured into it now 'exists' in its own pocket universe. That universe will never share any overlap or contact with our own. It will be a cosmos unto itself . . . now and forever."

There seemed no point in saying anything more after that. For a while, the two of them sat quietly. Finally, Alex excused himself and went off to seek his bed.

3.

Stan played with his friends, the numbers. He rested very still, and used a mental pencil to write them against the window. Equations stitched across the Milky Way. It did not take him long to see that Alex was right.

What they had done today was to create something from nothing, and then exile that something away again. Probably, to Alex and the others, that was that. The accounts all balanced. What had been borrowed was repayed. At least as far as *this* universe of matter and energy was concerned.

But something *was* different, dammit! Before, there had been virtual fluctuations in the vacuum. Now, *somewhere*, a tiny cosmos had been born.

And now Stan Goldman remembered something else. Something called "inflation."

Inflation . . .

Some theorists maintain that our own universe began as a very, very big fluctuation in the emptiness of all emptiness. And in that intense narrow instant, dense mass and energy burst forth to expand.

Only there was nowhere near enough mass to account for what we now see . . . enough to later make up all the stars and galaxies. "Inflation" is the term they use for that weird mathematical trick . . . a small bang leveraged itself into a Big Bang.

Stan watched the equations unfold upon his mental blackboard, and came to see.

Of course. The inflation was no accident. It was a natural result of the lesser creation. Our universe had its start in a tiny, compressed ball of matter no heavier than . . . no heavier than . . .

Stan felt his heart beat.

No heavier than the "pocket cosmos" we created today.

He breathed. That meant that somewhere, completely out of touch or contact, their innocent experiment might have . . . must have . . . initiated a beginning. A universal beginning.

Fiat lux. Let there be light.

"Oh, my God," he said, sitting there quietly, and he remained completely unsure which of a thousand ways he meant it.

THE FOUR FORCES

ESSAY BY
SHELDON LEE GLASHOW
SPECULATION BY
GREGORY BENFORD

THE FORCES OF NATURE
SHELDON LEE GLASHOW
HARVARD UNIVERSITY

*The more success
the quantum theory has,
the sillier it looks.*
Albert Einstein, 1912

FOUR FORCES

NEWTON'S THIRD LAW SHOWS HOW THE REST OF THE UNIverse affects the motion of a body of mass M. F is the applied force and A is the body's response, its acceleration. F = MA, what could be simpler? When no forces act, a body moves in a fixed direction at fixed speed. Otherwise, as for Earth in orbit or Newton's falling apple, the force of gravity plays its role and the motions are more complex. Newton's universal theory of gravitation offered an explanation of this force that survived for centuries, until it was superseded by Einstein's even better theory. But there are many other forces besides gravity: of the wind, the tide, electricity, magnetism, rivers, muscles, earthquakes, *ad infinitum.*

Physicists seek to explain all of Nature's forces in terms of the simplest possible beginnings. In this quest, we have been remarkably successful. With our present theory, all observed phenomena can be reduced, in principle though certainly not in practice, to the operations of four seemingly distinct and irreducible forces: gravity, electromagnetism, and the strong and weak nuclear forces. Even so, we are not entirely satisfied. Our goal is to reduce the number to only one ultimate and unifying force from which the others spring, much like the avatars of Vishnu. Today's four-force theory is only a base station for the final assault.

Gravity ordains the motions of large bodies. It holds our galaxy of billions of stars together and keeps planet Earth firmly in orbit about the sun, putting the seas where they belong and maintaining the integrity of the ocean of life-giving air about us. Gravity provides us with a home, but we are not ourselves gravitational creatures. Astronauts and cosmonauts showed that humans can work and play in a gravity-free environment. Someday, men and women may colonize space to breed and thrive in free fall. Of course, they would have to invent sports other than baseball, football and tennis, which depend more on the force of gravity than we do.

We of Earth are *in* gravity by accident of birth, but we are not *of* gravity. Life in all its aspects is an essentially electromagnetic phenomenon. Everything we see, feel, touch, hear or smell results from electromagnetic interactions among electrons and atomic nuclei. Coulomb's law describes the electric force between charged bodies that binds electrons to nuclei to form electrically neutral atoms. Chemistry is the study of the interplay among these atoms that produces molecules. Chemical forces result from the electromagnetic interactions among many electrons and nuclei following the rules of quantum mechanics. So also for material science, fluid dynamics, solid-state physics, and biology. Gravity explains how I am held to the ground, and electromagnetism explains why I don't simply fall through the ground. Every spring blossom pushing its way toward the sun displays the conflict between gravity and electromagnetism that led somehow to the evolution and the glory of life on Earth. So why do we need two *more* forces?

The tale starts with the serendipitous discoveries of radioactivity in 1896 and of the atomic nucleus in 1911. According to Abraham Pais: "Nuclear physics began with a nucleus without neutrons, beta decay without neutrinos. Matter was made of protons and electrons. There were neither weak nor strong interactions. In the beginning there was only electromagnetism. And, of course, there was gravity." Two distinct nuclear forces are needed to explain the existence and properties of atomic nuclei.

For most purposes, the atomic nucleus can be regarded as a tiny and structureless body bearing mass and electric charge. Yet, from the time of its discovery, few scientists thought of the nucleus as an elementary particle. The discovery of isotopes of atoms showed that there are far more nuclear species than there are chemical elements. How could so many different things all be elementary? Each kind of atomic nucleus is characterized by two integers: its atomic number or electric charge, and its atomic mass relative to hydrogen. Lord Rutherford christened the lightest nucleus, that of hydrogen, the *proton*, and he and his contemporaries believed that nuclei were made up of protons and electrons. In this unsatisfactory picture, electrons play two conflicting roles: they orbit the nucleus to complete the structure of the atom, and they are themselves nuclear constituents.

Things changed in 1932 with the discovery of a new nuclear constituent, the neutron. There are no electrons inside the nucleus after all. It is made up of neutrons and protons: its atomic number being the number of constituent protons, its atomic weight the total number of neutrons and protons. Simple!

What force could hold protons and neutrons tightly bound together as a tiny nucleus? Electromagnetism hardly affects electrically neutral neutrons, and it causes the protons in a nucleus to repel rather than attract one another.

Gravity, while it does provide an attractive force, is 40 powers of 10 too feeble. Another fundamental force is needed: a strong nuclear force to act as nuclear glue, to provide a short-range attraction among neutrons and protons.

Soon after natural radioactivity was discovered, physicists saw that it came in three varieties: alpha, beta, and gamma. In the alpha variety (called alpha decay), a parent nucleus emits a helium nucleus to become a lighter daughter nucleus. In gamma decay, an "excited" nucleus emits a high-energy photon or "gamma ray." Both processes were eventually understood as consequences of the electromagnetic and strong nuclear forces. Beta decay was the holdout.

A nucleus vulnerable to beta decay spits out an energetic electron in its act of transmutation, thereby posing two serious problems. The nucleus is made of neutrons and protons held together by the strong force. *There are no electrons in the nucleus to be emitted!* The second problem has to do with the law of conservation of energy, the physicist's first commandment. In beta decay, some of the available energy mysteriously vanishes, in seeming violation of this law. Wolfgang Pauli offered a daring resolution to the puzzle. He argued that *two* particles are emitted by a nucleus that beta decays: an electron together with a ghostly neutrino. The energy crisis is solved, since energy is shared by these two particles. Sometimes the electron is awarded a large share of the energy, sometimes only a small share. The invisible neutrino carries off the remainder.

Pauli was right, except that his neutrino turned out not to be quite so invisible as he thought. Today, beams of high-energy neutrinos are routinely produced and detected at accelerator laboratories. Neutrinos coming from nuclear reactors, from the sun, and even from 1987's new supernova have been "seen" by experimenters. My colleagues and I have suggested that the time may come when neutrino beams will be used to explore the interior of the earth to search for hidden deposits of minerals or fossil fuels. Gigantic particle accelerators, mobile and deployed at sea, will rove the earth in search of oil, proving the technological relevance of today's abstract and impractical discipline.

We know that the process of beta decay transforms one of the neutrons in a radioactive nucleus into a proton. At the same time, an energetic electron and neutrino spring out of the nucleus. These particles were simply not there beforehand. They were *created* by the action of the weak nuclear force, the fourth and last of the fundamental forces.

Each of the four forces plays a key role in the drama of life on earth. The strong force lets protons and neutrons bind together to form atomic nuclei. Electromagnetism holds electrons within the atom and lets atoms combine to form molecules, mice, men, and mountains. Gravity keeps our feet to the ground and guides Spaceship Earth in her orbit. The weak force plays its role offstage. It lets the sun and other stars burn hydrogen in their nuclear furnaces. Without the weak force, stars could not shine and all the matter of the universe would be in its pristine form. Our splendid planet, should it exist at all, would be a frigid and lifeless ball of pure hydrogen.

TOWARD A THEORY

Since the 1930s, scientists have known of the four forces and have believed that all the phenomena of nature ultimately depend upon these forces and no others. No mysterious astrological influences of the stars and planets affect our fate. A so-called vital force, once invoked to explain the mystery of life, has not been a serious scientific concept for a century. With the discovery of DNA and the emergence of molecular biology, we are close to unraveling some of nature's most guarded secrets: how a fertilized egg becomes a baby, how to undo a genetic flaw, how we think. All of biology, chemistry, cosmology, geology, and the other sciences result from the complex interplay of these four forces acting upon the subatomic constituents of matter. Knowing this, of course, doesn't solve the problems faced by the geologist, the psychologist, or the plumber. Knowing the rules of chess doesn't make one a grandmaster, either. But it helps!

Merely to identify the four forces of nature is not nearly enough. The physicist demands a precise mathematical framework from which he can accurately predict the effects of the forces and explain the wondrous spectacles of nature. The first such framework was Newton's universal theory of gravitation. Dealing with just one of the four forces, it nevertheless permitted very precise calculations: of eclipse times, of the motions of planets, and, lately, of the trajectories of intercontinental ballistic missiles. However, Newton's theory was wrong. Einstein devised a far more appealing and mathematically elegant vision of gravity, the general theory of relativity. Its numerical predictions differ only very slightly from those of its predecessor under ordinary conditions, but the differences are observed and Einstein's theory is confirmed.

The next great success dealt with electromagnetism. Maxwell's theory, developed in the midnineteenth century, provided a consistent and unified description of electricity and magnetism. It identified light as an electromagnetic wave and predicted the existence of other forms of electromagnetic radiation, such as radio waves, discovered in 1888, and X rays, discovered in 1896. Successful as it was, Maxwell's theory was wrong when applied to atoms. For example, one might think of the atom as a minute solar system where the electrical attraction between nucleus and electrons plays the role of gravity, but such an atom would be good for nothing. If it followed Maxwell's laws, the atom would radiate light, and in no time at all its electrons would fall into the nucleus.

Nineteenth-century physicists didn't know the rules, neither of quantum mechanics nor of the special theory of relativity. They had yet to discover that light could behave like a particle (the *photon*) or a wave, and that the same is true of an electron or a proton. They did not realize that the position and the speed of a body cannot both be known to arbitrary precision, that no body can exceed the velocity of light, that energy and mass are as intercovertible as dollars and yen. They would take a quantum leap into the twentieth century.

Quantum mechanics and special relativity are the two great pillars upon which rests our present understanding of the microworld. Ironically, their characteristic effects are practically unobservable in the everyday world. Relativity reveals itself only at speeds approaching that of light, and a jet aircraft travels at a mere millionth of that speed. Quantum effects are usually relevant only for very tiny systems like molecules, atoms, and their parts. Elementary particles may be confused as to whether they are particles or waves, but not falling pebbles or the ripples they produce in a pond. The failure of meteorologists to predict tomorrow's weather has little to do with Heisenberg's uncertainty principle.

Paul Dirac made a giant step toward a theory of electromagnetism that is compatible with both relativity and quantum mechanics. In 1930, he devised his famous equation describing the behavior of an electron in the presence of electric and magnetic fields. He discovered a curious spin-off of his arranged marriage between relativity and quantum mechanics: his equation demanded the existence of antimatter. Dirac deduced that there must exist in nature a particle just like the electron but with opposite electric charge. Dirac's predicted positron was observed in 1932. Its discovery was one of the greatest early triumphs of the newly born theory of quantum electrodynamics (QED). (Many other forms of antimatter have since been observed, including antiprotons, antineutrons, and even some antinuclei.)

Serious problems remained. Sometimes QED theory yielded infinite, and hence meaningless, results. Small effects observed in the laboratory could not be calculated correctly. The theory was polished and perfected by Julian Schwinger, Richard Feynman, and others. By the end of the 1940s, QED had emerged as a consistent and predictive framework for the interactions among electrons, positrons, and photons. Today, several of its predictions have been verified to a precision of ten decimal places. QED became a paradigm for the description of the other forces of nature.

Feynman introduced a simple pictorial language for the workings of QED. The theory deals with three types of particles: electrons, positrons and photons. In Feynman's notation, an electron moving from one site to another is denoted by an arrow going from left to right. An arrow going from right to left denotes a positron. A wavy line denotes a photon. A system involving lots of these particles moving in various directions and speeds can be depicted in terms of a complicated array of such lines, the primitive ingredients of Feynman diagrams.

So far, nothing interesting can happen: each and every particle simply moves along its own linear trajectory. The stage is set, but the action has not yet begun. A mechanism must be introduced to describe the forces, collisions, and interactions among the particles. Amazingly, everything that can possibly happen to our system of particles can be reduced to a deceptively simple interplay among Feynman's lines. (See Figure 1.) There is a vertex into which one arrow enters and from which one arrow leaves, and a wavy line emerges. It is the primitive mechanism for change, the root of all electric and magnetic forces, the "fundamental act of becoming" of QED. Depending upon how it is oriented, the diagram can represent any of the following: emission of a photon by an electron; absorbtion of a photon by an electron; emission of a photon by a positron; absorbtion of a photon by a positron; creation of an electron-positron pair by a photon; or annihilation of an electron-positron pair into a photon.

Figure 1. The fundamental act of QED. The broken straight path is a charged particle; the wavy line represents a photon. (Credit: Sheldon Lee Glashow)

Ironically, none of these six avatars of the fundamental act of becoming can take place as a real physical process. Each of them would violate the laws of conservation of energy and momentum. The massless photon, for example, cannot permanently transform itself into a pair of massive particles. But quantum mechanics allows departures from these laws over very short time periods. According to Heisenberg's uncertainty principle, there are fluctuations of energy given by Planck's constant divided by the time interval. A photon *can* become an electron-positron pair, but not for longer than 10^{-21} seconds. Thus, the fundamental act may enjoy a fleeting and transient "reality" as a part of a more complex but observable physical process.

Realizable physical processes are obtained by iterations of the fundamental act. Consider, for example, two electrons that exchange a single photon. (See Figure 2.) The diagram in Figure 2 is made up of two fundamental acts and describes the scattering of one electron by another. This is the Feynman diagram of the process that produces Coulomb's force of electrostatic repulsion

Figure 2(a,b). Two pathways for a collision between two electrons in which virtual photons are exchanged. (Credit: Sheldon Lee Glashow)

between any two electrons. The exchange of several photons leads to tiny corrections to Coulomb's law at very short distances.

A more complex diagram involving three fundamental acts (see Figure 3) shows a collision between a photon and an electron leading to the creation of an electron-positron pair. We say that electromagnetism is "mediated" by the exchange of photons between electrons and positrons. These "virtual" photons generate electromagnetic forces and can also lead to the creation or destruction of real particles.

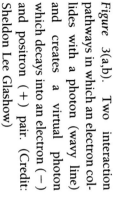

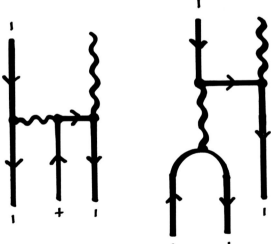

Figure 3(a,b). Two interaction pathways in which an electron collides with a photon (wavy line) and creates a virtual photon which decays into an electron (−) and positron (+) pair. (Credit: Sheldon Lee Glashow)

QED, a triumphant quantum theory of electromagnetism, was our model for the construction of an analogous theory of the strong and weak forces. All that was needed was to figure out who the players are: the particles that mediate the nuclear forces, and the basic constituents of matter that exchange these force-producing particles.

Once, it was thought that protons and neutrons really were elementary particles. The strong force was thought to be due to the exchange of "pions" between these "nucleons." But nucleons and pions were joined by innumerable cousins and nephews with a seemingly equal claim to elementary. Dozens, then hundreds, of new "elementary particles" were discovered at accelerator laboratories, their taxonomy recalling the catalog of the Bronx Zoo. In the early 1960s, two points of view competed. Some physicists believed that all these particles were in some sense truly elementary, while others, appalled by the teeming nuclear democracy, insisted on the existence of a small number of basic building blocks and a simple underlying force law.

In 1963, Murray Gell-Mann and George Zweig introduced the notion of quarks. They imagined that all then-known nuclear particles were made up out of just three species (or *flavors*) of quarks, called *up, down,* and *strange.* The force between quarks had to be such as to satisfy the following mysterious and originally inexplicable "quark commandments":

Nucleons and other "baryons" are made of three quarks!
Antibaryons are made of three antiquarks!
Pions and other mesons are made of quark and antiquark!
Individual quarks cannot be isolated!

Gell-Mann's ideas were on the money. Nuclear particles *are* made of quarks, although now we know that there are at least six different quark flavors, each coming in three *colors*. The color force holds quarks inextricably bound together to form the multitude of apparently elementary particles we see. The theory of this force, quantum chromodynamics (QCD), is patterned after quantum electrodynamics. It is the ultimate origin of the strong nuclear force and is an integral part of today's very successful Standard Model describing all of particle physics.

THE STANDARD MODEL

We didn't always believe in atoms. True, the atomic hypothesis demystified the laws of chemical combination, the behavior of gases, the nature of heat, and the beauty of crystals. Nonetheless, many nineteenth-century scientists thought of the atom as merely a useful mathematical construct. After all, no one had seen an individual atom.

So it is for quarks. No one has seen an isolated quark, and if our theory is correct, no one ever will. Individual quarks and the *gluons* that hold them together simply cannot be seen as isolated particles in their own right. They exist only as parts of the particles they make up. Several analogies may make this notion more palatable. A magnet has both a north and a south pole. Break the magnet in two and each fragment will have a north and a south pole. This attempt to isolate a magnetic pole is doomed to failure. (Others may succeed: there remains the possibility of finding a new kind of elementary particle bearing just one magnetic pole. Physicists have been seeking such a magnetic monopole for decades.) In the same way, a piece of string has two ends, never just one. So it is that each species in our elementary particle bestiary is made up of three quarks, three antiquarks, or a quark and an antiquark.

One trouble with the quarks as originally proposed was that they didn't seem to satisfy the Pauli exclusion principle, a primal law dictating that no two quarks (or other so-called *fermions*, such as electrons and protons) may occupy the same quantum state at the same time. Yet particles were found that consisted of three identical quarks spinning in the same direction. This apparent violation of Pauli's principle was resolved when it was realized that quarks possess a hidden attribute. Each flavor of quark comes in three varieties called *colors*. Gell-Mann's original three quarks became nine. Baryons are made of three quarks, one in each of the colors. The solution generated new problems. Why, for example, do we not observe particles made of three quarks of the same color, or two of one color and one of another?

All these problems solved themselves when physicists identified color as the arena in which QCD operates. In the fundamental act of quantum chromodynamics, a quark of one color emits a *gluon* to become a quark of another color. In the analogy with QED, gluons play the role of photons while quark color plays the role of electric charge. A glaring difference between the two theories is the fact that there are eight varieties (or colors) of gluon while there is but one kind of photon.

The force law associated with QCD consequently differs radically from Coulomb's law. At large distances the force between two quarks does not fall with the inverse square of the separation between them. It does not fall at all! It remains strong at large distances, thereby trapping the quark within the nuclear particle of which it is a part. Conversely, the color force becomes weak at distances very much smaller than the size of the proton. Thus, the three quarks within a proton can move about quite freely within their subnuclear prison, but they are absolutely unable to escape.

Today, we are convinced that all the hundreds of seemingly elementary baryons and mesons are made of quarks held together by gluons. The proton, for example, is simply the lowest energy state of a system of two up quarks and one down quark. Many other particles or states are produced when the constituent quarks wiggle or jiggle in one or another way. Not only does QCD make the glue to hold quarks together, but it explains the forces that act between mesons and baryons. Thus, the sciences of "elementary particle" physics and of nuclear physics have been reduced to the quantum chromodynamical interactions among quarks and gluons—just like the sciences of chemistry and atomic physics were once reduced to the quantum electrodynamical interactions among electrons and nuclei. So much for the strong force!

But how does a neutron turn itself into a proton in the process of beta decay? To complete our theoretical description of particle physics, we need a correct and consistent theory of the weak force. This was the thesis problem assigned to me by Julian Schwinger over three decades ago. Julian noticed certain suggestive similarities between the weak and electromagnetic forces. He believed that it might be possible to construct a unified theory describing them both. He was right, but the birth of the electroweak theory was preceded by a long and arduous labor.

As photons are to electromagnetism and as gluons are to the strong force, the electrically charged particles W^+ and W^- are to the force responsible for beta decay. These once hypothetical particles are intermediaries of the weak force. Unlike photons and gluons, however, these particles are very heavy. They weigh almost a hundred times more than protons. This makes them very hard to produce in the laboratory. It also makes it very difficult to understand how an analogy between the weak and electromagnetic forces can be implemented, since the photon is a massless and neutral particle with little in common with the W particle. The whole story is far too long to tell here, for it is intimately linked to our understanding of the microworld, to the birth of the universe, and to my own career as a physicist. Indeed, the full story would belie the title of this essay, for in today's theory the weak and electromagnetic forces are said to be unified, and four would become three. Yet, from another point of view, the four has become five, or even six! Much remains to be discovered before the end of the story can be written.

The electroweak synthesis predicted the existence of a second variety of the weak force, one mediated by a heavy and electrically neutral Z^0 particle. The new force is not an agent for the decay of any known particle. Its most striking effect is to permit neutrinos to scatter from matter while maintaining their integrity as neutrinos. At first, few physicists took this theory seriously. After all, the predicted "neutral current" effects had not been observed. (The truth was that no one had bothered to look for them!) More importantly, the theory seemed to be beset by infinities, just as QED had been in its early days. Then, in 1971, a young Dutch graduate student, Gerard 't Hooft, proved that the theory made sense after all, and the race for the discovery of the new kind of weak force began. Two years later, the predicted neutral currents were detected at the European Laboratory for Particle Physics, (CERN). Particle physics broke away from nuclear physics at about the time the laboratory was founded. It still retains its original acronym even though it never was the European Center for Nuclear Research. Conservative Swedes became convinced of the validity of the electroweak theory by 1979, when they awarded the Nobel Prize to Steven Weinberg, Abdus Salam, and me for our contributions to it.

A few years later, the elusive weak intermediaries, W^+, W^-, and Z^0, were produced and observed for the first time ever at the then world's largest accelerator at CERN. These particles behaved exactly as the theory said they should. For their triple experimental triumph, Carlo Rubbia and Simon Van der Meer won their very own Nobel Prizes. (See Figure 4.)

Ponderous W's and Z's are linked to massless photons by the electroweak theory. In today's cold and crystalline universe, the profound underlying symmetry between weak and electromagnetic forces is hard to recognize. It wasn't always like that. In the earliest moments of the big bang, when our infant universe was only microseconds old, it was hot beyond conception and burning bright, and the symmetry between the forces was manifest. Not since then has the weak force behaved in any way like electromagnetism—except in the tiny subnuclear world made accessible to us at the largest particle accelerators.

When a crystal forms out of a molten salt, symmetry breaking takes place:

When a crystal forms out of a molten salt, symmetry breaking takes place: While the original liquid is isotropic, certain directions in space are somehow singled out to become the crystal's axes as it solidifies. The rotational symmetry of the liquid must be spontaneously broken. In an analogous manner the symmetry between weak and electromagnetic forces was broken as the universe cooled down. The "direction" associated with the photon and its electromagnetic effects has been distinguished from the other directions, whose associated particles developed large masses. Indeed, the weakness of the weak force simply reflects the large masses of its intermediaries.

Traces of the underlying symmetry must remain. Some of these were the experimental results that led us to formulate the electroweak theory. For example, the weak force, like electromagnetism, is *universal*: it displays exactly the same intrinsic strength in beta decay, pion decay, and other observed processes. But the biggest clue remains to be found. According to our theory, for symmetry breaking to take place a new and unobserved particle must exist. It is named in honor of Peter Higgs, the Scots physicist who originated the notion in 1964. The Higgs boson is the sole survivor of a family of particles that thrived in the early universe. Survivor is hardly the word: the Higgs boson is a heavy and very short-lived particle, like its cousins the W and Z. To see this particle, and to study the force that *it* mediates (the fifth force?), we've got to make it at a giant particle accelerator, one larger than anything in existence. This is a primary goal for the superconducting supercollider that American scientists hope to build.

Quantum chromodynamics and the electroweak theory are the ingredients of the Standard Model, which provides a correct, complete, and consistent description of all known particle phenomena. Many experimental tests have been performed over the past 15 years, and the Standard Model has passed every single one. We seem to be stuck with a theory that works!

UNSOLVED PROBLEMS

Why don't particle physicists simply close up shop? We seem to have solved all the problems we set out to solve. Couldn't we save a lot of money and hard work by declaring our challenge met and our discipline dead? The trouble is that our theory really isn't good enough to solve some of the new puzzles that have arisen. And there remains Einstein's dream: a theory of physics that includes a consistent description of gravity along with all of the particle forces.

So far, we have direct evidence for the existence of five quark flavors: up and down, charmed and strange, and bottom. Our theory demands that quark flavors come in pairs, so we are absolutely sure that there exists at least one more flavor to be mated with the bottom quark: the elusive *top*. (Chances are that the top quark will soon be produced and observed by scientists working at the tevatron collider near Chicago, today's world's biggest accelerator.) In addition to the quarks, two obese relatives of the electron have shown up in the laboratory: the muon and the tau lepton. Each of these particles is associated with its own type of neutrino. This makes a total of 12 fundamental particles of the type called *fermions*, or particles which satisfy the Pauli exclusion principle. These could be called the "matter particles."

Other particles are exchanged between matter particles to produce forces. They are photons, gluons, W particles, Z particles, and the still undiscovered Higgs boson. These are the five fundamental "force particles." Generically called *bosons*, they are particles that do not satisfy the Pauli exclusion principle.

The search for the Higgs boson is the principal outstanding challenge to high-energy physics, and it has a special place in our theory as the spoor of symmetry breaking. When the universe was young and hot, all of our elementary particles were totally massless. The Higgs boson, as the agent of symmetry breaking, is ultimately responsible for the origin and the observed values of the masses of all the particles we see. How can we be satisfied until this beast is caught and catalogued and its properties known?

Count them up, and you find that there are at least 17 really elementary particles in our bestiary. Other methods of counting yield even larger numbers: Counting color, we get 36. Counting antiparticles and spin states, we get an astonishing 118. But even 17 is too large a number to take seriously. The ancient Greeks, for example, would settle for no more than four basic building blocks of matter. I, myself, would prefer just one.

Not only are there too many particles in our picture, but there are simply too many fundamental numbers—like the strengths of the various forces and the values of the masses of the particles. Again, about 17 of these numbers are simply not calculable from our theory. They have to be measured in the laboratory. Think of the microworld as a kind of universal television set with 17 knobs with which to adjust the color, brightness, tint, contrast, and even the channel. (Stay away from the power switch!) Each adjustment yields a slightly different version of reality. Things would not be so different, for example, if the muon were twice as heavy as it is. Muons don't seem to play much of a role in the workings of the world. Or so it seems.

But surely things must be just as they are in this best (and only) possible world. The Big TV is factory perfect and should have no knobs on it at all. Its creation was both rational and knowable. There must be a good reason for the proton to be 1,836 times heavier than the electron. At least, this is the majority opinion: a few physicists take the contrary view, that there are hordes of differently adjusted universes, a random one of which is ours. Most of us reject this possibility and feel that there must exist a better theory that tells us what particles exist and why they have the masses and other properties that they do. The Standard Model, with all its paraphernalia, simply must emerge from a unique and fundamental theory of supernal power and beauty. So we believe.

MORE PARTICLES, MORE FORCES

Dmitri Ivanovich Mendeleev organized all of the known chemical elements in a periodic table with seven columns. Three empty spaces in the table corresponded to undiscovered elements, and Mendeleev predicted what their properties would be. When his predictions were confirmed, his table became a central part of chemistry. Decades later an unexpected new element, argon, was found to be a 1 percent constituent of air. The discovery of several other "rare gases" followed soon afterward. Poor Dmitri insisted that argon could not possibly be a new chemical element since there was no place for it in his table. Reluctantly, and in the face of overwhelming experimental evidence, he was forced to make room for the new elements with an added eighth column. Perhaps there is a lesson to be learned for today.

Known matter particles can be gathered together into a kind of periodic table of quarks and leptons. (See Figure 4.) It has only four columns, each containing particles with identical interactions but different masses. Each row describes a "family" of quarks and leptons. The top row includes all the particles participating in the everyday world. The second and third families, the fruit of four decades of scientific endeavor, are particles whose ultimate relevance is not yet established. Is there a fourth family waiting to be found? We do not know, but the next generation of particle accelerators can answer this question. Are there missing columns consisting of new particles lying beyond our present vision? Have we fooled ourselves into thinking that all of nature's tricks have been exposed? Can anyone believe that the top quark and the Higgs boson are the only particles waiting to be discovered? The only way to find out is to look, and the only way we know of looking is to build bigger accelerators. These devices are cheaper and safer than missile systems or aircraft carriers, and they will tell us things that we otherwise could never know.

Electric Charge:	-1	$-\frac{1}{3}$	0	$+\frac{2}{3}$
The First Family:	Electron	Down Quark	Electron Neutrino	Up Quark
The Second Family:	Muon (1938)	Strange Quark (1947)	Muon Neutrino (1961)	Charmed Quark (1974)
The Third Family:	Tau Lepton (1975)	Bottom Quark (1977)	Tau Neutrino	Top Quark

Figure 4. The Periodic Table of Quarks and Leptons, showing the twelve matter particles in a regular array. The top quark remains to be observed experimentally.

Are there more forces left to discover? Perhaps an additional unanticipated force, one even weaker than gravity, produces tiny effects that have not yet been perceived. Recent experiments tantalizingly suggest the possible existence of a new subgravitational force, but the data are not yet very convincing. Perhaps more careful measurements will reveal effects that can be explained only in terms of a new force, a force that will wreak havoc with our Standard Model, which leaves no room for big surprises.

Another possibility is the existence of new and strong short-range forces exerting themselves in some unexplored nook of the microworld. *Technicolor* is the physicists' nonce word for this wild idea, but as yet not a shred of data supports the notion. Technicolor was originally proposed as an alternative to the Higgs boson. The superconducting supercollider, when it is built, will tell us which, if either, road nature follows. Meanwhile, three new accelerators have a good chance of spotting something new and exciting: The tevatron has just begun to study collisions at an energy of 2 trillion electron-volts, fully three times larger than have ever been achieved. CERN's large electron-positron collider is scheduled to begin operating on July 14, 1989, the two-hundredth anniversary of the storming of the Bastille. This machine will count the number of particle families and will identify *every* charged particle with a mass less than 50 billion electron-volts, and it has a chance to find the Higgs. Finally, a new type of accelerator is being built in Germany. This machine, called HERA, will study collisions between very energetic beams of electrons and protons: It will be the world's first electron-proton collider. Who knows what it will reveal? No one has ever built such a machine before.

A depressing but unlikely possibility is that no new forces or mystifying particles remain to be found at any future machines. Perhaps the Standard Model will survive intact. How strange we particle physicists be! We are the only scientists who pray that our theories will be falsified so that our heirs may build better ones.

EINSTEIN'S DREAM

What about that one and true "theory of everything"? We've taken a first small step known as *grand unification*, in which all of the elementary particle forces are gathered together into a unified theory of everything but gravity. This concise and elegant synthesis answers many puzzling questions, such as why photons are massless, why quarks and leptons come in families, and why the strong force is so strong. However, it leaves some of the juiciest problems unsolved: It doesn't say how many families there are, nor does it let us compute particle masses. The most striking prediction of the grand unified theory is that all matter must be very slightly radioactive. Thus, diamonds cannot be forever. This prediction has been put to the test in gigantic underground experiments searching for proton decay, one in a salt mine in Ohio, another deep under a mountain in Japan. So far, not one proton has been seen to decay. Unless this disappointing experimental situation changes, it seems we must conclude that our grand unified vision, gorgeous as it is, is mere mirage.

Perhaps we haven't been ambitious enough; perhaps the key to it all lies in a proper understanding of gravity. Find a deeper understanding of this most mysterious force, and all the rest will fall into place. Such a unified field theory was the unfulfilled dream that led Einstein down the Princeton garden path. He failed, but he didn't know as much as we do now. Perhaps the time has come to try again.

Thus far, we have given short shrift to the force of gravity, the force we sense every waking moment of our lives. Surely, it might seem, gravity is the strongest force of all, holding even planets and stars in its sway. True, the gravitational attraction of Earth exerts a very palpable force on our bodies, but what we feel is the effect of a thousand trillion trillion trillion particles acting in concert. The gravitational force exerted by just one subatomic particle upon another is entirely negligible. Gravity is by far the weakest of the known forces. We may require, for mathematical consistency, a quantum theory of gravity in which its force is due to an exchange of so-called *gravitons*. However, gravity is so very weak that its quantum nature simply can never be directly exhibited.

To prove this, let us consider the decay of a neutral pion. This particle, known for half a century, decays quickly into two photons. In principle, it could just as well decay into two gravitons. However, because the gravitational force is so weak, the probability for such a decay scheme is tiny: only one pion out of 10^{72} will suffer such a fate. Even if the entire mass of the Milky Way (all of its hundred billion stars) was magically transformed into zillions of pions, not even one of them would decay into a graviton. And even if an energetic graviton were produced, it could never be detected—it could pass through all the matter in the universe without suffering the tiniest interaction or deflection. The particulate manifestation of gravity, the graviton, is simply not an empirically relevant construct.

Nonetheless, mathematical consistency and logical completeness demand the existence of a quantum theory of gravity. However, until quite recently, there seemed to be an irreconcilable conflict between gravity and quantum theory. The tricks that worked so well for the other forces do not work at all for quantum gravity. Our immensely successful methodology may have reached its limits. Gravity, and the remaining particle puzzles, may force us well beyond our present powerful but limited paradigm. This is the context in which the *superstring* has blossomed, a promising, if still immature, approach to the problems of physics.

The Standard Model treats its fundamental particles as intrinsically point-like systems. Superstring theorists regard this assumption as not only wrong, but as the source of all our difficulties. Particles are not pointlike at all: they are tiny loops of string. Depending on just how the string twists and turns, the loop can appear as a photon, a quark, or any other of our erstwhile elementary particles. In reality, there is only *one* fundamental building block. Neat!

Why is space-time four dimensional? Perhaps it isn't, say the stringers. We can't sense the extra dimensions because they (as many as six of them!) are all curled up into a tiny ball. Theories based on these ideas have had one very great triumph: An apparently consistent quantum theory of gravity simply springs out of the formalism. Wow!

So much for the good news. While the best and the brightest young theoretical physicists have been struggling for years, they may have bitten off more than they can chew. The mathematical complexity of the theory has grown unmanageable: superstring theory depends upon mathematics so novel that it doesn't yet exist. Mathematicians, who thirst for new challenges, are among string theory's most ardent advocates. But there has not yet been much progress on the physics front. In particular, superstring theory has yet to emulate any of the many successes of the Standard Model. The infant theory has been unable to make even a single specific prediction. It is not yet subject to trial by experiment. No one will know whether superstring theory is truly nature's way until some brilliant theorist shows how a tiny superstring can appear to us as a familiar particle, or deduces QCD and the electroweak theory from the power of positive thinking. Nonetheless, it is clear that our aging Standard Model has got to be replaced by a more elaborate high-performance all-terrain vehicle, one with quantum gravity built in from the very start.

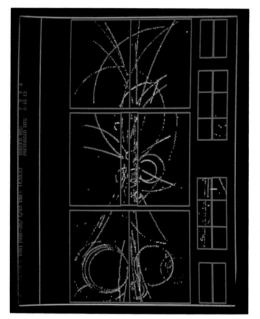

Figure 5. Computer-generated image of a neutral Z boson decay into an electron-positron pair. The Z boson carries the weak force. (Photo credit: CERN)

MOZART ON MORPHINE

GREGORY BENFORD

ILLUSTRATION BY
BOB EGGLETON

As a working hypothesis to explain the riddle of our existence, I propose that our universe is the most interesting of all possible universes, and our fate as human beings is to make it so.

—Freeman Dyson, 1988

All theory, dear friend, is gray,
But the golden tree of life springs ever green.

—Goethe, *Faust*

I READ A FRAGMENT OF GOD'S MIND, DURING THAT SUMMER when he seemed to be trying to stop me.

I realize this is not the usual way such proceedings go, with their pomp and gravity. But please bear with me. I shall try to talk of matters which scientists usually avoid, even though these are crucial to the unspoken rhythms of our trade.

I live in a small community spread before the Pacific like a welcoming grin, thin but glistening in the golden shafts of sunlight. That unrelenting brilliance mocked my dark internal chaos as I struggled with mathematical physics. I worked through the day on my patio, the broad blue of ocean lying with Euclidean grace beyond, perspective taking it away into measureless infinity. Endless descending glare mocked my gnarled equations, their confusion the only stain on Nature.

My habit was to conclude a frustrating day of particle theory by running on the beach. The salt air cleared my mind. The sun hung low and red and I pounded along crisply warm sand, vacantly watching the crumbling, thumping waves. I paid no attention to the small crowd forming up ahead and so when the first shot came it took me completely by surprise.

I saw the teenagers scattering and the scrawny man in his twenties poking the small silvery gun at them, yelling something I couldn't make out. I assumed as an automatic axiom that the gun was loaded with blanks; certainly it wasn't very loud.

The man started swearing at a kid near me, who was moving to my right. I was still doggedly running, so when the second shot came I was just behind the kid and the round went *tsiiip!* by my head.

Not blanks, no. I did the next hundred meters in ten seconds, digging hard

304

into the suddenly cloying sand and turning to look back only once. A third thin splat followed me up the beach but no screams—just more swearing from the skinny man, who was backing up the gray concrete stairs and trying to keep the pack of kids from following him.

From a hundred meters away I watched him fire one last time, not trying to hit anybody now, just holding the gang at bay. Then he turned and ran up onto the street beyond.

I thumped back down the beach amid buzzing spectators. It was evidently a drug deal gone bust. The kids had started jazzing the thin man around and he got mad.

The police caught him on the streets above. I watched them read him his Miranda rights . . . and unbidden, my mind gave me a tiny clue about the equations which I had labored over all day. Just like that.

Churchill once said that there was nothing as exhilarating as being shot at and missed.

Perhaps that explained the spurt in my research through the following week. I found some fresh mathematical tricks, a new conformal transformation. Problems rearranged themselves.

I had been pursuing a model for the universe which did not begin with any assumption about its dimensionality. We are used to our cozy three spatial directions plus ever-flowing time—four dimensions in all. When God made everything, was this choice forced? Could the deep laws governing matter work well in, say, six dimensions? Twenty-six?

The question reeks of arrogance, of course. Just *what* or *who* could force God?

Still, my imagination swept on freely. My pencil scribbled long chains of symbols as I sat on my deck and contemplated the beach below, where that *tssiip!* had flown past.

I interrupted my Muse to fly east and visit my parents on their fiftieth wedding anniversary. Alabama was sultry, the weight of its air somehow reassuring.

If you work in arcane labyrinths, conversations with parents circle around matters in which all are equally ignorant—politics, children, economics. I felt myself falling away from the glide of cool mathematics that, I knew, underlay everything.

I went with my father to the anniversary reception after that morning's church service. It was a moist, sunny day. I lazily breathed in the pine scent as my father pulled up at a stop sign. He started off and something darted in the corner of my vision. It was a car that a nearby telephone junction box had hidden from view, coming fast on the right. I yelled, "Dad stop!" as if it were one word. He hit the brake, and the other car smashed into our side.

The windshield cracked into diamondlike shards. Steel jabbed into my head. The pain did not register, but blood gushed down my face.

There was yelling and a spreading ache in my temple. My father pulled me across the seat, brushing glass to the floor. Shakily I stood on the tarry road and helped my father tear my shirt off. We used it to stop the bleeding. I kept saying "... like a stuck pig ..." in wonder at the cascade of blood that had soaked me.

The tight knot at my brow was a fist holding my life in. I leaned against the car and felt light, airy. I studied the geometry of the accident and saw that if my father had not stomped down on the brake they would have come smack in on my side of the car and probably right through the door. "It was *that* close," my father murmured to himself.

The people in the other car were badly shaken up. In the hushed moments following the big banging surprise, facts assembled like congealing particles. The other driver wasn't wearing shoes. Her car was borrowed. She had broken her hand. She sat in a red clay ditch, rocking and moaning.

My father took it all quite mildly, but my ears rang with alarm. I could smell the pine trees even stronger now. The broad-bladed grass, the azaleas, bright yellow flowers—ingenious implements of a propagating, abundant nature. This impossibly sharp world, and my persistence in it, demanded equally hard-edged explanation.

The vexing riddle of that waning summer stemmed from my reductionist impulse. I share it with all physicists.

The spirit of Einstein moves us still: we try to find the unifying principles behind the universe by looking for symmetries hidden in the laws that govern matter. The greatest scientists are unifiers—Newton, Einstein—and, indeed, nature often begins its grand works with a simple, unified start. In the beginning, a homogeneous ocean somehow differentiated into cells and microlife, predators and prey. A common ancestry of apes managed to break their smooth symmetry into such as we, with our complicated symbol-scribbling languages and cultures. It is a recurring theme: diversity from unity.

Our bias is to seek that primordial unity. We hope that all of nature once started with just such serene symmetry. A commanding single Law fractured as the universe expanded, splitting the unity, spilling forth the four fragmentary forces we now know.

And what odd forces they are. Gravity pins us to our solitary planet. Electromagnetism brings us light which whispers of far galaxies, of strange cosmologies. Stars glow in the boundless black, fueled by fusing atoms which obey the weak force. And underneath the seeming solidity of matter lurks the strong force, a glue binding nuclei.

I labored to find that single, unified parent force. No laboratory experiment can lead us to it, for the energies demanded must rival those of time's first thin instant. So it is up to argonauts on mathematical seas to chart the shadow curve of that Ur-Law.

Consider in turn the breadth of our universe; then the Earth; then a nucleus; finally, a thin wedge called a superstring. Each step downward in scale is by twenty orders of magnitude. That is how remote our theories have become.

Such smallness preoccupied me then. The image of a tiny wriggling string informed my nights, my dreams.

I sometimes awoke, my head still aching from the accident. I was uncomfortably aware that my mind was cradled in a shell of bone, my precarious reason hostage to blunt forces. Intelligence was besieged.

A friend of mine once referred to our brains as "meat computers." She was involved in the study of artificial intelligence, and as the aches slowly ebbed I often thought of her coarse, but perhaps true, remark. Yet my own head still bowed over the intricacies of theory.

In late September I was making my final plans to go to a conference in India when I developed stomach pains. My children had the same symptoms, a standard flu that was going around. I stayed in bed a few days and expected it to go away. I was doing pretty well, running a little fever, though the pain had moved down somewhat.

I went into the university for half a day to see my thesis students. Around noon I was sitting in my office when the pain got much worse. I couldn't stand up. I called a doctor near the university and made an appointment and waited out the pain. It subsided and I began to think life would resume its linear logic. But in the doctor's office I showed an elevated white blood count and a fever and some dehydration. When she poked my right side a lance drove through me.

She thought it might be appendicitis and that I should go to an emergency room nearby. I thought she was making too much of it and wanted something for my mild pain. I wanted to go to the hospital near my home, where I knew the doctors. She called an ambulance but I was pumped up by then and went out and got into my car and drove very fast, skating down the canyon road. The bleached hills lay beneath a hammering sun.

It was the real thing, of course. Soon enough I watched the fluorescent lights glide by as the anesthetist pushed me into the operating room. He said I must have a high tolerance for pain because the appendix was obviously swollen and sensitive. I asked him how quickly the drugs took effect. He said "Well . . .", and then I was staring at the ceiling of my hospital room and it was half a day later.

I had a good night, slept well. In the morning my doctor told me her suspicions had been right—that when the pain got bad in my office it had been the appendix bursting. By the time they opened me up the stuff had spread. I asked to see the appendix and they brought it up to me later, a red lumpy thing with white speckles all over the top of it. I asked what the speckles were and the aide said casually, "Oh, that's gangrene. It's riddled with the stuff."

The doctor said there was a sixty percent chance the antibiotics would not take out the gangrene that had spread throughout my lower abdomen. Mathematical probability carries little weight in the psyche. Of course I figured I would be in the lucky forty percent.

By the early hours of the next morning I knew I was wrong. A fever swarmed over me. I had stood up and walked around in the afternoon, but when the night nurse tried it with me again I couldn't get to my feet. I was throwing up vile sour stuff and the orderly was talking to me about inserting some tubes and then the tube was going in my nose and down my throat and a bottle nearby was filling with brown bile, lots of it, a steady flow.

I couldn't sleep, even with the drugs. There was talk about not giving me too many drugs for fear of suppressing my central nervous system too much. This didn't make much sense to me—but then, little did.

Events ran together. The doctor appeared and said the antibiotics weren't working, my white count was soaring. A man came by and reminded me to use the plastic tube with a ball in it that the nurse had given me the day before. You blew into it and kept a ball in the air to exercise your general respiration. It seemed dumb to me, I could breathe fine, but I did it anyway and asked for some breakfast. I wasn't getting any. They fed me from an array of bottles going into my IV, and wouldn't give me more than ice chips to suck on.

Quick, watery, white-smocked beings surrounded me. My fever climbed a degree every two hours and my wife patted my brow with a cool cloth and I wanted some food. I didn't see how they could expect a man to get better if they didn't feed him. All they did was talk too fast and add more bottles to the antibiotic array. They started oxygen but it didn't clear my head any. My IV closed off from vascular shock. A man kept punching my arms with needles, trying to find a better way in. Carefully and reasonably I told him to knock it off. And get me something to eat.

They tilted me back so the doctor could put a subclavial tube in close to my heart. It would monitor the flow there and provide easy access for the IV. Then I was wheeling beneath soft cool fluorescents, into a big quiet room. The intensive care unit, a large voice said. I lay for a time absolutely calm and restful and realized that I was in trouble. The guy with the breathing tube and ball was gone, but the nurses made me do it anyway, which still struck me as dumb because I wasn't going to stop breathing, was I? If they would just give me some food I would get better.

After the gusts of irritation passed I saw in a clear moment that I was enormously tired. I hadn't slept in the night. The tubes in my nose tugged at me when I moved. They had slipped a catheter into me, surprisingly painless, and I felt wired to the machines around me, no longer an independent entity but rather a collaboration. If I lay still with my hands curled on my chest I could rest, maybe, and if I could rest I could get through this. So I concentrated on that one irreducible quantum of fact, and on how blissful it felt after the nurse gave me another injection of morphine, on how I could just forget about the world and let the world worry about me instead.

I woke in the evening. I had been dreaming of giant cylinders and pyramids rolling and thumping on a cool blue plain, enormous geometric buildings jostling merrily on the ocean below my patio.

The next morning my doctor startled me awake. It was as though I had come in at midsentence in someone else's life. I was better. They had called in more exotic antibiotics, which had stopped the fever's rise, leveling it off at 105 degrees. But I was still in danger and the next day would be crucial.

The room still swarmed with prickly light. My wife came, wearing a peasant dress and pony tail, echoing her artsy college days. I made a joke about this which neither she nor the nurses could understand. At death's gateway there was nothing to do but wrap scraps of tattered wit about us.

She had brought my Sony and a case of tapes. They would shut out the hospital, which was real again, with its bustling all-hours brightness like an airport, its constant rhythm of comings and goings. I wanted to skate on that blue plain of my dreams; something waited there.

I had the nurse put the headphones on me and start a tape. She looked at me oddly and I wondered if I was making any sense. The swirl of a rondo swept me away.

They had me on demand morphine. Every hour or so I called for an injection and lifted off the sheets and spun through airy reaches, Mozart on morphine, skimming along the ceilings of rooms where well-dressed people looked up at me with pleased expressions, interrupted as they dined on opulent plates of veal and cauliflower and rich pungent sauces, rooms where I would be again sometime, among people whom I knew but had no time for now, since I kept flying along softly lit yellow ceilings, above crimson couches and sparkling white tablecloths and smiles and mirth. Toward the blue geometries. Mozart had understood all this and had seen in this endless gavotte a way to loft and sweep and glide, going, to have ample ripe substance without weight.

Physicists don't live in the real world. We have become so decoupled (another physicist's jargon word) that we regard reality's rub as hopelessly crude, an amusing approximation.

From tangible matter we slide easily down to tales of fields and particles. Rubbery, compliant, these fields follow clean differential equations.

Below those lie more profound truths: the symmetry groups which relate fields and particles through deft mathematical twists. Most particle physicists labor in this realm.

But now, I saw, there yawned a deeper level of abstraction: symmetry groups themselves were blunt beings, best seen as states realized in a ten-dimensional space-time. In this larger universe our dull doings in three dimensions, plus time, were as the crawlings of insects.

And still more: superstrings. Their dynamics defined the states possible in that ten-space. The ripple of their motions in that immensely larger universe sent tides lapping into lesser dimensions, wakes spreading like the whorls of passing ocean liners.

That was what I saw in the days that followed. It was all there. Abstractions, yes—but I also felt strumming kinesthetic senses, taking me where the mathematics led. I could tie the superstrings into knots, make of them what I wanted. Unimaginably small, they still had to follow the serene logic of mathematics. I *knew.*

When the doctor took the stitches out a week later she said casually, "Y'know, you were the closest call I've had in a year. Another twelve hours and you would've been gone."

In November I went to India anyway. I hadn't fully recovered, but it seemed important not to let a strange new sense in me, the calm acceptance of mortality, deflect me from life itself.

Without noticing it, I had lost my fear of death. The grave was no longer a fabled place, but rather a dull zone beyond a gossamer-thin partition. Crossing that filmy divider would come in time, but for me it no longer carried a gaudy, supercharged meaning. And for reasons I could not express, many matters seemed less important now, little busynesses. People I knew were more vital to me and everything else was lesser, peripheral.

Except the work. I spent time on the patio, watching the classical space defined by the blue sea.

My calculations took only a few weeks. They have proved successful in the limited ways theory can affect the world. Yes, they do predict the particles found in recent Supercollider experiments. True, they are fully consistent with the four forces we already know. Gravity emerges as a manifestation of events in a ten-dimensional space-time.

One of the deeper implications is that there is another kind of time. In that system, our truncated space-time forms a surface in the more general, superstring space-time. To that world, everything we perceive would seem like the surface of a soap bubble, wobbling in air. The bubble has no edge, no boundary—and so we will never, in that higher coordinate system, plunge through an abrupt juncture.

This implies that time, in the larger sense, is never ending. Of course it is not *our* time, but rather, the duration defined in higher spaces. The existence of this generalized time is perhaps the most startling deduction of the mathematics.

But what does this mean? We search for a completely unified theory, curling the fragmented forces of our hobbled universe into the Ur-Force. Still, even that is just a set of rules and equations.

What is it that breathes fire into the bare mathematics and makes a raw universe for them to describe? Now that we have achieved a unified model, we have in a sense answered the question first posed by the Greeks: *what is the universe?*

My answer is that we experience events in a higher dimension. Our perceived universe is the shadow of a higher realm.

Now we should turn to a grander issue: *why is the universe?* To attack this question is to ask to know the mind of God.

Can we? In comparison with the worldview which emerges from our recent discoveries, our earlier catalog of four forces seems comfy, domesticated. Gravity looms large in the model I have constructed because, though it is the weakest of the four forces, its steady pull can cause matter to collapse in on itself to infinitesimal size.

This may mean that we will never know whether our theories work. How can they be checked? We cannot see down to the skimpy size of a superstring, after all.

Only the chilly beauty of mathematics can lead us. But where does this winding path go?

After all, we cannot even solve exactly for the motion of three bodies acting under Newton's theory of gravity. In my theory, *no exact solutions are available for anything.*

So there is no certainty. Even the most lovely of all models gives us, in the end, a set of equations. But now these squiggles describe events in higher realms, in vast vector spaces where inponderable entities move to their own differential waltzes.

This is profoundly far from the realm of humanity. Yet we who do this are, as I learned, comically human.

We theorists have our homes with a view, our sufficient incomes, our digital stereos and foreign cars, our harassed, ironic wives or husbands—and blithely seem to have solved the paradox of being thinking animals. But what compass do we have, we who swim in the backwash of passing, imperceptible ocean liners?

In Agra I rose at dawn to see the Taj Mahal. By that rosy first glow it was as distant as a ghost.

It shimmered above the lush gardens, deceptively toylike until I realized how huge the pure curved white marble thing was. The ruler who built it to hold his dead wife's body had intended to build a black Taj also, across the river which lies behind. He would lie buried there, he planned, a long arcing bridge linking the two of them.

But his son, seeing how much the first Taj cost, confined his father to a red sandstone fort a mile away for the last seven years of his life. When he was too feeble to sit up, the old man lay in bed and watched the Taj in a mirror until the end.

I realize this has not been the usual sort of annual address given to this body. Please do not mistake my odd approach as a sign of disrespect, however. I deeply thank the Nobel Committee.

I have tried to speak of the human experience of science, because we are all finally encased in our individual, truncated selves. If the work for which you have honored me seems to raise more issues than it solves, that is our condition. We contend endlessly against pale immensities.

We seem so small. Yet we have a common, perhaps arrogant impression that we matter, somehow.

There is an old philosopher's joke:

What is mind? It doesn't matter.
What is matter? Oh, never mind.

But consider the tiny processes governed by quantum mechanics. There, matter is not inert. It is active, continually making choices between possibilities, following laws of probability. Mind is present, at least in the sense that nature makes choices.

Let us go one level higher, to our own brains. These fragile vessels amplify the quantum choices made in our heads by molecules. We apply the lever of size to underlying probabilistic events. We are magnifiers.

Now go to vaster scales. The universe itself shows some signs of design, at least in the choice of basic physical constants. If those numbers had come out differently, no life or even stable stars would be possible in the universe.

Or, in the light of my own calculations, consider the reality of other dimensions. Perhaps these dimensions are rolled up like tiny scrolls. Perhaps they simply lie beyond our knowing, except through the effects I have calculated. We do not know—yet.

Still, there emerges now evidence of mental processes at work on many levels of physical reality. We may be part of some larger act. For example, perhaps we contribute remotely to the universe's thinking about itself. We probably cannot know this with anything approaching scientific cer-

tainty—ever. The recent work of myself and others suggests, though, that higher entities affect our times in distant but profound fashion.

The equations can only hint, imply, describe. They cannot tell us why. I myself suspect that these besieged brains of ours matter. Somehow. Somewhere.

It is all very well, of course, to say that in some far dimension time has no end. But it surely does for us individually, through shootouts and car crashes and disease.

Yet we are given a glimmer of perception, through the Godly language of mathematics. Maybe, for creatures such as us, that is enough.

On the broad marble deck behind the Taj Mahal the river ran shallow. To the right lay a bathing spot for Hindu devotees. Some splashed themselves with river water, others meditated. To the left was a mortuary. The better-off inhabitants of Agra had their bodies burned on pyres, then tossed into the river. If one could not afford the pyre, then after a simple ceremony the body was thrown off the sandstone quay and onto the mud flats, or into the water if the river was high. This was usually done in early morning.

By the glimmering dawn radiance I watched buzzards pick apart something on the flats. They made quick work of it, deftly tearing away the cloth, and in five minutes had picked matters clean. They lost interest and flapped away. The Taj coasted in serene eternity behind me, its color subtly changing as the sun rose above the trees, its cool perfect dome glowing, banishing the shadows below. Somehow in this worn alien place everything seemed to fit. Death just happened. From this simple fact came India's inertia. I thought of Mozart and heard a faint light rhythm, felt myself skimming effortlessly over a rumpled brown dusty world of endless sharp detail and unending fevered ferment, and watched the buzzards and the bathers and felt the slow sad sway of worlds apart.

INNER SPACE/ OUTER SPACE

ESSAY BY
EDWARD W. KOLB

SPECULATION BY
RUDY RUCKER

INNER SPACE/ OUTER SPACE

EDWARD W. KOLB

FERMI NATIONAL
ACCELERATOR LABORATORY
AND UNIVERSITY OF CHICAGO

Had I been present at the creation,
I would have given some useful hints
for the better ordering of the Universe.

Alfonso X, the Wise

EVERY THINKING PERSON AT SOME TIME HAS LOOKED UP into the dark night sky and wondered about the universe. How big, how old? What is it, why is it? Where is the edge, the center? What is beyond, before? Every civilization has imagined answers to these questions and has employed people expert in such matters to answer them.

Twentieth-century experts who study such questions about the universe are scientists known as cosmologists. The word *cosmology* is derived from the Greek κόσμος (pronounced "cosmos"). κόσμος does not mean *enormous*, *immense*, *universe*, or even *billions and billions*. Rather, κόσμος is the Greek word for *order*. Modern cosmologists use physical law as a tool to bring order to an apparently complex and mysterious universe. The strategy is straightforward: learn the laws of physics by performing laboratory experiments, and explain the observed universe on the basis of these laws.

The idea of using our local physical laws, as determined by experiments done in terrestrial laboratories, to explain the entire universe did not arise until sometime in the seventeenth century. The most famous person to try this revolutionary approach was Isaac Newton. Everyone knows (I hope!) that Newton "discovered" gravity. More precisely, Newton discovered the law of gravity, which states that the gravitational force between two objects is proportional to the product of their masses and inversely proportional to the square of the distance between them. This law of gravity was confirmed in the laboratory by the famous experiments of Henry Cavendish. Newton made an even greater discovery than the law of gravity: he discovered the universality of gravity. Newton realized that the force responsible for an apple falling on his head was also responsible for the motion of the moon about the earth and the planets about the sun. He conceived of gravity as a universal phenomenon. Newton discovered that the forces responsible for the motions of the planets are capable of human comprehension and that they can be studied in terrestrial laboratories; this is an example of the connection between the "inner space" of the laboratory and the "outer space" of the cosmos. With a single sweep of genius, Newton freed celestial mechanics from the belief that crystal spheres, mechanical gears, and other sundry devices moved the planets. Is there anyone who can fail to appreciate the simplicity and beauty of the Newtonian view of the solar system? Many of his contemporaries complained that he had removed the hand of God from the heavens. I say he replaced a toilsome hand of brute force with a sublime hand of beauty.

Newton's realization in 1687 that heavenly forces are comprehensible on the basis of local physical law led to a revolution in thought as far reaching as the revolution caused by Copernicus's realization in 1543 that the sun rather than the earth is the center of the solar system.

The task before the modern cosmologist (and the reader) is the same faced by Newton: understand the laws of physics and apply them to the universe. I suspect a few readers are not familiar with modern physics. Perhaps some are afraid of physics. Some may not even know what physics is. To the fearful reader, I offer the following consolation: it isn't that bad. To the unknowing reader, I offer the following definition:

physics ['*fiziks*], *n.* 1: a subject that strikes fear and loathing in the hearts and minds of high school and college students (and some of their teachers). 2: something that is very difficult and should be avoided at all costs. 3: a career with low pay (but great fulfillment). syn: incomprehensible.

Now that we are all expert in physics, let us leave the terrestrial laboratory behind for a time and view the universe to determine exactly what it is we aim to understand.

BUILDING BLOCKS OF THE UNIVERSE

[The universe] is an infinite sphere whose center is everywhere, its circumference nowhere.

Blaise Pascal, *Les Pensées*

What is the universe made of? A simple answer might be that the universe is made of three things: matter, energy in the form of radiation, and space. General relativity connects the three on both local and universal scales, and it is impossible to study one without the others. Let us take each in turn.

MATTER

Cosmology is the study of the origin and large-scale structure of the universe. Here, *large* means larger than a galaxy. The distance from the earth to the sun is about 10^{13} centimeters (cm), or 93,000,000 miles. It takes light about eight minutes to travel from the sun to the earth. The next nearest star, α-Centauri, is about 10^{18} cm, or 4.3 light-years, away. Our solar system is about 30,000 light-years from the center of our galaxy (the Milky Way). Our entire galaxy of more than 100 billion stars is 100,000 light-years in diameter. Yet these scales are "small" to a cosmologist. The basic unit for cosmologists is a megaparsec, 3 million light-years or 10^{24} cm. A megaparsec is the typical distance between galaxies.

What does matter look like? How is it distributed in space? To the naked eye, it takes the form of stars. The stars we see with the unaided eye are all in our own galaxy. Only a sharp eye can see the fuzzy form of a few nearby external galaxies (the Magellanic clouds, 180 thousand light-years away; or the Andromeda galaxy, 3 million light-years away). In the early decades of this century, as telescopes and photographic techniques improved, we discovered that our Milky Way "island universe" is only one of countless galaxies in the universe. Our galaxy is not the largest, brightest, oldest, or youngest galaxy. Although the Milky Way is but a typical spiral galaxy, it is certainly nothing to be ashamed of; its majestic spiral arms would be a sight to behold from a million parsecs away.

Galaxies are basic building blocks for cosmologists. Some cosmologists (undoubtedly frustrated botanists) spend their lives observing galaxies and categorizing them by class (spiral, elliptical, irregular, and so on) and subclass. Since the stars we see in the universe are in galaxies, we must understand why there are galaxies and why they take the shapes and sizes they do. Although we have a qualitative theory of galaxy formation, the answers to such questions await a better understanding of the early universe.

Galaxies are not the only structures in the universe. In the past few years a new picture has begun to emerge. It is becoming clear that there are structures in the universe larger than galaxies. Some galaxies seem to be grouped into larger objects known as clusters. Even clusters of galaxies may be part of still larger groups known as superclusters. There is also evidence for giant voids in the universe, regions free of visible galaxies. These voids seem to form enormous bubbles surrounded by a thin film of galaxies. We are able now to see only the vague outlines of these structures, a hundred megaparsecs in size, containing thousands of galaxies.

In the excitement of discoveries about the large-scale structure of the universe, we should not lose sight of the fact that the most significant feature of the distribution of matter in the universe is not its structure, but its lack of structure: its smoothness. The situation is analogous to an ordinary cloud. On small scales there is substructure to a cloud: atoms, water molecules, and water droplets when viewed on progressively larger scales. However, on scales much larger than the distance between water droplets the cloud appears as a smooth distribution of matter. The same is true of the universe. On scales much larger than the typical distance between galaxies, say a dozen megaparsecs or so, the substructure is unimportant and the universe appears as a smooth distribution of matter.

The study of a smooth universe might sound boring, but smoothness has important implications. A universe that is smooth is said to be *homogeneous* and *isotropic*. A space is homogeneous if it is the same at every point, and it is isotropic if it appears the same in every direction. If our universe is homogeneous and isotropic, then we are led to the profound conclusion that we do not have a privileged view of the universe. The universe would appear the same to any observer living in any galaxy. If the universe is smooth, there is no special place in the universe, no boundary, no center.

We can be a little more specific about matter. We can observe its chemical composition. Since cosmologists study the universe on the grand scale, they cannot be concerned with the individual abundances of all 109 elements in the periodic table. We deal with a simplified periodic table of only three elements (the dream of many high school chemistry students): hydrogen, helium, and metals. Hydrogen and helium have atomic mass numbers 1 and 4. (Anything with a mass number larger than 4 is called a metal.) Most of the universe, about 75 percent by mass, is made of hydrogen. About 24 percent is helium, and metals comprise less than 1 percent. All the elements so important for life (calcium, nitrogen, iron, and so on) are but an incidental contamination in a universe of hydrogen and helium. We believe that hydrogen and helium were made in the first minutes of the big bang. Billions of years later, the first stars formed from the primordial hydrogen and helium, processed the primordial fuel to heavier elements by nuclear reactions, and then exploded and enriched the interstellar medium with "metals." The next generation of stars coalesced with metals from the debris of the first generation, processed them further, exploded, and further enriched the interstellar medium. In a real sense we are all star material. Any atom in our bodies other than hydrogen or helium was once part of a star!

The chemical evolution of the universe is an observational fact! Stars of mass about 10 times that of our sun rapidly "burn" hydrogen and helium to metals (in this case, iron) and end in a tremendous explosion known as a supernova. The debris of a supernova is much richer in metals than the surrounding interstellar material out of which the supernova was formed. We see that what goes into the star is different than what comes out. The chemical evolution of the universe is the first example of a feature we encounter again and again—*change*. The universe is constantly changing, evolving, developing. Modern cosmology has rejected the eighteenth- and nineteenth-century picture of the universe as static.

So far we have assumed that we can "see" all the matter in the universe. What we see is the light from stars, but there is no certainty that all matter is in stars. In fact there is evidence that most of the mass of a galaxy is *not* in the form of stars. We can "weigh" a galaxy just as we can weigh the sun. We determine the mass of the sun by measuring the rotational velocity of the earth about the sun, and we determine the mass of a galaxy by measuring the rotational velocity of stars about the center of a galaxy. The larger the mass of a galaxy, the faster the rotational velocity. When the mass of a galaxy is determined in this way, we find almost 10 times more mass than can be accounted for by the stars. There seems to be a large amount of *dark matter* in galaxies. This dark matter is not visible—hence its name. Not only is dark matter found in galaxies, but it is found in galaxy clusters as well. The nature of the dark matter is uncertain. We only know that it does not "shine" in any part of the electromagnetic spectrum. Perhaps dark matter is undetectable because it is not ordinary matter made of neutrons, protons, and electrons, but rather some undiscovered, weakly interacting massive particle. The possibility that the nature of most of the mass of the universe still awaits discovery is a sobering thought.

RADIATION

A view out of your window, day or night, suggests that the universe is awash in electromagnetic radiation—light. Visible light occupies only a small fraction of the total spectrum of electromagnetic radiation, special only because it is the part to which our eyes are sensitive. The visible electromagnetic radiation may seem important to us, but it is less than 3 percent of the total amount of the energy in electromagnetic radiation in the universe.

Most of the radiation of the universe is not in visible wavelengths, but in the invisible microwave region of the spectrum. In 1964, using a Bell Laboratories microwave communications antenna in Holmdel, New Jersey, Arno Penzias and Robert Wilson discovered that our universe has about 400 photons (light particles) per cubic centimeter with wavelengths of about 1 millimeter (the wavelength of radiation in your microwave oven is somewhat longer, a few centimeters). If your eyes were sensitive to these microwave photons, they would "see" about 10^{10} microwave photons per second pass through them. This is about 1,000 times the flux of optical photons averaged over all the universe.

The microwave background radiation permeates all of space. Even in the recesses of intergalactic space, there are 400 microwave photons in every cubic centimeter. These background photons have an intensity and spectrum like that of a thermal source of 2.75 degrees Kelvin (−454 degrees Fahrenheit). The temperature of the universe between the galaxies is not zero, but 2.75 K. The microwave photons are the oldest things ever detected. They are a fossil of the universe long before stars and galaxies ever formed.

The microwave background provides further evidence for the smoothness of the universe. The microwave radiation reaches us from all directions, and the radiation is the same in all directions to better than one part in a thousand. The only measurable departure from perfect isotropy is caused by the random motion of our galaxy toward the Virgo constellation at a velocity of 600 kilometers per second (1.35 million miles per hour). The isotropy tells us that when the microwave photons last scattered off the matter, the universe was *very smooth.*

Although the 400 microwave photons per cubic centimeter outnumber the nucleons by more than a billion to one (neutrons and protons have a present average number density of about 10^{-7} per cubic centimeter), the rest mass of the nucleons is so much greater than the average energy of the photons that today the universe is *matter dominated*—that is, the mass density of the nucleons dominates the energy density of the photons.

SPACE

The homogeneity and isotropy of matter and radiation must be reflected by the homogeneity and isotropy of space because according to Einstein's theory of gravity, the curvature of space is related to matter. The homogeneity and isotropy of the universe is so important that it has been elevated to the status of a principle, known as the cosmological principle. The cosmological principle states that there is no unique or special place in the universe—for example, there is no center, no edge, and no preferred location.

The shape of the universe is a fundamental question. Einstein showed that space is curved around massive objects. What about the geometry of the universe as a whole? Is the universe curved? Does the universe have a boundary? If so, what is outside the universe? Is the universe infinite or finite in spatial extent? The cosmological principle restricts the universe to certain shapes. A space that obeys the cosmological principle can be finite or infinite, can be curved or flat, but cannot have a boundary or a center. A center would be a special point, and the boundary would be a set of special points.

To see that the simple principle that the universe has no special point is powerful, let's start with an easy example: one spatial dimension. An infinite straight line is the simplest example of a space that has no special point. Every point on a straight line is equivalent. The straight line is an infinite space that is unbounded. There is no "edge" to the line; it goes on forever. Another example of a one-dimensional space that has no special point is a circle. A circle is a one-dimensional space that like the line is unbounded, but unlike the line has finite length. An unbounded space can have finite "volume" only if it is curved back on itself. Although the circle is a one-dimensional space, it is most easily visualized by drawing it on a two-dimensional flat space.

Examples of two-dimensional spaces with no special point are also familiar—the infinite plane and the surface of the earth. The infinite plane has infinite area and is unbounded. There is no edge, no center. The surface of the earth is an example of a space known as a 2-sphere (see Figure 1). It is unbounded, but it has finite surface area. If you walk in any one direction on the earth you eventually return to your point of origin (the space is finite), but you never encounter an edge (the space is unbounded). There is also no special point on the surface of the earth, at least not in the geometrical sense. If we wished, we could define Gretna, Louisiana, as the North Pole, although it is hard to imagine Santa living there. Although the surface of the earth is a two-dimensional space (any point can be specified by two coordinates—e.g., latitude and longitude), we picture the 2-sphere by embedding it in a three-dimensional flat space (the local space of ordinary experience), and in projection it can be drawn on a flat two-dimensional space (see Figure 1).

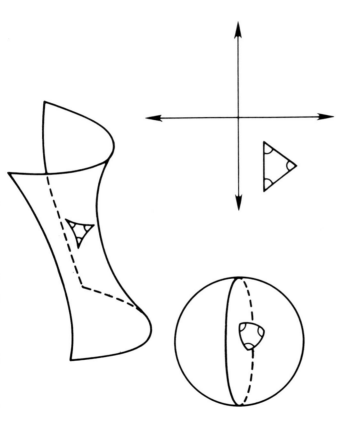

Figure 1. A triangle shows the lack of curvature of a flat space (the page), positive curvature (the 2-sphere), and negative curvature (the saddle). (Credit: Edward W. Kolb).

There is no problem visualizing an unbounded, uncurved universe with three spatial dimensions. Such a universe has no edge; it goes on forever. It has no center; every point is equivalent. It is also possible that our universe has spatial curvature and has the geometry of a 3-sphere. Just like the circle (1-sphere) and the surface of the earth (2-sphere), the 3-sphere has no boundary and no special point, but does have finite volume. The 3-sphere must be visualized by embedding it in four flat dimensions, and such visualization requires imagination.

There is another possibility for the geometry of the universe. Space may be curved in the opposite sense of the 3-sphere and have the shape of a saddle. Such a space is, of course, unbounded. It has infinite volume.

In principle, it is possible to measure the curvature directly and determine the shape of the universe. In practice, it is not so easy. If space is "curved" like the 3-sphere, the radius of curvature is greater than 10^{28} centimeters, or 10^{23} miles. The cosmological principle answers the question of whether there is a center of the universe—there is none. Neither is there an edge to the universe, even though the universe may have finite volume. If the universe is curved like a 3-sphere, then if you look out far enough into the universe, you might see the back of your head!

Whatever its geometry, the universe is expanding. The expansion of the universe was discovered in 1929 by Edwin Hubble. This discovery, the greatest of twentieth-century astronomy, was made by studying the spectra from distant galaxies.

Everyone knows that if light is passed through a prism, "white" light is separated into a spectrum consisting of different colors. If a pure element is heated until it glows, and that light is passed through a prism, the light present in the spectrum appears as a series of individual spectral lines of different color. The different colors of the spectrum correspond to light of different wavelengths. The longer the wavelength the redder the light. These spectral lines are a signature of the element. A spectroscopist can examine the spectrum and determine exactly what element is responsible for the light.

It was known before Hubble that spectra from distant galaxies were not quite identical to laboratory spectra. If the spectrum from a distant galaxy was examined in detail it was found that the wavelength of each line in the spectrum was slightly longer (redder) than the wavelength measured on earth (see Figure 2). Hubble discovered the connection between the amount of this red shift and the distance to the galaxy. He noticed that the red shift of the lines increased in direct proportion to the distance to the galaxy. (The distances used in Hubble's study were determined by other methods, most of which relied on comparing the brightness of "standard candles"—special stars and other objects—to the brightness of similar objects in our own galaxy.)

The red shift of light waves can be understood by an analogy with the

Figure 2. Spectra showing progressively greater line shifts to the red, due to the Doppler effect. (Credit: Edward W. Kolb)

Doppler shift of sound waves. If a source of sound waves, say an airplane, is approaching an observer, the detected wavelength will be shorter than if the source were stationary. If the source is receding from the observer, the detected wavelength will be longer. The sound of an approaching airplane is different from the sound of a receding airplane. The increase of the wavelength of light with distance to the galaxy (red shift) can be understood as resulting from the fact that the distant galaxy is receding. The more distant a galaxy, the faster its recessional velocity.

If all the galaxies are receding from us, does that make us the center of an explosion? The answer is no! The expansion of the universe is not an explosion of matter into empty space, but rather the creation of space! You can picture the expansion of the universe as what happens to a loaf of raisin bread when it is baked. Imagine the raisins as galaxies and the intervening bread as space. As the bread is baked, the distance between the raisins increases because space is expanding. Now simply imagine an infinite loaf of raisin bread. The distance between any two raisins increases as the bread is baked. In the infinite loaf there is no center and no edge. An observer on any raisin sees every other raisin receding from it, just as an astronomer on a galaxy 500 megaparsecs from us would see the Milky Way receding.

The study of the building blocks of the universe has led to two important conclusions. The first, the cosmological principle, resulted from the revolution that Copernicus initiated. The second, the expansion of the universe, was discovered in 1929 and was completely unanticipated. The expansion of the universe is yet another indication that the universe is not static, but dynamic. It is expanding, evolving, changing.

The cosmological principle has profound implications. Whatever our place in the universe, it is not a special location. We now know that the solar system is not the center of our galaxy, and our galaxy is not the center of the universe. Our galaxy is not even at rest with respect to the microwave background radiation. Perhaps the discovery of dark matter is the inevitable culmination of the Copernican revolution: Not only do we not occupy a special place in the solar system, the galaxy, or the universe, but the neutrons, protons and electrons that make up our body are but a small part of the total mass of the universe, and most of the mass is invisible to us.

The discovery of the expansion of the universe illustrates how deeply rooted is our view of the universe. In 1905, Albert Einstein examined the results of his calculations and realized that space and time were intimately connected and that the view of space and time held for millennia must be modified. In 1915, Einstein examined the results of further calculations and realized that space was curved and that the view of geometry maintained since the time of Euclid must be modified. In 1917, Einstein examined the applications of his beautiful equations to cosmology and realized that his equations predicted that the universe was expanding or contracting. But Einstein, educated in the nineteenth century, clung to the cosmological view of an infinite, static universe. Though he could modify his view of space and time and geometry to conform to his equations, he could not change his most deeply held beliefs about the nature of the universe. Instead of predicting that the universe is expanding, he butchered his beautiful equations to force them to predict a static universe. Later, when Hubble discovered the expansion, Einstein regretted modifying his equations and referred to it as the "biggest blunder of my life." If the imagination of a man like Einstein was bound by his view of the universe, how is ours prejudiced?

The idea that we do not live in a special place in the universe has upset a lot of people. Giordano Bruno was burned at the stake in 1600 for espousing such ideas. However, the idea was not scattered to the wind with Bruno's ashes. In my opinion, people become upset when they hear that we do not live in a special place in the universe because they confuse the fact that we do not occupy a special place with the idea that we are not special. But despite the fact that our location is not special, we are special because, on a small planet orbiting an insignificant star on the outer arms of a typical spiral galaxy, we look up into the immense cosmos, in awe but not in fear, and boldly attempt to comprehend it.

It is with these brave words that we start our journey to investigate the origins of the universe.

THE BIG BANG

For violent fires soon burn out themselves.
William Shakespeare, *King Richard II*

The universe is expanding and is full of radiation. These two observed facts are the cornerstones of the theory of the big bang. If the distance between points in the universe is increasing, then in the past the distance was smaller and the universe was denser. Just as a gas cools upon expansion and heats upon compression, the temperature of the universe changes. The universe is expanding and cooling, so when the universe was older it was hotter and denser. At the time of the big bang, the temperature and density were infinite.

In order to understand the present state of the universe we must understand the origins of the universe. What hope do we have of understanding what the universe was like 13.6 billion years ago? Well, we can follow the lead of Newton and take physical law as our guide. After all, in the seventeenth century people asked Newton what hope he had of understanding the motions of distant planets. Extrapolation of knowledge over great time and distance is possible if we understand the nature of physical law under the conditions encountered. Where the physics is simple, or at least understood, predictions can be made. For instance, the temperature on Mars next week can be predicted with greater precision than the temperature in Cleveland. Although Mars is distant, the physics of Martian weather is not complicated by the turbulence of a thick atmosphere.

Let us journey back in time to see what the universe was like. The temperature in our 13.6-billion-year-old universe is now 2.75 K. In order to illustrate the expansion of the universe, let us use as a reference a radio source known by the unromantic name of 3C84.0, which is presently at a distance of 100 megaparsecs.

When our solar system formed, some 6.5 billion years ago, the universe was already 7.1 billion years old and the temperature was 4.24 K. The universe was somewhat denser then (3C84.0 was at a distance from the earth of 65 megaparsecs). The universe at that time closely resembled the universe we observe today.

Quasars are the most distant (hence the oldest) astrophysical objects we observe. The light we now observe from the most distant quasar was emitted some 12.6 billion years ago, when the universe was only a billion years old and had a temperature of 13.8 K. The distance to our reference source (although the source probably had not formed yet) was a mere 20 megaparsecs. Quasars probably represent the earliest epoch of galaxy formation and do not seem to be forming in nearby regions now.

Prior to the quasar epoch, galaxies and stars did not exist, and the distribution of matter in the universe was very smooth. The mass density in galaxies today is about 10^{-24} grams per cubic centimeter, or about 100,000 times the present average density of the universe, 10^{-29} grams per cubic centimeter. Before the quasar era, the regions that would eventually form galaxies had a density only a few percent larger than the average density at that time. Over billions of years, these regions of slight overdensity accreted other matter by gravitational attraction and eventually grew to become the structure we observe. If the universe today is smooth on large scales, the early universe was *very* smooth on all scales. Although any tiny irregularities in density will inexorably grow, the nature of the resulting structure depends on the amplitudes and sizes of the irregularities. We must study the universe at even earlier epochs to learn the nature of the irregularities.

The table below shows some interesting developments in the history of the universe. The distance between any two points in the universe is proportional to the size of the universe. For instance, a point that is 100 megaparsecs away today, was only 20 megaparsecs away at the time of the formation of the oldest visible quasars.

History of the Universe

Epoch	Age	Size	Temperature
singularity	0	0	∞
super unity	10^{-43} seconds	10^{-32}	10^{32} K
grand unity	10^{-35} seconds	10^{-26}	10^{27} K
weak unity	10^{-12} seconds	10^{-15}	10^{16} K
nucleons form	10^{-4} seconds	10^{-12}	10^{12} K
nuclei form	1 second	10^{-10}	10^{10} K
radiation era	31,200 years	0.0002	15,800 K
atoms form	260,000 years	0.0007	3,850 K
hotter than hell	3.2 million years	0.004	718 K
comfort zone	12.2 million years	0.009	295 K
oldest quasars	1.2 billion years	0.2	13.8 K
solar system forms	7.1 billion years	0.65	4.24 K
now	13.6 billion years	1	2.75 K

The average temperature of the universe was a comfortable 295 K (72 degrees Fahrenheit) when the universe was about 12.2 million years old. The temperature of the universe was hot enough to boil water (although no oxygen was present to form H_2O) 8.6 million years after the big bang, and cold enough to freeze water 13.7 million years after the big bang. There is no cosmological significance to the comfort zone.

Earlier than about 3.2 million years after the big bang the universe was really hot. In fact, it was hotter than hell (assuming that the temperature of hell is near the boiling point of brimstone, 718 K). At that time the distance to 3C84.0 (or, at least, the matter that would eventually form it) was only 0.4 megaparsec.

A temperature of 3,850 K marks an important cosmological event. When the temperature was higher than this, the universe was so hot that any atoms of hydrogen and helium present would have been ionized (the electrons would have been stripped from the nuclei). Thus, atoms formed at the time when the universe reached this temperature. Before this era, the universe was a plasma of nuclei and electrons. This era was 260,000 years after the big bang, nearly 13.6 billion years ago. It was at this time that the microwave photons last interacted with the matter. The microwave background is a direct probe of the universe at this time.

The universe at the time of ionization was so dense that 3C84.0, today 100 megaparsecs distant, was then only 70,000 parsecs distant. Recall that our galaxy is today 100,000 parsecs in size. Although the universe at this early era was hot and dense compared to the present universe, the density and temperature were not extreme by laboratory standards. The average density of matter at the time that atoms formed was a mere 10^{-19} grams per cubic centimeter, or 10^{19} times less dense than water. A temperature of 15,800 K is routinely obtained in plasma physics laboratories. We have a complete understanding of physical law under these conditions, and it is with confidence that we can speak of the universe at this time.

Although the energy density of the radiation in the universe is today much smaller than the mass density of matter, earlier than 31,200 years after the big bang the density of radiation was larger. In the very early universe, matter played a negligible role in the dynamics of expansion.

The next important era encountered in the journey to the beginning of the universe is the era of formation of nuclei. When the universe was hotter than 10^{10} (10 billion) K, any nuclei present would have decomposed to their constituent particles, neutrons and protons. In this era the density of matter was still not very high, about 4 grams per cubic centimeter (about four times as dense as water). The energy of the particles present was high by normal experience, but is routinely reproduced today in nuclear physics laboratories. Since we understand the structure of matter under these conditions of density and temperature, we are able to make reasonable predictions about the state of the universe in this era.

One of the predictions we can make has to do with the chemical composition of the universe after primordial nucleosynthesis. If we start with an expanding universe of neutrons and protons at 10^{10} K, about three minutes later the neutrons and protons will be cooked into nuclei that are 76 percent hydrogen and 24 percent helium, exactly the proportions observed. If the universe had expanded more slowly than is predicted by the big-bang model, a smaller fraction of helium would have resulted; a slightly faster expansion would have resulted in too much helium. This is another example of the inner space–outer space connection. There is an interplay between the laws of nuclear physics (inner space) and the law of cosmic expansion (outer space).

Earlier than a second after the bang, the universe was hot and dense enough to produce all particles in copious numbers, even those particles with the most feeble interactions known, the neutrinos. These primordial neutrinos should have survived the big bang and be present today in the form of an undetected sea of neutrinos. The big-bang model predicts that in every cubic centimeter of space there are about 100 of each species of neutrino (100 electron-neutrinos, 100 muon-neutrinos, and 100 tau-neutrinos). These invisible weakly-interacting particles may, in fact, be the most significant in the universe. If a species of neutrino has a mass as small as 100 millionth of the mass of a proton, the lowly neutrino could be the dark matter in the universe, and the weak shall dominate the universe. In laboratories around the world physicists are attempting to "weigh" neutrinos to see if they might be the dark matter.

At a tenth of a millisecond (10^{-4} seconds) after the bang, the density of the universe was so high that nucleons were touching. Individual neutrons and protons did not exist as such, but for a brief moment the universe was as one giant nucleus. At nuclear matter density the mass of the sun occupies a sphere of 14 kilometers, and the mass of a galaxy is contained in a sphere smaller than the sun. The physics of nuclear matter is difficult, but many of its most important properties can be calculated with the aid of quantum mechanics, and the calculations checked by laboratory experiments.

Before the nuclear density era, the universe was so hot and dense that individual neutrons and protons could not exist as such, but broke up into their constituent particles, quarks and gluons. The universe before 10^{-4} seconds was a primordial soup of elementary particles: leptons (electrons, muons, taus, neutrinos) and hadrons (quarks and gluons).

How can we hope to understand the universe a microsecond after the bang? Every day, in a handful of particle accelerators throughout the world, scientists accelerate protons or electrons to tremendous energies and collide them. In these collisions we can recreate for a brief moment the conditions that existed in the universe 13.6 billion years ago. By studying the properties of elementary particles in high-energy collisions we can gain insight into the origin of the universe in the same way laboratory experiments of the seventeenth century measured the gravitational force and led to insight into the motions of the planets.

The highest-energy collisions we can study in the laboratory have an energy equivalent to 10^{16} K. This was the temperature of the universe about 10^{-12} seconds after the big bang. At this point our direct knowledge of the properties of matter ends, and hence we are able only to speculate about the universe at earlier times. To extend the frontiers of knowledge of early cosmology, it is necessary to achieve a deeper understanding of the fundamental forces.

Newton shaped seventeenth-century cosmology using the force of gravity. We now know that gravity is not the only force at play in the cosmos. In the twentieth century we have identified four fundamental forces: gravity, electromagnetism, the weak force, and the strong force. Most people are aware of the influence of the gravitational and electromagnetic forces. The less familiar strong and weak forces are just as crucial to our existence. The strong force is responsible for the nuclear interactions that bind neutrons and protons into nuclei and that bind quarks and gluons into neutrons and protons. The weak force is responsible for the transmutation of protons into neutrons. It is the action of the strong and weak forces in the sun that causes four protons to form a helium nucleus consisting of two neutrons and two protons, thereby releasing energy to power the sun. Our universe is shaped by an interplay of all four fundamental forces.

Although the four forces are fundamental, they may be related. There is historical precedent for the unification of seemingly disparate forces. Until the end of the nineteenth century it was believed that magnetic forces were distinct from electric forces. The pioneering work of Faraday and Maxwell in the last century demonstrated that electric and magnetic forces are different manifestations of a single fundamental electromagnetic force. This interplay of electric and magnetic phenomena is apparent every time you turn on an electromagnetic motor. In the 1960s Sheldon Glashow, Steven Weinberg, and Abdus Salam demonstrated that the electromagnetic and weak forces are related, and in fact are different aspects of a single *electroweak* force. Many particle physicists feel that unification is the path to deeper understanding and that all four fundamental forces are different aspects of a single force.

Unification of the forces has important implications for the early universe. Unification theories predict that at very high temperature the character of the fundamental forces is different from what is now observed. For instance, the strength of the electromagnetic force between two particles is observed to decrease in proportion to the square of the distance between them (like the gravitational force), while the strength of the weak force between two particles is

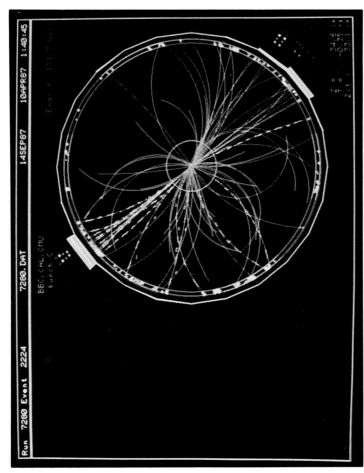

Figure 3. Computer-generated graphic of high-energy proton collision spilling out nucleons and heavy mesons from quark interactions. (Credit: Edward W. Kolb)

seen to decrease much faster with separation. At high temperature, however, electroweak unification predicts that the weak force should behave exactly as the electromagnetic force. According to unification theories, as the universe expanded and cooled the behavior of fundamental forces changed in a series of transitions. The transition of the electroweak force, according to unification theory, should have occurred around 10^{-12} seconds after the big bang. This electroweak transition is perhaps the last event in a series of unification transitions, the first of which occurred 10^{-43} seconds after the big bang, when the "super unity" between the gravitational force and the other forces was lost. Then, at 10^{-35} seconds, the "grand unity" between the strong and electroweak forces was lost. Finally, at 10^{-12} seconds, the weak force split from the electromagnetic force.

One exciting prediction of unified theories is that the unification transition may not have occurred everywhere, so there might be regions of the universe where the fundamental forces still retain their high-temperature character. An example of such a region is a *cosmic string.* A cosmic string is a very long, very thin region of space where fundamental forces have different properties. Strings produced in the grand unification transition might be present today as loops

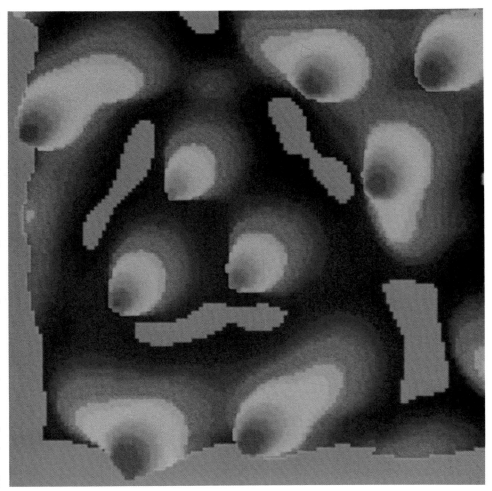

Figure 4. Atoms or galaxies? This image (by STM, of atoms on a silicon surface) could almost equally well symbolize the interaction of atoms or of protogalaxies in the early universe. (Photo credit: IBM)

of string that are megaparsecs in radius but only 10^{-28} centimeters thick. Cosmologists and particle physicists are still trying to understand the consequences of cosmic strings. One striking feature of a string from the grand unification transition is that it would weigh more than a million-billion tons per centimeter. A string only a few centimeters long would contain the mass of a mountain! Another interesting characteristic of such strings is that they can turn matter into antimatter. A proton passing through a cosmic string can turn into an antiproton. Other bizarre features of cosmic strings are just now being explored.

An understanding of the earliest moments of the universe requires an understanding of the nature of the fundamental forces at work. It is through recreating the conditions of the early universe in high-energy collisions at accelerator laboratories that we can learn the secrets of the early universe.

EPILOGUE

The Universe is full of magical things,
patiently waiting for our wits
to grow sharper.

Eden Phillpotts, *A Shadow Passes*

We have tried to paint a simple, beautiful picture of the universe based upon the big-bang model. We have direct evidence, in the form of the abundances of primordial hydrogen and helium, that we understand the structure of the universe for the last 13.6 billion years, starting one second after the big bang. We can use the inner space–outer space connection and apply the knowledge we learn in the laboratory to stretch our knowledge about the universe back to 10^{-12} seconds after the big bang. We seem to be on the verge of understanding a crucial transition in the universe, the electroweak transition.

Where should we stop? If we have a consistent picture of the universe for the last 13.6 billion years, back to a second after the big bang, is that enough? No. I think we won't stop asking fundamental questions about the universe until all the answers are in hand.

I often wonder what people in the next century will think of our attempts to understand the very early universe. Will they regard our ideas of grand and super unification with the same amusement with which we look upon the efforts of previous centuries, and think them naive? However they judge our scientific efforts, I believe that they will not judge us to have been lacking in boldness and imagination as we again attacked problems once thought to lie outside the realm of human comprehension.

I am grateful to the Department of Energy and the National Aeronautics and Space Administration for supporting my research. I would like to thank Professor Franco Occhionero for his hospitality at Osservatorio Astronomico di Roma, where this was written.

AS ABOVE, SO BELOW

RUDY RUCKER

ILLUSTRATION BY
BRUCE JENSEN

I'D BEEN OVERHACKING AGAIN. THE WARM CALIFORNIA NIGHT was real and intimate, *synaesthetic*, with the distant surf sound matching the pebbly parking lot under my bare feet, and the flowering shrub of jade plant in front of me fitting in too, with its fat loplop green leaves and stuffed yellow star petals knobbing along like my breath and my heartbeat, and the rest of the plants matching the rest of the world: the menthol-smelling eucalyptus trees like the rush of the cars, the palm trees like my jittering synapses, the bed of calla lilies white and wonderful as the woman waiting for me at home, ah the plants, with their smells and their realtime ongoing updates . . .

The old flash came rushing over me once again: astonishment at the vastness of the invisible world machinery that keeps all this running, awe for the great program the world is working out. *What a system! What a hack!*

I was stoned and I'd been overhacking and my eyes were throbbing and I couldn't remember what I'd said to Donna when she phoned . . . an hour ago?
. . . nor could I remember when I'd last eaten. Eat. I walked across Route 1 to the Taco Bell. There were some kids there with pet rats crawling out of their Salvation Army coats, nice middle-class kids no doubt, this being Santa Cruz. They wanted their burritos with no beans. *Beans are the worst,* one of them explained to the cholo countergirl. The back of the boy's head had a remarkable yellow and green food-coloring dye job. A buzz-cut DA with the left back half of the assembly language XOR operation, which is a little like MINUS. Green XOR Yellow is Red. If I let my eyes go out of focus I could see a strip of red down the back of his head. I didn't want to think about the weird screens I'd just been watching at my workstation in the empty Micromax labs.

334

The boy's rat poked its head over the boy's shoulder and cheesed its nose at me, *twitch twitch*, the long whiskers sweeping out envelopes of virtual surfaces. The beastie had long yellow fangs, though a festive air withal.

"You should dye the rat red," I observed. "And call him XOR. Exclusive OR."

"Beans are the worst," repeated the boy, not acknowledging. He paid for his beanless burritos and left.

"Your order, sir?" My turn.

"Four tacos and a large iced tea."

I ate the food out on the concrete patio tables. I poured on the hot sauce and it was really good. I liked being there, except I didn't like the traffic and I didn't like the wind blowing all the paper off my table. They give you a lot a lot of paper at Taco Bell. It's really obvious that the paper costs more than the food. But except for the wind and the traffic, I was feeling good. It was so neat to be getting input for free. When you're hacking, you're coupled to the screen, and all your input is from the machine's output, which all comes from the passage of time and from what you put in the machine. You're making your own world all the time. And then you go outside and there's all this great deep complex shit for free. The crackle of the thin taco shells, the faces of the punks, the wind on my face, and best of all—always the best—the plants.

Plants are really where it's at, no lie. Take an oak tree: it grows from an acorn, right? The acorn is the program and the oak tree is the output. The runtime is like eighty years. That's the best kind of computation . . . where a short program runs for a long long time and makes an interesting image. Lots of things are like that—a simple start and a long computation. In information theory we call it *low complexity/high depth*. Low complexity means short program, and high depth means a long runtime.

A really good example of a low complexity/high depth pattern is the Mandelbrot set. You grow it in the plane . . . for each point you keep squaring and adding in the last value, and some points go out in infinity and some don't. The ones that don't are inside the Mandelbrot set, which is a big warty ass shape with a disk stuck onto it. There's an antenna sticking out of the disk, and shishkabobbed onto the antenna are tiny little Mandelbrot sets: ass, warts, and disk. Each of the warts is a Mandelbrot disk, too, each with a wiggly antenna coming out, and with shishkabobs of ass, warts, and disk, with yet smaller antennae, asses, warts, and disks, all swirled into maelstroms and lobed vortices, into paisley cactus high desert, into the Santa Cruz cliffs being eaten by the ever-crashing sea.

The Mandelbrot set goes on forever, deeper and deeper down into more and more detail, except sooner or later you always get tired and go home. After I finished my tacos I walked back across Route 1 and got in my bicycle. It was a carbon-fiber low rider with fat smooth tires of catalyzed imipolex. I realized that I'd left my workstation computer on inside the Micromax building, but I just couldn't handle going back in there to shut things off. It had been getting too weird. The last thing I thought I'd seen on my Mandelbrot set screen had been hairline cracks in the glass.

There was a liquor store just before the turnoff from Route 1 to the long road uphill to our house. My friend Jerry Rankle had stopped by Micromax to hand me a little capsule of white dust a couple of hours ago and I'd swallowed it fast and robotlike, thinking something like *this'll get you off the machine all right, Will,* because I knew I was overhacking and I wanted to stop. I'd been the last one out of Micromax every day for a week.

"Lemme know how it hits you, Will," Jerry had said in his jerky stuttery voice, always on the verge of a giggle. He was an old pal, a rundown needle freak who'd once summed up his worldview for me in the immortal phrase, *The Universe Is Made of Jokes.*

"What is it, exactly?" I'd thought to ask, sitting there at my workstation, feeling the little lump of the pill in my gullet, suddenly worried, but not talking too loud just in case my yuppie boss Steven Koss was within earshot. "How fast does it come on?"

"Wait and see," said Jerry. "It's brand new. You can name it, man. Some H.A. biohackers in Redwood City invented it last week. Could be a new scene." H.A. stood for *Hell's Angels.* Jerry thought highly of H.A. drug suppliers.

Now, on my bicycle, two hours later, passing the liquor store, I realized Jerry's stuff was hitting me weird, worse than MDMA, this Tinkertoy crap some slushed biker chemist had biohacked together—I was grinding my teeth like crazy, and for sure it was going to be a good idea to have some booze to smooth the edges.

Basically, I was scared of going nuts just then, with the overhacking and the pot and the speed and now Jerry's pill on top of it. The images I'd been getting on the machine just before quitting were at wholly new levels of detail in the Mandelbrot set. These were new levels I'd accessed with brand-new hardware boards, and the almost impossible thing is that at the new levels the images were becoming more than two-dimensional. Partly it was because I was breeding the Mandelbrot set with a chaotic tree pattern, but it had also seemed as if my new, enhanced Mandelbrot set was somehow taking advantage of the screen phosphor's slight thickness to ruck itself up into faintly gnarled tissues that wanted (I could *tell*) to slide off the screen, across the desk, and onto my face just like the speedy octopus stage of the creature in that old flick *Alien,* the stage where the creature grabs onto some guy's face and forces a sick egg down his esophagus.

Wo!

So I'd left the office, I'd had my tacos and tea, and now calmly calmly I was taking the precautionary measure of picking up a cylindrical pint bottle of Gusano Rojo, a Mexican-bottled distillation of mescal cactus, with an authentic cactus worm (*gusano rojo means red worm*) on the bottom. I paid the Korean behind the counter, I got back in my bike, I took a few hits of Gusano Rojo, I tucked the bottle in my knapsack, and I started the rest of the way uphill, trying to stave off the pill by ignoring it, even though I couldn't stop the grinding of my teeth.

I held it all together until the last slope up to our house. The fatigue and the fear and the drugs started to clash really badly, and then the new drug kicked in top volume, fusing shut the sanity brain switch I'd desperately been holding open. It was nasty.

I lost control of my bicycle and weaved into the ditch. The bike's cage protected me, more or less, not that I noticed. The bumps and jolts were like jerky camera motion on a screen. When the picture stopped moving the camera was pointing up into the sky.

I lay there quietly grinding my teeth, like a barnacle sifting seawater, unwilling to move and to stir up more sensations to analyze. The patch of sky I could see included the moon, which was nearly full. Her pale gold face churned with images, though her outline held steady. Dear moon, dear real world.

My calm lasted a few minutes, and then I began to worry. My leg was throbbing; was I badly cut? A car would stop soon; I would be institutionalized or killed; I was really and truly going crazy for good; this would never stop; the whole crazy cozy womany world I leaned on was a rapidly tattering computer pattern on the nonscreen of the angry Void; and *actually* I was bleeding to death and too wrecked to do anything about it?!?!?

Wo. I sat up. The bike's front wheel was broken. I dragged my machine up the road's low sand embankment and shoved it into the manzanita chaparral. There was a tussocky meadowlet of soft grass and yellow-blossomed wood sorrel a few meters further in. All the plants smiled at me and said hello. I lolled down and took a hit off my pint. Donna would be worried, but I couldn't hack going home just yet. I needed to lay out here in the moonlight a minute and enjoy my medication. I was pretty together after all; the clashing was all over and the drugs had like balanced each other out. Though I was in orbit, I was by no means out to lunch. My skin felt prickly, like just before a thunderstorm.

And that's when the creature came for me—all the way from the place where zero and infinity are the same.

The first unusual thing I noticed was a lot of colored fireflies darting around, all red, yellow, and green. I could tell they weren't hallucinations because they kept bumping into me. And then all at once there was this giant light moving up the hillside toward me. The light was so big and so bright that the manzanita bushes cast shadows. At first I was scared it was a police helicopter, and I scooted closer to the bushes to hide. The light kept getting brighter, so bright that I thought it was a nuclear explosion. I didn't want to be blinded, so I closed my eyes.

And then nothing was happening, except there was a kind of hissing sound, really rich and complicated hissing, like a thousand soft radios playing at once. I opened my eyes back up and the light was overhead. It was hovering right over me, hissing and sputtering in a whispery way. I decided it was a UFO.

I knew the aliens could do whatever they wanted, and I knew they saw me, so I just lay there staring up at the ship. It was maybe fifty feet overhead and maybe fifty feet long. Or maybe a hundred and a hundred . . . it was kind of hard to tell. There were zillions of those fireflies now; and the ones high off the ground and closer to the ship seemed larger. There were thin tendrils connecting the fireflies to the ship so that the whole thing was like a jellyfish with bumpy tentacles hanging down, though by the time they got to the ground the tendrils were too small to see, so that it looked like the "fireflies" weren't connected. I reached out and caught a couple of them . . . they were tingly and hard to hold on to. My skin was prickling like mad.

I yelled, "Hello!" up at the UFO just so it would know I was an intelligent being. And then I was thinking maybe it had come especially to see me, so I yelled, "Welcome! My name is Will Coyote! I'm a hacker!" For the time being the mother ship just stayed up there, hissing and with all its tendrils wafting this way and that like beautiful strings of Tivoli lights flashing red, yellow, and green.

The ship itself was shaped in three main parts. There was a great big back section with a dimple in it, and then there was a smaller spherical section attached opposite the dimple, and sticking out of the front of the sphere section was a long spike kind of thing. It was just like—oh my God!—*just like a giant three-dimensional Mandelbrot set!* Though also like a beetle in a way, and like a jellyfish.

The UFO came lower and then some of the thicker tendrils were brushing against me. They felt shuddery, like the metal on a shorted-out toaster. I figured the prickly feeling I'd been getting was from invisible fine tendrils that I couldn't see. Could it be possible the thing was going to eat me like a Portuguese man-of-war that's got hold of a small fish? I screamed out, "Don't hurt me, I'm an intelligent being like you!" and the thing hissed louder, and then suddenly the hissing Fourier-transformed itself into a human voice. A woman's voice.

"Don't worry, William. I am very grateful to you. I wish to take you for a ride."

I tried to stand up then, but I was too fucking zoned. So I just smiled and stretched my arms up to the big UFO ass. UFO? This *had* to be a hallucination. Slowly, slowly, it came lower.

The tendrils were thick as vines, and the fireflies on the tendrils were as big as grapefruits and baseballs. Since this whole ship was a fractal, each of the firefly globs was a three-sectioned thing like the main body: each of them was a dimpled round ass part with a little antennaed head sphere stuck onto it.

This was absolutely the best graphic ever. I was really happy.

I took one of the baby Mandelbrot sets in my hands and peered at it. It was as warm and jittery as a pet mouse. Even though the little globster was vague at the edges, it was solid in the middle. Better than a graphic. I cradled it and touched it to my face. As the big mamma came lower I kept calm by wondering if she was real.

I stayed cool right up to when the giant ass landed on me and began pressing me down against the ground—pressing so hard that I could barely breathe. Was I like *dying* or some shit? Had I passed out, gotten apnea, and forgotten to breathe? I blinked and looked again, but the ass was still there; and right up against my face was the incredibly detailed female hide of a gigantic three-dimensional Mandelbrot set, man, like all covered with warts on warts and cracks in cracks and bristles 'n' bristles everywhaaar, oh sisters and brothers, and the whole thing rippling with every color of the rainbow and loaded with such a strong electric charge that my nose pricked and I had to sneeze.

The sneeze changed something. Everything got black. Now I was really dead, right?

"Welcome aboard, William," came the deep, thrilling voice of the mandelsphere's dark innards. "My name is Ma."

It was not wholly dark, no indeed—there were objects, but objects of such a refined and subtle nature that, likely as not, I would normally have walked right through them, except that here I had nothing else to walk into or through, so they became real to me.

It was not really dark, and it was not really small inside Ma. The space within was the mirror of the space without. While the outside of the Mandelbrot set's hide was crowded and entangled, the hide's inside was endlessly spacious. There being nowhere in particular to go, I sat myself down in a faintly glowing blue armchair and spoke.

"Where are you from?"

"I am everywhere; beyond all space, and within the tiniest motes. I am any size that wants me. You called me here."

"It's good to see all that programming finally pay off." I was giddy with excitement. "Can I get a drink?"

Faint shapes wafted around me, and then a long luminous beaker of yellow was in my hand. I sucked greedily at the pure energy fluid. This was the kind of rest I deserved after all that mind-breaking hacking: always shifting bits left and right to make bytes, masking the bytes together into register-sized words, generating lookup tables, finding room for the tables in RAM, feeding the output into the color display ports . . . I drank and drank, and my glass was always full.

One pale shape after another came to me, flowed over me, and gave way to the next one. Each was reading me like a book, accessing me like a hypertext, learning the nature of my familiar world. It seemed that each could sense me in a slightly different way. While they read me, I thought questions and they thought answers back.

The shapes were like different body parts—each an aspect of the single higher-dimensional entity called Ma.

According to Ma, the smallest and largest sizes were one and the same. That was her native habitat.

Ma needed my presence to easily stay at this size-level; for her it was more natural to exist as a quark or a universe. I was like a snag in a rushing river for her to hold onto.

Despite that, said Ma, there was only one thing at all, and that one thing was Ma.

"Am I you?"

"You are a pattern in the potentially infinite computation that is the universe; and I am the actually infinite end of said computation. I am all space and all time. The world you live in is happening; my essence is what comes before and after your mundane time."

"How long is the program that starts it all?"

"Two bits. One Zero."

"What about all the details?"

"You'd call it *screen wrap*. Patterns grow out and around and come back over themselves and make fringes. It adds up over the billions of years, especially when you remember that each point in space is updating the computation each instant. Each of those points is me; I'm the rule that runs it all; and looked at the other way, I'm the past and all the future."

"I can totally dig it, Ma. The universe has a simple code and a long rich parallel computation. There are infinitely many size scales, so in fact each orange or atom has everything inside it. Right on. What about uncertainty and Planck's constant, though. Is that a hassle for you, Ma?"

She got into a complex answer involving infinite dimensional Hilbert space—the human modes of thinking were new to her, so we had some back and forth about it—and the conversation drifted on. Talking mathematical metaphysics, lolling on my ethereal couch, sipping my invigorating energy drink, and with the eager phantom Ma figures mounting me like harem girls, I swore I'd never been so happy. But then, all at once, the joy ended.

"Two more people are here," said Ma's sweet voice. "One of them is—Ow!" There was a sputtering and a lashing. "They've torn off a piece of me," she screamed. "And now . . . oh no—"

There was a brain-splitting cry of pure agony, a pop, and then I thudded to the hard ground.

"Will! Hey, Will!" It was my wife Donna and my boss Steven Koss. They were proud of themselves for "saving" me.

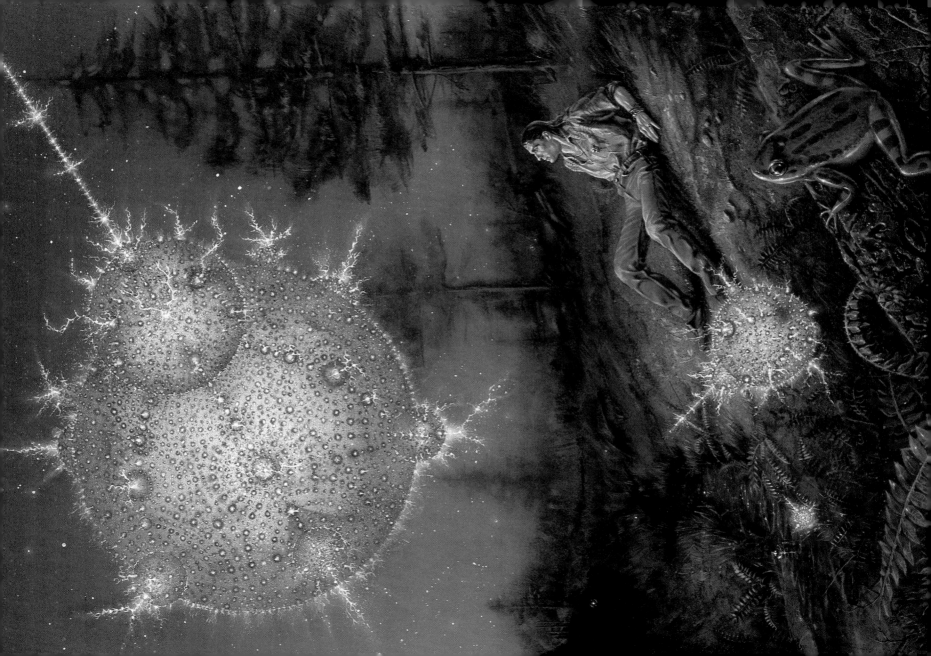

"Yeah," gloated Koss, stupid yuppie that he was. "I shot it with my Tazer." He held up a stubby box with two wires trailing out if it. "Was some kind of anomalous electromagnetic field, I guess, and my jolt disrupted it. You feeling OK, big guy?"

"Why did you shoot it?" I asked, sitting up. "It was so beautiful!"

"It was going for your wife!" he snapped. I noticed that he had his arm across her shoulders.

Donna's face was a white patch inside her long, hanging-down dark hair. "Are you all right, Will? What happened was I pulled off one of the baby globbies, and it started screaming and flashing checkerboard sparks." She held something cradled against her breasts. It glowed.

"You got a baby Ma?" I cried, getting to my feet.

Donna cracked her fingers so Koss and I could peek in and see a flowing, colored tiny Ma. Donna held it tight as a baby. Its little tail or spike stuck out below her hands. The tail was knobbed with tinier Mas.

"I broke it off the big one, and the big one got mad," smiled Donna. "Do you think we could keep this one for a pet?"

"Pet, hell," said Koss. "We can sell them."

The magic energy drink Ma'd given me had gotten my head back together pretty good. The three of us went on up to our house on top of the hill, Donna and I in our dingy Honda, Koss following behind in his Jaguar with my wrecked bike.

"I was really worried when you didn't come home," said Donna. She was driving and I was holding the baby Ma. Ma felt good to my hands.

"I called Micromax and nobody was there except that thing, that AI answering machine," continued Donna. She didn't sound particularly friendly. "So I decided to drive downtown and look for you. I just knew you'd be drunk and stoned again. God, I'm sick of you, Will. You never notice me anymore."

"Don't start nagging me, Donna."

"Oh, right. That's what you always say: *Don't talk, Donna. Be quiet.* Well, I've had it, Will, with your computer and your drugs. When was the last time you bothered to touch me? I need love, Will, I need someone who'll listen to me!"

What she said was true, but why did she have to start in on it now? "I hear you, Donna, loud and clear. Can you tell me more about how you found me?"

She sighed and shook her head and grudgingly told me the rest. "Halfway down the hill I saw this huge bright light UFO sitting on the ground. I got out and looked at it, and after a while I picked a bud off it. It got all upset. That's all."

"How does Koss fit in," I demanded. "Who told him to show up with his asshole electric gun?"

"Steven thought I was in danger," said Donna. "He cares about me. Not like you, Will, so stoned and hacked you don't know the first thing about me anymore. Steven showed up in his Jaguar right before I picked the bud. He said the stupid AI thing at Micromax called him to tell him a window was broken. And when he went there he found your terminal's glass all broken out too. He thinks the UFO thing came from your computer, Will."

"Her name is Ma, Donna. She's an infinite fractal from Hilbert space. This little one is all of her. Each of her bumps is all of her. She's every particle, and she's the whole world." I held Ma up to my face and kissed her warty tingly hide. Each time I kissed her she grew a little. Donna sighed heavily.

Back at the house, I couldn't get Koss to leave. He was all fired up with excitement from having killed something. Jock, caveman, yuppie—all the same. He preened himself in front of the disgustingly attentive Donna, laying down his moronic rap about what he thought had happened.

"I was in the exercise room working out with my exercise machine—hey, I need it every day, guys—and then the emergency phone's all ringing from our AI about a broken window. I get in my Jag, cruise down there, and find Will's fifteen thousand dollar Mitsubishi VGA with the front screen blown away. I'm wondering if Will's dusted-out friends've blown him away or what. I decide not to call the pig in, I board up the broken window—then outside I'm all *what's that light on the hillside?* I wind the Jag on up here and it's some kind of atmospheric plasma display. Donna's standing under it looking real fine—and she's got the idea to tear off a little bud from it, and all at once it's violent."

By this point Koss was pacing and pounding his hand with his fit tan fist, reliving the big play. "At the speeds I travel, you can't waste time saying why. You just react. I snapped my Jaguar's utility boot open and got out the heavy-duty stungun I keep in there in case of trouble. Sucker's got a gunpowder charge that shoots two metal fishhook electrodes twenty yards. Those 'trodes pack 150 volts! I aimed steady and I nailed that big mother right in its butt. FFFFFTT!"

"Big deal," I said. "Donna already told me."

"Let's tear another glob off that little one," said Koss.

"You better not," said Donna. "It'll get violent!"

"This little one can't hurt us," chortled Koss, snatching it out of my hands and tearing off a bud.

Little Ma screamed, but only I could hear her. She got an ugly cyan/white/ magenta for a few minutes, and her broken tendril shot out black and white sparks, but a minute later she was a calm red/yellow/green and the sparking spot had healed over.

"Check it out, Donna!" exulted Koss. "We got work to do!" He pulled off another bud and another. "Like artichokes!"

"How exciting," squealed Donna.

I just wanted to be alone with a Ma and grow it big enough to get inside again, but Koss got on my case about how I should write up a sample ad for the new company we were going to start. I told him to get fucked. Donna frowned at me and wrote an ad that was so bogus that I rewrote it. The finished version went like this:

WONDERGLOBS

The living Wonderglob is an object of unparalled beauty. Like God or the Universe itself, the Wonderglob feeds on YOUR attention—the more you look at it, the larger it grows.

Perhaps the most satisfying aspect of owning a Wonderglob is that you can HARVEST BUDS from it and, under our franchising agreement, SELL these buds to your friends! The initial investment pays for itself in a matter of weeks!

The Wonderglob dislikes electricity and is easily kept captive in our patented Wonder-tanks, whose metal-plated glass sides carry a small electric charge. The Wonderglob may be removed for play and meditation, but be sure to replace it in the Wondertank, particularly after harvesting.

We didn't happen to have any "patented Wondertanks" handy, but Donna had the idea of hooking a wire to the tightly woven steel mesh of our old djinkotl cage and keeping the buds in there. Djinkotls had been last year's fad pet—lizards or rodents or something—stinking and liable to bite. The Mas hated it; man, they were shrinking steadily. Meanwhile Koss was giving Donna lines of coke and jabbering about money. I couldn't tell if things were as bad as they seemed, or worse. I chilled and crashed.

I snapped awake at four a.m., the way I sometimes do. Like if I go to bed wrecked, the survival reflex wakes me as soon as the limbic systems reboot. I wake up to assess the damages. Am I in bed? Who did I phone? What did I break?

Donna wasn't in bed with me. I got up and went in the living room. There was Koss putting it to her right there on our rug, her legs wrapped around his dumb cheeks. My Mas are dying specks in a shitty cage and Koss here is putting it to my wife? While torturing my dreams for gain?

I picked up the djinkotl cage and headed outside. Koss and Donna barely noticed.

It so happens I know my woods like the back of my own prick. I went around the hill to a green boulder redwood gully, a special spot all ferned and purling, with small white flowers and soggy mosses and rivulets underfoot, and overhead clear sky and stars past the tall trees. I took the Ma buds out of the djinkotl cage—sixteen of them in all—and held them in my hands and mooshed down into soft trickly moss where living water could well in through my finger cracks and feed the ripped off and the newborn buds.

They drank the water avidly; they grew closer to my size. I could hear her/

their happy thoughts. Ma'd never tasted water at this size-level before. The newly harvested buds stopped at the size of oranges, while Donna's maimed original puffed up to woman size and continued to grow. Big Ma.

The spots where Koss had torn buds off were flat scars covered with a fine fractal down of new growth. Each of the new baby buds bore a single birth scar, a kind of navel hidden in the cheeks of her swelling behind. Ma's girls.

Sixteen is hex-ten. The girls lifted off and darted about. When they got farther away from me, they either got a lot smaller or a lot bigger. Some of them went high into the redwoods and on up into the sky, growing as they flew. There were quick blinks of brightness across the sky as one by one they maxxed out to cosmic scale. Others bumped down the gully towards the sea, dwindling to tiny bright specks in the water. A few hung around watching me and the main Ma.

And then the main Ma was big enough for me to get in her, so I did; I did it by hugging her against me until her shape slipped over me and I was back inside the endlessly vast interior of a fractal solid weird screen come true.

I wandered about in there at will. There were trees, there were boulders, but when you tripped over something it didn't hurt. I went up a nubby slope and found an ethereal armchair, same one as before, except now it was purple and it had wood trim along the arms. There was a glass of energy drink on the floor by the chair, and lying there on the left arm's wood trim was a monster jay with a book of matches. I fired up for sure. Breathing the smoke out, watching the tendrils, with a pink womany Ma shape on my lap, I forgot everything I ever knew.

And it was calm, and it was wonderful, until of course some new Nazi asshole was on our case.

"A loud machine," said Ma. "Coming closer."

If I peered closely at a little speck in the air near me, I could see out to the world outside. It was all there, right in that little speck, the hill, and the ocean, and Santa Cruz. Racketting towards Ma and me was an army helicopter with searchlights and with guns. From the speck's shifty viewpoint, I could even see the soldiers in the chopper, all peering down at our glow. They were getting ready to shoot us.

"Can we hide somewhere?" I asked Ma.

"Yes, William. I can shrink and I can jump in and out of Earth's space."

"Won't that hurt me?"

"Inside me you're already out of Earth's space. And as far as shrinking goes—infinity divided by ten is still infinity. My inside is always the same."

"Then let's go and get . . . inside the can of Geisha Girl crabmeat in my kitchen cupboard."

"It's . . . done."

I took my attention off the little worldview speck—which now showed strands of crabmeat, a can, and outside the can our kitchen. Cops in the house, talking to Koss and Donna.

That all happened yesterday, or maybe it's been two days. The longer I'm in here, the better I can see. At my request, Ma's got soft-edged computer graphics rippling over the endlessly unfolding surfaces around me—Escher images, Gosper hacks, Conway games—whatever I feel like seeing. It's like programming without ever having to touch a key. And with the energy drinks I'm never hungry. It's perfect in here.

I just hope no one gets hungry for canned crab.

CONTRIBUTORS

BYRON PREISS is editor of *The Planets*, *The Universe*, and *The Dinosaurs*. He is also coeditor, with Ben Bova, of the forthcoming book, *First Contact*. He has collaborated on books and computer software with Arthur C. Clarke and Ray Bradbury. His project, *The Words of Gandhi*, won a 1985 Grammy Award, and his monograph, *The Art of Leo and Diane Dillon*, was a Hugo Award Nominee. He resides in New York.

WILLIAM R. ALSCHULER is the founder and Principal of Future Museums, a museum consulting firm which provides program concept through final design for museums and exhibits which have science and technology content or are in related fields. Mr. Alschuler has a background in hard science, science education and engineering, including a Ph.D. in Astronomy and extensive teaching experience in the sciences and energy conservation at the university level. He is the author of published scientific studies in astronomy, and has a work in progress on the state of science museums, for which he has travelled and interviewed internationally.

RUTH ASHBY, associate editor, has taught English literature at the University of Michigan and the University of Virginia. She edits nonfiction, science and wildlife books, and books for young readers. She is the author of two childrens' books, *Time Machine #23*, *Quest for King Arthur*, and *Tigers*.

DAVID M. HARRIS, associate editor, is America's most successful unpublished author. When he is not writing or working in his garden, he has been an editor, agent, publicist, photographer, and ice-cream freezerman.

ALEX JAY is a designer and lettering artist. His design of the *Banana Republic Guide to Travel & Safari Clothing* book was exhibited in the 1986 AIGA Book Show, the Type Directors Club 33rd annual competition (TDC 33), and Graphis Design Annual 87/88. TDC 28 displayed his title lettering for the book *The Art of Leo & Diane Dillon*. He art directed and designed *Tales of the Dark Knight*, *Batman's First Fifty Years: 1939–1989*, which was published in September, 1989. His comic book

and graphic novel logos include those for *The Green Lantern Corps*, *The Adventures of Superman*, *The Mighty Thor*, *X-Factor*, Clive Barker's *Hellraiser*, Howard Chaykin's *American Flagg!*, Alfred Bester's *The Stars My Destination*, and William Gibson's *Neuromancer*.

DARREL ANDERSON has designed graphics for computer software and computer magazines. He has illustrated two children's books for Bantam and painted the cover for Time Machine #11, *Mission to World War II*. A respected painter, he resides in Denver, Colorado.

POUL ANDERSON was one of the first science-fiction writers to move to the San Francisco area, pioneering a major settlement. Two of his seven Hugo Awards are separated by a span of more than twenty years, testimony to his enduring quality.

ISAAC ASIMOV's total of published books has passed four hundred volumes. Although his Ph.D. is in chemistry, his popular non-fiction has covered almost every imaginable subject, from quantum physics to the Bible. He is a winner of the Hugo and Nebula awards for science fiction. Among his novels are the Foundation series (winner of a special Hugo for Best Science Fiction Series of all time) and the Robot series. He is also the father of the Three Laws of Robotics.

GREGORY BENFORD writes for the *Encyclopedia Britannica* in the areas of relativistic plasma physics and astrophysics. His fiction, equally highly regarded, includes most notably the novel *Timescape*, which won four separate awards. He most recently was nominated for a Nebula for *Great Sky River*.

MARCEL BESSIS has worked on the frontiers of modern cytology for the past thirty years, and has applied both the techniques and theories of cellular physiology to the problems of normal and abnormal blood cells. He is the Founder and Director of the Institute of Cell Pathology (INSERM), where numerous new techniques have been developed, particularly for the study of the living cell and of the single cell.

Dr. Bessis is currently the Director of the Laboratory for the Study of Cell Ecology, Paris. He is a member of The French Academy of Sciences, International Society of Hematology, The Harvey Society, The American College of Physicians, and The American Society of Hematology.

MICHAEL BISHOP's short fiction has appeared nearly everywhere, including *Best American Short Stories 1985*. He has accumulated two Nebula Awards and countless Hugo and Nebula nominations, none of them, so far, for his science fiction and fantasy criticism, which appears regularly in *Thrust*.

DAVID BRIN's second novel, *Startide Rising*, won both the Hugo and Nebula Awards. He was awarded another Hugo (his third, altogether) for *The Uplift War*, set in the same universe. When he is not writing, he is a teacher of university physics.

MICHAEL CARROLL is an astronomical artist, writer and lecturer. His art has been published in eight countries, and has appeared in *Time, Smithsonian,* and *Omni*. His articles have been published in *Astronomy, Sky & Telescope,* and the Japanese science magazine *Newton*. He lives in San Diego with his wife and two children.

JOHN COLLIER has won the Society of Illustrators' Silver and Gold medals, and is regarded as one of the most influential contemporary illustrators. His paintings are represented by major galleries and have appeared in major magazines.

ALVARO DE RÚJULA has conducted research and taught physics in various places around the world, including the French Institute for Advanced Studies near Paris, the University of Madrid, and the French and Spanish Nuclear Energy Commissions (CEN-Saclay and JEN-Madrid), the International Center for Theoretical Physics in Trieste (Italy), and Harvard University. At present he is a Staff Member at CERN, the European Center for Nuclear Research near Geneva, and a Professor of Physics at Boston University.

BOB EGGLETON was first drawn to science fiction by the movies, and would rather illustrate for science fiction than any other subject. He has been nominated for the Hugo Award numerous times, and has won two Chesley Awards. His work was includ-

ed in the first exhibition of American astronomical art to tour the Soviet Union. His long-term goal is to visit Mars and do some landscape painting.

GERALD FEINBERG is Professor of Physics at Columbia University. His research is in theoretical physics and he was one of the scientists who first proposed the distinction between the muon and electron neutrinos. He is also responsible for a theory of tachyons, hypothetical particles that travel faster than light. Dr. Feinberg has written five books for general audiences, including *What Is the World Made Of?*, a book about modern physics; *Life Beyond Earth* (with Robert Shapiro), which deals with possible forms of extraterrestrial life; and *Solid Clues*, a discussion of the future of science.

DR. ROBERT L. FORWARD was until 1987 a Senior Scientist at the Hughes Research labs, specializing in exotic physical phenomena and advanced space propulsion. Those of his ideas that can be accomplished with current technology he does as research projects; those that are too far out, he develops in his speculative science articles and science-fiction stories and novels.

WILLIAM M. GELBART has been Professor of Chemistry at UCLA since 1979. He has published approximately one hundred research papers and review articles in the areas of gas-phase photochemistry, light scattering from simple fluids, phase transitions in liquid crystals, statistical thermodynamics of surfactant solutions, and the properties of thin films and absorbed monolayers.

SHELDON LEE GLASHOW is the Higgins Professor of Physics and Mellon Professor of the Sciences at Harvard University. He has done groundbreaking research on the electroweak synthesis and the unification of the four forces. His many honors include the Alfred P. Sloan Foundation Fellowship (1977), the Oppenheimer Memorial Medal (1978), and the Nobel Prize (1979), awarded for his work in the unification of the electromagnetic and weak forces.

ALAN GUTIERREZ first began doing science fiction art in 1977, before he entered college. Before he had graduated, he had made his first

KEVIN JOHNSON is a native of Washington State. He started painting science fiction book covers in 1978, and has done well over a hundred of them. He is also the co-inventor of "The Supernaturals" toy line for Tonka Toys.

EDWARD W. KOLB is presently head of the NASA/Fermilab Theoretical Astrophysics Group at Fermi National Accelerator Laboratory in Illinois, and is a professor of astronomy and astrophysics at the University of Chicago.

The major area of Dr. Kolb's research is the study of the early universe in the first seconds after the big bang, when the extreme conditions of temperature and energy can be reproduced in the high-energy collisions of particles at accelerators.

LEON M. LEDERMAN received his B.S. from the City College of New York and his Ph.D. from Columbia University in 1951. His thesis assignment was to build a Wilson Cloud Chamber. In 1958 he was promoted to professor and took his first sabbatical at CERN, where he organized a group to do the "g-2" experiment.

Dr. Lederman was appointed Director of Nevis Labs at Columbia in 1961 and held this position until 1978. In 1979 he became Director of the Fermi National Accelerator Laboratory where he supervised the construction and utilization of the first superconducting synchrotron, now the highest energy accelerator in the world.

Dr. Lederman was awarded the Nobel Prize in Physics in December 1988 for his work on neutrinos.

PAMELA LEE is the first American artist whose paintings have flown in space aboard the space shuttle. They can also be found in numerous museums, including the Yuri Gagarin Museum in Star City, USSR, and the Pushkin Art Museum in Moscow, and have been published in the *American Illustration Annual*, *Art Direction's Creativity Annual*, and the *New York Society of Illustrators Annual*. Other work has been featured on book covers, television, and in the film, *Space Visions*.

RALPH McQUARRIE is best known for his work as designer/illustrator on the Star Wars tril-

professional sale. He moved to New York for several years to establish himself, and succeeded—he has done over a hundred book covers since 1983. He now lives in Arizona.

HARRY HARRISON has been an artist, art director, and editor. As a writer, he had a career as the author of numerous true confessions and men's adventures before leaving New York for Mexico in order to write his first novel. He has since written more than thirty-five novels, and has lived in nearly as many countries. His books have been translated into twenty-one languages. He was founding president of World SF. He received the Nebula award and the Prix Jules Verne for his novel *Make Room! Make Room!*, which was made into the film *Soylent Green*.

WILLIAM A. HASELTINE received his B.A. in Physical Chemistry from University of California in 1966 and his Ph.D. in Biophysics in 1973 from Harvard. Since 1980 he has been connected with the Dana-Farber Cancer Institute where he has been Chief of the Laboratory of Biochemical Pharmacology, the Laboratory of Molecular Studies of Cancer Cause and Treatment, and presently is Chief of the Division of Human Retrovirology. He also holds a position with the Harvard AIDS Institute.

Since 1969 Dr. Haseltine has won awards from the American Cancer Society, the Governor's AIDS Committee, the Leukemia Society and the Royal Society of Medicine.

LINN W. HOBBS is Professor of Ceramics and Materials Science at Massachusetts Institute of Technology. Dr. Hobbs is chairman of the Materials Science Degree Program in the Department of Materials Science and Engineering at M.I.T. His research interests are in the fields of radiation effects in materials (ceramics, metals, and organics), extended defects and non-stoichiometry in solids, high-temperature corrosion of metals, and multi-layer semiconductor devices. He has pioneered the application of transmission electron microscopy in many of these research areas.

BRUCE JENSEN recently adapted William Gibson's *Neuromancer* and W.R. Philbrick's *The Big Chip* into graphic novel form. He is an experienced computer graphic artist and painter.

ogy. He started working in film on the animated portions of the CBS News Special Events coverage of the Apollo missions. Other credits include design of spaceships for Steven Spielberg's *Close Encounters of the Third Kind* and *E.T.* His most recent work has involved design for the film *Cocoon*, and book jacket illustration.

RON MILLER was nominated for a Hugo Award for best nonfiction for *The Grand Tour*. He has also been art director of the Albert Einstein Planetarium at the National Air and Space Museum, and is a founding member of the International Association of Astronomical Artists.

PHILIP MORRISON took his Ph.D. in theoretical physics at Berkeley in 1940. For almost 20 post-war years he was on the physics faculty at Cornell. Since 1964 he has been at M.I.T, where he is now Institute Professor (emeritus). Among his accomplishments are serving on the Manhattan Project with J. Robert Oppenheimer; taking part in the Trinity test, the first atomic explosion; and watching the take-off run of the Enola Gay.

Dr. Morrison believes that physicists owe their fellow citizens two services: better understanding of physics, and independent comment on modern war and how to avoid it—by winding down the arms race. He has written several books and made films along both paths. Most recently he and his wife, Phylis, wrote and appeared in a TV series on PBS called The Ring of Truth, meant to look at how science knows what it knows: by the evidence, not by authority.

PAUL PREUSS began his writing career after years of producing documentary and television films. He recently published his eighth novel, *Hide and Seek*, the third in the Venus Prime series. He has also written a computer game, a television biography of physicist Albert Michelson, and reviews and articles for the *Washington Post*, *New York Newsday*, the *San José Mercury News*, and other newspapers.

JEAN PAUL REVEL was born in France in 1930 and came to Harvard University for his graduate studies in biochemistry. After post-doctoral studies in electron microscopy, he joined the Faculty of Anatomy at Harvard Medical School. He was appointed professor in 1969.

In 1971 Dr. Revel joined the Biology Faculty of the California Institute of Technology (Caltech) where he now is the Albert Billings Ruddock Professor. In 1973 he was elected President of the American Society for Cell Biology and he was also recently the President of the Electron Microscopy Society of America.

With D.W. Fawcett, Dr.Revel has contributed to our understanding of muscle structure, and with Elizabeth D. Hay, to examinations of the interrelationships between epithelia and mesenchyme. Starting from work originally carried out with Morris Karnovsky, Dr. Revel has been interested in the structure and function relationships in the so-called "gap junctions," a specialization of cell membranes important to cell-cell communication.

RUDY RUCKER is considered the leading mathematician in the cyberpunk movement. His writing alternates between fiction and nonfiction; his latest book, *Wetware*, won the Philip K. Dick Award. Recently, he has added computer software design to his repertory.

ROBERT SILVERBERG is a native New Yorker now living near San Francisco. Considered one of the best editors in science fiction, he produced the New Dimensions series of original anthologies and is coeditor of *The Universe*.

Among Silverberg's novels are the bestselling *Lord Valentine* trilogy, *Star of Gypsies*, and *A Time of Changes*, for which he won one of his five Nebula Awards, more than any other writer. He has also won two Hugo Awards, a Jupiter Award, and the Prix Apollo.

CONNIE WILLIS first published in 1978, and in 1982 won two Nebula Awards and a Hugo. Her work was described by the *New York Times* as "fresh, subtle, and deeply moving." Her story, "Schwarzchild Radius," in *The Universe*, was a Nebula nominee, and she recently won for her novella "The Last of the Winnebagos."

SELECTED READINGS

BESSIS, Marcel. *Corpuscles*. Berlin: Springer Verlag, 1974.

BESSIS, Marcel. *Living Blood Cells and Their Ultra Structure*. Berlin: Springer Verlag, 1973.

Blood Cells. Special Issue. *Therapy of Leukemias-New Approaches*. Berlin: Springer International, 1968.

DAVIES, Paul. *Superforce*. New York: Simon & Schuster, 1985.

DEDUVE, Christian. *The Living Cell*. New York: W.H. Freeman and Co., 1984.

EPSTEIN, I.R., et al. "Oscillating Chemical Reactions." *Scientific American*, March 1983.

FEINBERG, Gerald. *What is the World Made of?* New York: Doubleday & Co., 1977.

FEYNMAN, Richard. QED: *The Strange Theory of Light and Matter*. Princeton, N.J.: Princeton University Press, 1985.

GLASHOW, Sheldon Lee and Ben Bova. *Interactions*. New York: Warner Books, 1987.

HARRISON, Edward R. *Cosmology: The Science of the Universe*. Cambridge: Cambridge University Press, 1981.

HASELTINE, W.A. and F. Wong-Staal. "The Molecular Biology of the Human Immunodeficiency Virus." *Scientific American*, Vol. 256, (1988), pp. 52–62.

HAWKES, Peter W. *The Beginnings of Electron Microscopy*. Orlando, Fl.: Academic Press, 1985.

HAWKING, Stephen W. *A Brief History of Time*. New York: Bantam Books, 1988.

HEY, Tony and Patrick Walters. *A Quantum Universe*. Cambridge: Cambridge University Press, 1987.

KANER, R.B. and A.G. MacDiarmid. "Plastics That Conduct Electricity." *Scientific American*, February 1987.

LAYZER, David. *Constructing The Universe*. New York: W.H. Freeman and Co., 1984.

LEDERMAN, Leon M. and J. Steinberger and M. Schwartz. "The Two Neutrino Experiment." *Scientific American*, March 1963.

MINTZ, Beatrice. *Gene Supression in Neoplasia and Differentiation: The Harvey Lectures*. New York: Academic Press, 1978.

NEEMAN, Yuval & Yoram Kirsh. *The Particle Hunters*. Cambridge: Cambridge University Press, 1986.

OKUN, Lev B. *Quarks and Leptons*. Netherlands: North Holland Publishing Co., 1984.

PAIS, Abraham. *Inward Bound*. Oxford: Oxford University Press, 1983.

Physics Through the 1990s: Nuclear Physics. Washington, D.C.: National Academy Press and Physics Survey Committee of the National Research Council, 1986.

PICKERING, Andrew. *Constructing Quarks*. Chicago: University of Chicago Press, 1984.

PREISS, Byron, ed. *The Planets*. New York: Bantam Spectra, 1985.

PREISS, Byron, ed. *The Universe*. New York: Bantam Spectra, 1987.

"Replication and Pathogenesis of the Aids Virus." *Journal of Acquired Immune Deficiency Syndromes*. Vol. 1, (1988), pp. 217–240.

RIORDAN, Michael. *The Hunting of the Quark*. New York: Simon and Schuster, 1987.

SEGRE, Emilio. *From X-rays to Quarks*. New York: W.H. Freeman and Co., 1980.

STOCKDALE, I. "A Search for Neutrino Oscillations with Large Values of Delta-M-squared." Thesis. Rochester: University of Rochester, 1984.

The Way Things Work, Vol. 1. New York: Simon & Schuster, 1967.

TUCKER, Wallace and Karen. *The Dark Matter*. New York: William Morrow and Co., 1984.

TURNER, G. L'E. *Essays on the History of the Microscope*. Oxford: Senecio Publishing Co. Ltd., 1980.

WEINBERG, Steven. *The Discovery of Subatomic Particles*. New York: W.H. Freeman, 1983.

WEINBERG, Steven. *The First Three Minutes*. New York: Basic Books, 1988.

WEISS, P.A. *Dynamic Development: Experiments and Interferences*. New York: New York Academy Press, 1968.

WEISSKOPF, Victor F. *Knowledge and Wonder. The Natural World As Man Knows It*. Cambridge: MIT Press, 1980.

WILCZEK, Frank and Betsy Devine. *The Longing for the Harmonies*. New York: Norton & Co., 1988.

YOUVAN, D.C. and B.L. Marrs. "Molecular Mechanisms of Photosynthesis." *Scientific American*, June 1987.

ABOUT THE SECTION TITLE PAGES

Pages 20–21: A scanning electron micrograph of the head of a fly, showing its multi-lens eyes and microscopic hairiness. (Photo credit: © David Scharf, 1986)

Page 63: An oblique view of a layer of red blood cells (discocytes). Color added. (Photo credit: © Marcel Bessis)

Page 83: Test tube preparation of DNA material. (Photo credit: National Cancer Institute, Bethesda, Maryland)

Page 121: Computer image of an antibody binding pocket. (Credit: © Dr. Arthur J. Olson, Scripps Clinic, Department of Molecular Biology)

Page 153: *Atoms at an Exhibition*. (Credit: © Kenneth Snelson, 1988.)

Page 187: Super-conducting disk levitating above super-conducting magnet, with no electric energy being expended. (Photo credit: Science Photo Library)

Page 217: Looking down the long axis of a neutrino detector to be used in an experiment to see if neutrinos are truly massless. (Photo credit: Lawrence Livermore Laboratory)

Page 263: Electron-positron pair tracks in a bubble chamber. They spiral in opposite directions in the magnetic field because they are oppositely charged. (Photo credit: CERN)

Page 287: Computer-generated cross-sectional view of the intense particle-guiding magnetic fields of the proposed super-conducting super collider. (Photo credit: Science Photo Library)

Page 315: M82, a spiral galaxy with an active core. False color. (Photo credit: Science Photo Library)

ADDITIONAL ART ACKNOWLEDGMENTS

Page 1: Credit: James T. Hoffman, 1989.

Page 2: Illustration by Greg Spalenka.

Page 12: SEM image of house dust. (Credit: © David Scharf, 1981)

Page 133 (top), 167, 192, 229: William R. Alschuler with Elizabeth Wen.